The Complete Guide™
To Writing Fantasy: Volume One~
Alchemy With Words

TOM DULLEMOND AND
DARIN PARK, EDITORS

Save a Tree Program

At Dragon Moon Press, our carbon footprint is significantly higher than average and we plan to do something about it. For every tree Dragon Moon uses in printing our books, we are helping to plant new trees to reduce our carbon footprint so that the next generation can breathe clean air, keeping our planet and it's inhabitants healthy.

Dragon Moon Press
www.dragonmoonpress.com
Dragon Moon Press is an Imprint of Hades Publications, Inc.
Printed and bound in Canada and the United States. Released in 2003.

Copyright Acknowledgments
"Roots of Fantasy" copyright ©2002 John Teehan
"Bringing Characters to Life" copyright ©2002 Lea Docken
"How to Make Your Characters Real" copyright ©2002 Tee Morris
"Race Creationcopyright ©2002 Michael McRae
"World Building" copyright ©2002 Tina Morgan
"Writing Effectively" copyright ©2002 Milena Benini
"Plot Construction" copyright ©2002 Marko Fancovic
"Medieval Clothing" copyright ©2002 Lauren Cleeland and Kim Bundy
"From Fast to Feast" copyright ©2002 Michele Acker
"Healthand Medicine copyright ©2002 Michael McRae
"Magic" copyright ©2002 Tom Dullemond
"The Stories Within Your World" copyright ©2002 Valerie Griswold
"Religion" copyright ©2002 Julie Peavler-McCord
"Live fast, die young, leave a beautiful corpse. Maybe two."
copyright ©2002 Tom Dullemond, Michael McRae and Tee Morris
"Combat" copyright ©2002 Tom Dullemond
"Two Great Tastes That Taste Great Together" copyright ©2002 Tee Morris
"Humour in Fantasy" copyright ©2002 Darin Park and Rob Durney
"The More You Know, The Safer You Are" copyright ©2002 Tee Morris
"Market Resources" copyright ©2002 Tina Morgan
All interior illustrations copyright ©2002 Michael McRae.

The complete guide to writing fantasy / Darin Park and Tom Dullemond, editors ; authors, Darin Park ... [et al.].

Includes bibliographical references and index.
ISBN 1-896944-09-4

1. Fantasy literature—Authorship. I. Park, Darin. II. Dullemond, Tom, 1976-
PN3377.5.F34C65 2003   808.3'8766   C2003-910884-8

The Complete Guide™
TO WRITING FANTASY: VOLUME ONE~
ALCHEMY WITH WORDS

TOM DULLEMOND AND
DARIN PARK, EDITORS

Dragon
Moon

www.dragonmoonpress.com
www.completeguidetowriting.com

Dedication

This book is gratefully dedicated to the authors of its content and especially to those that read the pages herein.

You are the dreamers who craft fantasies that allow us brief escapes into wonderful worlds.

May your vision forever guide us into magical realms.

Contents

Foreword

DARIN PARK

DEFINING FANTASY

Fantasy. What is it? Is there a defining factor?

Well, if you're reading this guide then you already have some idea of what fantasy is and you're ready to plunge headlong into creating your own story or novel. The definition for fantasy is as varied as fantasy itself. Fantasy will not fit into a neat label. Let's see why.

Definition: Fantasy is about elves and fairies.

Wouldn't it be great if we could say that one definition covered it all? But we can't. Elves and fairies also run amok in children's stories. Then there are dragons and wizards and a host of other beings that could be included in the framework of fantasy.

Definition: Fantasy is historical.

That could very well be true. A great number of fantasies, including Tolkien's Lord of the Rings, could fall into the historical category. But there are endless possibilities for modern day fantasies, or fantasies that don't even include an announced time period.

Definition: Fantasy is all magic.

Fantasy does include the use of magic. But what about worlds where magic doesn't exist? What if it's a world like our own without science or magic, and people and beasts of all sizes and characteristics inhabit this world? Is it science fiction? Is that the qualifying ingredient? Magic? Even though that would make a nice generic definition to finally label our elusive "fantasy" category, unfortunately, it's not that easy.

Definition: Fantasy is about the fantastic that doesn't rely on science for explanations.

Since this definition is as close as we can possibly come to describing fantasy, let's expand on that. General agreement in the present day world of authors involved in the fantasy world is that fantasy is not science fiction. Fair enough. So, just what is fantasy?

FANTASY EXPLAINED

Loosely, fantasy is an applied mythology, a creation in the mind of an author of worlds or events that could not possibly exist in the scientific realm. There is the tendency to create a sort of mixed breed with stories such as "*Star Wars*" where there are laser wielding aliens and druids with some sort of magical force. But on the whole, science fiction and fantasy usually has a line of demarcation.

Fantasy uses devices such as magic, fantastic creatures that fly—no matter how improbable in the real world—historical settings, modern settings, and so on. They do have one thing in common. There is no scientific explanation of how these things are achieved. Instead, the author creates a base of rules that are used entirely in the world of his devising that would not apply to the normal everyday world. Science fiction applies technology and expands to try to "forecast" other devices that could possibly exist in the near or far future, in short, based on reality and possible scientific achievements. If there is a matter-transmitting device, it is grounded in "science" with an explanation of how it could be achieved. It has to be carefully written and described to make the process as believable as possible to the reader.

Fantasy uses this describing factor, as well, but it is based on rules entirely created for the world that's being written about; the author does not attempt to create the possibility of such things working in our real world. It is a self-contained compilation that engages the reader in fantastic things that live inside the mind and propels the reader into a world where imagination is the key.

In creating this book, authors with expertise in different fields were called upon to give you the best possible learning devices to create your world. You will be taken on a step-by-step process of character creation, race building, world building, magic and its uses; combat, weapons and armor, religion, mythologies and a host of other ingredients for a successful story. This in-depth look at fantasy will generate inside you a wellspring of ideas. With the resources contained throughout these chapters, you will find a way to create a believable world of your own, with living, breathing characters.

Welcome to the world of fantasy. Welcome to the world of your imagination. Welcome home.

Roots of Fantasy

JOHN TEEHAN

INTRODUCTION

The first piece of advice any professional writer gives to the aspiring writer is this-read! Read for pleasure. Read to know the market. Read to know what's been done before and how. Read for inspiration. Mine for source material!

And don't just read within the Fantasy genre. Read books of history. Books on law. Books on mythology and folklore. Read a few mysteries, westerns, and historical romances. Check out what's happening on the science fiction half of the shelf. Read the *Bible*, the *Bhagavad-Gita*, the *Sunflower Sutra*, the *Koran*, and the *Tao Te Ching*. Grab a stack of comic books. Read *Beowulf*, *The Canterbury Tales* and the works of William Shakespeare. Find good translations of Boccaccio, Dante and the Pearl-poet. Read James Hilton's *The Lost Horizon* and *The Razor's Edge* by W. Somerset Maugham. Don't forget to add Mark Twain—especially *A Connecticut Yankee in King Arthur's Court*. Explore lost worlds with Allan Quartermain in *King Solomon's Mines* and fourteen other books by H. Rider Haggard. While you're at it, grab a copy of *She*. Collect the complete works of Jules Verne, Edgar Allen Poe, Edgar Rice Burroughs, and even H.P. Lovecraft. Look for some old pulp magazines at a used bookstore.

Are you ready for a shocker?

It didn't begin with J.R.R. Tolkien. I'll pause for a moment while you regain your composure. It's true, you know. Modern fantasy did not begin with tales of hobbits and diverse companions gamboling across *Middle Earth* in search of an honest politician.

Unsurprisingly, the roots of modern fantasy are more subject to debate. Many feel, and rightly so, that they stretch as far back as Homer's *Iliad* and *Odyssey*, while some maintain that modern fantasy is more a creation of the Victorian era, with writers such as H. Rider Haggard or slightly later with Edgar Rice Burroughs.

Part of the problem is in defining Fantasy to begin with, and I'll tell you now that's one bear I'm not going to bait for very long. Damon Knight once said, when asked to define science fiction, "Whatever I point at and say is science fiction!" One could similarly do the same thing with fantasy. The rules are different from science fiction—despite how they're shelved in bookstores, fantasy and science fiction are distinct genres. Personally, I like something Ted White (past editor of *Amazing*, *Fantastic*, and *Heavy Metal*) let slip: "Fantasy is magic that works."

Granted, I've unfairly taken the quote out of context, but, nonetheless, that definition appeals to me. It's overly simple. It doesn't attempt to be all encompassing and it leaves room for a lot of interpretation. Nobody's feelings are hurt and everybody is offended all at the same time.

So did Fantasy begin with Burroughs? Haggard? Homer? What about Robert "Two-Guns" Howard and his hulking Cimmerian creation, *Conan*? In the end, it's all a matter of perspective. One could actually go much further beyond Homer to discover roots of fantasy in Mesopotamia with the stories of *Gilgamesh*, the first epic hero on record who possessed the strength of an army, tamed wild men from the forests and slew dragons in distant lands. Even then, it probably started much earlier than even that.

Imagine a prehistoric time. Cavemen and cavewomen sat around the fire and relayed the day's events. When they finished with the news of the day they'd start retelling stories of the past.

"One time," says Thog, "Thog hunt big mountain lion and kill it with club. Wham!"

Thog's friends have heard this story hundreds of times. They probably invented mathematics just to keep track of how many times he has told this tired old bean. Then one day Thog reaches the prehistoric equivalent to mandatory retirement age and his family leaves him to sit out his remaining years on a glacial shelf. With Thog and his tiresome story out of the way, his descendants decide they'll relate the story of Thog's adventure this way:

> "And Thog, son of Moot, approached the glowing river where the Goddess of the Hunt spoke to him and beckoned him to place his hand beneath the roiling torrents. Thog reached into the icy waters and took hold of the fabled Warclub of Goog and set forth to purge the hunting lands of the evil demon that was plaguing—"

And that's how it likely began: the mixing of the natural and supernatural worlds to tell the story of heroes combating forces greater than themselves.

Folklore. Legend. Myth.

So far as we know, these stories were never recorded. Thog could have found a magic spear instead of a magic club. Fortunately, however, there are plenty of other written sources we can look at. One doesn't even need to go back all that far to find some literary resources that relate directly to contemporary fantasy—only say, nine hundred years.

THE ROMANTIC TRADITION

Let's pay a visit to the twelfth century. Eleanor of Aquitaine's children (Richard the Lionhearted and the luckless Prince John) decide that locking their mother up in a tower is safer for the stability of Europe than letting her play politics. Locked away, and not the sort of noblewoman who gets much satisfaction from sewing daisies onto petticoats, she turns to literature as her comfort. In a time when troubadours and other poets depend upon wealthy sponsors for their livelihood, Eleanor is a medieval writer's dream come true. There was a price to pay, however. One has to write the sort of stories that Eleanor enjoys reading stories about kings and knights, damsels such as herself locked in towers, and oodles of love poetry with a dash of adventure thrown in for good measure. Thus were born the medieval romances. (For more on Eleanor, read *Eleanor of Aquitaine* and *The Four Kings* by Amy Kelly)

Over the next few centuries, the most common element of these stories involved some sort of troubled romance between two people of different social stations, usually a highborn woman and a low-rent man—most often a poor knight or squire. Love was a major theme, with much time spent between the two players composing long discourses on painful infatuation, unrequited love and the occasional veiled reference towards extramarital sex. At some point in the story the man would set forth on a heroic journey to prove his worthiness and the depth of his devotion. He'd swim the deepest sea, climb the tallest mountain, chop down the biggest tree with a silver spoon, all to prove his love was true. These quests often sent these poor heroes to foreign lands where they'd meet with many trials along the way. Sound familiar?

For settings, most medieval romances split into two main camps: those that dwelt on the British side of the Channel with stories of Arthur and the Round Table and those from the French side with tales of Charlemagne and his paladins. Both had their heroes in shining armor, their monsters and maidens, their magics and quests. However, unlike Arthur, Charlemagne (aka Carolus Magnus) is a verifiable figure in history, credited with founding the Holy Roman Empire and pretty much bringing civilization to most of Northern Europe. For some fascinating accounts into the life of Charlemagne and his court, consult *Two Lives of Charlemagne*, available from Penguin Classics. For an example of French romance with Carolingian characters, I highly recommend perusing *The Song of Roland*. For a Carolingian story by a more contemporary author, check out *Three Hearts and Three Lions* by Poul Anderson.

While the inspiration of Charlemagne played a significant role in the development of the romantic tradition, it is the story of King Arthur and his knights that has captured the most attention and has the most direct influence on fantasy today.

THE DEATH OF ARTHUR

Make a list of your favorite contemporary fantasy novels. Now go through that list and ask yourself how many of them contain one or more of the followings themes:

- · Commoner who is really a king
- · Old wizard who guides the hero
- · Enchanted sword or other artefact of great magic
- · A quest for a relic, sometimes a vessel, with powers on a god-like scale
- · Diverse companions

Perhaps a more difficult task would be to find the fantasy novels that don't include any of these themes. While each of the above has appeared in countless legends, fables and sagas over time, they've never before come together quite like they have in the tales of King Arthur. Whether or not Arthur really existed is almost immaterial by now; the real Arthur was most likely a Celtic war chief from around the time of the Roman occupation—meaning he didn't wear full plate armor and was probably as much pagan as Christian. Just the same, myth eclipses reality, and the spark that launched the popularity of the Arthur myth into the centuries that followed was set by a fifteenth century Warwickshire knight named Sir Thomas Malory (1405-1471).

If Tolkien is considered the father of modern fantasy, then Thomas Malory would rightly be considered its great-grandfather. He was something of a troublemaker, career criminal, and part-time highway bandit. While imprisoned for sedition and murder, as a nobleman and sometimes-member of Parliament, he was nonetheless permitted to visit a local library once in a while where he consumed its contents of romantic literature. By pulling together bits and pieces of previously existing Arthur stories [read Tolkien's translation of *Sir Gawain and the Green Knight*] with the traditions of the romance tradition, he compiled and created the stories that became *Le Morte d'Arthur* or *The Death of Arthur.*

By itself, Malory's opus wasn't a very organized piece of work. Fortunately a copy fell into the hands of a man named William Caxton who owned a printing press. As much as Eleanor inspired the tradition and Malory collected the stories, Caxton edited them into a form that remains unchanged to this day. (Never underestimate the power of a good editor.) With Caxton's presses running overtime, copies of *Le Morte d'Arthur* spread across England and France sparking a multitude of imitators and other Arthur-inspired stories.

The story of King Arthur didn't end with Malory any more than it started with him. Sir Walter Scott, the man who introduced Robin Hood to literature in *Ivanhoe*, composed *The Lay of the Last Minstrel.* Alfred Lord Tennyson took Malory's *Camelot*, full of murder, betrayal, incest and infidelity, and transformed it into a kinder, gentler *Camelot with Idylls of the King* suitable for a Victorian audience. Later came T.H. White's *Once and Future King* and *The Book of Merlin*, which enjoyed mass media popularity with the shortened Disney adaptation in *The Sword in the Stone* dwelling more on Tennyson's *Camelot* than Malory's, but the basic structure of the tale set down by Malory and edited by Caxton remained close to true.

The themes set in the stories of King Arthur are probably the single most important influences in modern fantasy and Camelot remains an open and viable playing field for many writers. More recent visitations to the Round Table include Mary Stewart's Merlin trilogy beginning with *The Crystal Cave*, which tackles the Arthur tales as a historical romance. One also should not overlook Marion Zimmer Bradley's *Mists of Avalon*, which tells the Arthur tale from the women's side and summons up more of the Celtic origins of the story.

Camelot lives on, and King Arthur, Guinevere, Sir Galahad, Sir

Lancelot, Sir Percival, Mordred, Merlin, and Morgana le Fey are not about to leave us anytime soon.

AGES OF GODS AND HEROES

Go back further in time and, depending on which culture you examine, you stumble across a period when gods and heroes roamed the Earth. Author David Eddings once suggested that pagans were more fun to write about than Christians, and he has a pretty valid point. While we are enchanted with Arthur's Christian knights and their holy quest to recover the Holy Grail, we find the old gods of the Norse people and the ancient Greeks equally entertaining. In some instances we find them even more entertaining as a wealth of legends, myths and folklore span the ages, giving these old world gods personalities and agendas not unlike our own, only larger in scope. The study of any culture's myths makes for one great epic story.

Take the ancient Greeks for example. Zeus is always slipping away from his wife Hera in search for some young maiden to molest, leaving half-god children in his wake like a sixties rock musician on tour. (A lot of children in these stories apparently suffer from irregular parentage.) Hera, rather than tightening the reins on her husband, punishes the maidens and their children, resulting in stories like those of Herakles. Then there are lighter stories, such as that of the Pleiades sisters who were placed in the sky by a protective Zeus to keep them out of the reach of Orion the hunter. And how can anyone forget that it was mythic Prometheus who provided mankind with fire and for his troubles spent the rest of his days chained to a rock with an eagle dining on his delectable innards?

Quite a collection of stories. All of them make for good source material. In how many contemporary fantasy novels do gods take a direct hand in the events of mortals? Quite a few. Myths have even proven to be popular in popular media. While shows like *Xena: Warrior Princess* or the *Legends of Hercules* make good folklorists purchase antacid in bulk, there's no question that modern audiences still feel an affinity for the days of yore, even if those myths and legends have been a bit bruised by Hollywood. I heartily recommend that before jumping into playing with ancient myths, you check out what the original myths are really like. *Bullfinch's Mythology* has long been the gold standard of myth-lore and you may remember reading dog-eared copies of Edith Hamilton's *Mythology* from high school English classes. Both are excellent places to start. [While you're at it, check out the story of the Trojan War and Odysseus in Homer's two masterpieces, the *Iliad* and the *Odyssey*, both packed with gods, monsters, heroes and historical figures. For the Roman angle, check out Virgil's version in the Aeneid.]

Myths and legends don't have to be Greek in origin to be enjoyable. You have a whole world to explore. Bullfinch and Hamilton both venture into Norse myths as well as Greek, and any good library will have collections of myths and legends from around the world. Start with Ainu creation myths and keep going until you hit the Zulu tales of Unkulunkulu. If that's too much to read at once, thumb through a copy of *The Dictionary of World Myth* by Peter Bentley for an overview and then select the folklore you wish to explore further. [While you're at the library, look for *Man, Myth, and Magic*, an encyclopedia set edited by Richard Cavendish.]

Before we move on, I should really take time to point you in the direction of *Beowulf* as well. Outside of "classical literature" (i.e., Greeks and Romans), Beowulf is probably the most significant epic hero of pre-medieval times. Like any good hero, when someone yelps 'help', he comes. In this case he ventures to Heorot Hall and, through bravery, wit, and godlike strength, slays Grendel, a monster who's been terrorizing the local populace. He then risks life and limb by swimming into a underwater cave to defeat Grendel's sorceress mother and later on defeats a dragon, taking a death blow that allowed him to die like a hero. While the monks who transcribed the original oral version of Beowulf slapped on a veneer of Christianity, the story is still quite laden with the presence of Northern Europe's pagan past. Beowulf is basically the European answer to Hercules and worth your time exploring. [While you're at it, take some time to consider the monster's point of view in John Gardner's novel, *Grendel*.]

On Fairy Tales

Between the worlds of epic poetry and romantic literature lies another world of literature with origins deeply set in the folk tradition. Partly myth and legend, partly parable, these are the kinds of stories told around the fire and later to children nestling in their beds, these are the fairy tales. Versions of these tales can be found in Celtic folklore and offshoots of Norse myth. Here, giants, ogres, elves, dwarves, gnomes, and dragons populate the land. The details vary from region to region, which only adds to the wealth of resource material. Most of the earliest material was never recorded, only bits and pieces found in various folklores and copied down by professional folklorists in pursuit of PhDs.

Of course that's only half of it. Not even half. The rest of the world of Fairy is easily accessible in the collected works of the Brothers Grimm and Hans Christian Andersen. One could easily make a career just by studying these alone; in fact, some people have. Any foray into writing fantasy should include reading through at least a standard collection of *Grimm's Fairy Tales* with its classic and often horrific stories of *The Bremen Town Musicians, Snow White, Sleeping Beauty* and *Little Red Riding Hood*. Probably more than Arthur or the *Iliad*, fairy tales enjoyed a wider popularity in their tales focusing on simple people just trying to survive in a world that held a lot of mystery and terror, not too much of a stretch considering everyday life for peasants in medieval Northern Europe.

Fairy tales went through an evolution of their own through the centuries; beginning with dark folktales of Jenny Greenteeth who would drag young children into the bogs of Ireland to the instructive *Aesop's Fables* and continuing on to Hans Christian Andersen's enchanting tales of *Thumbelina* and *The Snow Queen*. Fairy tales and purposefully fanciful tales such as *The Travels and Surprising Adventures of Baron Munchausen* blended into each other. The latter was at one time considered a revival, of sorts, of Jonathan Swift's *Gulliver's Travels*. [While you're exploring the Neo-Classical period, check out Voltaire's *Candide*.] Fairy tales later merged with the modern novel in works such the immensely popular *Peter Pan* by James M. Barrie.

Fairy tales aren't limited to the West. Every culture has its own collection. Again, this is a case where going to your local library for some research will pay off. If you're thinking of setting a story in a certain type of society, start looking for fairy tales from cultures close to your creation. [I will, however, personally recommend *Myths and Legends of Japan* by F. Hadland Davis and *The Trickster: A Study in American Indian Mythology* by Paul Radin as being good reads, either for pleasure or research.]

Whether you dismiss folklore and fairy tales as stories suitable for children only, don't overlook the fact that everyone was once a child and these stories affected the vast majority of us during our development. Fairy tales are as valid a resource as any other literary source for contemporary writers. Ask Anne Rice. Ask Patricia Wrede. I'm sure they'd agree.

THE ARRIVAL OF MODERN FANTASY

As we inch forward in our survey of literary roots for fantasy, we stumble across a number of authors ranging from the well known to the obscure who have had their influence in today's fantastic literature. H.G. Wells, Jules Verne, Lord Dunsany, H. Rider Haggard, E.R. Eddison, Edgar Rice Burroughs, H.P. Lovecraft, Robert E. Howard and Clark Ashton Smith are some of the better known of the names. There are others, of course, such as William Morris and James Branch Cabel, who deserve attention as well, but they're less known today and difficult to find in print, even in used bookstores (although with the recent explosion in small press businesses, some are now finding their way back into print). For a more comprehensive survey covering the early years of modern fantasy, look for a copy of L. Sprague de Camp's *Literary Swordsmen & Sorcerers: The Makers of Heroic Fantasy*.

Most of the modern fantasy writers took advantage of magazine and pulp markets for their stories (or were reprinted in them). Back then the definition of science fiction hadn't been firmly established—that wouldn't come until Hugo Gernsback and John W. Campbell made their marks. Instead, there existed a general theme of imaginative literature that featured stories set in places such as the "Third Hemisphere" (Lord Dunsany), the Earth's core (Jules Verne), the future (H.G. Wells), lost civilizations (H. Rider Haggard), Mars (Edgar Rice Burroughs), other planets (E.R. Eddison), Atlantis (Robert E. Howard), and the very edges of perception (H.P. Lovecraft). As the pulps evolved, other writers continued to explore strange new worlds. Clark Ashton Smith set his stories in a fictional land called Averoigne. Catherine L. Moore established the role of the modern female fantasy heroine in seven stories set in a quasi-medieval society. Fritz Leiber created Fafhred and the Gray Mouser, two adventurers who caught the imagination of the multitudes over the years and are still read today. Andre Norton still writes a fantastic fiction today after breaking into novels in the 1950s. [Grab her *Witch World* novels.]

Back then fantasy didn't exist as a distinct category of fiction. Science fiction (sometimes called "scientifiction") was still an emerging genre disdained by many and relegated to cheap magazine racks until changes in the paper market allowed for cheap paperback books to be produced. This resulted in a series of reprints of Edgar Rice Burroughs and a flurry of pastiches openly imitating the style and grandeur of Barsoom. I won't recommend any of the pastiches as they're generally derivative with little new to offer the genre, but they're fun reads when the mood is right. Ask around at your local used bookstore. For some later fantasy from that era check out the works of C.S. Lewis, a contemporary and friend of a certain modest Cambridge don who entered the picture in 1954 with a little story he had been noodling with for a few dozen years.

ON TOLKIEN

I can't get away with writing a chapter on the literary roots of fantasy without acknowledging the enormous influence John Ronald Reuel Tolkien (1892-1973) has had upon the field. Right or wrong, for many people, Tolkien is the beginning of contemporary fantasy. For one thing he was the most commercially successful. Almost fifty years after *The Lord of the Rings* first appeared, he remains consistent bookstore fare and with the twenty-first century releases of *The Lord of the Rings* movies, the resurgence of interest has boosted the books to the bestsellers lists once again. I know full well that *The Hobbit* came out first in 1937; and while *The Hobbit* was well received, it wasn't until *The Lord of the Rings* that a real impact was made on the fantasy market.

Tolkien's ability to create the believable, living and breathing world of *Middle Earth* is rarely matched even today. He began the tradition of including maps with novels and put such care into his world building that even his notes are avidly read by fans. Before the Klingon Language Institute was established, Quenyan, Tolkien's version of elvish, was the most spoken or studied fictional language (discounting artificial languages such as Esperanto and Interlingua). Many authors have sought to emulate him and his creations, making elves and dwarves common denizens of many fantasy worlds. Incidentally, Tolkien also popularized the "-ves" plural for "elf" and "dwarf" in storytelling—previously the plurals had been "elfs" and "dwarfs." He took characters and settings from sagas such as *Beowulf* and Finnish *Kalevala* and reinvented them into character types and landscapes that have become familiar in many novels since then. [If you really want to get in-depth with Tolkien, by all means, be my guest. Check out *The Tolkien Reader* especially *On Fairy Stories* and *The Letters of J.R.R. Tolkien*.]

The plot to *The Lord of the Rings* can be used (and has been used) as a road map for outlining one's own fantasy novel, as it contains all the essential elements for a good fantasy story. The hero, Frodo, comes from a secluded part of the world. He is a reluctant hero at the start, later gaining encouragement far beyond what would usually be expected of any normal individual. He has many and diverse companions to aid him on his way. There is an object of power—The One Ring—and he has guides for his journey, Gandalf and Strider. There's the theme of the hidden king (Strider becomes Aragorn) and even the theme of Evil mirroring Good (Orcs are Mordor's version of Elves, Trolls star opposite dwarves and Gollum is the antithesis of Frodo). After taking into consideration everything that's come before Tolkien, the Arthur tales, *The Song of Roland*, *The Canterbury Tales*, *The Odyssey*, "*Jack and the Beanstalk*", along with historical sources such as *The Battle of Maldon* and Tacitus's *Germanica*, *The Lord of the Rings* didn't so much break new ground as it repaved the old ground for the next generation.

That's not to say Tolkien was being unoriginal. Far from it. Never before had a story been put together exactly this way and received such unexpected worldwide acclaim. The debt contemporary fantasy writers owe to Professor Tolkien goes beyond measure. He helped define the current fantasy genre and created the necessity for a new category of books in publishing. Fantasy, while still shelved next to Science Fiction, became identified as a genre separate from Science Fiction, with its own rules, traditions and heritage. The modern writer who attempts to write in the fantasy genre and is not at least familiar with Tolkien's creations is like an inventor who builds a light-emitting device in order to illuminate his workshop without looking into all this talk about light bulbs. It's possible, but why would you do something that way?

BEYOND TOLKIEN

More and more fantasy novels began popping up following the success of *The Lord of the Rings*. Among those early fantasy novels was a first novel entitled *The Sword of Shannara* by a young man named Terry Brooks. Today he's a well known author who has shown up repeatedly on bestseller lists as each decade a new set of *Shannara* books crop up to entertain long-time fans and bring new fans to fantasy readership. More than any other book in the seventies, *The Sword of Shannara* was a direct descendant of the works of Tolkien. Populated by blond, sylvan elves and squat, suspicious dwarves, a wise druid and dark riders, the similarities are too numerous to count. However, rather than being dismissed as merely a Tolkien rip-off, the *Shannara* books were a smash success. Brooks was not writing as Tolkien; the plot was not the plot of *The Lord of the Rings*. It was a similar setting using similar tropes, but the story was original and entertaining. While Tolkien may have been the inspiration, the *Shannara* books went beyond being merely a pastiche and, instead, added to the development of the look and feel of fantasy literature that perpetuates today.

The seventies were good times for new fantasy writers. Another young man named Stephen R. Donaldson sold a difficult trilogy to Del Rey called *The Chronicles of Thomas Covenant*. This was undoubtedly a fantasy world populated by giants, monsters, magicians, and horsemen—there was even a magic ring—but it was unique in the sense that it introduced a very different sort of hero. Instead of starry-eyed youths like Frodo Baggins or Shea Ohmsford, Donaldson gave us a middle-aged leper with a very sour attitude towards life in general—so much so that he rejects the fantasy world he finds himself in and adopts the title of Unbeliever. While Donaldson surely was influenced by the trend in contemporary fantasy novels to focus on quests and clear conflicts between good and evil, he took a chance and experimented with a hero who was hard to like and harder to identify with, as for most of the story he doesn't believe in any part of the quest. Donaldson showed us that we didn't have to write about elves or dwarves to make good fantasy.

Other early blockbusters in the seventies booming fantasy field were Patricia McKillip with her *Riddlemasters of Hed* series and the already popular Anne McCaffrey dragon books, which were enjoyed as much by Fantasy fans as Science Fiction fans. Katherine Kurtz published the *Deryni* saga, which managed to create a strong Christian flavour in its magic system. By this point people were no longer feeling confined by Tolkien, but identified the overall archetypes in Tolkien's works and made them their own while at the same time drawing from a wide range of resources ranging from the *Bible* to Celtic mythology. Piers Anthony shifted from Science Fiction to Fantasy with his best-selling *Xanth* series. Drawing heavily from creatures from myth along with heavy doses of wordplay and puns, he created adventures in a unique world where using magic was as natural as breathing air.

Despite the odd nod towards occasional nostalgia, literature tends to move in a forward direction and builds upon what came before. The eighties and nineties saw more fantasy books hit the shelves. David Eddings appeared on the scene with his wildly popular *Belgariad* series and took his inspiration from the works of the medieval romance writers, along with a healthy dose of Jungian archetypes. Robert Jordan's immense *Wheel of Time* books added a bit of Eastern influences to a growing genre that was becoming ever more confident in telling epic-length tales.

In the eighties gaming had a significant influence on the genre as well. *Dungeons & Dragons*™ was a popular role-playing game that owed much of its inspiration to Tolkien's *Middle Earth*. This game's influence was carried into fiction as some writers found ways to bring the feel of gaming to the pages of fantasy novels. Among the most successful were the *Guardians of the Flame* series by Joel Rosenberg and Raymond Feist's *Riftwar Saga*. While the former's theme involved a direct transfer of human role playing gamers to a fantasy world, the latter was more self-contained in the fantasy world but heavily influenced by Fantasy role playing game settings. Around this time, the owners of *Dungeons & Dragons*™ began publishing their own series of novels set in official game worlds.

By the nineties and the onset of the twenty-first century, Fantasy took up as much space on bookstore shelves as Science Fiction, and the number of popular authors are too many to mention in a single chapter. Suffice to say that the literary roots of fantasy didn't stop at Tolkien. More and more authors began experimenting with worlds based less on medieval Britain or Celtic Ireland, and set their stories in alternative versions of medieval Spain (Lois McMaster-Bujold's *Curse of Chalion*), medieval France and Italy (Jacqueline Carey's *Kushiel* series), lands inspired by Australia, South America, and even the Arctic.

You're limited only by your own imagination.

A FEW VINES

Before closing this chapter I just want to mention a few other literary sources of importance to the development of modern fantasy. While bricks may be the most important part of building a house, it'd be a pretty shaky dwelling without supports and mortar. These resources aren't entirely fiction, but they've made their impact on the development of today's society and, by extension, may help you develop worlds of your own.

Become familiar with religious texts. The Christian *Bible* is a must for Medieval Fantasy, but I'd add surveys of Hebrew scholarship and the *Koran* as well. I personally enjoy reading Buddhist texts and the works of Lao-Tze. For some keen instructions on how to build a rigid society, check out works by or about Confucius. For some adventure, read the *Baghavad-Gita* and get the scoop on Krishna.

Include history and politics as required. *The Babylonian Code of Hammurabi* is the first recorded set of laws. China's *Romance of the Three Kingdoms*, while probably the first example of written fiction in existence, gives some great insight to feudal Chinese culture. [While you're at it, look for a copy of *The Travels of Marco Polo*.]

Don't forget the ever-popular strategy manual, Sun Tzu's *Art of War*. There's *The History of the Franks* by Gregory of Tours and *The Alexiad* by Anna Comnena (daughter of the Byzantine Emperor Alexius I). Read Machiavelli's *The Prince* and Heroditus's *Histories*. For more contemporary sources, I highly recommend *A Distant Mirror* by Barbara Tuchman for an amazingly detailed examination of fourteenth century European life.

Dissect myths in Joseph Campbell's *The Hero With A Thousand Faces* and *The Power of Myth*. For a good breakdown of archetypes in modern storytelling, obtain a copy of *The Writer's Journey* by Christopher Vogel. While exploring the world of Jung, check out the thoughts of Freud as well. When you're done with psychology, explore parapsychology. It may surprise you.

At this point I imagine you're wondering why our gentle editors haven't snuck up on me yet and pumped a large amount of sedatives into my arm. In all seriousness, however, the vines for research, inspiration and information stretch out as far as your imagination can take you. You now have a fairly good list of recommendations to start with, and I'm sure you've already come up with an equally valid list of influences and resources that I've failed to mention. Good! When you're writing fantasy you're not writing on a raft set adrift. You're writing amid a tradition that stretches all the way back to poor Thog, son of Moot, and his magic club.

Make use of it.

Wham!

CHAPTER APPENDIX: A READING LIST

Again I feel I should make this disclaimer.

The list below has a number of glaring omissions. They aren't glaring to me now, but they will be about a week after this is published. You'll probably see them right away. You'll notice right away that I've neglected to list your favorite source materials and authors. The point of this chapter isn't to catalog the immense number of fantastic works in the canon of worldwide literature, but, to point out some avenues of exploration that you may not have already considered. Fantastic stories are not new phenomena; in fact, they've been with us since the very beginning. When we write fantasy, we're both continuing a tradition and cutting new ground at the same time. To know where we're going, it's good to know where we've been.

Consider the works below as merely a starting place.

As for the groupings and the order of listing, I've tried to keep certain themes of literature together without worrying about when they were published; hence, John Gardner's *Grendel* is listed with *Beowulf* as *The Mists of Avalon* is with *Le Morte d'Arthur*. Don't worry overmuch about the grouping. Read the books instead.

SOME SOURCES:

THE ANCIENT WORLD TO THE AGE OF HEROES

Beowulf

Grendel (John Gardner)

Grettirsaga

Mythology (Edith Hamilton)

Histories (Heroditus)

Germanica (Tacitus)

Illiad (Homer)

Oddysey (Homer)

The Aeneid (Virgil)

Bullfinch's Mythology

Code of Hammurabi

Kalevala

MEDIEVAL WORLD TO THE ENLIGHTENMENT

The Alexiad (Anna Comnena)

The Battle of Maldon

The Squire of Low Degree

The Prince (Machiavelli)

Gulliver's Travel's (Jonathan Swift)

A Distant Mirror (Barbara Tuchman)

Eleanor of Aquitaine and the Four Kings (Amy Kelly)

Romance of the Three Kingdoms (from China)

The Travels of Marco Polo

Sir Gawain and the Green Knight (author unknown, referred to as the Pearl-poet)

Canterbury Tales (Geoffrey Chaucer)

The Parliament of Fowls (Geoffrey Chaucer)

The Exeter Book

The Song of Roland

The History of the Franks

Candide (Voltaire)

Ivanhoe (Sir Walter Scott)

ARTHURIAN TALES, THEN AND NOW

Le Morte d'Arthur (Thomas Malory)

A Connecticut Yankee in King Arthur's Court (Mark Twain)

Camelot (Lerner & Loewe)

Idylls of the King (Alfred Lord Tennyson)
Once and Future King and *The Book of Merlin* (T.H. White)
Mists of Avalon and others (Marion Zimmer Bradley)
The Crystal Cave and others (Mary Stewart)

FAIRY TALES AND SUCH

Grimms' Fairy Tales

Aesop's Fables

Peter Pan (James Barrie)

Hans Christian Anderson's Fairy Tales

On Fairy Stories (J.R.R. Tolkien)

FROM THE EARLY YEARS OF MODERN FANTASY

Jules Verne

H. Rider Haggard

H. G. Wells

J.R.R. Tolkien

Fritz Leiber

Edgar Rice Burroughs

Clark Ashton Smith

H.P. Lovecraft

Andre Norton

C.S. Lewis

Lin Carter

Lord Dunsany

Robert E. Howard

James Branch Cabel

Catherine L. Moore

L. Sprague DeCamp

RECOMMENDED CONTEMPORARY FANTASY AUTHORS

Piers Anthony

Terry Brooks

J.V. Jones

Jacqueline Carey

Raymond Feist

David Eddings

Stephen Lawhead

Elizabeth Haydon

Robin Hobb

Patricia McKillip

Robert Jordan

Guy Gavriel Kay

Katherine Kurtz Tad Williams

Stephen R. Donaldson

George R. R. Martin

Anne McCaffrey

Laura Resnick

Jennifer Roberson

Joel Rosenberg

Lois McMaster Bujold

RELIGIOUS TEXTS AND RELATED

The Bible

Zen Flesh, Zen Bones (Paul Reps)

Tao Te Ching (The Way of Life) (Lao-Tze)

The Koran

The Baghavad-Gita

SOME MISCELLANEOUS RESOURCE MATERIALS

The Hero with a Thousand Faces (Joseph Campbell)

The Power of Myth (Joseph Campbell)

The Dictionary of World Myth (Peter Bentley)

Man, Myth and Magic (Richard Cavendish, ed.)

The Writer's Journey (Christopher Vogel)

Myths and Legends of Japan (F. Hadland Davis)

The Trickster: A Study in American Indian Mythology (Paul Radin)

Black Elk Speaks (Nicholas Black Elk, John G. Neihardt)

The Art of War (Sun Tzu)

Characterisation:

BRINGING CHARACTERS TO LIFE

LEA DOCKEN

INTRODUCTION

Characters become. We get a story in our head and we have to tell it. We have to tell it because the characters are jumping around dancing and yelling at us to tell their story. And when I say their story I mean exactly that. It is their story. We are but the means to share them with others. The Muse strikes us with classic tales full of classic characters, and they simply become.

They live with us. They eat with us. They sleep with us. They watch television with us. They play with us. They do the dishes with us. They are with us when we—well, they are with us all the time. They will not leave us be. I imagine my Muse is hiding watching the proceedings and giggling to herself at my foolishness instead of opening the present she has given me. Yours is probably giggling away somewhere also. So, now that the Muse has given us our playmates and story ideas what do we do with them? We flesh them out and tell the tale we are supposed to tell.

Remember the last time you asked someone for directions? Did they have a hard time telling you how to get to their home or place of business? The last time I asked a friend how to get to his house for a party he and his wife were having, he ended up drawing a map. They lived in the country—once we got out of town there was no point of reference, but by following the directions on the map we knew exactly where we were going.

There are times when people ask me how to get to my house from a certain point and I have to sit and think really hard about how I drive from there to my house. And you know, at times it is really hard. I know how, but telling others the route I take day in and day out is not easy. Have you ever said to someone, "I drive that everyday but I can't think how to get to..." Frustrating, isn't it?

You do not want to leave your readers frustrated by not having well-rounded characters they can relate to. Yes, even fantasy characters need to have characteristics that we can relate to. This chapter on Bringing Characters to Life will be your map to making those pesky characters you live with day in and day out come to life on the page, so your readers will cry, laugh, and generally have fun with the story you are sharing with them.

CHARACTER BEGINNINGS

Your personal Muse sends you an idea and characters to help you fulfil a story idea and share it with others. The great question is: "What do you do next?" The question is answered by the way you work. Some people like to outline characters before they go any further and some like to take time to mull over what they are like. Cutting a picture from a magazine, or downloading a picture from the net, or drawing the character is another way. Then there are those who just carry a picture in their mind. It is so firmly planted an earthquake could not uproot it. So as long as a system works for you, use it.

The above methods are only a start. There is so much more to do: deciding what the character is like, choosing a name, deciding who is good, bad, in between, deciding who is going to be the action hero, the heroine, deciding who is going to be a flat character or a character just because one is needed in a scene—and so forth. Whew! Are you tired yet? You can't be because there is more—lots more.

Remember that you are making the character as real to the reader as he/she is to you. Listen to what he/she is telling you. Have a chat over morning coffee. Yes, there may be times you may feel schizophrenic but hey, you are a writer, you're supposed to feel crazy at times.

Work with one character at a time. Begin with names. Names are never easy. You may go through several changes before you hit upon a name that feels right to you and your characters. And there will be times the first names you think of will be the right names. Your writers' group may hate the names you have chosen and your friends might laugh out loud, but if you love and adore the names, and they just feel right, keep them. You may want to use A, B, C, D, etc., as placeholders for each character until you can come up with a name.

How do you choose the names? Some names just pop into your head. If the name popping into your head works for you then by all means use it. For those who have trouble with name popping there are many resources that generate names. Check out the World Wide Web. The Internet can provide many name-generating sources. You may like the baby name books found at the checkout counters and magazine racks at grocery and discount stores. *The Character Naming Source Book* is a great book for names and meanings. Read the obituary column and jot names you like in a notebook. If you are walking through the mall or are at a restaurant and hear a name that interests you, write it down in a notebook. All writers should carry a handy dandy notebook with them at all times.

You want the name to fit the character and the character to fit the story. Once you begin to really flesh them out, he or she will fall into the story and the name will fall gracefully to them. After the naming, numbering, or placeholding—such as A, B, C for the characters—it is time to really start working on fleshing the character out to seem as real as possible.

You will find getting the story partially written is an asset in bringing your characters to life. It can be a foundation to build from. In this way the character begins to grow as you write, and will result in making your characters convincing to the reader. Within the first twenty to fifty pages of the WIP (Work In Progress) the main characters will probably show up. Work on each in turn. Some writers write the whole story. Then when the WIP is finished they go back and test and flesh out characters' needs. Some writers are talented enough just to write and have the characters come to life there and then.

There are several tricks you can use which will help you know your characters intimately. First, initiate each one of your creations with a name. Then begin bringing each character to life by working on these eight steps: Timelines, Back-Stories, Dreams, Closets and Clothes, Where They Live, What-Ifs, Character Profiles and Semantic Mapping. Many other methods float around. You can hunt them down if you wish. However, these eight steps will bring your character to life and give you a base for your writing.

You may wish to work through your character as you read this chapter, or you may want to read it first and then go back and work on your character. Either way is good. Have fun

EIGHT STEPS TO BRING CHARACTERS TO LIFE

1. TIMELINES

Timelines are a way to get to know your characters through the events in their lives. The year they were born, important events that happened within their lives and so forth and so on. Doing a timeline for several different characters will show certain events overlapping within the characters' lives. You will find it an interesting phenomenon.

Timelines can be a frustrating experience at times. If you want the perspective of the age of Mesopotamia and want to work a Timeline starting at 2700 BC, aging the characters 'backwards' can be confusing and fun. The important thing to remember about timelines is that the character has to be born, age, go through certain life events, come to a critical climatic stage within the story, and live happily ever after or die. The ending for the character is up to you. The timeline ends at the end of the story or the end of the character's role in the story. Some writers think it is important to do a timeline for every character in the story, even the static ones that just appear in a scene as window dressing. I do not. Write the timelines for your major characters and perhaps the characters that support the main characters and be done with it. Otherwise you will be bogged down in timelines and won't get any other writing done.

So, your timeline will look something like this:

1960 Joh was born, triplets, two sisters were with him. A Wise Woman (or Witch) raised them until their fifth birthday.

1965 On his fifth birthday Joh was sent to military school and his two sisters were sent to a girls' boarding school, separating him from his sisters and his mother.

1970 Joh turns ten, graduates from middle studies with honors and begins secondary studies concentrating on philosophy and magical law.

1972 Joh begins puberty and dreams about his siblings and the horrible separation. As yet he does not understand the significance.

1975 Joh is still plagued by dreams so real he wakes up screaming. He is beginning advanced studies.

1980 Plagued by nightmares about his sisters, Joh graduates

with honors. He takes his place in the high ranks of Advocates.

1985 Joh begins his search to find his sisters.

You may begin your story at any time within the timeline you are writing. Your Timelines can be as short or as long as you want depending on your character and his role in the story.

The above Timeline was done in modern time as a point of reference. Alternatively, you might look for an aging process outside of historical references. For your fantasy character the years may look something like this:

· 0   Joh was born

· 5   Joh began school

· 10   Joh had his first crush

· 15   Joh graduated with honors—etc.

2. BACK-STORIES

Once you have the Timeline done it is easier to do Back-Stories. Back-Stories will rarely be used in the story, if at all. However, Back-Stories are essential in order for you to be able to see and show your character as a live person. The personal history you will write will give you the needed insight into what makes your character tick. Write your Back-Stories before the WIP. Take a minute and think of one of your friends. Think about what you know about them. You'll have more information on your friends than you originally thought. Let your characters be like your friends, even if you don't like them personally. Find out all you can about them and write down their stories. Back-stories give your characters life. Your characters come to the page with their own history. Listen carefully, hear what they tell you and see with your mind's eye what they are showing you. Write everything down. Refer to the Timeline if you get stuck. Include all the details you can in the Back-Story. Write until you feel everything has been told to you. And remember to do a Back-Story for each one of the important characters in your book.

Let us take a look at Joh's Back-Story based on the timeline given above.

Joh was born to a poor family in the Northern Mountain Village of Kahm. He was the youngest of eight children. Actually he was the youngest of triplets. Two girls and Joh were born on the eve of February 29th, 1960. A legend was told in the mountains; any multiple births on the 29th of February in a year ending in zero were psychically linked and the children were marked for Mystics. Joh and his sisters Mara and Nari were doomed from birth. Their parents, poor villagers, could hardly provide food for their normal children and now they were expected to feed three witches.

His parents consulted a Wise Woman of their village, never realising she, too, was a twin born on a February 29th in a zero year many, many years ago. Her sister died in childbirth, which gave the Wise Woman a strong psychic connection to the netherworld. She immediately saw the future of all three children and knew they needed to be away from the family for that future to unfold. The Wise Woman told the parents that Joh must be sent to a military school in the town of Lugh and his sisters to a girls' school at Sophie. On their fifth birthday, the three children were to go to the schools. The Wise Woman would support and care for the children until then.

For five years the Wise Woman cared for and raised the triplets as her own. The children loved her as their mother and they knew no different. Soon the fateful day came. Joh and his sisters cried and threw tantrums as they were separated from one another. Young Joh made a promise that one day he would find his sisters and they would never be separated again.

Joh entered the Lugh School of Military Tactics. He catapulted through the subjects and moved through all the levels quickly.

The Back-Story continues until you come to the place where the character enters your main story. You can see that by comparing the Back-Story to the Timeline you can toggle back and forth filling in the Timeline as needed or jotting notes to the side. Or you could leave it, as the Back-Story has filled the Timeline in for you. But if you are working with only a Timeline you'll want all the information in case you need it.

Three other characters were introduced in the Back-Story example. If you were writing this story you would want to pursue Back-Stories on these additional characters. The first step is a Timeline on each. The second step is Back-Stories. If you get stuck, resort to Semantic Mapping or Webbing. We will discuss this trick later in the chapter.

The more Back-Stories you write the more in-depth your understanding of your characters will be. Aren't Back-Stories wonderful? As you get acquainted with the people in your story, an idea of the conflict and obstacles your characters will have to overcome should start to form.

You have a very long way to go yet before you have a good story. The ideas are forming and evolving as you get to know your characters. And before you realise it, your story will be blossoming and fleshing out with a very solid foundation.

3. DREAMS

Dreams are very intimate and can tell us a lot about others and ourselves. In his book on writing, The Weekend Novelist, Robert J. Ray suggests using dreams as a way to get to know your characters. It is a great way to delve into your character's psyche and see what is really going on inside. In the case of the example Joh, his dreams mentioned in the timeline would be the trauma of separation from his birth sisters. By pretending you are the character you can write a dream they had in your journal or tell the dream to a friend or therapist. A dream may look something like this.

> I woke up screaming last night from a dream that I had. I was in a fog holding on to something soft and small in both hands and all of a sudden I was being pulled away from it. Being pulled away from them.

> They started screaming "No! Don't go! Don't go! We can't live without you, Joh! Joh! No! Let go!"

> And then I started yelling, "Mar! Nai! I am coming. I will save you! Let me go!"

> I was pulled away by some unknown force, screaming and crying, "No! No! Mar! Nai! I am coming! I will find you!"

> Then I woke up. I do not know who these people are. I do not know what is pulling me so hard. I must find these two—I do not know who they are or where they are. They come every night to me. They get closer. The other night I almost saw them. I wake up screaming and crying.

The dreams may change as the character progresses, playing a major role in the action, plot or conflicts of the story. Any questions you have regarding your characters can be answered as you work through your character sketches. Once you begin to bring your characters to life the story develops dramatically.

Dreams are only one way. As the creator you could do a series of therapy sessions with your characters. Or you could do interviews, or the characters could write journals. There are all kinds of ways to get to know what makes your characters tick.

4. CLOSETS AND CLOTHES

Closets and clothes may not seem important to you but your characters want to look good and fit into the style of the day, or have their own style. No matter what the period, whether they are in an Alternate Universe, a Renaissance Fantasy Period, a Middle Ages Period, a SF Romance Fantasy, or an era you make up, dress is important. It is also important to decide if their clothes are computer-generated, kept in trunks, in wardrobes, clothespresses, trunks, or hung on racks. What your character wears will tell the reader who your character is. We learn a lot about people by the way they dress.

Style is important. Start by thinking about your style of dress. What is yours: artistic, romantic, eclectic, conservative, gypsy? What style would be good for your characters? What colors do you like to wear? What are your characters' favorite colors? Think of your favorite movie or book character. How do they dress? What style of clothes do they wear? What colors do they like to wear all the time? What do their clothes tell you about them and the story? Anything? The type and style of dress will tell the reader a lot about the character and the story. And may even give clues to the conflict the character is facing within the story. So, the way you dress your characters will tell the reader a lot about the characters.

As the author you will gain insight into the character by taking a peek into where clothes are kept. As a result, it will be easier to write about that character as you progress through your story. Will your character have a closet, a trunk or a rack? Or is the clothing computer-generated? Will he or she wear just one outfit or have two thousand to choose from? How many pairs of shoes do they have and what type? In your character sketches, write about where your character keeps his/her clothes. You will most likely not be using this scene in the story you are writing. However, by writing about the clothes, and where and how clothes are kept, you will produce a deeper look at the character inside your own mind. This transfers to the WIP and will flesh out your characters even further. The example below will give you an idea on how to proceed.

Joh opened the door to the clothespress. He sighed. He did not have much in the way of dress clothes and the dinner was to be a black gown affair in honor of the Templar's wife's birthday. He would have to choose carefully. There were a lot of dark jackets and trousers, although none were extravagant. They would have to do. He was a poor student, and although apprenticing under the Templar did bring in some extra monies, it was not enough to engage a tailor to make a proper black gown dress jacket and trousers. One of these days, Joh thought, I will be able to hire the best tailor in the country and I will wear the best of the best— no more hand-me-downs or making do. Joh sighed as he reached for the indigo suit with the dark aquamarine collar and cuffs. Maybe if he wore a dark shirt under the jacket, he would fit in. Joh smiled as he handed the outfit to his personal groomer, the man provided to him by the Templar, and headed for the bath that only the Templar's favorites could use. Being the Templar's star student and right-hand man did have its advantages as well as disadvantages.

Here we see a not so struggling student. Joh has been taken under the Templar's wings and is being groomed for a high position. Joh is being spoiled and coddled just enough to whet his appetite. We get a glimpse of what he will become some day and by using his thoughts on clothing another facet of his characterisation is brought to light.

5. Homes, Apartments and Worlds

The type of houses, apartments and world your characters live in will tell you a lot about them. When filling out profiles for characters one of the basic questions will be about where they live, the type of home and the street in general, the immediate neighbors, and the car he/she drives, if any. Other chapters in this book go into detail about world building, but remember that environment plays an integral role in character development.

Joh came home tired. He had been in court all day with only a noon break and was exhausted. It would not have been so bad except today was just the beginning of what was turning out to be an exceptionally long and complicated trial. All he wanted was to open the door and step inside his home. He opened the door to the whitewashed adobe house and let the rush of cool air envelop him. He kicked off his sandals and delighted in the feel of cool red tile against his feet as he made his way to the bar to make himself a tall cold drink.

6. The 'What If' Game

A fun thing to do with characters is play the 'What If' Game. Ask your characters questions. What if you liked asparagus? What If you lived at night and slept during the day? Would that make you a vampire?

With the character Joh as an example, play the 'What If' Game. You would ask questions like these:

· What if Joh was despised by his teachers and only accepted by the top marks he made?

· What if Joh was the Templar's right-hand man through a testing process only and not hand-picked?

· What if the Templar hated Joh and only put up with him

because the system said he had to?

- What if Joh despised the Templar?
- What if Joh vowed revenge on all of those who got in his way?
- What if the woman he loved and understood more than anyone was his sister and he did not know it?
- What if his sisters died in childbirth?
- What if he never got the breaks discussed previously?

How would these things change the story? How would it change Joh? You see, the 'What If' Game can go on and on. Not only do you have to ask the questions, you have to answer the questions too. It's a great thinking game, and once again you get to know each character and more about the story they are telling through you.

You can play the 'What If' Game with whatever you write; poetry, story, books, etc. It really works wonders and gives you the advantage of developing a full understanding of the characters you are writing about.

7. CHARACTER PROFILES

Next to Back-Stories, this is one of the most important things you will do for your characters. Profiles range from the simplistic to extremely complex. Once you choose a Character Profile, you will find it keeps evolving as you use it. It evolves because you will change it to fit your needs for almost every story you write.

Many books line the bookshelves of libraries and bookstores with all sorts of handy-dandy information on creating profiles. The main information you might be interested in, so that you may create your own character profiles, is listed below. Feel free to add what you need or delete what you feel you do not need for your particular story. However, keep the entire list as a master profile, just in case you need to use other aspects for different stories.

Title Of Book	Name Of Character
Age	Height, Weight And Body Type
Eye Color	Hair Color And Hair Style
Skin Tone	Physical Condition
Distinguishing Features	Physical Imperfections Most Likely To Change
Gestures	Ethnic Group
Family Background	Religion

Parents	Siblings
Neighborhoods	Income
Growing Up	Education
Skills, Talents	Short And Long Term Goals
Short And Long Term Wants And Needs	Introvert Or Extrovert
Eccentricities	Type Of Temperament
How He/She Handles Anger Or Rage	Admirable Traits
Negative Traits	Habits
Prejudices—Good And Bad	Things That Irritate
Things That Make Character Uncomfortable Or Embarassed	Most Painful Things In Life/ Traumas From Past
Political Leanings	Sense Of Humor
Fears	Phobias
Friends	Enemies
Major Probems To Be Solved (At Least Three)	Solutions To Problems (At Least Six)
Lessons Learned	Chronology Of Actions From Beginning To End Of Story—At Least One To Twenty

Cobble together whatever you need for your character profiles. It is an ever-evolving process. As you work on the profiles you will find things you do not need for a particular character in a particular story so just skip it. When you have time, review the profile and decide if you will need to use the item in the future. If not, get rid of it.

Look for these major items in any profile you choose: title of work, name of character, age, body type, coloring of hair and eyes, physical characteristics, body language and gestures, race, culture, religion, education, occupation and skills. Do not hesitate to take any character profile ideas and make them your own.

8. SEMANTIC MAPPING

Semantic Mapping is a trick to use whenever you get stuck on a character or characters. Use it whenever the ideas are just not gelling. It's a simple way to get ideas rolling. Some people call Semantic Mapping, "Webbing." Whatever you call it, it works. It is another paper and pen

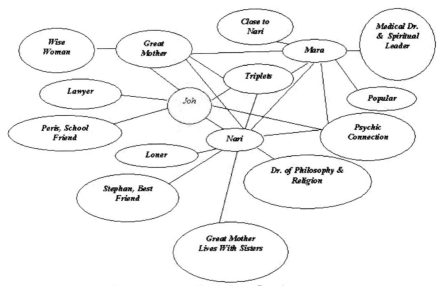

play and it's a terrific way to get the juices flowing.

Here is what you do. Draw a circle in the centre of the page. In the circle write the name of the character that is giving you problems. Draw a line from the centre circle outward. At the end of the line draw another circle. Inside that circle write the name or idea or whatever pops into your head regarding that character.

In the example, I have highlighted Joh, the example we have been working with, as he is the centre of the Semantic Map. And on and on the Semantic Mapping goes until ideas run out. You may find you need more then one sheet of paper for one map. Just keep going until you are finished. One idea relating to another idea leads to a different idea relating to the same one, a new one, or a different idea.

TYPES OF CHARACTERS

There are many different types of characters filling the pages of your book that come to aid you in telling your story. In many ways, you are a casting director as well as the writer, and in your hands you have to juggle the lead players, the supporting characters and the extras. The intricate handling of these characters is what makes your story develop and progress. Some characters appear only in one paragraph and some are seen throughout the whole book, depending on whether the characters are just window dressing or have an ulterior purpose.

The point of view (POV) character is from whose eyes the story is being viewed. The POV character may be a minor character, a major character or a narrator telling the story.

The Protagonist is the main character of the story, who the story is about, the character we remember when asked about the story, and generally thought of as the good guy.

The Antagonist is the bad guy, the one who is the opponent of the protagonist or the enemy of the hero of the story.

For a more intricate look at characters you can refer to a paper by James Patrick—"You and Your Characters" at: http://www.sfwa.org/ or the 'Living World' chapter in this book.

DEFINING CHARACTERS THROUGH CONFLICT

You will never go through life without conflict and problems to solve and neither will your characters. The characters you bring to life will always have some type of conflict or problem, and the meat of the story can sometimes be the solving of those problems. Your characters are defined mostly through conflict and adversity. As your characters work towards a solution, they become breathing, living entities and bring the reader into their world.

The character I chose to work with, Joh, started off with conflict. Joh's conflict is who he is versus what he has been brought up to be. And as the story develops, Joh will discover he has more than one problem to resolve, just like people in the real world. As a writer, you have to decide the predominant problem that needs to be resolved. And, of course, your characters will resolve more than one conflict within the story before they resolve the main conflict.

SUMMARY

Getting the writing process started is the hardest part of creating wonderful characters. Hand in hand with getting started is using the knowledge gained through writing and reading the reference books that line your bookshelves. Do not get stuck in all the various worksheets, formulas, and research the books recommend. Your most important job is to write the story and bring those characters who are in your head to life on paper. They do not have to be perfect people. Who wants to read about a perfect character?

You want your characters to be fallible, to have a not so perfect complexion, to be gangly, to have a wee bit of a stoop. You want your men to be engaging, but that doesn't mean they have to be perfectly handsome. You want your women to have some "bitch" qualities, and perhaps only type twenty-five words a minute and not be able to cook. Think about your favorite actors. Are they shorter than the norm? Perhaps their noses are a bit crooked? Perhaps their faces are not symmetrical? Maybe their figures or physiques are not up to the model image. How about your favorite characters in the books you read? Do they have flaws in looks as well as personality? It's the qualities that aren't perfect that make people so intriguing.

So, throw your books out. Box them up and put them in the attic. Stack them and use them as end tables. Put them on shelves where they can stay out of the way and yet be grabbed when you need a reference. Getting lost in the swampland of methodology is not where you want to be. Your characters won't find you and you won't get any writing done. Writing and populating the story with engaging characters are your two main goals. Do not thrash in the quagmire of perfection and never get anything written.

Start writing. Start journalising. Write ditties. Write about anything and everything. Listen to your characters and write what they are telling you. Jot down notes whenever you can. Always carry your handy-dandy writing notebook wherever you go.

Writing scenes will take you into your WIP without even realising it and then you are on your way. At about fifty pages, stop, find your characters and begin to flesh them out more by using the methods discussed.

You do not need to use all of the methods discussed all of the time. Why? All the methods all the time for each and every character is overkill. You will be able to recognise and discern some of the characters without having to do the eight-step method. World building, religion building, race creation, magic, health or any other fantasy world creation will bring you closer to your characters. This is the point where you have to feel your way. You will find that each step overlaps the one before it as you build your story and your characters. Just as your life story spills into the lives of others, so will your characters'.

You need to do a Character Profile on the main character and the major supporting characters in your story. The main characters should have a thorough profile but the supporting characters can be as simple or as extensive as you like.

Always do Back-Stories for each main and major supporting character. By doing Back-Stories you will become intimate with your characters and bring that intimacy to the pages of your book or story. A character may show up in your Back-Story you had no idea about and he/she may become an integral part of your story. As a creator you can never be completely sure what will happen once you set the stage in motion. That's what makes it so interesting.

Timelines for all characters are very important, as it will help you track developments easily.

These Eight Steps can be done in any order. You can do Dreams first, Timelines last and Character Profiles in the middle. You can go straight down the line if you feel it is needed. Do what feels best and makes the most sense to you at the time.

If you want to bring your characters to life, the reader needs to relate to them. You want the reader to laugh and cry with the characters you create. Begin to think about the characters that you are drawn to when you watch TV. How do you relate to them? Why? Are you drawn or repelled by certain characters? These are questions to ask when watching *Buffy*, *Star Trek*, *Beast Master*, *Xena*, *Hercules*, *Six Feet Under* or *The Sopranos*.

Why do you cry during scenes with Buffy and Angel but not with Buffy and Spike? Why do you laugh at *Ally McBeal* and cry when you watch *The Practice*? Why do you watch *Frasier*? *ER*? *Judging Amy*? What draws you to these shows? If you only watch the news stations think about what makes them so interesting to you. Is it the personal conflict that's evident in most news stories?

What kind of movies do you like? Why? What is it about that character that draws you? Do you watch soaps? What draws you to the daytime dramas? Many people watch soaps because the characters are so intense. Whether it's a classic movie or even a news program, take notes on the characters, especially paying attention to which characters are evolving, which ones are window dressing and which are just there for support. Note the ones who make you emotional. Become aware of the characters and where they fit according to type and how they relate to you as a writer when you read your next book. As you read, ask yourself what you would do differently and why. Ever wonder how their lives progress after the story ends? How would you have changed the story? Could you have developed the characters better?

Be aware of what is going on around you. Be aware of the characters on TV, in the books you read and the movies you watch. Be aware of how much time you are spending on getting the characters perfect instead of listening to the characters and writing the story they have to tell through you.

The Eight Steps to Bringing Characters to Life will give you fully developed characters in no time. You will be able to write the story and not get stuck in a mire of 'how to' books. You will be able to work with the Muse and the characters that are dancing and yelling at you inside your head. And you will be happy because you have accomplished something great. You'll have written a character driven story with the help of your personal Muse and the people in your head. Not only is it a great story, it's a story with characters you created. Fantasy characters with human frailties, needs, conflicts, failures, and the whole gamut of human experience, giving them the ability to be larger than the page upon which they are written. It is those larger than life characters that will stay with the reader long after they've read that final sentence.

WEBSITE RESOURCES

- http://www.writerswrite.com/journal/jun00/gak14.htm
- http://www.absolutewrite.com/novels/articles1.htm
- http://teenwriting.about.com/library/weekly/aa072701a.htm
- http://teenwriting.about.com/cs/creatingcharacter/
- http://www.fictionfactor.com/articles.html
- http://www.runesofao.com/roa/webdoc2.htm
- http://www.sillybilly.com/write3.html
- http://www.concentric.net/~pcbc/awritingtips.html
- http://www.wtamu.edu/~jcraven/Enneagram.htm
- http://www.9types.com/
- http://www.musecreations.ca/vanessagrant/
- http://www.musecreations.ca/vanessagrant/
- http://www.babynamer.com/
- http://www.panix.com/~mittle/names/
- http://www.flatearth.com/utilities/namegen.asp
- http://spitfire.ausys.se/johan/names/default.htm
- http://www.poewar.com/articles/adversity.htm
- http://www.globalserve.net/~pjduane/characterbuilding.htm
- http://www.eclectics.com/articles/character.html
- http://www.sillybilly.com/objecti.html
- http://tritt.wirefire.com/tip8.html
- http://www.sfwa.org/writing/character.htm
- http://www.q-ten.co.uk/artsotm/resources/characters.html
- http://www.ideafisher.com/creative.htm
- http://www.actioncutprint.com/chart.html
- http://www.creativepurrsuits.com/reststopnews/characterchart.html
- http://www.keirsey.com/
- http://www.hobgoblin.net/resources/createlink1.asp
- http://www.twc.org/forums/ASF00159.html

Always keep a Great Heavy Dictionary and Thesaurus by your side. Always keep a writing manual handy. I prefer *The Gregg Reference Manual.*

I am never without the *Self-Editing for Fiction Writers*. Since my first love is poetry I always have a Rhyming Dictionary by my side.

BIBLIOGRAPHY

Browne, Renne, *Self-Editing For Fiction Writers*, Harper Collins Publishers,©1993 Editorial Department Harper Collins, ISBN 0-06-270061-8

Busteed, Marilyn, *Phases of The Moon*, Shambhala Publications, ©1974 Marilyn Busteed, ISBN 0-87773-056-3

Cameron, Julia, *The Artist's Way*, Putnam's Sons, ©1992 by Julia Cameron, ISBN 0-87477694-5

_____, *The Vein of Gold*, Putnam, ©1996 by Julia Cameron, ISBN 0-87477-879-4

_____, *The Right To Write*, Putnam, ©1998 by Julia Cameron, ISBN 0-87477-937-5

Campbell, Joseph (ed.), *The Portable Jung*, Viking Press, ©1971 by Viking Penguin, ISBN 0-14-015-0706

Card, Orson Scott, *How to Write Science Fiction and Fantasy*, Writers Digest Books, ©1990 by Orson Scott Card, ISBN 0-89879-416-1

Charles, Ann, *The Story and Its Writer*, Bedford Books of St. Martin's Press, © Bedford Books of St. Martins Press, ISBN 0-312-03469-5

Elbow, Peter, *Writing With Power*, Oxford University Press, ©1998 by Oxford University Press, ISBN 0-19-512018-3

Faraday, Anne Dr, *Dream Power*, Afar Publishing A.G., ©1972 by Afar Publishing A.G., ISBN 0-425-16059-9, http://www.berkley.com

Goodman, Linda, *Love Signs*, Ballantine Books, ©1978 by Mannitou Enterprises Unlimited Inc., ISBN 0-449-90185-8

_____, *Relationship Signs*, Bantam, ©1998 by Golden Mountain Investments, ISBN 0-553-58015-9

_____, *Star Signs*, St. Martin's Press, ©1987 by Linda Goodman, ISBN 0-312-95191-4

Grant, Vanessa, *Writing Romance*, Self Counsel Press, ©1997 by Vanessa Grant, ISBN 1-55180-096-9

Kenyon, Sherrilyn, *Character Naming Source Book*, Writers Digest Books, © 1994 by Sherrilyn Kenyon, ISBN 0-89879-632-6

McCutcheon, Marc, *Building Believable Characters*, Writers Digest Books, © 1996 by Marc McCutcheon, ISBN 0-8979-683-0

Novakovich, Josip, *Fiction Writers Workshop*, Story Press, ©1995 Josip Novakovitch, ISBN 1-884910-03-3

Ray, Robert J., *The Weekend Novelist*, Dell Publishing, ©1994 by Robert J. Ray, ISBN 0-440-50594-1

Richardson, Cheryl, *Life MakeOvers*, Broadway Books, ©2000 Cheryl

Richardson, ISBN 0-7679-0663-2

Sabin, William A., *The Gregg Reference Manual* 9th Edition, McGraw Hill, ©2001 by McGraw Hill Companies, Inc., ISBN 0-02-804046-5 ISBN 0-02-804048-1

Swain, Dwight, *Creating Characters: How To Create Story Book People*, Writers Digest Books, ©1990 by Dwight D. Swain, ISBN 0-89879-662-8

Tanner, Wilda, *The Mystical Magical Marvelous World of Dreams*, Sparrow Hawk Press, ©1988 Wilda Tanner, ISBN 0-945027-02-8

Webster, Richard, *Aura Reading for Beginners*, Llewellyn Publications, © 1998 Richard Webster, ISBN 1-56718-798-6

Wilde, Stuart, Sixth Sense, Hay House Inc., ©2000 Stuart Wilde, ISBN 1-56170-501-2

Zuckerman, Albert, *Writing the Blockbuster Novel*, Writers Digest Books, ©1994 by Albert Zuckerman, ISBN 0-89879-598-2

Living World:

HOW TO MAKE YOUR CHARACTERS REAL

TEE MORRIS

When it comes to a study in characters, how they work, and when "stock" characters (something we will discuss in this chapter) ascend beyond their "stockiness," I recommend that everyone run out to their local video store and rent *Galaxy Quest*. If you have never seen this hysterical science-fiction comedy, *Galaxy Quest* centres around a cast of a *Star Trek* style television show.

Our heroes (who just play heroes on TV, mind you...) find themselves leading a far-off galactic civilisation that patterned their entire society from transmissions of their television show. "Character study" is beautifully summed up in a scene between Guy (an actor who appeared in one episode as an expendable Ensign) and Fred (one of GQ's regulars who played the Ship's Engineer). Guy hastily decides to single-handedly take on an entire platoon of hostile aliens in order to buy Fred and the good guys time to save the ship. The scene plays out like this:

Guy: "I'm just a glorified extra, Fred. I'm a dead man anyway. If I'm gonna die, I'd rather go out a hero than a coward."

Fred: "Maybe you're the plucky comic relief? Did you ever think about that?"

Guy: "Plucky?"

With this exchange, along with other numerous scenes throughout the movie, writers David Howard and Robert Gordon not only poke fun at actors, Science Fiction, and fans of Science Fiction, but also present an excellent study of characters. Characters, major and minor, remain at the heart and soul of any plot. They are what drive the story and keep the audience interested. Without solid characters, that audiences can relate to, feel and sympathise with, a story goes nowhere and audiences move on to another work.

Now while this is a guide to writing, I will be bringing a little more to this table from another passion in my life—acting. Now don't get me wrong. Science Fiction, Fantasy, Non-fiction, it doesn't matter to me. I love writing, but my degree was in Theatre. You may not think that there is a connection between writing and theatre, but both walk hand-and-hand in the world of media and entertainment as both are character driven. Actors and writers work on a daily basis with characters to capture their audiences, so don't be surprised if you hear me refer to scripts of stage and screen as well as books. What makes a good book is good writing. The same can be said for scripts on the big and small screen. You want to make a good movie? It all begins with a well-written script.

THE ESSENTIAL CHARACTERS

A story of any kind needs a subject. This subject can be a variety of characters. The Hero, the Damsel-in-Distress, the Villain, or perhaps the subject of the story can be the storyteller themselves. So how about we take a closer look at the people who keep the story moving forward?

THE HERO

Don't let this masculine, macho header fool you. In our post-*Xena* society, the Hero can also be a Heroine. Male or female, the term "Hero" is no longer limited by the boundaries of gender. This is a good thing!

Why not have females take control of your story? The popularity of the afore-mentioned warrior princess has only crystallised the demand for female heroes in Fantasy, a genre plagued with delicate, frail vestal virgins chained in a dungeon somewhere, hoping beyond despair that her valiant knight will rescue her from harm. While strong female characters are relatively new to the Fantasy genre, female heroes have been present in literature since Ancient Greece. Athena was the Goddess of War and hardly the "damsel-in-distress" in Greek Mythology. In Viking folklore, the Valkyries were hallowed as mighty warriors in service to Odin. It would be the Valkyries that would select the heroes worthy to enter Valhalla. In more modern times, Wonder Woman came on the scene in the comic books. Sixty years later, Princess Diana has never looked better! So while you may think the term "hero" applies only to men, think again.

To better understand what makes a hero, let's start at the beginning with the *Merriam-Webster Dictionary*'s definition of the word hero:

Hero: 1 a: a mythological or legendary figure often of divine descent endowed with great strength or ability b: an illustrious writer c: a man admired for his achievements and noble qualities d: one that shows great courage 2 a: the principal male character in a literary or dramatic work b: the central figure in an event, period, or movement 3 plural usually heroes: SUBMARINE (2) 4: an object of extreme administration and devotion: IDOL

Now, apart from definition three (unless you are planning for your story's hero to be a hoagie) the definition of hero is clear. Even while definition (2a) defines the hero as the "principal male", definition (2b) refers to the hero as a central figure, meaning your hero, by definition, does not have to be male. Heck, the hero doesn't even need to be human! It can be an intelligent computer, a dog, a cat, or an alien life form. Man or woman, animal or vegetable, Dwarf or Orc—your hero is who you make it.

Now that you have defined your hero, what kind of hero is your hero? You have a few options available here for what kind of central character you create for your Fantasy or Science Fiction adventure.

The Classic Hero

These kinds of heroes are the tried-and-true, pure-of-heart, and scary-perfect souls that step up to the plate and save the day for a living. You have Hercules, the child of Zeus, who faces his twelve labours and comes out standing tall with an "Okay, what's next?" attitude. King Arthur and the Knights of the Round Table (not the Monty Python "k-niggits" but the classic *Le Morte D'Arthur* knights, pure of heart, battling their human frailties to overcome adversity. And, of course, the Man of Steel himself—Superman. Faster than a speeding bullet, Superman can reverse time, push back tidal waves, stop earthquakes, and still make an appearance at the Little League World Series to throw the first pitch. They are the embodiment of all that is good. We look to the Classic Heroes as role models. The Classic Heroes are what we aspire to be. With clean living and following in their footsteps perhaps we will become what they represent.

THE SWASHBUCKLER

While the Classic Hero is what we aspire to be, the swashbuckler is who we really want to be.

They are the "bad boys and girls" of the heroes, also referred to as the anti-heroes. Swashbucklers possess many of the good qualities of Classic Heroes, but they are having way too much fun breaking the same rules that Classic Heroes try and uphold. Swashbucklers usually include Privateers, Pirates, Rogues, Highwaymen, Gamblers, Scoundrels, French Musketeers (three of them, in fact), and Mercenaries. So where can you study a classic swashbuckler in action?

Two words, one name: Errol Flynn.

While those of you who know Errol Flynn from the classic film *The Adventures of Robin Hood*, he is even more the swashbuckler in the pirate film classics, *Captain Blood and The Sea Hawk*. He's brash, swaggering, and full of bravado. Nothing fazed him, even when he faced insurmountable odds. In the genre of Fantasy, you have Terry Brooks' Cephelo from *The Elfstones of Shannara*. Always with the one-liners, cocky, and truly happy in the light of his own brilliance, he is a "Rover" with his own set of rules on how to handle what life throws at him. If you are looking for a good female swashbuckler, Eretia, Cephelo's daughter in *Elfstones...* is a terrific beginning. She fits this profile with her blunt, brash way of handling situations and people who cross her path. In more modern Fantasy settings, look no further that the Indiana Jones-esque gunslinger, adventurer, and tomb raider, Lara Croft. The rules of privilege take a back seat to her whims as she breaks the rules any and every chance she gets! Same can be said for The Chosen One, Buffy Summers. She has been blessed with the gifts and supernatural abilities of The Slayer, but her concerns are more towards who will take her to Sunnydale High's Senior Prom and if her outfits are with the latest tends. Regardless of her flippant attitude, she is still *Buffy, The Vampire Slayer*. Buffy sidekicks, spin-kicks, and stakes the agents of evil while still managing to be a teenager, always searching for the best way to throw her grown-up watcher off balance.

Now perhaps you think these qualities would not make a hero likeable. But it is that "rebellious" and confident attitude that makes these reluctant heroes so charming. There is also a lot of room for growth in these characters. You can keep the edge with these characters throughout your story, then give a slight polish to their personality in its finale. Not exactly grow them up, but simply make them wiser to the world you have built around them.

THE DARK HERO

You know the old saying "You can't make an omelette without breaking a few eggs?" This could be easily said for The Dark Hero. The Dark Hero is not reluctant or an overbearing egomaniac. For some of the Dark Heroes in literature, it could be argued that they are common vigilantes. It could also be argued that some Dark Heroes are sociopathic in nature. They are usually driven by some kind of tragedy or traumatic event in their life that turns them against the laws of society and, in some rare cases, nature. These heroes don't break the rules. They simply disregard them to get the job done.

Now when I describe a hero that has suffered a trauma, disregards the laws of society, and does what is needed in the name of justice, a "dark knight" probably springs to mind. Millionaire Bruce Wayne does fit the profile. Witnessing the death of his parents, followed by falling into a cave and disturbing a family of bats, was the foundation for the creation of the detective vigilante hero, Batman. Another character who easily falls into this category is Paul Atreides in Frank Herbert's *Dune*. Driven to the deep deserts of Arrakis after the assassination of his father and coups led by House Harkonnen and financed by the Emperor Shaddam the IV, Paul becomes "Muad'Dib." In the beginning, he is nothing more than a revolutionary, but as the story unfolds so does Paul's evolution into a messiah. While he does use his powers to liberate the desert-planet Arrakis, Paul also uses his new found abilities to literally hold the universe for ransom. Finally, there is the druid sorcerer Allanon. Throughout Terry Brooks' *Shannara* series, Allanon serves as a guardian and guide over the books' heroes, but he protects the Olmsford descendents with magical tactics and moralistic decisions that gives one pause, even from those benefiting from the sorcery. For a druid so high and revered of his order, Allanon gives no thought for discipline, and his reckless, careless disregard for the repercussions of his methods makes his darkness all the more chilling.

The Dark Heroes are perhaps the toughest of the heroes to write and base a story around, as they can become so dark they may turn their audiences and have them rooting for the villain. The Dark Hero needs to be out-of-control to an extent, all the while remaining likeable and keeping the audience on their side, even if they are ultimately doomed to succumb to their weaknesses.

While these three categories are good starting places for you in creating a hero, keep in mind you can always create heroes established in two of these categories or in all three. Take Wolverine, for example, from Marvel's popular *X-Men* series. Clearly, Wolverine is one of the more popular mutants featured. Why? Perhaps it is his darkness that makes him popular. He believes in getting things done, regardless of the consequences. But he is hardly a Dark Hero, as he does tend to accept counsel from Professor Xavier. So then he becomes a bit of a swashbuckler in his flippant nature.

Then you have the enigmatic Stryder (who is actually Prince Aragon) from J.R.R. Tolkien's *The Lord of the Rings*. He breaks rules and traditions by turning his back on a throne that is rightfully his. His hard edge and nature coming from being a Ranger makes him appear as a swashbuckler. When you discover his reasons for turning his back to the crown, he appears more as the Classic Hero.

So keep this in mind when creating your hero. You are not limited to your three types, but merely given a launch pad. Either stay within those confines, or shake-and-bake to create your own unique hero category. Also, try not to limit yourself to merely one hero. You can, if you so desire, have a number of heroes of all types leading your readers through your story. (Baggins, party of nine, your table is now ready.) Do be warned, however, that the more heroes and villains you incorporate, the greater a challenge your story becomes to write (more on the "Cast of Thousands" later in this chapter). You will want to feature everyone's abilities and special skills, but if you're not careful, your Fantasy novel becomes more of an exercise of "one-upmanship" where your heroes are showing off how their power is better than someone else's. Make sure if you do incorporate multiple heroes that, unless the story demands otherwise, you make them part of a team.

THE DAMSEL-IN-DISTRESS (OR DiD)

From here out, we will be referring to the Damsel-in-Distress as a DiD, because much like the hero this term is not gender-specific, nor should it apply to an individual. Let's say, for example, you want to try a bit of the conventional roles but in reverse genders. This would make your Damsel-in-Distress a Dude-in-Distress. Or let's say you want to avoid the whole person-in-peril formula and you make it a single hero hired to save a nation. Then you would have a Dominion-in-Distress. Usually, this is what a hero faces—someone or some place in serious trouble. (Of course if you're *Farscape's* John Crichton, you may have to face a different DiD—the Dominar-in-Distress, depending on what Rygel has got his grubby little hands into!)

A DiD, especially in today's modern society, carry extremely negative connotations. While Fantasy novels are often set in a far-off chivalrous time, the thought of a demure, virginal lady in white (yeah, same girl from the beginning of this chapter...) watching from a high tower window her hero approach, his sword held aloft, to face the demon horde in order to save her from the villain, is enough to make the most romantic roll their eyes in disgust. There is the burning desire to have the villain sneak up behind the wide-eyed, helpless damsel and just give her a good shove out of that window.

A DiD, however, do not have to fall into this trap. Male or female, they can also play an active part in the story. They can be one of the heroes of the story, if you so desire. The DiD can start off as part of the adventure, only to be captured or caught under a spell of the villain, and it is up to another in the Hero's party or the Hero himself or herself to rescue their compatriot.

As mentioned in the introduction of this section, the DiD can also be a country, continent or world in danger. In *The Lord of the Rings*, a looming threat of unleashed evil faces *Middle Earth*. In Robyn Miller's *MYST* series, the "book realms" were threatened if essential elements to keep the worlds intact were not corrected by the Creators. Making the DiD a realm or a world presents its own set of challenges for the writers. There is a risk of keeping the reader detached from the hero's struggle. If you do so, the reader loses touch with the hero, so when he or she proclaims boldly before The Council of Elders, "The Demons of Tyrian are threatening the Realm of Shisheros!" The reader could easily say, "Yeah, so what?" I don't know anyone who lives in Shisheros?" How can you care about a realm or a world that is distant and a collection of strangers to you? Going back to the example of *The Lord of the Rings*, do we really care about *Middle Earth* or are we more worried about Frodo, Sam, and the guys? By making the DiD something other than a person or people featured in detail, the audience runs the risk of caring little for the realm and even less for the story. Make certain to always remember who is driving the plot and holding the readers' interests—the characters.

Now that you have the DiD, be it a guy, a girl, a group, a realm, or a combination of the previous, and you have your heroes in place, your basic plotline needs to be mapped out. Now perhaps you're thinking, "Wait a second, this is sounding somewhat formula..." and you know what—you're right. All stories, no matter how innovative or original the plotline sounds, has a basic formula in place. An example of a classic formula that is still considered tried and true:

A meets B—B tells A of an undiscovered destiny—A goes on a journey with B at A's side—A meets C who tries to stop A from discovering destiny—B helps A overcome C—A discovers destiny.

Now this may sound like a pretty cliché formula, but this is the basis for numerous Science Fiction and Fantasy classics. If you doubt it, plug in the following names for A, B, and C:

- A=Galen, B=Ulrich, the Wizard, C=Vermathrax (Dragonslayer)
- A=Willow, B=Madmartigan, C=Queen Bavorda (Willow)
- A=Harry Potter, B=Albus Dumbledore, C=Voldemort (Harry Potter)

Following a formula does not necessarily mean your story is contrived or trite. The formula is merely the basis for your plot line. Without a formula you have a random series of events strung together and linked thinly by a series of events. In other words, a story that goes nowhere fast. A formula gives you the writer a sense of focus.

Now we have a hero and a DiD. All that is left is someone to start up trouble. We call that character the villain!

THE VILLAIN

For some authors, actors, and audience members, the villain is not only essential to the story but sometimes more important to develop than the Hero. The villain is the hero's reflection, the opposite that creates the conflict in the story. The villain can also be a lot of fun to create. Now let's go and take a look at the definition of villain:

Villain: 1: an uncouth person BOOR 2: VILLEIN 3: a deliberate scoundrel or criminal 4: a scoundrel in a story or play 5: a person or thing blamed for a particular evil or difficulty

Merriman-Webster's definition is pretty dry, but the villain has to be the equal antithesis to your hero. Villains are the instigators of the distress the Damsel, Dude, or Domain find themselves in. Without a clear villain, your readers have no focus for the struggle your heroes will face.

Much like the heroes, I have taken villains and broken them down into several sub-categories. These villainous types can be combined to create one super-villain or mixed-and-matched to create your own villain. Remember the sub-categories of "utter badness" are merely reference points for you in creating your story's villains.

THE CLASSIC VILLAIN

Supreme Evil—a total embodiment of our fears and insecurities. And similar to the term hero, the term villain can be either a man or a woman. This type of villain is the person that silences a room when he or she enters. With a look, he or she can silence an argument. With a gesture, they can kill. Villains are sociopaths or psychopaths of the most dangerous magnitude in that they act with a purpose, and care little about who or what is in the way of their goals. They are different from the scoundrels and swashbucklers who disregard the rules of society for fun. Classic Villains break the rules because they believe the rules are a hindrance, and this is something that makes the line between the Dark Hero and the Classic Villain so very thin. And like DiDs, Classic Villains can be either individuals or entire races. Examples of the Classic Villain include Lucien Blank in Danielle Ackley-McPhail's *Yesterday's Dreams*, Prince

John and the Sheriff of Nottingham from numerous tales of *Robin Hood*, and the Morlocks from H.G. Wells' *The Time Machine*. Classic Villains are sometimes thought to be two-dimensional, but they are no more two-dimensional than are Classic Heroes.

There are trends with some writers to make the Classic Villain redeemable as George Lucas and his crew did to their Classic Villain, Darth Vader. When you do this with a villain (of any kind) you take the chance of cheating the audience. You have spent page after page creating this evil presence only to reduce him or her to a "warm fuzzy" at the story's climax. It all depends on the story you create, but know that redeeming your villain in the story's climax can work for you or against you.

The Supernatural Villain

The Supernatural Villain is the embodiment of evil rooted in some sort of dark sorcery or paranormal power. Their intimidation and evil comes from breaking the laws of nature. In some rare cases, there are rules and limitations to their supernatural abilities, but it is these rules and limitations that set up these villains for vulnerabilities. Ray Bradbury's Mr. Dark from *Something Wicked This Way Comes*, Anne Rice's Lasher from her *Witching Hour* Trilogy, and the evil wizard Voldemort from the *Harry Potter* series all share these qualities. Even the Antichrist has made appearances, both in Stephen King's *The Stand* and Tim Lahaye & Jerry B. Jenkins' *Left Behind* series. These Supernatural Villains can be the hardest adversaries for your Heroes to overcome...

...as well as the most difficult to write.

Think about it. If you create "ultimate power of Evil", how can your hero stop it if you establish it as unstoppable? In creating your nemesis, you need flaws that your hero can either exploit or can undermine the Supernatural Villain's progress. Citing an earlier mentioned work, Danielle Ackley-McPhail's *Yesterday's Dreams* actually has two types of villains at its heart. First there is the Classic Villain of Lucien Blank, but working through him is a centuries old, dark entity named Olcas. The entity does have a consciousness of its own, complete with memories of when it was in its corporal form. Regardless of its power—and its power is immense— Olcas cannot act against the race he avenges against without an agent. Lucien Blank, through a great expelling of Olcas' black magic, became that agent; and now they cannot carry out their desire without each other. The symbiotic relationship they share is the Supernatural Villain's flaw, and an opening for our heroes whether they are aware of it or not.

Flaws are essential in Villains and in Heroes alike. We will discuss flaws later in this chapter.

THE BOND VILLAIN

Let's face facts—no villain is more fun to watch in action than a James Bond Villain, and I mean the classic James Bond villain. Who does not recall with delight the exchange between Auric Goldfinger and James Bond as an industrial laser is slowly inching its way up to Bond's body?

James Bond: "Do you expect me to talk?"

Goldfinger: "No, Mr. Bond, I expect you to die!"

Now I know you're thinking, "Um, I'm writing Fantasy, not campy James Bond spy stories," but I can assure you it is very easy to create your own Bond Villain for your Fantasy novel.

The Bond Villain lives life with a passion and does nothing on the small scale. They have an entourage wherever they go and money is never an issue. In many cases, the Classic Villain and the Supernatural Villain are either motivated by their own ambitions and desires, or driven by their nature, therefore beyond the control of their own actions. A Bond Villain, however, knows that what they are doing is wrong and they love it. They enjoy it. They are ecstatic in watching the hero or heroes suffer. As they are usually wealthy, privileged, and self-indulgent, they are addressed formally by their full name. For example: Ernst Stavro Blofeld, Hugo K. Drax, William H. Gates. (Wait a minute—I'll have to check that last name. I think he appears in a more obscure Bond film.) There is a hint of the Swashbuckler in a Bond Villain, tinged with a sinister overtone, and they refer to the hero only by their last names or by their title and then their last name. (Etiquette is everything to Bond Villains.)

Their motivation can be summed up in two words: world domination.

The one constant flaw in a Bond Villain is their ego. World domination indicates that in the eyes of a Bond Villain the world would be a better place under his or her rules. These kind of egomaniacs will trip themselves up as they refuse to believe anyone their true equal. They love the sound of their own voices, pontificating right to the bitter end.

Bond Villains are easy to spoof, a joy to create, and so much fun to play with in a story. It will amaze you how easy it is to incorporate the qualities of a Bond Villain into a Classic or even a Supernatural Villain. Just remember when writing a Bond Villain the prime directive: it is so very good to be a bad guy.

A RIVAL

A Rival, while classified as a villain, is not outwardly evil. Be it a rival opponent, a rival party, or a rival nation, the struggle here is either openly confrontational or "passive aggressive" in the way of politics. This kind of villain can be either the focal point of the novel or a secondary foil against the heroes. Terrific examples of rivals are the Klingons, Cardassians, and the Borg (along with a few select other races from both sides of the Wormhole) from the *Star Trek* universe. These races continue to harbour ongoing confrontational relationships with the Federation, therefore making them political and ideological rivals.

When the rivals are individuals, they can be family members or competitors of the same trade. In *Raiders of the Lost Ark*, archaeologist Indiana Jones' rival was fellow archaeologist René Belloq. The female pirate Morgan Adams faced off with her uncle, Dawg Adams in the swashbuckler film, *Cutthroat Island*. In both films, the rivals were not blindly evil but simply the competition for the final prize. Their villainy takes form in their tactics to thwart the heroes. Rivals and Bond Villains are "kissing cousins" in many ways. Both love one-liners and wordplay as seen here in Cutthroat Island:

Dawg Adams: Why aren't we moving?

Sailor: We can't leave yet, Cap'n. We haven't put enough food on board.

Dawg Adams: Then we need less mouths.

(Dawg then shoots the complaining sailor)

Rivals also enjoy breaking the rules. When your story pits a Swashbuckler against a Rival, you can imagine the chaos that ensues. As the Bond Villain is driven to rule the world, the Rival is out merely to rule their corner of it. In most cases, it is a matter of pride and ego in getting "one-up" on the hero.

So what exactly makes a Villain of whatever kind a truly unforgettable Villain? Charisma. In creating a villain, you create an intensely charismatic individual. They know how to charm you and win your trust, thereby gaining an ally and an instrument in their own personal agendas. Of course, when it comes to charismatic villains, Dr. Hannibal Lechter remains a favourite of many, even though he eats people. Another maneater of a villain who uses finesse to win friends (only to suck them dry, so to speak) is Anne Rice's *Lestat*. So when you create the Villain or Villains of your work, keep in mind their charisma. It comes in many forms and can even give your Villains a sensitive edge. You could even create your villain to be somewhat likeable, giving the audience a twinge of sympathy if he or she falls.

Now that we have the heroes, the DiDs, and the villains in place, we are ready to begin to work on your story. Now depending on the kind of writer you are, you can create supporting characters as you go. These supporting characters are also referred to as "stock characters." These are the "old reliables" that you can find in just about every story published. To make these characters original, well-rounded, and unique rests in how much time (and how many pages you're allowed) to develop and involve them in the story.

STOCK CHARACTERS

The term "stock characters" has many origins. *Commedia del Arte* theatre performers claim they were the first to "create" these characters, but they were really the first to make the term refer to characters that have existed since the dawn of the story itself. These characters are not "non-essential" (Stock characters have feelings too, you know) as some would argue, but merely serve minor roles in the plotline. You might have your heroes, DiDs, and villains, but it's the stock characters that round off the adventure.

Some writers avoid "stock characters" because they find them too cliché. We find, however, that these same writers are actually using "stock characters" because without them, the end result would be a very one-dimensional story. Good versus Bad for Kingdom. Well, joy. How about some colour? Some depth? Friendships? Anything! That is what "stock characters" are—the finishing touches to your heroes, villains, and DiDs.

THE SIDEKICK

Much like the Bond Villain, the sidekick has been parodied time and again, but still remains a staple in any good story. Why? The Sidekick gives the Hero a playful foil, someone to share ideas with, and maybe even share a bit of the glory. Many of the greatest and most unforgettable characters of Science Fiction and Fantasy have been a duo, a Hero and his faithful Sidekick. Bilbo had Gandalf guiding his way in *The Hobbit*. Sully would have a tough time getting the job done for *Monsters, Inc.* if Mike was not keeping his training intense. And just how much trouble would Captain Kirk have found himself in, if it were not for the logic of Mr. Spock? So, when creating a Hero, leave room for a potential Sidekick, as they bring a lot to the story.

Villains have their Sidekicks as well, but they are referred to as Henchmen. If you have a Bond Villain for your story, better start working on a cleverly named Henchman. Auric Goldfinger had his Oddjob (and I would be amiss not to mention Dr. Evil employed a hysterical parody of Oddjob, named Randomtask in the first *Austin Powers* film). Where would Count Dracula be without his own henchman, Renfield? Even in the legends of King Arthur, Morgana did a lot more damage to Camelot and The Round Table with Mordrid at her side. There is always room for a Sidekick or Sidekicks, and they can range in classes and trades. What makes the Sidekick work is the camaraderie shared with the Hero, even if the Sidekick is just waiting to get in a good shot and the Hero's square jaw. This is the common thread that bonds them together and pulls them both through the adventure.

THE TURNCOAT

This character can either be a loveable weasel who gets their comeuppance in the end of the story or could be the stranger that proves to be reliable, loyal, and steadfast only to show their true colours in the end. These characters, however, run the risk of being picked out right away as traitors, so the challenge in writing these characters is making them appear faithful without their betrayal of the Heroes seeming forced. Usually, Turncoats are just that—informants, spies, and "street urchins" trying to profit from both sides of the story's struggle and not get caught. Turncoats cannot be trusted, but sometimes the Heroes are given no choice. Other times, the Turncoats provide a bit of comic relief only to wind up double-crossing the Heroes. They can also be agents of the Villains, sent to win the trust of the Heroes in order to foil the Hero's plans from the inside. They might even be friends of the Hero, blackmailed into betraying him or her because of loved ones held captive by the Villain (see Dr. Wellington Yueh from *Dune*, who's supposedly unbreakable loyalty training was subverted by the Villain's schemes in order to destroy the Hero's father). Regardless, the Turncoats usually get it in the end and in many cases in the most horrible way imagined, to the delight of the readers.

THE ALL-KNOWING ORACLE

Quick—picture an omnipotent presence that has all the answers to Life. Don't think about it. Just picture it. Chances are, you came up with a bright, blinding light of angelic proportions. Or maybe you came up with a craggy, old man or woman on a rocking chair, slowly enjoying a pipe of tobacco while staring off into the distance. Something like that? But how many of you came up with a bartender that looked a lot like the guy who played D-Day in *Animal House*? Or did you come up with a kind, sweet lady in apron and oven mitts baking Oatmeal cookies?

All-Knowing Oracles have been constant stock characters since the days of Greek and Roman Mythology, and are still prevalent in today's Science Fiction and Fantasy. They appear in many forms (such as the earlier examples of the Bartender and the lady baking cookies were

Oracles from *Quantum Leap* and *The Matrix* respectively) but they share two things in common: they know all and because they know everything they are not saying anything. If you work the mystical know-it-all (because for the lack of a better term that is exactly what they are) into your story, make certain they don't spell it out for the Heroes or the Villains. They should serve as guides, not Information Kiosks that can tell your Heroes where to be, when to be there, and what to do when they get there. Give your Heroes through the Oracle just enough tidbits to stay in the game and (hopefully) win it on their own.

THE LOVE INTEREST

In many cases, the DiD becomes a Love Interest. If the story permits, a Sidekick or another Hero becomes a Love Interest. Then there are bold and daring writers that make one of the Villains a Love Interest. You can also make another character appear—a lost love, old boyfriend, old girlfriend—and they can indirectly affect the Hero's judgement. Now don't forget, Villains need love too. Sometimes, Love Interests can lock the Hero and Villain into love triangles. Romance is a part of the Fantasy arena; that much is certain. The necessity of involving a love interest is strictly up to you and the demands of the story.

THE MENTOR

It can be a "father figure," a "mother figure," or simply an individual who has seen the world several times over and now chooses to take a Hero under their wing. The Mentors are a lot like the Oracles in that they posses a great amount of knowledge, but they do not have all the answers. What answers they do have they give freely without cost. In their Life's experiences, they know the consequences of certain actions and try to protect their protégés from harm. Mentors are commonly depicted in Fantasy and Science Fiction as teachers, yet they still consider themselves students. Sometimes, their words are heeded. Oftentimes, their advice falls on deaf ears and they assume a more active role in the story (as in they will once more pick up the sword or grasp the enchanted staff once more) and help the Hero or Heroes back on the right track.

These are just a few generalisations of "stock characters" and from these generalisations can come many variations on a theme. This is where you come in as a writer. It is your words, your descriptions, and your characterisations that will make these characters—currently obvious and predictable on the surface—original and particular in your Science Fiction or Fantasy creation. It can begin in their outward appearance and then run deeper. How do these characters walk? Are they well spoken?

How are their thoughts given word? Are they verbose or curt? The more questions you can ask and answer about your characters, the better rounded they become.

THE DOSE OF REALITY

So here you are with a collection of characters, diverse in their make-up and spanning the globe of your world. They are staring back at you, wordless and dumb, simply waiting for those final touches. These final touches make or break your characters and it is these final touches where many new authors fail. How do they fail? Simple—they don't apply them. No one likes frailties or weakness in their characters, because these beings you breathe literary life into are like extensions of yourself, and so new authors tend to create the "perfect" individual, a character that is pretty, witty, and unstoppable. The end result is an individual the reader does not connect with (on any level) and quickly loses interest in whatever their outcome is in the story.

Your characters are all part of you, extending from word processor or pen and finding a home on paper or CD or ephemeral bit stream. It becomes an issue of ego. You want to create that Classic Hero, the embodiment of everything you aspire to be in life. Yet before your Hero heads into the Great Wide Unknown, you must understand and accept that he or she cannot go without some kind of vulnerability or flaw. Even though it's neat to think that this hero will face the opposition without a worry, it eventually becomes rather dull to hear about a Hero conquering evil without so much as a single tarnish on his armour or a hair out of place.

So while you are staring at your characters and your characters stare back, let's just touch base on some doses of reality and some things to think about when creating a cast for your Fantasy novel.

AVOID THE INVINCIBLE CHARACTERS

Even the Classic Heroes need chinks in their armour. All Heroes need some kind of fault or failure to make them Heroes. By overcoming this fault, the Hero becomes all the more heroic.

Now I have known some self-defensive writers who say about their characters, "My knight, Sir Stabs-a-Lot, does have an affliction. He's allergic to spicy food. If he has anything hotter than fresh horseradish, he has an allergic reaction." That is not a character flaw. That is a medical condition. In acting, we call this "raising the stakes." We increase the risk of the situation or scene by making our character's condition or outcome direr. So let's get back to Sir Stabs-a-Lot and his medical condition. How could we raise the stakes? Well, let's say instead of it being horseradish, why don't we say he has taken a vow of purity to his deity and refuses to take a life unless in combat. Therefore, he becomes a vegetarian. While on his quest, he runs out of provisions. No water, no food. He is close to death. Then crossing his path is a bunny rabbit.

Does our Hero take this innocent life to save his own?

Frailties make a character. Frailties make a hero not only likeable, but also easier to relate to.

Take the current literary juggernaut that is *Harry Potter*. J.K. Rowling's boy-wizard prodigy has proven himself to be formidable in the ways of magic, but is he a star student of Hogwarts? Hardly. Harry's a jock! He gets average grades (below average in the case of Snape's Potion Class) and sometimes he even misses homework assignments. Get him on a Quidditch field and he is in his element. Had J.K. Rowling created him as the perfect kid, with the perfect parents, with the perfect G.P.A., and captain of the Quidditch team, chances are Harry would not be as popular as he is today. In the case of *The Lord of the Rings'* Frodo Baggins, there is the fact he has never been outside the Shire. Now, on his first trip out, he is heading through all the various lands of *Middle Earth* to challenge the dark wastelands of Mordor. You bet he's scared!

Even with the great swashbuckler, Errol Flynn, the faults made the man. Captain Geoffrey Thorpe in *The Sea Hawk* was a brilliant tactician, a master swordsman, and a man who knew no fear. Except when it came to talking to women. He would get horribly shy, awkward, and tongue-tied. Audiences love reading about far-off lands; however, audiences enjoy even more the hero who overcomes adversity, both in the world and in themselves, to win the day. There is something gratifying in that kind of personal victory, and something we can relate to, even in the most powerful of Heroes.

Whatever shortcomings you give your characters, even if they are fantastic in nature, make them believable. Make certain whatever ails them continues to hinder them from beginning to end until you find the time for your Hero to either overcome it or use it to their advantage. Outlandish hindrances are about as believable as characters that possess none. Let's say, for example, the writer in question for Sir Stabs-a-Lot agrees to raise the stakes but remains on the "food allergies" theme. The writer is just being stubborn if the argument is "An affliction weakens his character." This is a common mistake and a silly matter of pride that new writers succumb to, often. The writer proclaims "Okay, then instead of allergic reaction to horseradish, my Hero cannot eat Chinese food! If he does he'll die!"

I ask you—how many orders of Moo Goo Gui Pan are your characters going to trip over along their way to the summit of Dark Mountain? And don't tell me, "They deliver!" Most Chinese restaurants I know only have a ten-mile delivery area, and the summit of Dark Mountain is not in there.

In the above case, your character might as well not have any afflictions. On the other extreme, do not burden the character with shortcomings. Just find that happy medium with your character, and don't worry about weakening your character. In their frailties, find convictions. This way the character will grow stronger, just on a different level.

AVOID A CAST OF THOUSANDS

Now I have described a wide variety of characters in the above sections. Does this mean your story has to have ALL of these characters? Absolutely not. When first-time writers begin a novel, they usually have "favourite" stock characters in mind that they immediately want to incorporate. As the story progresses, the temptation to bring in other characters grows. If you are not careful, your manuscript-in-progress will teem with major and minor characters. You may create so many in your cast that your Sidekicks have Sidekicks, the Love Interests are distant relatives with the Mentors, and there are so many Heroes and Villains involved that the story resembles an episode of Challenge of the Superfriends. Audiences will need a play card just to keep up with everyone!

Sometimes, the story—especially if it is epic fantasy—tends to demand the large cast of characters, but note how these casts are handled. They make their appearance, speak their minds, and leave. Very little is given into their background or in their motivations. All they do is say what is needed or do what is needed and then they are out of there! Minor characters are kept minor. The focus of your story, be it epic fantasy or a simple short story, always remains on the major cast members. When creating your story, keep the number of characters under control. Details should be reserved to the essential characters while minor characters continue the flow of the story.

Your readers should be able to figure out who is who. If you have a story with so many involved that chapters need to be read or reviewed twice, there is a serious problem. A solution to this problem is to keep a "flow chart" of who is in which scene and track their actions and interactions with other characters. This way, you know who is contacting whom, and in the end you can see if there are too many characters involved or if any characters repeat themselves. Another advantage of the flow chart is to keep track of who is where and what happened to them on their exit. This allows you to perhaps bring them back in a later scene, or in a later book if your first one proves to be a success. To create a character, major or minor, and then have them "disappear" with no good reason can be frustrating for the reader. Know your chartacters' entrances and exits, like any good Stage Manager. You want to make sure that your cast does not miss a cue, that they are ready to enter, and know when to leave.

THE BORN-TO-DIE STOCK CHARACTERS

Imagine yourself at Star Fleet Academy on the day where graduates are receiving their assignments. Now imagine that awkward moment when you see those few honour students receive red shirts and are told grimly, "You're assigned to the Enterprise." The Kiss of Death. It is the same kind of moment you share at the old abandoned summer camp with that bosomy blonde best friend of yours who loves to wear shirts cut way too low and skirts cut way too high. She just had a fight with her boyfriend and tells you she is going for a walk to cool off. She might as well rip off that top and show off the birthmark covering her back that, oddly enough, resembles a bull's-eye.

Writers and fans of Science Fiction and Fantasy always laugh at the thought of these characters, but still they crop up and draw attention—as well as crossfire—to themselves. These stock characters are known by Trek fans as "Expendable Ensigns," but I prefer the term "Born-to-Die" (BtD's).

While there are uses for BtD's (cannon fodder, primarily), these are characters that should be used sparingly. In Fantasy, especially if there is a war, there will no doubt be a body count. In that case, BtDs are needed. BtDs are excessive, however, if you go out of your way to build a team of individuals to head off for adventure and describe all in detail, save Wendyll Willkomen who "doesn't talk much and hefts his haversack over his shoulder with a gruff grunt."

"Right," thinks the reader. "So this one is the first to get the mace-in-the-face."

When you create your characters, your last thought should be, "Now how is this one going to buy the farm?" even if death is very much a fact of this character's life. But depending on the mark you want to make with your story, every character be it a major or a minor one, faces death. While killing off major characters is always risky, the deaths of major and minor characters always carry more impact with the readers. You establish a bond between the character and reader, so that when the character is lost, not only do the other characters in the book feel it—your audience feels it as well. BtD's should not serve as a substitute for the death of another character you've worked hard to develop. If your story warrants such a poignant moment, then let the character's death occur with dignity (or shame, depending on the circumstances) for the death of a major or minor character should have an impact on all levels. Don't be afraid of death. Simply accept it as a possible fate of the character's destiny and then move forward from there.

THE ADVENTURES OF MARY SUE, GARY STU, AND ENSIGN JONES

Right, as much as I hate to admit this, my writing partner and I broke this prime directive of Fantasy writing that I'm about to talk about.

In our work, *MOREVI: The Chronicles of Rafe and Askana*, the lead character of Rafe Rafton was actually a character I played between 1998-1999 at the Maryland Renaissance Festival. This swashbuckler was a real delight for me to play, and I put a lot of myself into the character. Truly, Rafe Rafton was an extension of myself and we shared many common interests. As for Askana Moldarin, Lisa Lee was playing this persona on an Internet RPG, Askana being the embodiment of a "feminist movement" if it ever hit her Chinese culture and hit it hard.

Unexpectedly, between this alter ego of mine and this alter ego of hers, Miss Lee and I wound up writing an adventure. Technically, this makes us guilty of pushing the "Gary Stu/Mary Sue" envelope of creating characters. As it is with acting, budding authors tend to escape in their writing. Nothing wrong with that, until it becomes a self-indulgent ego trip. In the case of Mary Sue and Gary Stu characters, authors place themselves (characters that look, sound, and act like them) into perilous situations and manage to come out victorious in the end with all the glamour and gleam of the Classic Hero. While this may seem like a harmless exercise, it can get out of control. As the Hero is you, the Hero will have no faults or frailties. In Time Travel stories, Gary Stu's and Mary Sue's tend to change history or at least influence it, always for the better. The story becomes less of a struggle against adversity and evil and more of a deep-sea dive into "Lake Me."

While you may think, "People don't really try to get that stuff published," the folks at Paramount are all too familiar with Gary and Mary but refer to them by another name—'Ensign Jones'. In the documentary, Trekkies, the script team for *Star Trek: The Next Generation* talk about the numerous 'Ensign Jones' scripts they receive. The plot lines are frighteningly similar. The crew is in trouble, stranded on a planet of hostile aliens. Ensign Jones (usually played by the scriptwriter) bravely steps forward to save the day. Deanna Troi or Beverly Crusher is feeling lonely and amorous? Ensign Jones (usually played by the scriptwriter) bravely steps forward to save the day. A Cardassian stun beam knocks out the entire crew, all save for Ensign Jones (usually played by the scriptwriter) who, due to partial loss of hearing and poor eyesight, is impervious to the frequencies of the stunner. The ensign bravely steps forward...well, you get the idea. (On a side note, is my theory these Ensign Jones scripts inspired the *ST:TNG* script "Hollow Pursuits", introducing one of the most beloved of *Star Trek*'s minor characters—Reginald Barclay. So, some good can come from bad.)

So, if my partner and I did this crime, how did we land the publisher? Simple, we changed the names, gave the characters vulnerabilities, and even played around with our own dreams and doubts. It is possible to take a Gary Stu or Mary Sue concept and make it work with a lot of development and a lot more honesty. To make Gary or Mary real, you have to not only explore what you wish to be, but what you are in the real world. Fears, insecurities, and failures all contribute to building characters that readers respect and love. That is another reason why Gary's and Mary's are so hard to write. They can become a hard reality check for you, the author. So in that case, the Gary's and Mary's of the Fantasy genre work. When the stories become an exercise in unrestrained gratification, a line is crossed and the reader will catch it. No one wants to read your personal fantasies, although some questionable publications might want to indulge if they are racy enough.

But in the case of Lisa and myself, the characters of *MOREVI* (all of them, not just Rafe and Askana) are extensions of ourselves, and do tend to go into the good and bad of who we are in the real world. This is nothing unusual for, as stated earlier, characters comes from somewhere inside of us. The same can be said for the characters of *Harry Potter* from J.K. Rowling, the characters of *Kushiel's Dart* and *Kushiel's Chosen* from Jacqueline Carey, and the characters of the *Shannara* books from Terry Brooks. Unless these characters come from your heart and soul, they will lack the heart and soul to pull readers along with them through the adventure.

You now have the building blocks for characters, characters that are not caricatures. This chapter offers a blueprint for you to mix and match "character genres" and create the Heroes and Villains you would like to see in your realm. Then along with the major characters, you can create minor characters to serve as brothers or sisters-in-arms, guiding lights through the oncoming darkness of doubt, or simply a reason to come home from the long, perilous journey. Then once you have the cast built, work on making these Super Heroes and Super Villains less Super and more Human. From the weaknesses of both the Good and the Evil come relationships and rivalries that audiences embrace and refuse to relinquish.

Now we actor-types have exercises, and while they may seem "method" on the outside I have found a little "method acting" can go a long way, especially in writing. Here are some exercises you may want to try with your own characters:

Pick two central characters (Heroes or Villains, doesn't matter which) and then jump back in time to five years before your story begins. Where are they in their lives? Who do they know? Have they met their sidekicks yet? What are they doing with themselves? Did a major event happen in their lives at this age? Once you have the details worked out, jump even further back. Maybe another ten years? Once those two are completed, try this exercise with two other characters.

Have an "interview" with one of your characters. Ask them hard-hitting, probing questions. Prohibit yourself from having the character reply with "No comment" and one-word answers (unless deemed appropriate, for comic effect.) Record facial expressions and ticks. Really dig deep into the character's psyche.

Pick two characters and jump them ahead in time of your story's timeline, say five or ten years. Where are they now? Married? Living? Happy? By jumping ahead, you can have a better idea of the character's behaviour and fate in your present story.

Summary

By working with these exercises, finding frailties and strength as well as ironing out details in character building, you can create real and engaging characters for your story. You may also find that these exercises in building your characters may assist you in building your worlds. Perhaps at this point you have already built your universe and now you are creating the characters for it. If you are the kind of writer that works with characters first and then builds the world around them, go for a ride with these three exercises offered here. You will find the reward for your characters and your world most gratifying.

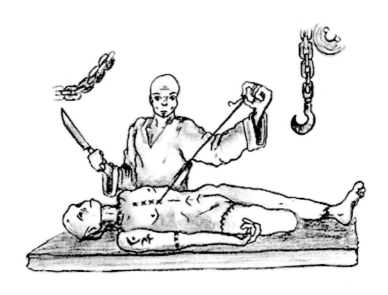

Race Creation

MICHAEL McRAE

"Land of our birth, we pledge to thee
Our love and toil in the years to be;
When we are grown and take our place
As men and women with our race."
~ Rudyard Kipling, The Children's Song

INTRODUCTION

As a consequence of our ability to use reason, we arrange our environment into categories on the simple basis of 'like' and 'unlike'. Cognitive boxes labelled 'man' and 'woman', 'black' and 'white', 'tall' and 'short', help us make sense of a relatively chaotic universe.

Based on certain differences among us, such as peculiarities in language, ceremony, custom, skin tone and facial structure, we arrange ourselves into cultures, nationalities, communities and races.

The traits we choose to classify ourselves with vary depending on what we see as relevant, and what social groups we nominate as significant. To some, difference might be decided by hairstyle. To others, cuisine may be a barrier. Others will be declared as different because they worship a different deity, or speak in another language. Personal stereotypes associated with diversities such as skin color and language arise after the initial process of 'differentiation' occurs, hence you cannot nominate a Jew as being a miser until you have declared a way of defining a man as a Jew.

We have therefore created races as a way of defining ourselves on the basis of a whole range of differences.

There is essentially no such thing as race in biology, as the classification cannot be supported by genetics or breeding compatibilities (and the term 'population' in the scientific sense fails to offer the same connotation as 'race'). Hence 'race' is a term created solely to represent characteristics that separate mankind according to differences a society sees as significant. These differences can represent characteristic themes or traits in a story.

Most forms of literature employ individual character types to move a plot or to represent certain themes. In the Fantasy genre, writers have the option of using different races as an additional device. Gnomes in the *Dragonlance*™ series often represented technology. Nobility is commonly a trait represented by elves. Hard work is associated with dwarves and thievery by such races as halflings and kender. As will be shown, race creation plays an important role in shaping the overall structure of your fantasy world.

This chapter aims to encourage you to be both imaginative and critical in your creation of the interacting societies that will populate your fantasy world. It will discuss what it means to have different cultures, races, languages and even species coexisting in a given area, how to develop believable cultures for them and even how to make that cliché race of elves a little more unique.

WHAT IS A 'RACE'?

To create a race for a fictitious world, we must first understand what we, as fantasy writers, mean by the term 'race'.

As stated in the introduction, races do not exist in biology. The levels of classification used to sort life forms on Earth are Kingdom, Phylum, Class, Order, Family, Genus and Species. Humans are accordingly organised as thus: Animalia, Chordata, Mammalia, Primate, Hominidae, Homo and Sapien. Beyond this are 'sub-species' (modern humans are of the sub-species 'sapien', so technically our scientific name is homo sapien sapien), which is where the now extinct Neanderthal man differed from us (homo sapien neandertalis). There is really nothing lower when it comes to diversity, except for a 'population'. Genetically, populations hold little significance. You can distinguish a population by marking the presence of a particular trait, however, it is impossible to look at two organisms and declare them to be from two different populations on the basis of their genes. There is as much, if not more, genetic difference within a given population than between them. Therefore, the definition of race cannot be made with the use of science.

In the past, the term 'race' was applied to any society that differed to your own in terms of culture and heritage. While today the French and English people are of the 'Caucasian' race, in the eleventh century nationality did not exist—the populations of England were not English, but rather of Celtic, Saxon, or Norman heritage. Likewise, the French were Frankish, Norman, Gaelic or Gothic. These were essentially the 'races' of man.

As nationality became a concept with the rise of national borders, the term race became based on physical characteristics more than cultural ones.

Negroid meant you had dark pigmentation, broad facial features, and curly hair. Asian indicated less pigmentation, straight hair, broad faces and something called the 'epicanthic fold' (giving the narrow appearance to the eyes), and Caucasians were declared to have minimal pigmentation and narrow faces. It could be argued that there are other races, based on more detailed variations in morphology—Pacific Islander, Hispanic, Middle Eastern and Native American people have characteristics that are unique to those of their heritage.

One of the distinguishing features of epic, or high, fantasy is its reflection of historical sociology. It takes traditional myths, social structures and cultures and uses them as foundations for fictitious societies. Mervyn Peake's *Gormenghast* trilogy echoed the typical 18th and 19th century European metropolis. J.R.R. Tolkien's literary works reflected ancient Norse and Saxon heritage. Even Lewis Carroll's *Alice in Wonderland* parodied the political and social etiquette of the 19th century through modified nursery rhymes and children's stories.

Since typical fantasy encompasses historical mythology as if it were a reality, mythological creatures should be classified in similar ways, according to the society it resembles. In other words, what is an 'elf' to a 'human'? Do you declare it a 'race' using modern terms of morphology, or historical terms of culture? There is no certain answer to this. It truly depends on the style of your story.

If you are reflecting a historical setting you should create races with both modern and historical concepts in mind, but refer to the unique aspects of a single race primarily on the basis of culture. Hence an elf in a medieval-type setting is any individual who first speaks 'elf' and reflects 'elven' culture and, secondly, looks like an elf. If you are setting it in a scenario that reflects the modern age, an elf is any individual that has the physical characteristics of an elf, regardless of culture or heritage.

Taking all of this into account, we can define race as being 'a population of people who share the same heritage and culture and possess similar morphological traits'.

Tolkien's dwarves resembled the ancient Norse concept of dark elves, or 'swartalf'; short, twisted creatures that lived underground where they mined precious minerals. Tolkien created a race that differed to the others in '*Middle Earth*' by way of language, culture and morphology.

Where, then, does the boundary exist between race and the next classification? By this I mean that a dragon, which is usually intelligent in epic fantasy settings, would be different in terms of language and culture, and morphology. But can you apply the same concept of race to it? You might not think that it matters much, but it is worthy of consideration when you start to design the various societies of your world.

Back to stark reality for a moment—two races of humans can breed and produce children that are 'viable', in that they can produce more children themselves. Two species within a given genus of human (if another species of homo existed) could breed and produce children, yet they would have a high chance of being sterile. For instance, horses and donkeys can produce 'mules', which are sterile animals. Any two genuses within a given family of animal would not produce offspring at all from a successful mating. For example, nothing would result from a mating between a domestic cat (*Felis silvestris*) and a panther (*Panthera sp.*), two genuses within the Felidae family.

So, if elves are a race akin to humans, their mating could produce viable offspring. What if a dragon (gods-forbid!) mated with a human? If there is a way, either magically or physically, you could have this happen, what would be the result?

In short, we can define a race as being any population of individuals who differ from other races by way of culture, heritage and/or morphology. Beyond this, it is up to you to decide what boundaries are placed.

This might seem like a complicated way to make a race, but when you start to define how races would interact politically, what events occurred in their history, how wars were fought and won, all of this will make that job so much easier.

Template versus Unique Races

In his novel *Perdido Street Station*, China Mieville establishes a society where strange races interact in a weird, pseudo-technical world. Each race is based on a creature that originated in a myth from somewhere around the globe. Vodyanoi are Russian water spirits, and as such are bloated frog-like creatures that live and work in the city's river. The Khepri, on the other hand, are bug-headed women who are based on the Egyptian sun god, Ra. Garuda are winged creatures that look like the Indonesian eagle-men of the same name.

However, within the story nothing historically cultural is reflected in any of these races. Each race within Mieville's world is inspired solely by the physical description of the original mythological creature; not the cultural mythology attached to it. This was an interesting, and significant, decision for the author to have made, as will be addressed later.

A number of fantasy stories have elves displayed as human-like creatures that are beautiful, regal and conduct a very noble society. In the mythology from where they are taken, the word 'elf' comes from the Germanic 'aelben', meaning 'white one'. In these myths they range from ethereal creatures of beauty that toy with the affairs of mankind (while retaining a sense of dignity) to being rather bitter, malevolent creatures that set out to accomplish evil deeds. Fairies (from the latin 'fatum', meaning 'fate') were originally regarded as creatures to distrust, not tiny butterfly people who sang at the bottom of the garden. Hence the figures in mythology have always played a role in inspiring the races of fantasy worlds, even if they are not directly translated across.

Here we will discuss the benefits of using a pre-made template race versus the benefits of creating one yourself. The choice between using mythological races over unique creations is not to be made lightly. It has major repercussions that should be considered.

TEMPLATE RACES

Present day High Fantasy stories often feature cliché races influenced by J.R.R. Tolkien's *Middle Earth* series. Elves, dwarves, hobbits (or halflings), dragons and dark miserable creatures like orcs, goblins and ogres all populate the realms created by countless fantasy writers.

Other stories 'borrow' from other cultures—the djinn from Islamic folklore, the mogwai from ancient Chinese children's stories or even beasts such as seraphim or leviathans from the *Bible*. The question is this—is there an advantage to using pre-fabricated races, be they mythological or contemporary in origin, within your story?

The answer is 'Yes.' When people read about elves, they assume they are reading about noble creatures. Goblins are mean, giants are dim-witted and fairies are small and untrustworthy. Stereotype is the key word here, and it pays to be aware of the stereotype behind the mythological creature you are wishing to use.

This does not mean you are restricted to describing the typical elf in your story as noble or your dwarves as hard working miners. It does mean, however, that you must be aware of the impression the word 'elf' or 'dwarf' makes when presented in a fantasy setting.

Remember this: readers will make assumptions about what you write where they are not explicitly presented with an alternative explanation.

Simply referring to an army of halflings marching across the landscape will not inspire much hope, or fear, in any seasoned fantasy reader. Humour, maybe, but certainly no expectation that such an army would be too effective. The reader will assume this from the conventional stereotype of halflings. So without saying anything, you have already said a great deal.

A template race can reduce the need for detailed descriptions. Compare the above halfling army with 'The Bod-gani soldiers marched across the landscape'. The reader will make no assumptions, as the name 'Bod-gani' presents no information that can be based on an established convention. You will, however, need to provide more detail concerning the Bod-gani race. You are forced to establish the convention that it lacks, and you must do this without writing a complex history five chapters long.

On the other hand, you may wish to use a template race for another reason—contrast. As stated earlier, races are often used to represent a characteristic, personal trait or a plot device. Elves, when portrayed in an epic fantasy setting, are expected to be noble. Therefore, when a reader is presented with a typical high fantasy elf working in a mine, they are forced to ask questions. Again, you have no need to explain it in terms of being an unusual situation as much as if it was a Bod-gani dancing in front of a Wittwambla, two names that carry no conventions to supply a connotation.

Humans, as a Fantasy race, carry perhaps the greatest connotations of all. There is a range of things to consider when highlighting humans as a single race. Philosophically, what do humans represent in your story? Progress? War? Sin? Enlightenment? How this is approached depends on the focus you choose to use in your plot. Humans are generally used as an anchor through which the reader can relate to the created world. The reader can often assume the emotions felt by a human protagonist better than if the protagonist was a dark-elf, or a goblin. The use of humans as a race depends on context to a greater degree. As we have studied ourselves intently throughout history, the traits we associate with being 'human' have varied with the context. We cause war and incite peace, destroy nature and save it, worship intelligence and wallow in ignorance, and exult in religion and turn towards sin. Hence the human race is perhaps the most flexible of all templates. Choosing the traits relies on knowing the context of your story.

Remember that you are not obliged to use all of the traits of any single template race. Templates should be a starting point only—feel free to change whatever you feel necessary. Just be aware of the aspects you want to portray.

Template races are useful on the sole basis of having a pre-established convention. By being aware of the stereotype associated with any given race, or mythological creature, you can make a significant statement without saying a single word.

UNIQUE RACES

Maybe you don't like the idea of using elves and dwarves to represent the differences between the nobility and working classes in your story. Perhaps the baggage it carries from Tolkien's *Middle Earth* is too much for your own world. Or you might even like the idea of playing 'Grand High Creator' and making a race of beings on your own. Whatever the reason, some of you will choose to start from scratch in order to create races that are unique to your story.

The following step-by-step guide is just that—a guide. It is not a dance, nor is it a recipe. So it should not be used as such. If you come up with a name first, or a physical description, run with that. Follow this process in principle and try to understand the concept behind each step.

And remember, above all, be creative.

STEP ONE: EMBODIMENT OF THEMES

Often, this initial step is either neglected or unwittingly accomplished without any real contemplation by many inexperienced writers. It should be asked: 'What types of society do I want to introduce to my world?'

Note, the question is not: 'What races exist in my world?' You have a finite amount of space to develop your plot and explore your themes. Why have a war-like race in a novel that never touches on war? Or thieving imps when it is not necessary that somebody have something stolen? You have to look at the themes and ideas contained in your novel concept. Plot movements and character concepts should also play major roles in creating race ideas.

> Example: For the purposes of this chapter, I will give the following example: a fictitious plot addresses commercial enterprise, betrayal and sexism. I wish to make only three races, each of which will embody one of these themes.

STEP TWO: INTERACTIONS

Decide what it is your races will embody and how they will interact. Are there two races opposing each other? Are there many races fighting together? Are they at peace? Are they symbiotic? In short, what do your racial groups represent in regards to one another?

Remember, earlier I mentioned the difference between a 'race' and a 'species.' At this point, consider the relationships held by your various nameless races. Can they interbreed? Are there half-races? What is the relationship of half-breeds to their parent races?

Don't forget you still have yet to name the races and describe them in detail. You might think it strange to describe their relations before detailing the races themselves, however, the whole point of having different races in your story relies on the interactions between them. Finishing this step before moving on will keep this point a priority.

> Example: There are three main races in this fictitious story—one represents trade, another sexism, and the third, betrayal. The first two races can breed to produce infertile offspring, which are regarded as 'impure' by both groups. These two races rarely mix on good terms—they compete with each other for the favor of the third 'god race', which is to be used to convey the betrayal in the plot.

STEP THREE: MAJOR NON-PHYSICAL CHARACTERISTICS

You should have a good idea by now how the races mix together, and what they essentially represent. Now is the time to fill in the smaller details.

- What is their political structure: Monarchical, tyrannical or democratic?

- What is their social structure: Hierarchical, anarchical or gender-dominated?

- Are they agrarian? Do they herd animals? Are they slave traders, nomadic, oceanic, or technologically advanced? Is there a mix of many different societies or of different histories?

This is truly the 'make or break' stage for your race. For example, if you have a war-like race, or a character that represents a society that uses intimidation to get its own way, describing them as 'diplomatic' would conflict with the rational idea of 'war'. Again this is where assumptions come in. The reader will make associations between certain themes and traits based on stereotypes: intelligence—diplomacy, war—totalitarian regime, commerce—technologically advanced. Again, that does not mean you cannot have a war-like race run by a democracy. However, you should be aware of any contrasts and address them accordingly.

For example, why is the nomadic race of female-dominated shepherds you made technologically advanced? There should be a good reason.

Having a basic understanding of global history can help here. It is not exactly cheating if you decide to base any of your races on a past culture, after all. For example, at this point you might want to refer to the Aztec cultures if you have a society that might benefit from certain Meso-American cultural traits.

> Example: Race 1 (traders), is technologically advanced, has a monarchy and is matriarchal, and is loosely based on Renaissance France. Race 2 is patriarchal to an outrageous extent (sells its women into slavery), while Race 3 has no sexes, is dominated by a single god-being and refers to all of its individual beings within its society as 'I'.

STEP FOUR: NAME

Unfortunately, this is where many people start. That is not to say it is always a bad thing, necessarily. However, be aware of the power a name contains. Many inexperienced writers will be led by their race's name to create their novel, rather than the other way around. A name will contain the very essence of your race—every time it is mentioned in your novel, a range of characteristics will be represented which will embody everything that your race is.

Again, assumptions play a massive role. You should use these to your advantage.

A name will act on two levels—as a physical descriptor (its sound can convey a physical characteristic) and as a cultural descriptor (its sound will convey a cultural characteristic). An aggressive warrior race called 'Fliffs' does not really work—the word 'fliff' sounds light, soft and not exactly warlike. Again, calling a race of leprechaun-type creatures 'Xai-Ko-Rotan' is questionable, as the word has connotations of Oriental cultures. Hence the reader might assume certain Asian characteristics where they are not provided.

Names are formed in direct relation to the language of a race. Short, sharp words can represent a lack of intelligence, while complex, flowing speech, filled with poetry carries connotations of high culture and advanced intelligence. Words that echo other words, whether in spelling or phonics, also convey connotations. Brogs, for instance, automatically gives rise to images of squat, animalistic, unintelligent creatures, by mere association with the words 'dogs' or 'frogs'. Lewis Carroll used this extensively by way of a poetic device called 'portmanteau', where two words are combined to convey the essence of each word. For example, 'Snark' is a combination of 'snake' and 'shark', and implies a sly, cunning creature that is hard to catch (*The Hunting of the Snark*, 1876).

Hence be aware of what your race's name conveys. A good way of testing this is to ask several people what comes to mind when you say the name. If they say 'evil' when your race essentially represents good, you might have to rethink things.

> Example: Race 1, the technologically advanced race, are 'Fe Rayalise' (Romantic sounds to imply a French sense of early industry). Race 2, the sexist ones, are 'Bruls' (using the word 'brute' as a base) and the god-like race, Race 3, are the 'Vorpalis' (using the word 'vorpal', from Lewis Carroll's Jabberwocky, which implies something sharp and dangerous. Romantic ending, '-lis', again gives a sense of old-world mythology).

Step Five: Physical Description

Here is the truly fun part. Get your crayons and start scribbling!

In fact, this bit should write itself. By now you should have something of a vague mental image of your race, especially if you have followed through each of the above steps. What must be remembered here is that physical characteristics always impact on the personal characteristics.

Recall our earlier example of China Mieville's *Perdido Street Station*. Avoiding the cultural connections with his races was a bold move on the writer's behalf, but one that was made intentionally. Hence the description of the Khepri (Bug-headed) society within the story was well detailed to avoid having people familiar with Egyptian folklore make false assumptions. In the end, nearly everything about the Khepri mythology was reformed. Bug-headed people were no longer exotic sun gods, but rather strange grotesques with unique biological attributes.

The trick here was in using physical characteristics to create the race, not the name or the template mythology. Hence this stage can be rather important—the physical description must fit the essential design of the race. A race that is characterised by a lack of dexterous limbs will need a good reason to be technologically adept. Likewise, why would your race of warriors be small and weak, with rabbit ears?

Perhaps they are. But again, it must be reasoned within your story as to 'why' they are like this.

It may seem odd that Mary Gentle used rats as the physical bodies for the tyrannical aristocracy in her novel *Rats and Gargoyles*; after all, rats are dirty sewer-runners, not bureaucratic nobility. However, the contrast of rats in high society highlighted the dirty, fetid connotations the image of a rat carries, hence made these aristocrats seem all the more intellectually conniving, and politically 'rat-like'. The image of her race conveyed the theme more than any other trait.

> Example: The Fe-Rayalise are tall, with tiny black eyes, human-like except for the black fur that trails down their

backs. The Brul have males that are totally covered in that same black fur, but have females that are smooth skinned. The Vorpalis are essentially dark-cowled shadows that rarely show their true forms.

STEP SIX: FILL IN THE FINE DETAILS

It is possible to approach this step in two ways. First, sit and write the details in note form until you are happy that your race is tuned to perfection. Refer to actual cultures of the past, and use it as a guide. This works well for those who appreciate a detailed plan to be present before they even start the first chapter. However, the downfall here is that you might create more details than is required for the novel. Sure it's fun having the complete family lineage of the present ruling monarchy mapped out in minute detail, but are you going to use all of it? It may be exciting to have a sports game unique to your race being played halfway through the story, but will it simply be an out of place event that has little or no connection with the rest of the plot? Pre-detailing to a large extent may tempt you into including some things in the story that have no relevant place, to your detriment.

Secondly, you can leave this step to write itself. If you have a solid concept of what your race entails, the small details will fill themselves in, as they are needed. The trouble with doing things this way is that it relies on you, as a writer, having confidence in your creations. They need to be real enough in your own mind for the fine details to write themselves. A mix of the two methods might be the most beneficial.

What details am I talking about? Language, cuisine, history, leisure, hunting, transport, weaponry, pets, sayings, greetings, customs, superstitions, beliefs, rituals, festivals, education systems and so on. These are the things that personalise any single character that is influenced by their racial heritage.

> Example: To use one of the example races, the Fe Rayalise greet each other by touching foreheads. They worship the Vorpalis during a holy week of fasting followed by feasts. Children are given to selected relatives for education. Pets are forbidden, sport is often violent (gladiatorials are favored), and they wear perfume that is extracted from the anal glands of desiccated baby dragons.

SUMMARY

The segregation of character types into 'races' in literature is something unique to speculative fiction. Fantasy and science fiction stories often use the convention of race to describe a theme or to embody a particular trait they wish to use in the course of their work.

To extensively describe what the term race means within the fantasy genre would take more than a single chapter. However, a simplistic definition would follow these lines:

A race is any population of individuals who differ from other populations by way of culture, heritage and/or physical morphology.

How closely you follow this definition is up to you. There are unfortunately no hard and fast rules to the 'do's' and 'don'ts' of creating races for your fantasy realm. It depends a great deal on the intention behind your story. Is it supposed to be realistic? Is it a pseudo-myth? Are you recreating a legend or rewriting actual history? These are important things to consider when choosing the character types and the races for your fantasy world.

By being aware of the details proposed in this chapter, the races portrayed in your story will work much more effectively.

World Building

TINA MORGAN

CREATING A NEW WORLD

Creating a new world can be a daunting task or a work of passion, depending on your personal tastes and talent. No matter how you view the process, setting is a vital part of your story. Your characters do not exist in a void, so you must decide when and where they live—or haunt as the case may be.

> When: can be anytime from the dawn of creation to the far off future.

> Where: can range from remote wilderness of an unknown world, modern concrete jungles or unexplored galaxies.

Fantasy is not confined by location or time like other genres. Your choices of setting are unlimited.

Start with the Basics:

Time: when the story takes place: prehistoric, pseudo-medieval, futuristic, and anytime in-between.

Magic: who uses it, where does it come from, can it be taken away, consequences to user

Physical: earth-like or alternative, ecology, architecture and building materials

Inhabitants :human, non-human, animals-earth based, mythological or something new, domagical creatures exist in the open or hidden

Society: laws and government, arts and recreation, education, religion, vocation, money or barter

TIME

A large percentage of fantasy stories take place in pseudo-medieval settings so a good portion of this chapter will be dedicated to that. However, alternative history, modern fantasy and futuristic fantasy may be options you would like to explore as a writer.

Pseudo-medieval settings are the most prominent in the fantasy genre. As a result, it is important that you are accurate in your portrayal of a medieval world. Technology must be consistent: a printing press cannot be invented until after a written language and paper. Characters must fit the time frame and social structure. Feudal societies were common and the average citizen was disposable to the nobility that ruled the land.

One of the attractions to the medieval setting is the lack of technology. Characters must rely on magic and their wits to survive. Traveling by horseback has a romantic appeal that is lacking in most subway excursions. Chivalry and a strong code of honor capture the writer and reader's imagination.

Medieval settings do not have to be limited to British or Celtic locations. Norse, Russian and Asian myths provide a wealth of inspiration and information for creating a variation on the theme. Middle Eastern cultures are rarely used, partially because of the constant religious conflict in the area, but it is an alternative worth exploring. However, if you are publishing in an English-speaking nation then odds are your audience grew up being educated in Anglo-Saxon based history. For that reason, it's easier for them to relate to the feudal societies and European settings of so many fantasy novels. Stepping outside this imaginary boundary gives a writer new opportunities for creative expression.

Because of the number of fantasy novels set in medieval times, most fantasy readers have a good idea what life was like during that period. Many readers enjoy renaissance festivals and role-playing games. They will spot mistakes and if there are too many, they will discuss them in book and writers' groups on the web and in person. This kind of negative publicity can harm book sales.

Several chapters in this book deal with the medieval setting and there are some informative sites include Life in a Medieval Castle: http://www. castlewales.com/life.html and medieval Life (not in-depth but a nice overview) and http://www.medieval-life.net/.

There is a drawback to the medieval setting and reader knowledge. Because of the reader's preconceived ideas, it is difficult for a writer to create a pseudo-medieval world on another planet. The common misconception will be that the story is somehow still taking place in feudal Europe.

From the very first page, the writer must differentiate their world from earth. If you fail to make this distinction, the reader will be pulled out of the story the first time your character behaves in a manner that is inconsistent with medieval social mores. This can be very difficult to do and still avoid the infamous "info-dump".

Add small details to your setting and character development that informs your reader they're not on earth anymore. If your protagonist is a woman with a serious political agenda that can be accomplished in a pseudo-medieval setting without her resorting to bribery or sexual favors, then state from the beginning that she's the mayor of her town or the ruling party's advisor. Make it clear from the start that this is no ordinary lady-in-waiting serving a patriarchal society.

Alternative history is often combined in the fantasygenre because editors are not sure how to classify it. Purists would argue that changing history does not automatically put a story in the fantasy category. Orson Scott Card defines the genre in his *How to Write Science Fiction and Fantasy*: "If a story is set in a universe that follows the same rules as ours, it's science fiction. If it's set in a universe that doesn't follow our rules, it's fantasy. Or in other words, science fiction is about what could be but isn't, fantasy is about what couldn't be."

If your story is set in a world that only differs from ours in that a certain historical event did not occur, then it probably is not fantasy, but if your story is about sprites living in lower Manhattan and how they've hidden from us for all these years, then you're writing fantasy.

When starting the story from the assumption that a certain event did not occur, then you need to follow that thought process through. If Columbus did not "discover" America, what would have happened to the world economy at that point? What if the Vikings had been more open about their trips across the northern Atlantic? This would change not only the culture in Europe but also in the Americas. The government and economy would be different because of the different influences.

Alternative history can also include the human race's many attempts at exterminating the different races and religions. Creating a plot consisting of one of these genocide attempts being brought to an end by a superior magical force is an interesting challenge. The events you are changing happened in the real world and they need to be considered carefully. Changing WWII so that the holocaust ended before it began requires a great deal of finesse. If you devalue the human suffering that has taken place, you risk losing and offending readers.

Fantasy has a worldwide appeal. If your intentions are to write purely as a hobby, then play with history all you want. If you intend to seek publication, consider your reading audience. Sometimes even the death of a single person can touch the lives of complete strangers: Princess Diana, John F. Kennedy, and Mother Theresa, just to name a few. Changing or eliminating an event like: Chernobyl, Three Mile Island, or the Holocaust, can alienate your reader, particularly if your audience has a close affiliation to those events. If you negate the importance of that trauma, you risk losing credibility.

Recent history has been well recorded. Failure to research the event in question will result in a sloppy story that will pull the reader out of the realm of believability. The Internet provides swift access to information. It also provides history enthusiasts with a place to meet and discuss world events. Joining an on-line group can be a valuable source of information and reference referrals.

A few good sources of inspiration are as close as the Internet or your local library. For those unable to view the History Channel, they have an informative website http://www.historychannel.com or A&E at http://www.biography.com/ does as well.

A&E's biographies can also be found in their print magazine. If you will be using a historical figure as one of your characters, be sure to take the time to research their personality, education level and social standing. What may seem like a prejudiced attitude in our modern world may have been the only politically and socially acceptable choice in their time

Another approach to alternative history or modern settings is to add magic to our world. In doing so, there are some considerations to take into account. If magic has existed all along, then you must decide if it is practiced openly or in secret.

If your magic community exists alongside the 'real' world, how does it escape detection? What are the consequences do the magic users face if they are discovered? In J.K. Rowling's *Harry Potter* series, she explains how the wizarding community remains hidden by giving the "muggles" false memories if they are exposed to magic. Other characters, like the Dursley's are so afraid of what other people will think, they don't talk about magical members of their family. Or in the case of Hermione, her parents are very proud to have a witch in the family, but are assumedly protective of their daughter and kept the secret for her safety.

For magic to exist in the open there must be consequences to our society and if not, there needs to be a valid reason. Wizards walking down main street USA (or any other country) would have an effect on that country's economy and social structure. There would have to be a way to enforce laws on a wizard bent on destruction. If a wizard could change ordinary items into gold or jewels, it would wreak havoc on the economy. What would happen to the divorce rate if wizards and witches could be paid to create love potions? Would nuclear weapons have been invented as weapons of mass destruction?

Incorporating current events into your story line can be a very tricky proposition. While we can guess the outcome of any of the current political conflicts in our world, we cannot accurately predict the exact conclusion. The human race is too full of variables. Some events may seem monumental at the time they are taking place, but by the time an author has finished a story, they've faded into history and been replaced by larger events. The event may also have become anathema to publishers.

Modern settings, like alternative history must take into consideration their audience the risk of alienating them. However, science fiction and fantasy have a long history of challenging perceptions and some of the best stories fly in the face of social conventions.

The futuristic setting often pushes a story into the realm of science fiction because of the emphasis on the technology involved. However, many stories blur the lines between the two genres. Before 'midichlorians' were introduced into the *Star Wars* saga, it could be argued that the movies incorporated elements of both SF & fantasy. The Death Star and FTL drives giving it strong science and technology, and the Force bringing in strong fantasy themes. By trying to dispel the 'myth' around the Force and giving it a scientific explanation, the fantasy is removed from the series.

If magic were the force that made the ships fly between the stars and not anti-matter engines, the fantasy theme could be strengthened. For that matter, futuristic settings do not have to include star ships at all. They can take place on distant planets, either with new species or with Terran colonists. The scientific details of how the colonists arrived on the planet can be overshadowed by the magical creatures and wizards the earthlings encounter on their new world.

Armageddon stories are popular futuristic themes and often fall back on the technology angle, but they too can be manipulated to fit a fantasy format. The magical creatures that have remained hidden in our 'real' world could be forced into the open. Elves could be a vital part of every community as they strive to help humanity rebuild the devastated earth. Wizards could form domes to protect the citizens when technology failed. The possibilities are only limited by your imagination, but to keep the story in the fantasy realm, the magic must play a larger role than the technology.

MAGIC

Developing a magic system for your novel requires careful consideration. First, magic needs consequences. If there are no drawbacks to using magic, then everyone would use it and you would have anarchy. Your characters' abilities must be limited so that there is a conflict to be resolved. If six hundred pages into the novel, your protagonist suddenly remembers he can just 'wish' the antagonist into the fires of hell, most editors are going to reject your novel.

WHO OR WHAT

Start with who will use magic in your world. A limited few or everyone and everything like in Piers Anthony's *Xanth* series? Then decide where their magic comes from: the universe around them, god/demon-given or life force driven. If all the creatures of your world are capable of working magic to some degree, does the magic all come from the same source? Unless your animals are intelligent, they are not going to understand the consequences of life-force magic. This could lead to accidental deaths or mutations. If life-force magic is used, can the wizard take the power they need from an unwilling victim?

Your wizard(s) position in society should be considered as well. Plot will determine if you need a large, organized group of wizards or a limited number of secret magicians. What role do your magic users play in the government or religion? Are they permitted or required? Do your wizards have to obtain a license to work magic? A registry of magicians or mutants is a common theme in futuristic fantasy.

Not being able to work magic in the open restricts access to resources. If a spell requires certain herbs to work but the herbs have no other uses, then a renegade wizard won't be able to walk into the local apothecary and buy them, nor grow them in their garden. Shape shifting in public could be taboo or part of a ritual depending on the rules your story requires. A good grasp of how magic works within your society allows for stronger characterization and fewer mistakes requiring rewriting.

Once you know who or what will be using magic in your world, you can decide how that use will affect them. Life-force magic should leave the wielder weak if it's coming from their body/soul. Constancy is once more an issue. If you start the novel with your protagonist able to maintain a spell for only a few hours but end the story with a three day long battle with repetitive magic use, then there needs to be a reason why your hero was able to maintain this constant drain. Options could include finding a magic restorative plant/elixir, using another person's life force, making animal/human sacrifices or a gradual growth in your protagonist's abilities.

TECHNIQUE

Once you know who will be using magic, then decide how it will be performed. Herbs and strange ingredients like 'eye of toad' are often used for potions. Ritual magic can take many forms. Katherine Kurtz based the magic in her *Deryni* novels on Catholic ceremonies and prayers. Holly Lisle used life-force magic invoked by rituals in her *Secret Text* trilogy. For a variation, her protagonist sketched a magical shopping cart on special paper in *Minerva Awakes*. The dark arts of demonology and necromancy can give your writing a sinister feel.

Instinct only goes so far. In order to perfect any natural talent, there must be some sort of training. How your magicians are trained will depend on Magic's role in society. If your magicians are limited in number and must stay hidden from the rest of the population then one on one mentoring makes more sense than a secret school. If the location of a secret school is discovered by hostile forces, a large majority of your wizards could be lost in one attack. This might suit your plot needs but it's not very practical. Secret societies rarely take such a large risk with their limited membership. To use such a plot device, your wizards must have a logical and strong reason for gathering together.

POWER

Some writers favor puberty as a milestone for magic to grow or reveal itself for the first time as opposed to being present at birth. Regardless of when the character realizes their potential, they may or may not be able to increase their strength through learning, practice or working with other wizards. Your characters may be limited by laws, sex, heredity or social taboos.

Vulnerability can play an important role in your plot. Can your characters 'lose' their magic or have it taken away from them? Just as age and illness affect our mental and physical strength, it should also affect your characters' magical talents. If a virgin has more power or special abilities, rape or consensual sex must alter those traits.

A wizard cannot be all-powerful. If all he has to do is wave his wand and every obstacle become inconsequential then there is no conflict and no story.

No matter how your characters use their magic or how it interacts with other creatures and forces, it needs to follow a set of rules. Consistency is invaluable in the magical universe. Without that, magic becomes the miracle elixir that revives wounded plots and rescues poorly developed worlds.

Patricia Wrede has an excellent list of questions to consider when creating your fantasy world. They can be found at the SFWA website:

http://www.sfwa.org/writing/worldbuilding1.htm

A very nice article with tips about culture, geography and magic systems can be found at: http://www.artofbuilding. eqsdesigns.com/frodpo/library.html

PHYSICAL

Fantasy and science fiction often share the same shelves in the bookstores and often the same readers as well. This makes your task of creating a physical world for your characters a bit more daunting. Faking the science could get you laughed off the shelves.

ALTERNATIVE EARTH

More than one early SF/fantasy story took place on Jupiter's moons. Io and Ganymede were popular locations for space age colonists. There are some problems with this scenario. Jupiter is a gas giant. In order for a planet made of light hydrogen and helium atoms to exist, the temperature has to be below freezing. If Jupiter is frozen because of its distance from the sun, then its moons must have a similar temperature range. Factor in Jupiter's fast rotation and magnetic field which collects charged particles from solar wind and you have radiation belts that accompany the planet in its orbit. Jupiter's moons pass through these belts, resulting in severe radiation storms on their surface. Not only is Io frozen, it's surface is scoured with radiation. Not a very habitable planet for humans. So no matter where you create your world. It can't be the moon of a gas giant unless your magicians or scientists have found a way to protect its inhabitants.

Another common variant on the earth theme is multiple moons. This too can create some serious problems. We know that our moon is responsible for our ocean tides. With multiple large moons, a world would have very complex tidal patterns. How would this affect sailing? How far inland would the tides come each day? The variables are staggering. Going in the other direction provides another interesting twist. Without a moon to stir deep oceans, there is a good possibility they would become stagnant. Imagine a planet wide swamp. Imagine also, nights lit only by starlight, no large ghostly white orb to set the mood as your lovers embrace or to light the cemetery where your teenagers have dared each other to spend the night.

Not to be forgotten when creating your universe, the biggest factor in whether or not your world is habitable; its sun. We know stars come in all sizes just as planets do. Some are giants that produce bright white light with heavy amounts of ultra violet light. Most of these are short lived. Evolution would have to be accelerated for humanoid species to develop before the star burns itself out. If you take the deity approach, would a deity create a solar system where his/her children's existence would be limited?

Multiple star systems are also tricky. Your planet has to orbit the stars in the temperate range (between boiling and freezing) to be habitable. If your planet orbits too close to the second star, its temperature could rise dramatically from morning to night. One hundred degree temperature swings are going to have a dramatic effect on the type of life the planet can support.

ECOLOGY

All the world is intertwined. We've discovered just how true that is as our civilization encroaches on land formerly dominated by wild animals. Species become extinct for lack of habitat. So too is your world going to be changed by what your societies actions. If one species decimates another, that will impact their environment. Too many chemical pesticides in our own world have led to a shortage of honeybees. A problem fruit growers are struggling to find ways to combat. Removing a species leaves a hole in the eco-system.

If you create new magical creatures or use mythological stand-ins, these will also affect the earth's ecology. For example, a large herd of centaurs requires sufficient amounts of food. Bending at the waist to plant fields would be very difficult for a centaur. They would be more likely to forage for food. Foraging requires large areas of forest. Your centaurs either have to find a way to grow their own food, become nomads or will be very combative toward travelers through their range.

One very common error world-builders make is creating a world with too many predators. Large predators need sufficient prey animals or they face starvation. Not matter how impressive all those multi-fanged monsters may look in your own mind, you either have to eliminate few or give them more prey to eat than just your characters. Unless your characters live in a vegetarian society, man is the biggest predator of all. Throughout the ages, humankind has killed off large predators because of the competition for food sources.

Another mistake is the mindless, rampaging horde of ogres, trolls, goblins, or other fantasy nasties. If your armies are pillaging and burning everything in sight, how are they going to find food for themselves?

Poisoning water supplies can backfire if your army is forced to retreat. If your mindless horde wins the battle chances are, they'll turn on their masters because they've burnt all the fields and there's nothing left to eat. You can't compare mindless hordes of sentient creatures with swarms of locusts. The locusts die out once they've eaten everything. Sentient creatures will eat each other to survive. (Think the Donner party on a grand scale. Mass cannibalism is not a pretty thought.)

Think about the creatures, big and small that will roam your world. You may be able to find a similar eco-system here on earth for a model. Explore your local library or university. Most of all don't be afraid to ask questions in this research stage of your world building.

CLIMATE, GEOGRAPHY AND POPULATION

The tilt to your planet's axis will change the weather patterns and is another alternative to consider. If your world does not tilt, then it will not have seasons. How will this affect your society? How would they view death and birth? Would they still see the same cycles we do without the seasons to reinforce this philosophy? How will this affect the plants that grow on your world?

Erosion can be fast or slow depending on the forces at work. Repetitive violent tides, storms or flooding could make sea or river travel difficult. Without water transportation, the distribution of food and goods could be significantly slowed or even halted. This happens even in a world with extensive ground travel like our own. Large ships can carry heavier loads than airplanes and are cheaper to operate, but they do need harbors in which to dock.

The amount of farmable land will determine the population your land can support. Remember that not all land is capable of supporting food crops. Mountain ranges, lakes, rivers, forest and deserts will limit the amount and type of plants that can be grown and harvested. Mountain communities are going to be smaller than those on fertile river basins unless you have adequate transportation systems to bring food into the area.

Transportation will be a major factor in where your people live. Modern suburban society can spread out because of modern governments, law enforcement, availability of food supplies and transportation. Medieval societies would have clustered closer together. Towns and villages would have only been a mile or two apart to allow for foot traffic. Most of the population would have lived in or around cities, towns or villages for security.

How do you determine how many people your world can support? 14th century France had a population density of 105 people per square mile. Germany averaged 87 people per square mile. Italy with its hills and rocky terrain came close to Germany with 86. The British Isles only had 42 people/sq. mile. Compare the type of land you're creating with these countries and you'll have a rough idea of a reasonable population.

The maximum arable amount of land on earth is approximately 66%. That allows for a maximum of 120 people per square mile with medieval technology. The more forests, rivers and lakes that cover your continents the lower the population will have to be.

MAPS

Many novels begin with a map in the opening pages, but is this necessary? Current trends lead us to believe that it is. However, most of us aren't mapmakers nor are we experts in geography. Thankfully, we don't "have" to draw a map to get our work published. What we need is a well-crafted story and the ability to sell it to an agent or editor.

You many find sketching a rough map to be a useful tool in keeping track of your hero's travels. The details can be as simple as a rough circle or square to show the country/continent and dots for the major points of interest: cities, towns, ruins, dangerous mountain passes, or forests that your hero will actually come in contact with. Just enough for you to remember that if your hero travels west at the start of the story, he's going to have to travel east to get back to where he/she started. Or that in order to get from point A to point D, he/she has to cross river E.

Even if you are dealing with a modern or futuristic setting, towns and cities will be built on the main routes: major road intersections, low river crossings, mountain passes and sheltered harbors. Communities of every size need access to goods that are not made or grown in their region.

Working with a co-author, I find it helpful to have a map of our world and rough layouts of the major castles. This helps us keep our writing consistent. It also makes it easier to co-ordinate battles.

There is help if you want to create a more detailed map. Many role-playing game sites give directions on how to build your own world. Don't discount them because it is for a game and not a novel. Many game players spend extensive amounts of time researching and building their worlds. Some of the best sites I've found for information over world building are linked to game playing sites.

> http://www.hut.fi/~vesanto/link.useful/worlds/world. creation.html (some of the links are broken and some are for shareware, but the site is full of links and information, well worth visiting)

> http://www.geocities.com/Area51/6902/ (scroll down the page past the personal comments and you'll find a nice selection of links and programs from building universes to languages and society)

http://www.dungeonmastersguild.com/world_campaign_
building_main.htm (breaks down building a world into
some very basic steps. Aimed at role-playing but useful to
the fantasy writer as well.)

http://hiddenway.tripod.com/world/ (nice collection of links,
some repeated on the other sites but a must visit site.)

STRUCTURES

Structures lead us to the man made part of our physical world. Unless
your characters are camping in the wilderness, they probably live in some
sort of structure. Buildings will typically be made out of materials at hand. In
sparsely wooded areas, sod or adobe will be the common building material.
Stone castles will require a quarry and the technology to make hard enough
tools to cut the given stone. Plank construction requires tools to cut and
smooth the wood, as well as a place to dry it evenly so it does not warp.

Space station materials must be imported from nearby planets or be easy
enough to transport into the area. The ability to repair damage or rot to any of
these structures depends on the availability of replacement parts. When dealing
with limited resources, mankind must become practical or fail to survive.

Not only do you need materials to build your keeps, castles, forts and
space stations, but you also need defensible positions. Even in medieval
times, 'location, location, location'... was a major selling factor. All
kidding aside, your king, queen, or warlord must be able to defend his
seat of power or be overrun by his/her enemies.

Castles and fortresses were often built on higher ground with a physical
barrier as a deterrent: moats-water-filled or dry, motte-bailey-earthen
and wooden structures that made it difficult for the enemy to approach
unseen, etc. Trees were removed from the immediate vicinity to clear a
line of sight and also to build doors, gates, bridges or catamounts and
other defensive obstructions.

The outer wall of the castle was often wide enough to allow for soldiers to
shoot arrows and to carry boiling pitch and large rocks. Doorways were limited.
Multiple entrances left the fortress open to attack. Narrow slits in the walls
allowed for archers to rain arrows (sometimes burning) down on the attackers.
Boiling pitch was used to soak battering rams and siege engines. Burning
arrows could be used to set these and the brush in the dry moat on fire.

Practicality is an issue for space living as well as medieval castles.
Everything has a use because of limited space on a ship or the limited
hours in a day for the medieval society. Communal living requires storage
for food, tools, weapons etc. Personal space would be minimal. Neither
medieval folk nor futuristic astronauts would have the clutter that exists
in modern homes.

http://www.castles-of-britain.com

http://www.castlesontheweb.com/search/Medieval_Studies/

http://www.castlewales.com/listings.html (very nice site with lots of historical information and castle layouts.)

CONTINUITY OF PHYSICAL STRUCTURES

Your medieval world is not going to have the variety of architectural designs that you see in your average 21st century city or town. Regions will have their own distinctive style. A Japanese pagoda is not going to be seen in downtown 12th century London or Paris. Styles do change over time but a modern geo-dome is not going to appear in typical medieval settings.

Your structures should also reflect the values of your society. If you have a highly religious society, decide if it would allow carvings of its deities or if statues are forbidden. Is the society separated? If men, women or children live in different quarters then there will be dorm-like buildings reflecting this practice.

The history of your society will determine not only the style of architecture but also whether ruins exist in your world. If you choose to have your protagonist exploring a new wilderness that has never seen intelligent life, then he/she better not stumble upon any ruins without some serious explanation.

INHABITANTS

This may be the hardest part of our world building. We must resist the urge to inhabit our planet with impossible creatures just because it suits our idea of danger, beauty or weirdness. Winged creatures are not very likely to evolve in a complete water world. The majority of the inhabitants would be gill breathers. If you take away the animals in our world that exist both on land and water and look only at the creatures living in the oceans, not very many breath through lungs. Whales and porpoises are the only animals that breath through lungs, give birth and die in water without ever coming onto land. Snakes, lizards and other cold-blooded creatures need heat to warm their bodies; they aren't going to evolve on an ice planet. Nor are ice planets likely to have inhabitants as we know them. In our world, polar bears live on fish, seals and small animals. Most of those small animals live off vegetation. If your world is completely covered frozen, the odds of vegetation existing are slim.

Different climates will affect your humanoid species as well. Their style of dress will reflect the weather in their region. Desert dwelling people will find it harder to cope with snow and ice even when dressed for the temperature. If you are dealing with a culture that doesn't travel a great deal, will they be prepared for extreme differences in weather? If you use a species with more hair, how will they adapt to a temperature change? Do they shed? What if they travel to a warmer region than they evolved in? Would they shave or cut their hair?

Asking questions is a good way to keep the creative juices flowing. Look at your creatures and ask yourself if they make sense in the world you've created.

Another important question to ask yourself is, 'why would I assume that an alien creature, raised in totally different circumstances, climate, culture, would walk, talk and think the same way as my other characters?' Too often aliens are used to highlight the shortcomings in humanity. We really don't need to resort to that. Mankind has plenty of shortcomings on it's own.

Keep a few factors in mind when creating your creatures and societies: ecology, environment (hostile?), gravity, atmosphere, sunlight, culture, history, and violence? Do your creatures have time for creativity to bloom or is all their time dedicated to survival? http://www.infinityplus.co.uk/nonfiction/blueheart.htm (Alison Sinclair gives an in-depth account on creating her water-world. Lots of good information if you're interested in this type of setting for your inhabitants)

Once you've decided on the type and variety of your inhabitants, give careful consideration to why you've created/used these particular races. Do not fall into the fantasy stereotypes: elves are good and in tune with nature, trolls are big and stupid, dwarves live under big mountains, etc. These are not only cliché but they also show a lack of attention to detail.

One of the best-known examples of stereotypical races in SF/fantasy is *Star Trek*. Klingon are violent, Vulcans are wise, Ferengi are thieves, Romulans and Borg are villains. Don't misunderstand me; I'm a big fan of the series. *Star Trek* broke a lot of racial barriers in the first series and it continues to do so in it's numerous spin-off programs. However, their aliens fall into stereotypes. *Star Trek* the only series to do this. In many ways, it simplifies the writers' job. Need a violent tempered antagonist? Grab someone from race X. Need a wise teacher? Race Y fills the void.

Can a race of near-clones exist? Possibly, but the odds are against it. Take into consideration the vast cultural differences between an Australian Aborigine and white-collar worker from Los Angeles. They are extremely different because of their physical and social environment but they are both human. Both are capable of learning complex philosophies and mathematics, both have learned to live in their society. Now, if man's intelligence allows him to adapt to such different settings, why would your sentient race evolve in a stereotypical manner? Shouldn't they show just as much diversity as humans?

SOCIETY AND DAILY LIFE

Society will play a major role in how your world functions and in your character development. Throughout history, it has been proven that the societies with the best engineers are those ruling the planet at the time. The Romans created a road system that enabled their armies to travel faster than their enemies. The Spanish freed up the shipping routes with their bigger boats but were overtaken by the Dutch with their faster, smaller boats. Who will rule the space ways? It will depend on who creates the best spaceships and/or other ways to travel.

Sounds more like science fiction than fantasy doesn't it? Not necessarily. Consider this, if your world is ruled by wizards, who is going to be in control? The nice guy who's an ineffective ruler or the not-so-nice guy with the ability to feed his people and protect them from invasion? Given the choice of living with the iron-fisted ruler, eating and being safe from harm or living with the benevolent ruler who's fields are barren and with invading armies who are decimating the population, most people are going to choose to eat and keep their families safe.

Whether your character has a choice in where he/she lives is up to you and what your plot dictates. Your character's role in society will have a major impact on how he/she acts or reacts. Creating new societies is as complex as creating the world itself. Everything is inter-related. So you must make a few decisions:

Type of government: Feudal, manorial, aristocratic, oligarchy, democracy

Level of technology: Types of transportation, manufacturing, how it affects everyday life

Magic: Where it fits into the system, respected, feared, criminal

Education: Public school systems, private schooling, apprenticeships

Crime and Punishment: Who governs the laws,-government, religion, mages

Business: Government controlled, trade unions, international/ interstellar cartels

Money: Coins & currency, barter or do they use a credit device-something that can be scanned by a computer?

Medicine: Doctors, priests, wizards, shaman-who is in charge?

Arts and Entertainment: Does the average person have time to enjoy creative pursuits? The type of entertainment your characters enjoy?

Since most fantasy novels are set in the medieval world, the feudal society is the most common. You can choose a different government and play with the options if you're creating a new world.

How do you know how many people should be in a small village or a large town? What is your character's place in society? What type of job might he/she be doing or training for? S. John Ross's, Medieval Demographics Made Easy, is an excellent article over the estimated sizes of population. The following figures are used with Mr. Ross's permission.

Villages   20 to 1,000 people.

Towns   1,000-8,000 people.

Cities   8,000-12,000 people

Big Cities   12,000-100,000 people

In the 15th century, some of the largest cities were: London-25,000-40,000, Paris-50,000-80,000, Genoa-75,000-100,000, and Venice-100,000+. Moscow had a massive population of over 200,000.

To help you decide what types of business your town, village or city needs, estimate the population and use the chart below.

Business	SV	Business	SV
Shoemakers	150	Butchers	1,200
Furriers	250	Fishmongers	1,200
Maidservants	250	Beer-Sellers	1,400
Tailors	250	Buckle Makers	1,400
Barbers	350	Plasterers	1,400
Jewelers	400	Spice Merchants	1,400
Taverns	400*	Blacksmiths	1,500
Old-Clothes	400	Painters	1,500
Pastrycooks	500	Doctors	1,700**
Masons	500	Roofers	1,800
Carpenters	550	Locksmiths	1,900
Weavers	600	Bathers	1,900
Chandlers	700	Ropemakers	1,900
Mercers	700	Inns	2,000
Coopers	700	Tanners	2,000
Bakers	800	Copyists	2,000
Watercarriers	850	Sculptors	2,000
Scabbardmakers	850	Rugmakers	2,000
Wine-Sellers	900	Harness-Makers	2,000
Hatmakers	950	Bleachers	2,100
Saddlers	1,000	Hay Merchants	2,300

Chicken Butchers	1,000	Cutlers	2,300
Pursemakers	1,100	Glovemakers	2,400
Woodsellers	2,400	Woodcarvers	2,400
Magic-Shops***	2,800	Booksellers	6,300
Bookbinders	3,000	Illuminators	3,900

*Taverns and Restaurants **These are licensed doctors. Total doctor SV is 350 (doctors can be substituted for wizards, or priests, whomever does the healing in your world ***Magic shops would be places to buy potions and herbs not magical weapons and armor. (SV= support value-the number of people required to support that type of business)

The rest of Mr. Ross's article can be viewed at:

http://www.io.com/~sjohn/demog.htm

http://www.geocities.com/unicorn7uk/writing.html   is   an interesting site for information on clothes, culture, magic, laws, etc.

RESEARCH

As you create your world, don't forget to research the basics. Many fantasy stories include horses as the mode of transportation. Unfortunately, too many writers have limited knowledge of horses or they base their knowledge on inaccurate portrayals in movies and books. One best selling fantasy author made a very large mistake in his narrative. The character shoved his sword into his horse's girth. A mistake such as this can shatter the entire novel's believability for an equestrian.

This diagram show's how a saddle fits on a horse's body. The girth is the band that holds the saddle on the horse.

The girth/cinch encircles the horse's body right behind the front legs. In order to keep the saddle from twisting to the side or under the horse's abdomen, the girth must be tight. Not just snug, but tight. Trying to shove a sword into the girth would cut the horse's side and/or the girth itself.

The horse is not going to tolerate this.

Consider the length of a sword. Even a short sword is close to 27 inches in length. (3/4 of a meter). Now, imagine this 27 inches of steel running along the side of the horse's body. Even if the sword

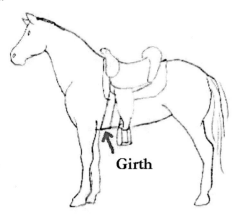

Girth

could be sheathed in the girth without the horse rearing and bucking, the rigid length of metal would severely hinder the horse's movement.

Referencing the parts of a horse can prevent mistakes such as describing a well-made horse as having deep withers, or a cut on the front leg bleeding down the horse's hock.

The average reader might not pick up on mistakes like these but horse owners/riders will. They will be quick to point out the mistakes to their friends as well. Their friends don't have to be horse owners/riders to appreciate the mistakes and to tell their friends. This is one case where word of mouth can be detrimental to book sales.

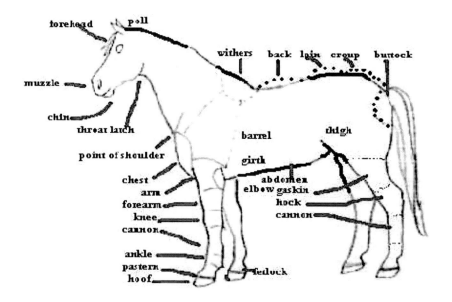

To often writers have their horses travel impossible distances in one day. The exception to this would be if you create a new type of horse with special traits or powers. If you decide to give your horses special qualities, this needs to be mentioned from the very beginning and not thrown in at the last minute as a save because you realized that your hero cannot possibly reach the battle in time if his mount lacks the ability to travel at twice the normal speed.

The average horse can travel 25 to 30 miles in one day. This will not be done at a run. Most of the distance will be covered in a trot, a gait that your rider will probably not enjoy. Endurance horses are trained to make 50, 75 even 100 mile trail rides in one day. However, this requires special diets and extensive training for horse and rider. A rider with considerable experience will know how to ease the strain on their own body while riding long distances but they will still be sore if they are riding farther than normal. The muscles on the inner thigh and buttocks will take the greatest amount of punishment, but the lower back, calves, knees and hips will also feel the strain.

Horses must be walked after working up a sweat. They need to cool down slowly or risk serious health issues. Horses cannot regurgitate, so if they overeat, they are prone to stomach problems, which can be fatal. A sudden change in diet consisting of grass or grain that is too rich can cause stomach problems as well.

Horses do not lap water. They are not dogs or cats. They suck water up into their mouths. While their lips don't pucker like a human kiss, they do tighten. Some horses like to immerse their entire muzzle into the water while they drink.

Mare = grown female horse

Stallion = grown male horse able to sire foals

Gelding = castrated male horse

Foal = either sex under one year

Filly = female horse up to two years

Colt = male horse up to two years

Most writers have a limited amount of time to research all the facts they need to include in their stories so how do you find what you need in a quick and easy manner? One solution is to read non-fiction books aimed at a mid-grade level audience. The facts are given in very simple easy to follow answers without a lot of extrapolation to slow your research.

For writers in the USA, contact your local county extension office and ask if you can purchase a 4-H circular. Horseless Horse, Basic 4-H Horsemanship, or Basic 4-H Horse Science would cover a lot of very basic information as well as giving you diagrams of horses, tack and other equipment. Most of the circulars are less than $5.00 and a worthwhile investment if you intend to use horses in very many of your novels.

Summary

World building can be a time consuming and daunting task, and when you're done, the odds are, you'll still have forgotten something. If you believe our world was created by the Christian God, then you know it took him seven days and he's omniscient. Humans aren't. If you believe in evolution, then you know it took millions of years for our world to reach this stage in its development. Do you think that it is possible for one person to create entire galaxies? It could take more than a lifetime to consider all the little details that go into making a world.

Fortunately for us, we don't have to know ever little detail. What we do need is the ability to picture our world as a real entity. Our societies need to make sense and our ecology needs to be balanced or have a reason why it's not. The clearer our vision is of our world, the easier it will be for us to convey it to our readers.

There is such a thing as 'too much information' in our stories. Our readers don't need or expect us to tell every little detail of our characters' days and lives. They want the highlights, the exciting and important bits. We do not need to go into detail about every seam of our characters' clothes nor how each plate was handcrafted in a kiln nor how one jungle vine is choking out the plants around it. Unless, that has a bearing on the plot and is vital to the setting.

We don't want to surprise or confuse our readers. If our protagonist wakes up with a knife in her hand, they're going to want to know where she got it. If you described the room as she went to bed, a reference to the knife under the pillow would be appropriate. The amount of lint on the floor really isn't.

Resist the urge to show the reader all the work you've put into your world building. If you've spent hours/days/weeks creating new and fantastic animals, don't draw attention to them by having your protagonist act like they're something new, when they're supposed to be a commonplace creature in their world. Pulling your reader out of the story with long drawn out descriptions does not endear your story to them. They want to be immersed in your world. Let them travel through it with your characters without giving into the temptation of playing tour guide.

BIBLIOGRAPHY:

Orson Scott Card, *How to Write Science Fiction and Fantasy*, Writers Digest Books 2001

Lee Masterson, *Aliens and Faeries: Non-humans Acting Badly*, http://www.fictionfactor.com/articles/aliens.html 2001

Michael McCollum, *World Building for Fun and Profit, Part 1, The Art of Science Fiction, Volume II, Chapter 4*, June 2001 http://www.scifi-az.com

Michael McCollum, *World Building for Fun and Profit, Part 2 The Art of Science Fiction, Volume II, Chapter 4*, July 2001 http://www.scifi-az.com

S. John Ross, *Medieval Demographics Made Easy: Numbers For Fantasy Worlds* http://www.io.com/~sjohn/demog.htm 1993, 1999

Steven Savage, *A Way With Worlds* http://www.seventhsanctum.com Weekly Column November 1999 to October 2000

Patricia C. Wrede, *Fantasy Worldbuilding* Questions, http://www.sfwa.org/writing/worldbuilding1.htm 1996

Fantasy Without Cliches

WRITING EFFECTIVELY

MILENA BENINI

THE MAGIC OF STYLE

So you've got the best, most original story in the world, peopled by lovingly created, profound characters. But if you don't tell your story in an effective, convincing and moving way, it will all fall flat. The style of writing, as well as being your personal signature, is the primary medium for your story. In this chapter, we will look at all the different elements that make up style, how to choose among them and how to avoid the pitfalls of clichés.

LANGUAGE: ALL ABOUT BRICKS

In the art of writing, language is the main construction material, the brick without which no amount of planning and mortar will create the building of your story. And, just like in architecture, there are many different kinds of bricks at your disposal. To be able to choose the one most appropriate for your purpose, you must first learn all about bricks.

Know your language. Many aspiring writers believe that spell-checkers and grammar checkers can spare them the boredom of learning the basic rules. Bleep—wrong! Although it's true that copy-editors need to earn their salaries, profound knowledge of language provides the author with a much greater range of building material. Moreover, nowadays, all writers live and work—and (try to) sell—in a buyer's market. Most editors won't even read a semi-literate story. And they'll be perfectly right not to. If you can't be bothered to learn the basics of your craft, you'll never make a good craftsman.

Always bear this in mind: just like all other arts, writing is a craft first, and can only become art later.

We will not concentrate here on the basic rules of grammar, as this is not our purpose. However, we will look at one often-encountered mistake and misconception: the problems in the usage of passive voice.

PASSIVE VOICE

First of all, please remember that passive voice is not just any verb form using the verb "to be." Many people tend to mix passive voice, which comes with the past participle (ending mostly on —ed), with progressive tenses, which also use the verb "to be" but come with the present participle (ending always on —ing).

Arthur was lifting a sword.—This is past progressive, in active voice. Progressive tenses are used to talk about actions that last longer, or take place while some other action is also happening. Other examples of progressive tenses are: The dragon is breathing (present), they were standing (past again), I will be reading (future), etc.

The sword was lifted. This is past simple in passive voice. Notice that this is not the same sentence as above. Past progressive passive would be, "The sword was being lifted." Other examples of passive voice are: Gaul was taken by Caesar (past), we were told to stay away (past), the plane is lifted by wind (present), the dragon will be slain (future). Notice also that passive sentences with the actor (whoever performs the action) will include "by" as the introduction: this was written by me.

While this confusion in naming things doesn't really matter in writing (it's not important to know what something is called if you're able to use it correctly), sometimes it creates problems because of the widespread belief that using passive forms in writing fiction is somehow wrong. Let me tell you this: passive is a perfectly legitimate verb form in fiction.

Problems start only when you use it too often, or in the wrong places. When in doubt, use this simple principle.

Passive voice should be used:

·   when you want to stress the action itself and not the actor;

·   when you don't know who the actor is; or

·   when you prefer not to reveal the actor.

Let us look at some concrete examples. The rule above was stated in the passive voice. True, I could have put it in active, saying "you should only use passive voice" instead, but my point wasn't about what you should do: what I wanted to stress was the usage of passive voice. By putting the sentence into passive, I eliminated you from the process entirely, and achieved greater width of the rule: it's not only you who should use passive in this way. The same goes for me and anybody else.

You can encounter many similar situations in fiction writing as well. Say, for example, that your story includes an enchanted castle. The race that had constructed the castle is believed to be extinct. Notice the passive voice here: everybody believes that the race is extinct; the focus is not on those "everybody", however, but rather on the (implied) fact that the belief is wrong. There are some members of the race still hiding in the ruined corridors of the castle. When your heroes spend the night in the castle and, in the morning, discover that someone had taken their saddlebags, you are perfectly right in saying, "The saddlebags were gone." This is also passive voice. The focus of your sentence here is on the fact that the saddlebags are missing, and that's why it's stated in passive. Neither your heroes nor your readers know at this point that it was the last of the Mawheekans who had taken them. In fact, at this point, your heroes are probably not even sure whether someone had indeed taken the saddlebags, or whether they had simply been too tired the night before and so left the saddlebags somewhere else. What's important at that point is only that the most important thing in those saddlebags, the Jewel of the Ing-Lysh crown, is gone—another passive, but also the shortest, most effective way of stating the situation.

Finally, while we're on the subject of language, always remember this. Language is an important element in the construction of the world. Language is how we shape our thoughts and feelings; that means that it will reflect certain attitudes and beliefs of the speaker. Think about Japanese, for instance, where there are separate pronouns for 'female I' and for 'male I'. Japanese also has different verb forms for speaking to your social peers, to your social superiors, and to your social inferiors. This is a reflection of the Japanese culture. Think about such things when you think about creating your own languages. You don't have to construct entire languages, of course, but adding a little touch here and there will go a long way in creating exactly the atmosphere you want.

Remember, also, that not everybody speaks the same language. In worlds with little or no communication, your characters will need to know many languages before they can venture further than their own village; in a world where trade is widespread, there will probably exist a lingua franca, which most traders can use to communicate. The emphasis being on most, not all: there will still be places where anyone who has traveled far enough from home will be lost without the help of an interpreter.

Skipping over such problems because they seem like problems is the mark of a sloppy writer; a really skilled one will integrate the matters of logic—such as language-barriers—in her story and make them plot points. This is something that is rarely seen nowadays. Use the hole in the market to your advantage.

Style: The Art of Laying Bricks

Literary discourse—that form of expression that we recognize as "literary" and not "everyday" communication—is just a fancy name for what we most often refer to as "style." (Actually, "everyday communication" is also a style, but that's irrelevant for our purposes.) To talk about (literary) style, we will, therefore, look first at what it is that makes us recognize a piece of writing as belonging between the covers of a book and not on a piece of paper magnetted to the fridge door.

If you think carefully, you'll realize that, especially nowadays, the very fact that we've found something between the covers of a book is, at the same time, the only sure way to determine that it belongs there. So, the rule of thumb to remember about style is this: Style can be anything.

Isaac Asimov (who, despite his own excellence as a writer, tended to give out rather offhanded, sometimes downright wrong advice on writing) once said that the only good style is no style at all—i.e. the kind of style in which the reader will not notice deliberate choices made in the process of writing. This is, of course, absurd by the time the story reaches the reader, there's no way to hide the fact that it is, indeed, literary discourse that they're reading. Even the decision to stay as close as possible to "ordinary", "everyday" communication is, in itself, a stylistic decision. One with a limited range of usefulness, too. Certainly, if you want people to concentrate on your ideas and not the way in which you present them, it's only common sense to try and not draw their attention away by floral phrasing. On the other hand, atmosphere in literary work is mostly created by departing from the common ways of expression, even if it's just a tiny departure. And if you are trying to create an epic story reminiscent of Homer's *Iliad*, for example, using a journalistic, simple, close-to-everyday style will work against you. Thus, we come to the second rule of thumb: Choose the style most appropriate for your story.

Of course, that may not always be easy. Let's say you are writing a humorous fantasy set in the middle ages: will you go with a conversational style usual in humor, or a flowery, lengthy tone of medieval literature? The answer is—it's up to you. Being chatty and lowbrow can make the text sound closer to your readers. On the other hand, the contrast between a highbrow tone and people falling on their faces in the mud can heighten the humorous effect. So, both options—and any number of other solutions—have their good and their bad sides. You must decide which one you're more comfortable with.

Before making your decision, there are two more things that you should be aware of: Whatever style you choose, be sure that you'll be able to keep it up all the way through. It's very important for style to be consistent throughout your work, whether it is a short story or a 150,000 word novel. (Unless, of course, there are overwhelmingly good reasons to change the style at some point, remember that nothing is ever written in stone.) While in short stories it may be possible to keep up a highly constructed style all the way through, it is much more difficult to do in a long work. If you are not comfortable with your style, no one else will be, either.

The other thing to remember is that dialogues, letters and other character-generated words in your work can be completely different from the words that surround them. You can use Hemingwayan hard-boiled style as narrator, and still have your minstrel of a main character never utter a sentence under twenty-five three-syllable words. In rhyme.

TAMING THE ELEPHANTS

Basically, the elements of style can be divided into two really rough major categories: the big stuff, and the small stuff. The big stuff includes all the general elements that are present all the way through your work. This means that they are mostly structural things, such as chapters, titling, choice of POV—all those things that help organize your work into a coherent whole.

People often agonize over these things: in a way, they're right. The same story will seem very different if told in the past or the present tense; in first or third person. Those are big decisions. At the same time, it's good to remember that, although it may seem strange at first, the bigger the stuff, the easier it is to change. This is because the big stuff is—well, big, and therefore easily noticed. The rule of thumb would thus go something like this: Structural decisions are like elephants. They can do a lot of damage, but, properly used, they're a great help. Also, you have to be blind not to notice them.

Although there are a lot of things that make up structure—paragraphs, chapters, amount of dialogue, construction of sentence—the most important elephant, at which we'll take a closer look, is the choice of Point of View (POV).

There are many POV's and POV combinations. The most widespread, nowadays, is close or limited third—the kind of POV that keeps a false distance from the main character (he did, she thought), but remains limited to the "event horizon" of that same character.

It's good to remember that it wasn't always like that: POV's are subject to fashion, just like everything else. Some periods preferred first person POV, others leaned towards third omniscient.

The choice of POV also depends on the genre and length: short fiction, for example, lends itself more easily to experimental and unusual POV's, such as the second person. And "noir" mysteries wouldn't be the same without the trademark first person voices of its jaded, world-weary detectives. In fantasy, however, there is no such firm rule on POV.

What's important, however, is always to bear in mind that POV's, like everything else, must remain consistent throughout the work. And, also like everything else, they all have their good and their bad sides.

Another thing to bear in mind when deciding on the narrator is the fact that, regardless of the actual POV, there can be two types of narrators: reliable and unreliable ones. A reliable narrator is usually the assumption with which the reader will start: they'll open the book and start reading ready to take anything you tell them at face value. However, you are under no geas to tell the truth, the whole truth, and nothing but the truth.

If you do decide to lie or omit things from your main narration, though, always remember two things: 1. at some point, you'll have to reveal the truth, so you had better come up with a convincing vehicle to do so, and 2. if you don't establish early on that your narrator is not reliable, your readers will feel cheated. This is particularly important if you're not using first person narrators, whose lies the readers will accept more easily. However, you can get away with lying with almost all limited POV's. Let's look at them more closely.

Whether first, second or third person limited POV's have this all-important characteristic: they're limited. (You never would have guessed, right?) This means they're wonderful for all plots that demand certain actions or thoughts to be hidden from the readers.

Making the lack of information convincing often makes trouble for new writers. The main character should never merely overlook something, especially if that something is a vital element of the plot. Well, actually, this can be done, but it's not easy. You can pull it off using one of the two techniques:

a) make it look as if it's not something that's vital for the plot. If the way to overcome the Evil Lord de Variapinta is to trick him into opening the red door instead of the green one, then the fact that all members of the de Variapinta family become color-blind by the time they're thirty should be mentioned before we find out the thing about doors. At that point, the information can seem like just a mildly interesting fact, easily missed in a bunch of family gossip your heroine hears from an overly talkative second cousin of de Variapintas. However, when the time comes for your heroine to put two and two together, she had better do so!

b) offer something even more interesting/ important/urgent at the same time, and have the character go after that. At the moment, when your heroine finds out about the dragon lurking behind the red door, have her also find out that she's really the long-lost heir to the kingdom of Ing-Lysh. This is a perfectly legitimate reason for her to ignore the dragon information, at least for the time being.

A much worse mistake than heroes who miss some vital bit of information are heroes who see all they need to see, but fail to come to the inevitable conclusion. If you do that, your readers will feel doubly cheated: nobody wants to read about heroes who are obviously less intelligent than an average person. Well, with the repeated caveat that nothing is ever written in stone. If your plot hangs on Lord de Variapinta's ability to control elevated minds, making one of your characters the village idiot can work—as long as you make sure that the wise old wizard Dabbler doesn't behave like another idiot as well. (At least not until de Variapinta's mind-control starts...but you get the picture.)

Limited POV's are, of course, a good way to make sure you can pull off tricks such as these. All-knowing, all-seeing narrators à l'ancienne, by their very definition, have all the information at their disposal. (This, too, can have its uses, as we'll see later.)

Aside from this, limited POV's have another very important characteristic, which is also one of the main reasons why they're so popular: they are a lot easier for the readers to identify with. This comes from the fact that, while limiting the readers' data input to the observations of one person only, they also give direct, intimate contact with that one person's thoughts and feelings. After a chapter or two spent in somebody's head, the readers will feel as if they were visiting an old friend.

Even with limited POV's, there's still the choice between third and first person narration. So now we will take a closer look at each, to find out what their good and bad sides are.

THIRD PERSON

This is, at the moment, the most popular of all POV's. There are many reasons for this, but the main ones can be summed up like this: third person limited POV has all the advantages of a limited, close POV, with none of the disadvantages of the first person. This means that you get to provide your readers with the sense of closeness, without actually having to go "all the way."

Limited third is a highly versatile little creature. It can fit naturally with almost any tone, atmosphere or genre. Unlike first person, it also provides you with the opportunity to use two similar, but still distinct voices—that of your main character, as demonstrated in dialogue and occasionally specified thought—and 'your own'—i.e. the voice of the narrator.

Limited third does have its downsides, too: it's very easy to slip from it unintentionally, for example. Look: "She turned away and left. De Variapinta watched her until she disappeared down the stairs." At first glance this seems like a perfectly natural thing to write but, unless de Variapinta is your POV character, it's slipping from POV (if she turned away, how could she know that he watched her?)—and that's a major no-no.

As with all limited POV's, there is also that eternal source of headache, the problem of character description. Newbie writers often try to solve this by having their POV character stop before a mirror (pool, polished shield, dead dragon's eye) and contemplate their blond hair and green eyes. This is one of those things that you should not do. (Unless there's a good reason for it, like for instance your character being a self-obsessed slicker or going out for her first courtly presentation; even then, however, it's more likely they would contemplate their clothes and hairdo, not their features as such.)

How to solve this? Generally, it is better to avoid solid chunks of description regardless of the POV issue. Instead, you should try inserting little bits of description into the action. Be careful, however, to avoid nonsensical false tricks, such as "She pushed her blond hair out of her eyes." With limited third, this is highly tempting to do, but it's also highly irritating to read: how often do people actually think like that? You push hair out of your eyes, not your curly red hair. Here's another good rule to remember: If you're in somebody's head, stay there.

You can, on the other hand, do something like this: on her way to the courtly presentation, have your character meet someone. If it's a friend, she can comment on the fact that, "that green dress goes wonderfully with your eyes." (And then your POV character can consider her blond hair and wonder whether a darker shade of green would have set it out better after all.) Or it can be an enemy, and she can offer a biting comment, such as, "you know, if I had such light hair, I'd use makeup. Your eyebrows are almost invisible; it makes you look like a rag doll." This technique is additionally useful as it helps you flesh out the situation. The character is immediately placed in the court, and we see her be high enough to have enemies; she's also attractive enough to produce jealousy. From there on, it's your call whether you want to make her a self-possessed beauty that will disdain the biting comment, or a self-doubting ninny who will step into the main hall on the verge of tears. But none of these additional elements can be presented nearly as effectively if you just have her stop before a mirror and admire herself.

Generally, remember this: interaction is always better than mere action. (And conflict is usually the best kind of interaction.)

All in all, any limited POV—and close third especially—can easily lure you into offering huge chunks of data-dumps and telling-instead-of-showing. Both of these are, on the whole, things to avoid. However, third close is probably the easiest to sell, and it's relatively easy to write. In other words, here's another rule of thumb: when in doubt, use close third.

FIRST PERSON

Let's put the bad stuff first: first person POV is very difficult to do well, and most editors nowadays prefer not to see it—unless, of course, there are overwhelming reasons to use it. Those reasons will most often pertain to the amount of information available to the POV character, the specific way of thinking of that character, or to some other element particular to that character.

Thus, for example, if your main character is a dragon or an elf, telling their story in first person can be justified—provided that their mental outlook is different enough. If your dragon is going to think and/or perceive the world exactly the way humans do, there's no reason to complicate things and go with the first person. If, on the other hand, dragons have some distinguishing characteristic—such as, for example, being unable to tell humans one from another, or seeing sound as color—then it may be a really good idea to go directly inside your dragon's head. Telling a story in third person with the POV character unable to tell those who surround him apart would look entirely unconvincing and very awkward; if you tell it from the first person, your readers will buy it a lot more easily. Look:

> "One of the soft-skinned approached me, waving its shiny claw. I hit it with my tail. I had seen my friends slain by those small, silvery points. Soft-skinned claws were dangerous."

If you tried to put the same thing into third person, it would sound awkward and distant.

Another thing that you may use the first person for is setting the tone. Remember what we said about fashion: using first person narrative, it will be much easier to create a false-noir atmosphere, or to give your story an eighteenth-nineteenth century feeling. Conversely, of course, you can use it for parody: if your story deals with a dragon who investigates crimes for a living, giving him a first-person voice will instantly transfer his cave into a dingy office with a bottle of bourbon hidden behind a rock.

EVERYTHING ELSE

Everything else includes omniscient narrators, epic or impersonal narration, and all possible combination of POV's, as well as that rarest of beasts, second person POV. While they are not very popular at the moment, and are perhaps best reserved for short fiction, there is some very useful stuff here, as well.

First, let us look at omniscient narration. This is the kind of narration where the author—and therefore the reader—has access to the thoughts and feelings of all characters, or at least a vast majority of them. Although lately this technique has earned the derogatory name of "head-hopping", it is in fact a perfectly legitimate technique. There is nothing inherently wrong with it and, in fact, many classical works were written using omniscient narration. The problem stems from the fact that head-hoppers are a lot more difficult to write well.

Just like the readers, the authors, too, have a tendency to bond more closely with some of the characters, and pay less attention to others. This often pulls the authors into describing a lot of the things from the POV of Character A, only to jump into the head of Character B for some little detail. This is a bad thing, and deserves the name of head-hopping. It indicates laziness on the part of the writer, and tends to confuse the reader.

Real omniscient, on the other hand, isn't like that at all: it divides its attention equally among a large group of characters. This is why it is most suited for "ensemble" productions, i.e. stories where a more or less large group of characters shares the importance. Think about high fantasy quests: they are usually excellent examples of ensemble productions. So if you've got a story like that, omniscient may just be the right choice for you. Remember, however, that it may not be everybody's cuppa. Choosing an omniscient narrator is a risk. It may well be worth taking, but deserves careful consideration.

Distant POV is, in fact, exactly the opposite: it's the kind of narration in which readers are never allowed to peek directly into any character's thoughts and feelings. A distant narrator will be reduced to describing what characters do and say. You can think of it as the militant wing of the show-don't-tell school.

The good side of such an approach is the high level of mystery you can keep. Reading a distant-narrated story is more like watching a movie, where you've only got access to the information you'd get in real life, without that mind-reading ability that makes literature so utterly different from any other medium.

The bad side of distant POV is that reading a distant-narrated story is more like watching a movie, where you've only got access to the information you'd get in real life, without that mind-reading ability that makes literature so utterly different from any other medium. In other words, the effectiveness of such an approach will depend on your skill as an actor and director. In distant POV, you can never write, "She was afraid," nor even, "She looked afraid." Instead, you can write, "She shivered, her eyes widening." This can be pretty encumbering, particularly if you have to keep it up for one hundred thousand words.

Finally, there is the mongrel of mongrels, mixed POV. Although this may seem like the most exotic of combinations, it isn't (the most exotic is second person). Mixed POV's can be very practical tools, and can go down well with the readers, too. The most often encountered combination is first/third, where part of the story is told from the first person perspective of one character, while the rest is told from third person, usually closely focused on another character.

This kind of technique does allow you to take the best of both worlds, of course, but it also brings along a double set of pitfalls. However, especially with a large cast of important characters, it may be a very good solution. It makes distinguishing among characters easier (Princess Grunhilda from third person, Sam the Dragon from first), and it allows you to change tones from one part to the next.

You can do the same thing using just close third and limiting your 'access-allowed' heads to two or three. Be careful, however, to use clearly defined switch-points, such as chapter breaks or those famous three-star dividers in the text. Remember that your readers tread through the story as if they were stepping through unknown, uncharted country. It's only fair to provide them with some pointers along the way.

Oh, and there's the by now infamous second person. As this handbook focuses on writing fantasy, there's only one thing to be said about using second person POV: don't. Well, all right—unless you're writing a short story. Only short fiction can survive experiment successfully. But even then, think twice before writing in second person. And then decide against it.

TREES AND FORESTS

The thing about the trees and forests is this: while structural things—paragraphs, chapters, choice of POV—all influence your style, they are so big that few people will notice them, provided you do the small stuff right. This applies equally to writers as to editors and finally readers. In fact, the rule goes even further than the infamous trees that make you miss the forest; it's the undergrowth that will catch the attention of most of your readers. The rule of thumb is here, therefore; do sweat the small stuff.

Of course, problems arise from the fact that there is so much of the small stuff; one hardly knows where to start. We will try here to look at some groups of small stuff, and mention some of the most often encountered unnecessary mistakes. If you've ever been in a forest, you'll know that the really tough plants are always the smallest ones, anyway.

We'll start with a very small plant indeed; although it's so widely present everywhere that the life of the forest would become impossible without it—words, or vocabulary.

Choice of words is immensely important. A lot of people, especially when they write fantasy, have this tendency to use "old" words, for example. While this is not a bad idea in and of itself, you should bear in mind one thing, of which you're probably sick and tired by now: whatever your choice of vocabulary, make sure you remain consistent. If you don't feel comfortable in Elizabethan English, it's better to leave it out all together than to forget it halfway through and slip into contemporary lower-Manhattan dialect. (Unless, of course, there is an overwhelmingly good reason to do so, which is always possible. The golden rule remains nothing is written in stone.)

Also, make sure that you really know your chosen dialect. The number of young authors who try to reproduce second person-English (thees and thous) without really knowing how to do it is incredible—and quite as incredibly irritating for those of us who actually know something about it. If you're creating a language variation of your own, there are many things to beware of. Here are some of the most usual.

THE TOLKIEN SYNDROME

This is a very dangerous problem. Its symptoms are too many made-up words that sound as if they had been created by having a five-year-old with a flu read off an eighteenth century map of Norway. Its characterized also by strange spellings (with plenty of y's instead of i's, more e's at the end than is usual, and most final c's turning into ck's) for which there is no justification.

You should always remember that Professor Tolkien was, in fact, a trained professional in the art of linguistics and, just as with any other trained professional, you should not try to repeat his feats at home. Moreover, bear in mind that Tolkien went directly to the sources, i.e. medieval languages, and worked his constructions from there. Deriving things with tons of fantasy reading as your only support is really the derivation of a derivation. While it may be a very post-modern procedure, it is also a highly risky one, as chances are you'll end up with something sounding as if it would dearly love to be Tolkien but very obviously isn't.

THE SMEERP SYNDROME

The great late Damon Knight, who strongly objected to people calling their small, big-eared, short-tailed, fluffy animals, smeerps—when they could perfectly well have called them rabbits instead, invented the name for this. Agreed, if you are inventing a world different from our own, by all means call whatever is really different by a really different name. Just make sure you don't merely call a horse a glymph.

If you were consistent in this technique (and you know how important consistency is!), you would have to call houses oompahs, and people brthdls. That's perfectly all right if your brthdls are, on average, four feet five inches tall, have three legs, ride on half-amphibian three-legged glymphs and live in small sacks suspended over water they call the oompahs. If, however, your people are people (two legs, two hands, two ears, one nose, not taking into account any possible losses due to dueling) who ride on horses and live in houses, have the honesty to call them people who ride on horses and live in houses. It will be easier both on you and on your readers if you don't produce a book that's half written in what is, in the end, a foreign language to both of you.

The smeerp syndrome is, in fantasy, particularly often encountered in measures, due to fear of anachronisms. Yes, meters and kilograms are relatively recent inventions. However, using miles as a word—ordinary as it may seem to you—does not necessarily make it the 'contemporary mile'. If you are definitely not comfortable with that, go with 'Royal mile', or 'league', or simply use a very large number of 'feet' or 'steps'. Greeks and Romans both found feet and steps acceptable for their measurement system; ancient Egyptians additionally used forearms for architectural and textile-producing purposes. Not to go into any more detail, measures using parts of human body do seem to be a very natural way to develop the measurement system, and there is nothing wrong with that.

At the same time, few authors realize the inherent anachronism of people who, in ancient times and especially in worlds without churches, wait for 'hours' or close their eyes for a 'second'. Despite the fact that principles of the clock have long been known both in theory and in practice, the idea that time should be divided into chunks smaller than 'morning', 'afternoon', and 'night' spent most of its life constrained to very narrow scientific circles. If your plot demands precise time co-ordination for your guerilla attack on the dragon's lair to succeed, the best course is probably to look for a different plan, or to have your forces co-ordinate with one another by magical means. Just don't have them agree to meet in two hours; not, that is, unless you have a very different kind of world.

Generally, the best way to avoid anachronisms is to know your own world in and out. If it's not based directly on an existing historical period, make sure your readers realize that and—no less important—make sure you explain how the differences came about. No, you don't have to provide detailed scientific explanations; making sure that if your hero owns a wind-up clock, the uses of the spring are also felt in other areas of life, will be enough. On the other hand, if you use an existing Earth period and/or culture as the basis of your world, make sure you know enough about it—and, again, make doubly sure your readers realize your knowledge is well-founded. Do not, however, write a historical exposé. That's a perfectly legitimate literary form as well; it just isn't fantasy.

THE A'POSTROPHE SYNDROME

That's the kind of situation when all the names and/or words have an apostrophe in them, for no other reason than to make them look different. Now, here we come to a somewhat delicate linguistic territory, so be patient for a while.

Remember: in English and most other Western languages, an apostrophe is merely a sign that something has been omitted. (Remember the use of apostrophes in Anne McCaffrey's naming of dragonriders? That's the correct usage.)

In some other languages, an apostrophe may be used to transcribe sounds that do not exist in English. If this is the case with your apostrophes, well and good, provided you find a place to explain it all—and even then, think twice about using apostrophes over some other system of transcribing that particular sound. Also, do be careful to be phonetically consistent in your use of the sound: if it's a vowel (i.e. it is a parallel to a, e, i, o, u and it creates syllables, because there are no syllables without a vowel), make sure it remains used as a vowel throughout. If you make it a consonant stand-in, make sure it doesn't create any syllables of its own anywhere along the way. The majority of your readers may not have the linguistic knowledge or phonetic skills to articulate this, but, believe me, they will feel that "something" is wrong. Human minds—not to say human guts—do know a lot more than we are generally aware of.

THE CAPITALIZATION SYNDROME

Having thus reduced Prynce Ch'ar'minge and his Megasmeerp to a mere Charlie on a horse, you might feel that the sense of dignity is beginning to lack. Many authors try to make up for this by capitalizing left and right: Mere Charlie thus goes to fight Lords of the Evil House of de Variapinta on his trusted Fire Horse, wielding a Runesword and holding a Mirror Likeness of his beloved Princess in his Pure Hand, while she awaits on Mountain Rainbow, in the Castle of the Colorful Dragon, hoping that the Jewel of the Ing-Lysh crown will help him.

First of all, remember that capitalizing common nouns, such as swords, mountains, hands or smeerp-droppings does not make them seem any more magical; it just makes them stand out a little, and even that effect is lost after a few pages, reducing what you envisaged as a Magical Object to a mere day-of-the-week-look-alike. Also, remember the warning from Vonda N. McIntyre: every single word you capitalize will make its way to the cover blurb of your novel. While most blurbs are inherently silly, there's no need to fuel it further by personally supplying the silly-material yourself.

Furthermore, if something you write about really has a magical quality, it will not need your capitalization to stand out. Real cool doesn't need to advertise. (Think about the appearance of Luke Skywalker in the opening sequence of *Return of the Jedi*: the simple black does much more for his impressiveness than a flashier, gold-studded Elvis-in-Vegas set would have done.) Reducing the Mirror Likeness to a simple likeness that Charlie wears in a medallion around his neck, and then having it wink at him when he hesitates before the red door, will have much more effect.

THE ENGLISH SPEAKER SYNDROME

This problem is particularly apparent with writers who do not speak another language: all of their made-up words and names sound as if they were derived from English. It's only natural, of course, to lean on your mother tongue when working with words but, if you want to create something that will sound original and different, you have to go further. It's usually also a good idea to know exactly where you are going.

In the creation of your own language, start with geography. Is the country you're describing a warm coastal place? In that case, look at Mediterranean languages. They are very many and varied: the Romance languages (Italian, Spanish, French, Portuguese); Slavic (Croatian, Bosnian, Montenegrian, Serbian); Greek, Albanian, Arabic. Choose any one of those languages as the basis for your future constructions—and then find someone who knows the language in question to check your constructions. Have them make sure you didn't inadvertently use any dirty words or created an otherwise wrong or funny construct.

Of course, you are not trying to re-construct an existing language, but every construction you do make, based on an existing language, will sooner or later reach someone who speaks the language in question and you never know what kind of a slip-up you may have made. In our global-communicating world, it's silly to leave yourself open for such a situation, as news spreads quickly. Remember the fiasco that Ford suffered when they tried to market their Nova model in Spain: they advertised it as No-Va, and wondered why it wasn't selling. The Spanish, on the other hand, wondered why anyone would want to buy a car named "doesn't go."

Forests and Trees

Even if you don't make up your own language, there are still a lot of little things that lurk in the corners of the writing world. Here is a short overview of the most dangerous of those beasts.

Redundancy

Redundancy is the kind of situation where people (usually automatically) use two words or a whole construction when just one would do. Some typical fantasy redundancies include huge giants and tiny dwarves. Small giants are not exactly an often-encountered species; and, except in Terry Pratchett, neither are large dwarves. In other words, be careful not to describe the same thing twice. It makes your prose unnecessarily wordy for one—and it will also make a lot of people laugh, exactly because they will come across your huge giant and wonder where his smaller cousins can be found.

Just like everything else, redundancy can be used to a certain effect in dialogue. Be careful, however: whoever uses a lot of redundancy in speech will automatically be marked as a pompous, boring kind of person.

Almost Just

The almost just syndrome pertains to all those "little" words that create unnecessary clutter in your prose, indicate lack of precision, or drop into your writing directly from your speech habits. They are modifiers and half-modifiers such as 'almost', 'similar to' and 'half', or false groupers such as "a kind of" and "a sort of." When you use them too much, you will end up with a lot of vague statements, such as, "He was half-afraid" and "She wore an almost yellow dress." In most cases, they make it seem as if you were unable to think of the right word: half-afraid is better stated as 'anxious' or 'worried', and 'almost yellow' is ochre, light brown, the color of sand, or off-white. It can even be burnt sienna, or, if you feel particularly creative, it can become burnt Licenna—most people will recognize the reference.

As always, no rule is absolute. Sometimes, using half-modifiers and false groupers can be the best way of putting things; just make sure you're aware you're using them, and be careful not to use them as an excuse not to have to think of the right words.

Another group of almost just symptoms are apparent modifiers, words with no real meaning, such as "just", "really" or "only." The easiest way to get rid of the plague is to run a search-replace routine on your text and see how many hits you get. Words such as these often wriggle into your writing from your spoken-language patterns. Remember, in spoken communication, we all use some words as mere indicators that we're thinking about something, placeholders which tell other people we haven't given up our turn in the conversation yet. In writing, however, there's no need for such placeholders, and they should be eradicated ruthlessly.

Obviously, this rule does not apply to dialogue, where you want to reproduce speech patterns. However, remember that written dialogue not only needn't, but also mustn't really be exactly the same as real-life speech; you need to make it more coherent and condensed, or else you'll end up sounding like some sort of a highbrow literary experiment. (Unless you're writing only about Oxford language professors speaking in class, which is a rather rare situation in fantasy.)

The same thing also applies to direct reproduction of thought. The people who tried to do this—i.e. provide an exact reproduction of human thoughts in literature—called this process the stream-of-consciousness writing, and were mostly called James Joyce, Virginia Woolf and William Faulkner. The results were eight hundred page books about people falling asleep. In short: don't.

If you must have specific thoughts of your characters reproduced in the text, try to keep it down to a few sentences, and make them much more coherent and systematic than thoughts usually are. No one will blame you for that little bit of un-realism.

PONTIFICATION OF EXPOSTULATION

Very often, people start from the wrong assumption that literary expression is marked by the usage of strange, long words. While there is truth in it—you can, indeed, use some words in literary context that would sound very unnatural used in everyday speech—the most important thing to remember is this: You don't have to use long words to be a writer.

Furthermore, many people seem to believe that using the same word twice in a row is somehow a bad thing, so they go to extraordinary lengths to avoid it. Bleep—wrong! Once you've found the perfect word for something, stick to it.

While this rule may sound utterly obvious at first, remember how often you've read a book where, for example, the main character was once called Charlie, only to become the "fair-haired warrior" in the next sentence. This is an irritating habit indicative of young writers and Gustave Flaubert fans. (Flaubert was reputed to go over every page of his manuscript to make sure no same word appeared on the same page twice.) If your prince is called Charlie, then call him Charlie—unless you're speaking from the perspective of one of Charlie's courtiers, in which case it's all right to call him the Prince. But no one, not even Charlie's mum, will ever think of anyone as the fair-haired warrior. This kind of description went out with Homer. It clutters the text needlessly, and makes the prose stuffy, stilted and mildly amusing to read.

Summary

There. Of course, we didn't say nearly all there is to be said about writing and style. We did, however, look at the importance of language in writing, we discussed the elements that make up style, we learned all the good and the bad sides of different POV's, and we looked at a fair number of 'small' things that can make your writing be that much more (or less) effective, including the problems of language-creation and more general problems.

At the end, there are these rules to repeat, as they are the most important ones: Always be consistent. Nothing is ever written in stone. And, as you may have guessed, the final rule, springing from the two above: You can do anything, provided you know that you're doing it and have a good enough reason to do it.

Acknowledgments

The following people have, over the years, given me excellent advice on writing, either in public or private communication: Steve Alghieri; Andrew Burt and all the lovely people at the Critters Workshop; Debra Doyle; Marko Fancovic; Liz Holliday; Damon Knight; Krsto A. Mazuranic; James D. McDonald; Vonda N. McIntyre; Lucy Schmeidler; Sherwood Smith; Jonathon Sullivan; Mike Totty; Tad Williams; Roger Zelazny. I may not have always agreed with them, but their advice never failed to open some sort of a new door for me. For this, I owe them an eternal debt of gratitude.

Plot Construction

MARKO FANCOVIC

The plot is the most essential part of your story. Actually, it is the story. It's what happens. It is what readers will tell each other when they (hopefully) recommend your work to another reader: "I've just read this good one about .... in which this-and-this happens." It is also one of the hardest parts of writing, of making a story, and one fraught with pitfalls for a fledging writer.

Well, hard it is, but hardships build character, right? This hard part, actually, not only builds character but is also built by characters. Good characters can make a story. Put a bunch of interesting people together, imagine in what relation they are to each other, and something interesting is bound to happen. One of my friends, a comics writer, had a pretty straightforward approach to plotting, based on characters: have as many characters as you can cram into a storyline, and then add even more, because they will make the plot interesting. Anytime the roster of characters gets too big to handle, just make a massacre that kills off half of them, and then continue with the plot, basing it on surviving ones.

Sounds ingenious and easy, but it isn't. You have to be really good at characterization pull off that kind of stunt, and even he wasn't that good all the time; his plots tended to be rather lousy. While this gimmick might come in handy if you're stuck with a plot into which you have worked too many characters, it is better to stick to a firm plot and follow the rules. (Also, too many massacres will absolutely ruin the chances of selling the film rights, because that much blood brings at least a PG-13 rating and drives away the kiddie audience.)

One of the first rules is that the plot has to be made out of basic elements, and there's no room for surplus. You are probably acquainted with that old adage by the master Russian dramatist Chekov, which goes something like this: "If there's a gun hanging on the wall in Act One, it has to go off by Act Three." Old Anton Pavlovich gave a very sound bit of advice there. Don't have any surplusses, guns (i.e. any kind of props) that don't go off, in your storyline.

Stick to basics for starters. You build a story by having a protagonist, who's nice and clean and wholesome and changes his/her socks regularly (OK, maybe doesn't do the socks bit now, but sure will, by the time we're through with him/her). There's also the obligatory antagonist, who might change his socks regularly but that is because he gets the poor opressed slave women working in appaling conditions to do his laundry. Something like the asthmatic breath beneath an iron mask is also a good idea, but who doesn't know everything about that bit? Asthmatic breath/ iron mask is a wonderful prop, but only if the mask gets to be taken off at the end. Remember Chekov!

Throw in the love interest, add seasoning (sidekicks /allies/enemies/ props) and all the building blocks for the plot structure are there. The classic structure of the plot was good enough for many generations of classic writers, both genre and mainstream, so it ought to serve you well too.

OK, let's get it over with: three acts, plus a beginning (prelude) and an end (resolution). In the prelude, before Act One, you introduce the protagonist, the antagonist, the story objective (primary goal), you try to generate empathy for the good characters and enmity towards the bad guys. The starting (inciting) event of the story, one which changes the protagonist's world, is not just desirable but actually necessary.

In act one the protagonist starts the pursuit of the first major subgoal and you have to introduce the first plot twist. Your hero (or heroine) has the first major confrontation with the antagonist, preventing him from possessing the primary goal (and/or the love interest). Act two contains the second subgoal and the second plot twist; this time it's the antagonist who prevents the protagonist from possessing/achieving the primary goal/love interest. Act three has the subgoal and the plot twist number three. In this act, at some point, the antagonist has laid his (or her) dirty hands both on the primary object and love interest at some point. In the climactic scene the protagonist and the antagonist fight over them.

After the climactic third act comes the resolution. The objective is achieved, love interest saved from the fate usually worse than death/ kissing a Wookie/whatever, and the celebration, fireworks, drinking binge and similar revelries can start, perhaps tinged a little with sorrow as the fallen faithful comrades are buried. Yada. yada, yada, that's all folks! (Until the beginning of the sequel.)

Some people add various things to this structure, calling the inciting event the first goal which makes some plot have a "two-goal structure" or whatever, but this simple analysis is good enough for all the practical purposes. This plot structure has sometimes been changed or disrupted or diverted from or twisted by skilful writers. Those are trained professionals—don't try that at home, kiddies. To change any bit of the structure of the basic plot you have to have not just the writing skills and experience that most beginners don't have, but also a very very very good and valid reason. And no, "because it seems like a good gimmick" is not, repeat not, and never was, a good enough or valid reason.

This cut-and-dried recipe might, to a frightened and inexperienced eye, sound too schematic. Well, to add juice to the whole recipe, and make plots convincing and lively, there are also some classic aids. Ladies and gentlemen, welcome ye aulde friende, ye tried-and-tested plot devices! There your love for various gimmicks can run amok without spoiling the structure of the plot; as a matter of fact, if done right, plot devices act as lubricant that can make even a cloddily done plot move along smoothly and without any visible Frankenstein stitches.

One of those plotting aids that takes some knowledge of the rules to be fully utilized is the running joke. Everybody who has ever watched movies or read entertaining fiction is familiar with the concept. It's wonderful for defining characters, especially the supporting ones who basically always have to say the same thing because that's what they were actually inserted into the plot to do, to be the stereotypes that help the plot along. However, strict rules that you have to follow, if you want it to work, are the following: even spacing (always the same amount of time/ pages/events between repetitions), a limited number of repetitions (six or seven works the best), and the obligatory payoff in the end; the last occasion of the running-joke-repeated gag has to be different and mean something else to drive the point home. Sometimes the payoff can be a useful plot device not just to finish the running joke, but to move the plot along more smoothly.

A classic example of the running-joke-as-plot-forwardment occurs in that masterpiece western, Howard Hawks' *Rio Bravo*. The reformed-drunk-gunfighter Dude (Dean Martin) constantly tries to roll himself a cigarette, but his hands shake so badly that he's just spilling tobacco all over the place. After his mediocre attempts, the sheriff Chance (John Wayne) takes pity on him several times, and hands him a rolled cigarette. In the end, the whole group leaves the relative safety of the jail building inside which they're besieged, and ventures out on the street-because they've run out of tobacco.

Using plot devices that might be called "catalyst" is a very good idea if you have a somewhat lumpy plot where the transition from one event to another, both being essential to the plot, is a bit contrived. A good example of a catalyst occurs in the movie *Cat People* (the new Paul Schrader version), in the scene of Nastassja Kinski's first transformation into a panther. The scene required the transformation from a girl in a postcoital relaxed mood into a wild beast. It was smoothed by a single thing-a fly. We see Kinski lying in a sitting position with her eyes open. A fly's buzzing is suddenly heard, and she starts to follow the insect's flight with her gaze. The movement of her head is somewhat catlike, and in one moment she just makes a very sudden move to swat the fly. Her hand, which was a girl's hand when it started to move, lands on the bedcovers in a contorted position resembling a claw and the transformation starts. Had it started while she was lying in the relaxed position, it might have seemed contrived, but the insertion of the fly made it go smoothly. Remember that fly whenever your plot requires something done suddenly.

A best-be-avoided plot device is the flashback, going back to the past to dig up some unsavoury thing you want your readers to know. In explaining the intricacies of the plot, it is, just like in moviemaking, better to show, not tell. Make brief explanations that hint at broader things in your dialogues and let the reader's imagination fill in the blanks. Don't turn their heads backward. Keep flashbacks where they belong, in the province of lousy movie directors. Even masters like Sergio Leone had some trouble in making the blasted things work as intended and not look too contrived and strained. If you think you're more skilfull a storyteller than old Sergio, go ahead and use flashbacks, but don't say we didn't warn you.

A classic plot device that needs to be modified for use in fantasy is a "McGuffin", which owes its name and existence to Alfred Hitchcock. "McGuffin" is the thing that protagonists strive for and fight about, central to the plot, while it's completely irrelevant what it actually is. In most spy movies, the secret plans being stolen/recovered/copied are just secret plans; whether they're plans for a submarine or an airplane or a dental drill does not matter at all, as long as they're coveted. Fantasy, being a different kind of fiction, full of magic stuff, its McGuffins have to actually have some specific powers. The best example of a "fantasy McGuffin" is the One Ring in *The Lord of the Rings*. The whole plot hinges on it being the most powerful thing in the world, but its powers are such that the protagonists dare not use them. Except for a few minor invisibility incidents (with just one serious consequence), it might well have been an inert ring of plain gold. So, we might call it a McGuffin. But if you invest special and important powers into a prop, remember that it has either to be used or have a very good reason for not being used. (Yup, it's Chekov and the gun again.)

Let's have a look at how such devices would be helpful in the plots, whose structure we have discussed. You might divide almost all fantasy works into four plot categories. However, that task is made Gargantuan by the fact that ye aulde fantasy novel will usually have elements of at least two of those plots, if not all four and then some, at one moment or other.

The four classic plots are the quest plot, the restoration plot, the reluctant hero plot and the treasure hunt plot.

In a quest you have a character (more often a whole cast of characters) striving to accomplish a task. Some of those might be reluctant heroes, which is a schtick that usually works: some schmuck either has special powers that he didn't want in the first place, or is just in the right place at the right time (hey, it worked for Bogie's Rick in Casablanca) but does not want to get involved in the whole mess. However, having his grandmother/grandfather gang-raped by Tartary horsemen or some such drastic measures usually brings them round, and then you can have them do the hero stuff as required. Restoration is the return of the rightful king/heir to the trone, defeat of the occupying/opressing foreigners and a general return to the good ol' times. Warning: often accomplished by a quest and/or done by a reluctant hero.

It is no wonder that those classic plots are often jumbled together; they are by now worn so threadbare that using any single one as a theme is akin to that quaint Japanese custom known as seppuku (or hara-kiri if you prefer vulgar monikers). The one most suitable for usage alone is the treasure hunt, always good for a short story or a subplot. Remember Robert E. Howard's classic stories? In about half of them Conan was chasing some loot buried or hidden somewhere with some guarding supernatural nasties added just for the kicks-always fun to read if they're done right. Besides, it shows kindness to your character. After all you've pulled him/her through you might at least fill the poor wretch's pockets with some werewithal. Feel free to mingle all those plots; the more plot threads, the more interesting the plot is, as long as you don't have to commit too many massacres to keep the unruly plots in line.

Summary

And for the final word of warning, we will return to my friend who's so fond of numerous casts that he had to have at least one massacre in every plot. He lives in a country where foreign movies are subtitled, and he had a grandmother who did not read all that well. Once, in an act of grandsonly kindness, he played a whole movie for her on his VCR, pressing the pause button every second or third frame so the old lady could slowly and laboriously read her way through the subtitles. After that, she pronounced it the best movie she had seen in her life, although the film in question was below-mediocre (I think it was one of the later sequels/prequels to *The Planet of the Apes*). But she understood what was going on, and for her it made that the best movie ever.

No matter what your plot is, and how convoluted its intricacies might be, make sure that your readers know what is going on at each and every moment. They don't have to know why it is happening, but making clear what is happening is essential. Lots of gibberish makes the readers put the book away and lose the patience necessary to reach the last page. Clear and understandable action makes them interested in the plot and engrossed in the reading. That leads to good reviews, good sales and good reputation. You bring joy to those who've read your work, which is why you started writing in the first place and the only right way to make money writing (things sell better if they get good recommendations). Speaking of money, if you followed all the plotting rules, used the plot devices well and had a moderately original idea to start with, I would like to read your book. Could you send me a complimentary copy, please?

Medieval Clothing

Lauren Cleeland & Kim Bundy

Introduction

Whether your fantasy story is set in present day, the future, or the traditional medieval era, the clothing worn by people in the story can enhance the mood and help establish the setting. Writers often hear, "Show, don't tell." Clothing is one tool you can use.

Non-medieval Fantasy Clothing

Fantasy stories are often thought of as being medieval in tone and setting. However, speculative fiction, weird fiction, etc. have broadened the definition of what is fantasy. It crosses all time eras, all cultures and imagines new fantastical places not of Earth while still being fantasy. Folk and fairy tales from India or Japan or Central America qualify, as do stories on other worlds or dimensions. Wherever and whenever your story takes place, there are three things to keep in mind about your character's clothing:

1) What are the clothing styles influenced by? Religion, law, personal choice, the climate? All are valid ways to enrich the story by the characters' feelings concerning their clothing. What fabrics are available or are manufactured from local animals and plants? What is traded?

2) Be practical. There's nothing wrong with sexy or unusual clothing, just think through what the restrictions of a particular style would be. Imagine yourself wearing it for a day. Would it bring unwanted attention from strangers? What kinds of weather or situations would this clothing be unsuitable or ideal for? Does it fit the creature/character's body shape? How do they get it off and on around wings, tails or unusual limbs?

3) Be consistent. Each character or culture choices in garments helps define it. Be consistent with what they're wearing, making deviations according to situations and appropriateness for each particular character. If a character's shape changes, what happens to his clothes when he changes? None of these things need be explained outright in the story. They can be portrayed through the character's reactions, movements and cause/effect. Take care to describe clothing but don't let it get out of hand. More than a paragraph or two at a time begins to interfere with the story causing readers to begin skimming.

MEDIEVAL FANTASY CLOTHING

Medieval clothing, referred to as garb or period clothing by re-enactors and gaming enthusiasts—a large section of the fantasy reading public—gives instant notions about your characters' background, social status, financial status, culture, and job description. Again, be consistent and don't get carried away with long descriptive passages of what everyone in your story is wearing every time they wake in the morning. A quick paragraph or two should suffice. You can tuck in bits of information on clothing through your characters' actions: Cara smoothed her velvet skirt; Tristram adjusted his sword belt; the warlord pulled on his leather gloves as he spoke.

There's no need to become an expert on medieval clothing. A working knowledge of some basics is to the writer's benefit. There's truth in the saying, "It's in the details." Fantasy readers do know a bit about period clothing from authors who've come before you. Clothing should never stop the reader in their tracks or otherwise detract from what the story is about. Be certain to get the small details right. Take buttons for example. Originally, they were used as ornamentation, like jewellery. Jewellery and accessories are useful tools also. Poison rings, a chain belt, which is later used for a weapon, small dirks tucked inside boots or a bodice sheath or as part of an elaborate necklace, are a few examples. Don't be afraid to use them—let your characters use them when the need arises. Forgetting about an item can trip you up. The reader won't forget and you certainly don't want them saying, "Hey! What about...."

Accessories can be a source of unintentional comic relief if care is not taken in choosing them. It's a nice idea for a woman to pin up her long tresses with a pair of daggers—until she draws them and shears off her hair. Any blade dull enough not to slice delicate hair strands won't be much good as a weapon. A bit of common sense is helpful to think through the potential pitfalls, restrictions and possible consequences of any garment or accessory.

WOMEN

When we consider the medieval time frame, we're covering over four hundred years (from 1000 to 1500). While clothing styles didn't change as quickly then as they do now, styles did evolve.

Earlier periods saw similar styles and fabrics between both peasants and nobility. Jewellery primarily served to set the nobles apart, though gem cutting didn't come about until the fifteenth century. Gold and silver threads were used, but being spun of precious metals, only by the rich. Then as road building got better and new trade routes established, new choices for colors and fabrics opened up. As information was exchanged, so were clothing styles.

Because nobility had first access to the new trade goods, the separation between noble or court wear and the everyday man's clothing became more prominent. Certain colors fabrics and styles became reserved for those with the right to wear them. Linen, muslin and sailcloth might have been used, depending upon where one lived. Silks, velvets and the most expensive, taffeta, were seen with more frequency on nobility. Oftentimes, royalty would 'hand down' her gowns to her attendants, who then passed them on to younger maids. Nobility did their best to copy the latest styles of the court using less expensive fabrics and jewellery. Used clothing always found other uses: Slaves tended to wear cast off under tunics and undergarments. The Scandinavians used worn out clothing as boat caulking.

Women's shoes and hose changed little throughout the medieval era. Ladies wore hose of knitted wool gartered at the knee and with low cut leather shoes. Striped hose were a favorite of the ladies. The late 1200's saw pointed toes come into fashion. Undergarments began as simple under tunics, often serving as nightgowns. Smock sleeves were added and then varied. These later versions, typically of linen, were also called kirtles or chemises.

Cloaks were another staple throughout the medieval period. Their length and style depended upon where the woman lived. Throughout the middle ages, cloaks increasingly became more adorned and constructed of heavier fabrics. Mantles are fancy indoor versions of a cloak, typically used for special occasions. The medieval woman did use cosmetics of various sorts, including chalks, soot, and powders which they used spit or water to make into a paste. Wigs date back to early Egyptian society and denoted wealth. Perfumes or pomades were used as well.

Sashes or belts were worn in various forms to hold up or pouf out fabrics. Rope-like belts in some religious orders denoted rank. Purses, worn by both men and women, were carried on the belt. Sheath gowns and tunic styles were called 'Doric Chiton' by the Greeks and 'Stola' by the Romans. Most women's tunics and surcoats were similar to men's except for in length and adornment.

Fur became a popular trim, lining the insides or edges of sleeves and as collars. Fur-lined outer-tunics were called a Pelicon. Certain furs, like ermine, were reserved for those of status.

The Cyclas of the mid thirteenth century is a sleeveless outer garment worn over the gown (also called a sleeveless surcoat). When cut low, they showed off a woman's hips—thought to be a daring sign of her fertility in some cultures. These deep armhole openings were sometimes fur lined. They evolved into sideless versions, held together beneath the arms with wide lacings (these lacings also allowed the gown to be 're-sized' during pregnancy).

The early twelfth century saw long sleeve widths, which were sometimes knotted to keep them from dragging the ground, called a Bliaut. Styles varied by country. Corsets came into being around the mid twelfth century.

Headdresses varied widely from culture to culture. Sometimes they were used to denote a woman's station in life, position in her religion or society, or her availability. Hairstyles, too, served similar purposes. Women drew their cauls up around the head into shapes, sometimes wiring and shellacking them into hearts, butterfly wings or horns. Wimples and veils concealed features, as well as giving excellent protection from the sun and elements.

One interesting note: women seldom wore aprons as we know them. Aprons, constructed of leather at the time, were a working man or craftsman's garment.

Children

The easy answer to this question is that children wore exactly what the adults wore, and the amount of adornment and embellishment was directly related to the status of the child's family.

The more complex and more difficult answer to this question is that childhood was an interesting and misunderstood period of life during the Middle Ages. There is much debate today on just what place children held in their families' societies, etc. Evidence can be accumulated to support a number of theories that is conclusively convincing. One fact is evident: children were as important, as loved, as cherished and as anticipated five hundred years ago as they are today. The heartache associated with the high infant mortality rates may or may not have played a part in the prevailing thoughts as to handling children and infants.

A great many people today would consider the way children were handled as cruel, uncaring and even abusive. On the contrary, those of the Middle Ages might very well think we today are being cruel and lackadaisical in our upbringing of our children, failing to give them the strength to survive what life dishes out.

Aside from that, there are perhaps some titbits to be gleaned from the sadly under-researched area of infancy and childhood that can offer some ideas or stimulate a completely new way of presenting children in the world of fantasy writing. Infants who did not die at birth and were not exposed by the head of the household would have been swaddled in many cultures, among them the Jewish and European cultures. Swaddling was done immediately after birth and continued for some months, perhaps even for the first year in some areas. Swaddling cloths were strips of linen or wool that were between three and six inches in width and from two to twenty feet in length. These strips were wound tightly about each limb and then crisscrossed about the child's body. In some cultures, the genital area was left open for the addition of a 'buttock's cloth' or wrapped to hold diapering material in place. Diapers were not changed often—one reference makes note that diapers in medieval times were not changed more than every few days.

Buttock cloths were made of flannel, linen or cotton and sometimes covered with an animal pelt to give it a bit of water resistance. Absorbent materials such as grass, moss, leaves, wool or cotton padding were often added to the interior of the cloth. Some cultures did not bother with a diaper at all and practiced a form of infant toilet training, by timing or attempting to time bodily functions.

When children began to move about on their own, they were moved from swaddling clothing into short dresses or tunics. Boys and girls were dressed alike up to age six in some cases. The association with gender identity is a relatively new concept. In fact, traditional boy and girl colors are less than fifty years old.

Medieval paintings and sketches of children show them dressed as mini-adults. Paintings of young children show them all wearing gowns and bonnets, even when old enough to stand on their own.

As children grew to an age when their chores would be defined by their gender and they took on more and more gender-identified roles, their clothing would change to simulate the looks of their parents. Girls would begin wearing chemises and kirtles or gowns; boys would begin wearing tunics and breeches or leggings.

Young girls were often allowed to wear their hair down and free, but the closer they came to an age when they could be betrothed (around eight years and sometimes earlier), they began requiring restrictions and their hair would often be bound. A married woman was rarely seen without her hair bound, adorned or tucked completely beneath a headdress and wimple. Some cultures required strict veiling of young women of marriageable age, especially in the presence of suitors or their betrothed, not allowing the bride to be unveiled until the final wedding ceremony. This was true in Spain—a practise that may have been a leftover from its Muslim occupation—and was particularly practiced among its royalty.

Children's clothing was made from the same materials as adult clothing, very often homespun and homemade. With the increase in trade, cloth of differing variety was available. There is some controversy over whether those in lower classes wore anything other than simple colorless clothing. It has long been assumed that this was the case, and yet there is strong evidence that this was not necessarily so, as dyes from plants were readily available in most areas. Needlework was not something strictly forbidden to the lower classes and it is quite possible that humans, being human and loving adornment, spent time adorning their attire, no matter what their station in life.

It is interesting what little information is available on children and infant clothing, and opens a world of possibilities for the person creating their own world. Stop a moment and think; look around your world. What is at hand that can be put to use for a child? Perhaps this moss, or not those leaves, because they leave a terrible rash, which makes the babe cry incessantly? What cloth do I have? What talent do I have? Is thread a treasured item? Is it possible to dye clothing the color of the flowers that grow on the side of a mountain? Are children's clothes simply practical? Is it hot or cold? A child born in a cold climate would have much greater need of clothing than a child born in a tropical environment. Are children allowed to play or must they be kept still and silent? What type of garment would allow that? Or perhaps on your world, children hold a special place and their garments are required to reflect that status.

There are a few things to remember: diapers—even cloth diapers as we know them—were not a reality until the 1800's. The diaper and safety pins were not invented and manufactured until 1880. Disposable diapers began appearing in various but not truly disposable versions in the early 1940's. Women entering the work force gave birth to the diaper service; they no longer had time to launder and prepare diapers themselves.

Pampers brand disposable diapers were first marketed in 1961. The advances in both diapers and disposable sanitary pads are the result of world wars and women entering industry. Women and children were not confined to the home any longer and likewise their personal hygiene products had to be mobile.

Another thing to remember during the middle ages: very few noble women actually nursed their own children. Children were often turned over to the care of a wet nurse, and this in many ways led to the high infant mortality rate, strict contracts were drawn up for wet nurses, restricting their behaviour, the nursing of their own children, etc. But children still succumbed to malnutrition, disease and neglect. There are examples of wet nurse contracts available online at the ORB site.

This is not to say that wet nurses were generally bad, for there were highly prized and excellent wet nurses. Children were often carried in slings while the mother or wet nurse went about with chores and duties.

In some ways the lack of definitive information on the clothing of children is a dream for the writer, for they can create what clothing they wish, or they can stick to the concept of children simply being mini-adults. Either way, the possibilities are endless so toss a few children into your story and listen to the belly laugh of a child stumbling through the thick lush grass of a mountain meadow.

MEN

In discussing men's garments, let's focus on clothing instead of armor, though certainly a man's choice of armor, or his lack thereof, influenced his mode of dress. Some types of tightly woven felt were known to slow a blade.

Men were more fashion-oriented in the Middle Ages. Shoes and hose were similar to the ladies, though men sometimes wore wooden patens over boots to keep their feet dry. Most were constructed of soft leather, sometimes painted. Woollen men's hose came up higher than women's to tie at the front and back. In later times, a codpiece was added and at formal times even embellished. These later years saw partitioned colors and patterned hose become popular with the ladies and then the men (just about the only time when women's fashion influenced men instead of the other way around).

Beneath the hose, men of all social classes wore a baggy kind of underwear called Braies. Made of linen, they wrapped around the legs with the ends drawn up the front crotch area to be tied with drawstrings. The excess material was rolled around the waist, which might seem silly to us now, but it played an important role in connection with some other garments and mail leggings.

Men's shirts, again of linen, began as simple tunics and evolved in length and sleeve styles from there. The over tunic also started out in simple patterns, at times belted to pull the lower half of the garment into a skirt-like design. Their length and hem styles varied significantly, depending on where a man lived.

Dagged edges of various shapes appeared in the early twelfth century, becoming more elaborate and intricate in design through the years.

Men's accessories seem to be culturally related. The crusades brought oriental influences in fabrics and clothing styles. Around 1199 heavily embroidered cuffs and gauntlets became popular. Trousers were laced with leather binds up to the knee. Men wore belts of cord or leather or metal.

Felt hats changed shape often and hood tips began short and lengthened into what was called a liripipe. Sometimes the long liripipe was draped across the shoulders or around the neck. The late thirteenth century brought out turban styled hats, adorned with feathers and sometimes crowns. Armbands with streamers and embroidered sashes edged with "folly bells" came about during this time also.

Cloaks began rectangular in shape, often pulled through a metal ring and with the ends knotted. As circular cloaks came into use, so did cloak pins, brooches and cording ties. Hairstyles and the acceptance of facial hair changed more quickly than clothing styles did, going from short to long and back again. Again, a man's culture and station in life determined his choices. Men balanced fashion and practicality in the medieval years. So should you as a writer.

RECOMMENDED RESOURCES:
BOOKS
The Writer's Guide to Every Day Life in the Middle Ages: The British Isles from 500 to 1500, Sherrilyn Kenyon, Writer's Digest Books ISBN 0-89879-663-6
This book is a great quick reference and includes information on shoes, hair styles and garment fabric types and colors.
Patterns for Theatrical Costumes: Garments, Trims and Accessories from Ancient Egypt to 1915, Katherine Strand Kolkeboer, Costume & Fashion Press ISBN 0-89676-125-8
Don't let the title fool you. This book contains basic sewing patterns but is filled with drawings of people wearing garments. It shows what each piece is called, suggests fabrics, how it's worn and how it's constructed. There are also samples of decorative trims and fabric designs.
Medieval Wordbook, Madeleine Pelner Cosman, Facts On File, Inc. ISBN 0-8160-3021-9
A dictionary of sorts, this book gives you a reference for medieval items, names, ideas, and famous persons.

The Rule of the Templars: Studies in the History of Medieval Religion, Volume IV, J.M. Upton-Ward, The Boydell Press ISBN 0-85115-701-7

Specific to the Knights Templar, this book reveals what garments were worn by each rank of the monk-knights. It explains what they were forbidden to wear and the significance of some pieces.

Costume 1066-1966, John Peacock, Thames & Hudson, Ltd. London ISBN 0-500-27404-5

Simple explanations, but good illustrations to show at a glance, the evolution of styles for both men and women.

What People Wore: 1800 Illustrations from Ancient Times to the Early Twentieth Century, Douglas Gorhsire, Dover Publications ISBN 0-486-28162-0

ONLINE RESOURCES

As writers we dream and create. We take the knowledge we have and we increase it, and then we transform that knowledge into an entirely new reality. But where do we get that basic knowledge? Where do we go to find delectable titbits that can morph our idea into brilliance?

Some of us delve into books, browse through museums, speak to others with expertise and some of us scout the web. Yes, the web.

While a caveat is necessary, for there are websites which, to state it nicely, are pure fantasy, there are others that are treasure chests full of gems. And, for medieval fantasy lovers, the web is literally loaded with information.

To help those who are interested in creating believable worlds of medieval fantasy, we have compiled a resource list of some of the most amazing sites. So, ease into your chair, fire up that computer, crack your knuckles and grab hold of that mouse. Now close your eyes and take a deep breath. Slowly, open your eyes and click. Behold the treasure trove of the medieval and Renaissance worlds!

The Costumer's Manifesto is perhaps the premier site for costuming information on every age imaginable. This site is loaded with links, articles, information, patterns and knowledge. It should be a first stop for anyone researching the middle ages, or dress in general. Enjoy!

http://www.costumes.org/pages/medievalinks.htm

StitchWitch provides a page crammed with pattern and costume designing information. This site will be especially loved by those with a skilful needle.

http://stitchwitch.hypermart.net/

Medieval Clothing. This one is a nice little site that covers a number of clothing topics. While the information is geared to a younger audience, its simplicity offers a nice foundation. The site was put together by Jim Cornish, a teacher at Gander Academy and offers links to a learning site.

http://www.stemnet.nf.ca/CITE/medieval_clothing.htm

Medieval Clothing Pages: Articles by Cynthia Virtue is a veritable dream for the researcher of medieval garb and headdress. The author is an active member of the Society for Creative Anachronism.

http://www.virtue.to/articles/

This is a link to a site owned and operated by Annenberg/CPB Lerner.org. There is a link to this site on the Medieval Clothing by Jim Cornish above.

http://www.learner.org/exhibits/middleages/clothing.html

Clothing of the Ancient Celts-Scotland 1100-1600 AD by M.E. Riley is an excellent collection of articles and information on clothing of the Highland Scots.

http://www47.pair.com/lindo.Scotland.htm

Lothene Experimental Archaeology-Early Medieval Clothing Patterns with Illustrations by the Lothene Research Group is a wonderful site, with links to other Scottish information and dedicated to researching specifically for re-enactors specifically interested in Scotland.

http://www.lothene.demon.co.uk/crafts6.html

Medieval Clothing by an unknown SCA compiler is a good site, with a great deal of information; unfortunately it is also loaded with pop-ups that can be irritating and distracting.

http://victorian.fortunecity.com/manet/394/page21.htm

Historical Renaissance Fantasy Medieval Clothing Costumes Roman Gothic Tudor Elizabethan is a site owned by House of Anoria. This is a catalog site and House of Anoria creates and sells these items, but it is filled with PICTURES! It is often helpful to actually see an item of which one usually only reads a description.

http://www.houseofanoria.com/

Wind Mills-The Medieval Project is a learning and educational experience full of information. There are a variety of topics. This site is a collaboration effort and is based in Turku, Finland. Check it out!

http://www.tkukoulu.fi/WindMills/en-windmills.html

Your Guide to Medieval History at about.com by Melissa Snell. This site includes a monthly Knightly Newsletter filled with articles, links, quotes and news. An excellent resource, this about.com site is a listing of links to a number of web pages on a number of sites that span several cultures and time periods. The first site is listed by Author and Historian, Nancy MacCorkill who owns her own site (listed later).

http://historymedren.about.com

Misperceptions about Medieval Clothing is a short article addressing some of the common misperceptions about clothing in the medieval era.

http://www.carillion.eastkingdom.org/basic_garb.html

 This site by Drachensteing Treasures specializes in jewellery for SCA events.

http://www.dragonsjewels.com/

Celtic lovers will especially enjoy the two following sites by Nancy MacCorkill and Reobert Gunn. While these two sites are particularly history sites, the information is superb and the writing is a joy.

http://members.aol.com/Skyelander/

http://members.aol.com/sconemac/

And, finally two of the best sites for medieval primary sources and other information would be:

ORB: The Online Reference Book for Medieval Studies. Entering this site will unfold an amazing and fascinating world for medievalists of all abilities and interests. The reader should take special interest in historian Paul Halsall's site, The Medieval Internet Sourcebook.

http://orb.rhodes.edu/

And, hosted by Georgetown University is The Labyrinth: Resources for Medieval Studies. This site, like ORB, is literally a researcher's heaven.

http://www.georgetown.edu/labyrinth/

In closing, here is a reminder to pay attention to the content of the sites. One can find excellent and accurate information and one can find sites that create their own information from misperceptions, or worse, perpetuated from the misperception of another site and simply repeated.

The sites here are by no means the only sites on the Internet, but they are good, sound sites that will give you many paths to follow in your pursuit of medieval information. The sites should provide the researcher/ writer with a strong foundation of knowledge from which they can dream a world uniquely and exquisitely their own in detail.

MISCELLANEOUS

Catalogs such as those put out by Museum Replicas and Chivalry Sports are great for clipping pictures for use as characters.

Patterns, particularly those available at many Renaissance fair vendors or through Renaissance/Chivalry Sports. These patterns are well worth the $25.00 price, even if you don't sew. The pattern instructions often include detailed information on types of fabrics, how and why the piece was worn, and other tidbits of history. They include information on typical accessories for each particular style.

SUMMARY

Whether your fantasy world closely resembles medieval history or has unique qualities of its own, consistency is the key to believability. Be aware of story possibilities opened by garment types, associations (religious, social and cultural) with them, availability and usefulness as plot devices. Let your character's clothing enrich your imagination and your stories.

Medieval Food

FROM FAST TO FEAST

MICHELE ACKER

INTRODUCTION

Unless you've done major research into the medieval time period, and even if you have, you will find that the topic of food is generally overlooked. A little understood subject, fantasy writers, especially beginning writers, tend to gloss over the lack of information by pretending it doesn't matter. They will either overlook it altogether and refuse to let their characters eat on camera, or else they will make their characters eat nothing but stew, and drink nothing but tea or water. Not only is this inaccurate, it's downright boring! Life, even medieval life, does not consist of stew alone.

Considering the popularity of medieval settings in fantasy novels, this would seem to be an essential consideration. And certainly it should be. Food was very important to people in the Middle Ages, not just as a way to survive, but also as a means of expressing their religious beliefs and as a way of controlling others, either by the giving of food or by the denying of it. Complex laws were put into place to prevent people from stealing food or cheating their customers, and punishments were swift and merciless. Elaborate rituals and special dishes and cutlery were observed at feasts of the rich and the well to do. Nothing was overlooked or taken for granted.

Religion ruled most aspects of people's daily lives in the Middle Ages. Its importance was second to none, extending even into the types of food eaten on certain days, and the rituals involved with fasting. Over time, those laws changed and mutated to accommodate those who no longer wished to follow them, though a few of those laws have travelled with us into the present. Then as now, the rich made the rules and the poor were forced to follow whether they liked it or not.

This chapter will cover some of these issues and will hopefully leave you better informed about a subject that was so vitally important to the people who lived in that time. Then perhaps we can see more interesting and accurate depictions of life and food in the Middle Ages.

NOT JUST A BOWL OF STEW

WHAT THE POOR PEOPLE ATE

If you are able to find information about food and life in the Middle Ages, you will likely find that most of it focuses on the rich and the banquets they gave. This is because they were so well documented. The importance of food and the power it gave were major considerations for the wealthy. The number and variety of dishes they could offer their guests was of paramount importance. Of less concern was survival.

Survival, however, was the overriding concern of the poor, as well it should be. The basic peasant, concerned with sustenance, not profit, produced most of their food and drink from easily cultivated grains such as barley, oats and rye. Wheat was much too valuable for personal use; instead it went almost exclusively to market. The combination of barley and rye, or wheat and rye if the wheat could be spared, made a heavy, dark loaf of bread that was eaten in large quantities by men, women and children alike. The bread was eaten both plain and as a sop to soak up cabbage water flavoured with vegetables and garlic.

Poorer peasants preferred barley pottage even over bread. Because there was no milling needed to create the staple, it was more economical and cut down on wastage. Barley grains were allowed to sprout in a damp, warm place then boiled in a pot full of water. The water was then drawn off, sweetened with a little honey and either drunk as barley water, or fermented into beer. Peas and beans were sometimes added to provide a little protein, and when they could afford it, a little fat bacon or salt pork as well, along with onion and garlic from their garden.

Foods eaten depended significantly on local conditions. Peasants, without access to diverse marketplaces or without the means to purchase what they couldn't grow, had to make do as best they could, foraging from the land if necessary, especially during times of famine. Spring and summer provided the biggest variety to an essentially bland diet. Vegetables such as leeks, cabbage, lettuce, spinach and parsley were readily available. Nuts, berries and roots were foraged wherever they could be found, and anything the least bit edible ended up in the cook pot. Fruit trees bore apples, pears and cherries, and though eaten raw by rich and poor alike, most medieval 'dieticians' advised cooking as it was thought raw fruit was unhealthy.

As many meals as possible were washed down with weak ale, either brewed, or bought from neighbors. Water was drunk as well, but only when there was nothing else, as the quality of the water left much to be desired, especially in the city. Though London tried its best to regulate water usage and keep the supplies as clean as possible, the rivers and streams were common dumping grounds for all types of garbage from the emptying of chamber pots, to the run off from the production of beer, to the blood and offal from numerous slaughter houses. Besides being low in vitamins, minerals and other essential ingredients, medieval peasant diets were also low in calories, which made the drinking of ale a benefit, both for health and for recreation.

When it came to meat, most medieval households kept chickens and pigs, though they seldom ate the meat themselves. Like wheat, animals were a cash crop and were much too valuable to waste on one's own family. They were usually sold to pay the rent or other incidental expenses. A more common food, cheap and readily available to all, was cod, or stockfish. Caught and air-dried on board ship, it was easily transportable and lasted for years. It was a staple of peasants and even the well-to-do bought and ate it during the forty days of Lent, when no meat was allowed. Before preparation, it had to be hammered for a full hour to soften the flesh then soaked for two more. Herring was also a staple on religious fish days and during Lent, and more flavourful and desirable than stockfish, though more costly.

Most households couldn't afford their own ovens, so bread dough, prepared by the housewife or cook, was taken to bakeries and baked in their ovens for a nominal cost. Bread, such a major part of everyday life, was a very busy and thriving business. Bought, baked and eaten by every class of society, it was such an important trade that its baking and sales were governed by some of the toughest food laws devised in medieval times. While most bakers were honest, there were cheats and swindlers as well and it was prudent for the homemaker or steward to pay close attention to every transaction.

Unscrupulous businessmen could be found in other trades as well. In order to make a small profit for themselves, cooks in large households were known to sell their cooking waste products—intestines, skin and other unusable parts of various animals—to bakers to be baked into pies and sold to the less well-to-do. This resulted in so many tainted pies, that a law was finally passed in 1379 forbidding this practice.

Unless a law was violated, the poor had little recourse to change practices they considered unfair. Born into a very strict hierarchy or cast system, they had little ability or opportunity to change the course of their lives. Medieval people believed very strongly that everyone and everything had its place and the poor were poor because God wished it so. Each person was thought to occupy the place that God had planned for him or her and to attempt to change things was a very serious business, fraught with fear and superstition. Any change was well considered, well planned and well documented in case of future problems.

Along with that belief, was the belief that to aid those who were truly poor and helpless was a mark of Christian charity and large households made a point of showing off that charity after feasts as a way of making themselves look more pious to their guests. To this end, the table at a banquet, no matter the number of guests, was always well laden, not only as proof of their good fortune, but as insurance that there would be plenty of leftovers to be given away after the meal. Trenchers, the bread used as plates and soaked with meat juices and various sauces, were gathered up in a basket after the meal, along with any other food that was not kept for the servants and taken to the back door to be handed out to any who were waiting.

THE TYPES OF FOOD EATEN

No list of the types of foods eaten by medieval peoples could begin without the mention of spices. Imported into England and Europe from the East, spices were an expensive luxury. Easily the most valuable item in any kitchen, they were kept in a special cupboard under lock and key and doled out to the cooks in carefully measured and recorded amounts. For those who could afford it, every effort was made to get away from what was considered peasant foods and peasant tastes. People ate to their station and unlike the people of today, would not by choice eat coarse bread or raw vegetables

At banquets, this hierarchy was even more pronounced. Guests were not treated equally. Instead they were served exactly as their rank or station demanded, no more and no less. To do otherwise, was to invite censure and ridicule from others. To this end, understated elegance had no place in a medieval society where opulent extravagance was the norm. The wealthy flaunted their wealth and nowhere was this more apparent than at the banquet table. A good host wanted to be seen using the costliest, most expensive ingredients he could afford and the liberal use of spices was one of the ways he was able to accomplish this. He wanted to be able to shout to the world, 'Power bought this'.

Made into sugar-coated comfits (small tidbits), spices were served sometimes after a big meal once the guests had retired to a smaller room. These tidbits might include candied orange peel, red anise, rose-sugar and citron. Along with comfits was served a heavily sweetened and spiced wine made by steeping the chosen flavourings, including cinnamon and sugar, first in wine, then heating and straining the resultant mixture.

The more popular and expensive spices included: sugar (a costly import, and was not as easily obtainable as honey which could be produced by local bees), ginger, cloves, nutmeg, cumin, mace, cinnamon, citron, coriander and saffron. Used not only to flavour their recipes, spices were also used to decorate and change or enhance a dish's color. For instance, white sauces were colored red with coriander, or yellow with saffron. Pepper was also considered a spice. It grew in India and Ceylon and was imported to Europe. Not as expensive or as hard to obtain as some other spices, it was very popular and spice merchants had no problem selling all they had in stock. Mustard, considered the poor man's spice, was locally grown and therefore the most often used of all the spices, especially in dishes of the middle and lower classes.

Certain assumptions have long become accepted fact concerning medieval cooking and eating habits. Most people assume, for instance, that medieval food was very fragrant and heavily spice-laden, perhaps to disguise the fact that the food had 'turned' or was not as fresh as it could be. This belief is enforced when you look back on medieval recipes to find that little clue is given as to the quantity of spices or herbs used in a particular dish, the number of different ingredients alone suggesting strong taste. Yet, when you look closer, you find that those few who do give quantities suggest sparing amounts: a pinch of this, a sprinkle of that, a touch, 'to taste'. It can also be inferred through medieval medical texts, that over-spicing was not recommended and moderation in all things was counselled for good health and long life. So, rather than being wildly spiced, it was much more likely that medieval dishes were only mildly fragrant. We also know that instead of being the gluttons modern people think them to be, medieval people actually ate very little of the generous helpings set before them at a banquet. The show of so much food was less for hunger's sake than to prove a host's wealth and status.

Salt, an essential item, contributed to the food and general health of the city more than any other element except water. Not only a spice for cooking, it was used to preserve everything from butter to meat to fish. Without it, most meat and fish could not be stored over the long winter months when fishing and butchering were difficult or impossible because of climate and law. Any city close to both water and salt preserves became a major seaport that grew and thrived.

Herbs, easier to obtain than spices, were an important part of every kitchen. They added a more subtle touch to cooked dishes, and for most cooks, there was a wide variety to choose from. Used by themselves, or sometimes mixed with spices, they also helped color and disguise foods during a banquet. These herbs included, but were not limited to: parsley, mint, cress, primrose buds, various flowers and flower bulbs such as daisies and roses, dandelions, red fennel, pennyroyal, borage, marjoram, fava blossoms, chickweed, thyme, radish, chervil, sage, garlic, purslane, onions, leeks, rosemary, hyssop and tansy leaves. Herbs were also well known for their medicinal properties and made up a whole series of curatives for various illnesses and wounds.

Large households who bought spices and herbs in great quantities, would spend hours chopping and grinding and preparing them for use in cooking. Smaller households would usually buy theirs already pounded and ready for use, since they didn't have access to the wide range of tools available to the apothecary. Sauces, too, could be bought already prepared, as could various other foods such as bread, pre-roasted rabbits or fowls, sausages or meat pies.

The distinction between herbs and vegetables was a fine one, with little difference between the two. Items that today we would consider vegetables, such as onions, leeks and spinach, medieval cooks considered herbs. More recognisable vegetables included: cabbage, beets, turnips, green beans, carrots, celery, artichokes, parsnips and winter squashes. Legumes such as peas, fava beans, lentils, fasoles (similar to a black-eyed pea), and vetches were also popular at all times of the year. Dried peas and beans, like the potatoes of today, added bulk to a meal. Cooked down to a puree, they were sometimes thickened with breadcrumbs or eggs, depending on the wealth of the household, and served as a type of vegetable pudding. Vegetables, combined with onions, were also used to stuff fowl and meat dishes.

Fruit made up an important part of the medieval diet. While more common fruits, such as apples and pears, were served raw at banquets, they were not thought important enough to garner much notice. However, imported items such as dried currants, raisins, dates and figs showed a host's taste and refinement and were served whenever possible. Imported during the winter and especially during Lent, they were expensive, but fairly easy to obtain and brightened a bland winter diet. On the other hand, citrus fruits, such as oranges and lemons, were rare and expensive luxuries and were much treasured when they could be found.

Other fruits available included: quince, strawberries, plums, cherries, medlars, St. John's Bread (carob), mulberries, gooseberries, peaches and pomegranates when they could get them. Grapes were not only used to make wine, but were eaten raw and cooked into various dishes to give them a sweet-sharp piquancy, and as with herbs and spices, certain fruits were sometimes used to color sauces and various other cooked dishes.

Though much of the available fruit was eaten raw, medieval 'dieticians' frowned on the practice, claiming that raw fruit was unhealthy, and recommended thorough cooking. Certain types of apples and pears stored well when laid in beds of straw and were brought out to roast in the ashes of fires during cold evenings. During Lent, when meat was not allowed, fruits were substituted in certain dishes and baked whole inside pies crusts called 'coffins'. Unlike the soft, flaky crusts we make today, medieval piecrusts were hard and tasteless and were used as a type of cooking pot, were not meant to be eaten.

Nuts were used in profusion and at every stage of cooking, as both ingredient and as garnish or decoration. Medieval cooks delighted in making their dishes look either as close as possible to the original animal— as when swans and peacocks were roasted, then painstakingly decked in their own plumage before being served—or as different as possible from the ingredients that made up the dish. For example, taking the stomach of a pig, stuffing it with meat and spices and roasting it on a spit, made a mock hedgehog, further disguised by covering the whole with fried almonds, like imitation quills. Ground into a powder, nuts could also be used to thicken sauces into a pudding like consistency. Popular nuts included walnuts, chestnuts, filberts, fir-pine seeds and of course, almonds.

During Lent, no butter, eggs or meat products could be used, so alternatives had to be found. Foods had to be fried in oil instead of lard (animal fat) and meat stock could not be used for stews or sauces. Since dough and pastries could not be bound together with eggs, water—or if they could afford it—almond milk had to be substituted. Blanched, ground and steeped in water, almonds produced a milk-like liquid that gave interest and nourishment to a meatless diet. It didn't spoil like regular milk and the almonds could be steeped more than once to yield several batches, making it affordable for most households.

Milk, enjoyed in moderation, could be and was supplied by goats, sheep and cows, the type used dependant on affordability, availability and the requirements of the recipe and the cook. Prudent households, if they could afford it, preferred to own their own milk animals, as those forced to buy theirs from others had to be careful that what they were buying was fresh and not diluted with water. Curds from spoiled milk were considered a medieval delicacy and the milk was sometimes treated by adding verjuice (the juice of green, unripe fruits, usually grapes, but sometimes crab apples), ale or wine to make it turn. The curds were then placed in a bag and hung, allowing the whey to drain into a dish. The resultant mass could then be served plain or with sugar and ginger, or divided into sections and colored with different herbs.

Eggs were a much loved staple of the medieval diet and were used for everything from binding various ingredients together, to painting or coloring food a rich, golden color, as an ingredient itself or as a cure for sick hounds and children. Produced from all types of fowl, chicken eggs were the most common and the easiest to come by, and even peasants kept chickens so they would have a ready supply of the nutritious food. Not only chicken's eggs were used though. Other birds' eggs, especially those of the sparrow, were considered to have aphrodisiac effects and were gathered in large quantities.

Unlike the cooks of today who use butter to make pastries and cookies and also as an ingredient in other dishes; butter was seldom used in medieval times except as a spread on bread, as a glaze on some types of food, or as a substitute for lard or oil to fry foods in. In order to preserve the butter and keep it from becoming rancid, it was covered with salt. When needed for cooking, the salt was either washed off, or the butter was melted and clarified, much as we do today.

FISH EATEN

Fish, allowed any time of the year, but especially during Lent and on religious fast days, was a major staple and so fishing was a vigorous and profitable trade. Because they lived in the water and not on land, fish were thought to have escaped God's curse on Adam after his fall from grace, and were therefore allowed by the church when meat was not. Herring was easy to catch, easy to salt, preserve and store and inexpensive to buy. Nourishing and plentiful, it was the most common fish eaten during Lent. Cod, or stockfish, even easier to preserve and store than herring, was also eaten during Lent, by the poor for their nutrition and by the wealthy for the flavour they added to other dishes.

Bass, bream, brett, brill, carp, colin (sea cob), codling, conger, dace, dogfish, doree, eel, flounder, garfish, gurnard, gray and red mullet, haddock, hake, halibut, keeling, lamprey, ling, loach, luce, shad, mackerel, minnow, perch, pickerel, pike, plaice, ray, roach, salmon, skate, smelts, sole, sturgeon, swordfish, tench, thornback, trout, tuna, turbot and whiting.

Anything that swam its way close enough to be caught was fair game for the medieval fisherman, unconstrained by the endangered species laws of today. Walrus, seal, porpoise, dolphin and various whales, though mammals were considered fish and served as such alongside cod and herring. Crustaceans and molluscs were also considered fish, as they lived in the water free of God's curse, and included crayfish, crab, lobster, mussel, oyster, scallop, shrimp, and whelk (sea snail). See the chart for other types of fish eaten.

With this kind of variety, courtly medieval food certainly never suffered the monotony of taste generally ascribed to it.

But even with such variety, the taste of fish soon paled on the medieval diet, especially during the forty days of Lent. In an effort to find some way to break free from the restrictions of sanctity and sin, even for a moment, clever clerics and laymen ensured the enjoyment of their favorite foods by changing the laws of natural history and making up their own. For instance, the 'barnacle goose', though forbidden during Lent if a mere goose, was often allowed because everyone knew that barnacles were fish, and it was widely believed that these geese laid their eggs, surrounded by protective barnacles, on underwater logs, making them an almost half fish, half flesh crossbreed. Fetal rabbits, not having been born yet, were considered 'non-meat' and were allowed as well, and even though beavers were obviously flesh, beaver tails were considered fish as their main function was to help the animal to swim.

The king of every meal, every banquet, every feast, was meat. Anything that could be caught, hunted, snared or trapped was eaten and enjoyed by those who could afford it. Along with basic meats such as beef, mutton and pork, you could expect to find recipes for fawn, kid, coney, rabbit, ox, beaver and bear. Young animals, such as veal, or coney (immature rabbits), were more highly prized than older ones and the very young even more so. Infant rabbits, called 'suckers', were a long time favorite.

Birds of all shapes and sizes augmented this enormous variety of feast ingredients. Along with the more common chickens, geese, and the young of each, it was a fairly easy matter to raise, trap, catch or hunt smaller fowl with arrows or hawks. These included: bittern, bustard, crane, curlew, dove, eagle, egret, gull, heron, lark, mallard, partridge, peacock, pheasant, pigeon, plover, quail, sparrow, shoveler, snipe, sorcell, stork, swan, teal, whimbrel and woodcock. With no controls on the number of these birds killed or eaten, sadly some species, such as the bustard, were hunted to extinction in the middle ages.

Medieval cooks wasted very little food. Every part of the meat or fish was eaten or utilised for some other purpose. Fats were used for frying and sautéing. The wings and necks of birds made up several noble delicacies. A pig's stomach, stuffed with meat and spices and covered with fried almonds made a fanciful mock hedgehog. Swim bladders from fish were removed and cooked with stuffing and sauces. Livers of whales, sturgeon and dolphin, once salted and cooked, were greatly enjoyed. Daintees (deer testicles) were considered a choice treat and were served with a sweet-sour sauce. Hoofs and feet were boiled to produce gelatine used not only as a cool contrast to a 'hot' food, but for artistic embellishment as well. For instance, fish served this way appeared to be 'swimming'. Bone marrow enriched and thickened tarts, and blood was used, not only with other ingredients in the making of various dishes, but alone, it was used as a coloring agent to turn sauces black or brown. Giblets, feet and bones were boiled together to make meat or fish stock that was saved for future use.

And as a selfless act of Christian charity, any food left over from a banquet that was not given to the servants, was gathered and given to the poor as a way of ensuring the banquet's host his allotted place in heaven.

LAWS AND LARCENIES

MEDIEVAL LONDON'S FOOD LAWS

Food markets flourished because they provided the raw materials for recipes that households could not grow, catch or raise for themselves. They furnished both varieties of choices as well as ostentation of exotic and expensive imports that even the wealthiest could not provide for themselves. Town dwellers and other lower class residents were even more important to the success of a market, as unlike the rich, they bought much more food than they raised.

A large market, such as those in medieval London, could provide everything from raw grains, to costly spices, to fully cooked 'convenience foods' such as pre-baked pies or pre-roasted meats or fowl, and they were all subject to carefully controlled 'victual laws', some of the toughest seen before or since. Not only did these rules control the prices, measures, quality and competition for merchants, but they prohibited unsanitary practices, punished severe and petty larcenies, set special hours and places for selling specific products, investigated allegations of illegal practices and enforced trials and punishments to fit the crime.

Bread was the glue that bound all classes together, from the rich to the poor to the strictest clerics, and its near universal acceptance and importance in the marketplace gave important clues to the sophistication and orderliness of London's food markets. The laws governing bread sale and production were some of the toughest known and were established, not because bakers and other merchants were particularly abusive of the laws, but as a way to protect both the patrons, as well as the reputations and profits of those merchants who did follow the rules.

Four different types of bakers predominated bread sales in the market. Bakers sold bread they baked themselves to households large and small, regraters bought already baked bread wholesale and resold the loaves to their own customers, public bakers ran huge ovens to which ovenless households brought their own dough to be baked, and pie bakers sold ready-to-eat pastries filled with fruit, meat, poultry or fish.

All commercially sold bread, even horsebread—oat and bran cakes baked for horses—had to be stamped with the official seal of the baker. This showed that the baker complied with the laws set down and also ensured that a customer would have some redress against said baker in case he was cheated as underweight or inferior bread could be traced back to its maker. Prices and measurements were set as to the size and type of bread sold, and numerous distinctions were made between the different grades of bread ranging from white to dark to specialty breads colored and flavoured with herbs.

Punishments for circumventing these laws was swift and just and could include confiscation of goods, confinement for a time in the pillory (a stock used to confine a person's wrists and neck), or being pulled through the streets tied to a sled-like device called a hurdle. For instance, a baker accused of selling underweight loaves could have their bread confiscated to feed prisoners at Newgate, or they could be made to sell future loaves at a loss as a warning. Another, accused of weighting down a cartload of loaves with an iron bar slipped into one so the cart would weigh heavier, would have one of the loaves, along with the bar, tied around his neck and locked in a pillory while a town crier called out his punishment. Another baker who baked bread with good dough surrounding rotten, might share his fate, and have the rotten bread burned beneath him as well. Any baker accused of the same crime three times was forbidden to sell bread in London again.

Public bakers sometimes practiced another type of petty larceny. In all bakeries, a flat board, called a moulding board, was provided to allow customers to shape their dough before placing it in the oven. A few ingenious bakers devised a way to cut and conceal a hole in the board so that it could not be seen from above, and when the unbaked dough was placed on top, the hole was opened and a baker's helper, unseen by the customer, would scrape free some of the mass, leaving the loaf shortened. The pilfered dough would then be added to, and then used to bake bread that was sold to others. Once this was discovered, moulding boards were banned from use.

Pie bakers were governed by other laws, guaranteed to preserve quality and prices for their wares, for instance, they were forbidden from buying 'garbage' from the kitchen of wealthy lords and baking them into pies, or baking beef into a pie and selling it as venison.

The laws governing the sale of wines were almost as stringent as the laws for bread. Prices were predetermined and any wine sold could be pre-inspected by the buyer before money ever changed hands. The buyer, or a single member of a drinking party, could also check the tuns, or pipes of wine, and the wine measures in the cellar. Some wines could be sold for immediate drinking, while others could only be sold in sealed containers and still other, local wines, could not be sold in the same tavern as certain foreign wines for fear of contamination or mixing. Mixing wines was not only illegal but was considered unhealthy and dangerous. With special dispensation, some wines were allowed to be combined, but only if their original components grew together, for instance, one Bordeaux grape with another.

Some wine merchants were known to mix pure wine with spoiled, or tried to disguise bad wine with strong spices. The punishment if caught, was to make the merchant drink his foul brew. Ale brewers were not exempt from greediness either. Ale was sold by the single quart, the two-quart and by the gallon, but to increase profit, some hucksters thickened or raised the bottoms of their containers with pitch, making the measures short. Those who made the wooden vessels, Coopers, sometimes made them out of unsound wood so the ale brewers would have to replace them more often. These would often crack and split, causing uneven measurements and putting the ale brewers at risk of losing their stock.

Then, as now, there were also those corrupt officials who could be bribed. Alehouses that were accused of some imagined offence, would pay off the investigators to prevent seizure of stock or other punishments.

London's food markets' guiding order was that certain things could only be sold at certain times in certain places. For instance, codfish caught on one side of London Bridge, had to be sold at a certain spot, only after 10:00 a.m., while shellfish could not be sold in a shop at all; they had to be hawked through the streets. Wine from France could not be sold in the same tavern as wine from Crete. These rules even extended to the types of shops any particular area could have. Some areas contained enclosed shops with windows and stalls, or had windowed extensions that allowed for more display space. Other areas allowed permanent and temporary stalls to be set up in front of, or between shops. Some food fairs could only be set up during special occasions and had to be shut down the rest of the time, and still other merchants were not allowed to have shops at all and like shellfish vendors, had to peddle their wares through the streets.

All commodities sold in medieval London's markets were carefully weighed and measured, using systems that were astonishingly accurate, effective and standardised, even compared to today's references.

Medieval Feasts
Customs, Manners, Food & Surprises

Feasts were an important and necessary part of medieval society. It was a visible demonstration of wealth and bound both guest and host together with ties of power, dependence and mutual obligation. Nothing was stinted at a feast because the generousness of a host gave valuable clues as to his resources and the place he held in society. His guests were chosen with equal care as the number and calibre of the diners was just as important to appearances as the food he served.

Guests in turn needed and desired to be invited to these banquets. A person's importance was based just as much on who issued him invitations as on whom he invited to his own feasts. Seating at a feast was important as well and the closer a guest was placed to the 'salt' (the ceremonial salt container on the head table), the higher his significance became. To be dropped from a guest list was the ultimate disgrace and guests would sometimes do anything to keep that from happening. An invitation was seen as a form of reward for good service or a favor rendered, as the lack of one was seen as punishment for a slight, either real or imagined.

As with everything in medieval society, appearances were all important. Except for the table, which was covered, everything else set out for use was the finest that the household could afford. Cups, serving plates and saucers were of gold or silver, or silver gilt. If made out of lesser materials, they were at least trimmed and embellished with the valuable metals. Drinking cups were sometimes made from elegantly decorated coconuts or ostrich eggs, that while not gold or silver, were at least rare enough that they were prized as unique conversation pieces. Pottery too, if fine enough, was also coveted and displayed with pride.

Some of the most valuable objects were not placed on the table for use, but were displayed instead on a cupboard. Guests would admire the pieces while at the same time noting which items were new and which were missing, as sometimes a host was forced to sell off pieces to pay bills or to secure a bribe. The fineness of the serving pieces used for each guest was another indication of the guest's status. Those at the high table—a table placed crosswise at the end of the room on a raised dais with the others placed perpendicularly beneath it—were given the finer dishes, while those at the lower tables made do with leather, pottery or ashwood tankards, cups and bowls.

A feast began long before the guests arrived with the preparation of food in the kitchen. Because of the threat of fire, kitchens in wealthier homes were set away from the main house, and food had to be brought from the kitchen to the dining area when it was ready to serve. Cooks were proud of their creations and took great care to ensure that all cooking surfaces were as clean as possible, since a dirty pan might ruin a dish that took hours to prepare. Scouring the insides with straw and ash from the fire cleaned pots and pans, while leaving the outside blackened. Cloths and towels and lots of water were kept in the kitchen to keep hands clean.

The tables were usually formed by using long, rectangular boards on trestles so they could be easily removed once the meal was over. They were wiped free of dust, and then fine linens were placed over the top, sometimes lapped end over end so they would drape to the floor. Even the linen was the finest the host could afford and must be clean as well, since using dirty or stained linen was a mark of disgrace. Because whiteness was so important, elaborate rituals evolved to help keep tablecloths clean, extending even to the church teaching that any man sinned who didn't have manners enough to keep from soiling the table linens. To this end, hands were washed before the meal, after the meal and sometimes between each course; with servants carrying warmed and sometimes perfumed water to each guest. Fingers were either placed in the bowl to wash or held above the bowl while water was poured over them, careful not to splash other guests. To keep the tablecloth from becoming wet, it was protected by a sanap, a long wad of towelling stretched along the table's edge and under the diners' hands. In order to help keep the linen clean, serving vessels for food and drink were carefully washed and wiped on the outside so they wouldn't leave spots, and guests were enjoined not to wipe their hands or knives on the cloth unless they first cleaned them with bread.

Even more important than the tablecloth was the bread. Bread was one element that was always present at any meal and the type of bread served each person, as well as its quantity and its freshness, told as much about a guest's importance as where he was seated. For instance, eight little white rolls might be placed before the lord or an important guest, while other guests would only receive four. At the lowest positions, rolls would be replaced by loaves of bread and one loaf would sometimes have to be shared between two people. The sharing of bread brought other considerations into play. For instance, it was considered bad manners to bite sections of bread from the loaf. Instead they must be cut or even torn, though tearing was frowned upon. And once a slice of bread was dipped into a sauce, it could not be dipped again—a fresh one had to be cut.

Bread was used not only for eating, but also for serving. Medieval hosts seldom, if ever, used individual plates for each person. Instead, they used flat sections of bread called trenchers. A trencher was usually made of bread that had been aged for several days so that it was stable and firm enough to hold up, and was about half a foot wide and four inches high. It soaked up the juices and gravies from the meal and after each course, was cleared away and new ones cut. At the end of the meal, all the trenchers, bread parings and leftovers were given to the poor.

The most important guests had their trenchers prepared for them by servers, who ranged them before the diner side by side in a little square with a smaller one set to the side to be used as an individual saltcellar. Salt and the serving of it had its own rules of etiquette. Food could never be dipped directly into the saltcellar, instead, the tip of a clean knife was used to dip some out and place it on your trencher. Because everyone used salt, it was placed on all tables then cleared away when no longer needed. However, the main saltcellar, called the Great Salt, was placed with great ceremony on the head table next to the lord of the manor and was left from the beginning of the meal to the end. Made of the costliest materials, they were a delight to the eye and the closer a guest sat to it, the greater his regard.

Manners were shaped by circumstances. When at home a man might have his own dish to eat from and his own cup to drink from, but at a feast he was often forced to share with others. Two people, and sometimes three, might be forced to drink from the same cup so it was very important that certain rules be followed. The cup must be held at the bottom of the bowl and no thumb or finger could touch the edge. Before drinking, the mouth must be empty and wiped clean and after drinking, the cup should be turned before being offered to the next person so that no two mouths touch the same spot.

Dishes were shared as well as cups, and sometimes as many as four people might have to serve themselves from the same platter or charger. Because of this, it was considered rude for someone to root around in a dish for the choicest meat, or take too much of a sauce leaving none for the next person. It was much preferred for a diner to select his meat quickly and considerately. This could be done with a knife for spearing the meats, but was most often done with just the fingers. A choice slice would be picked off the plate, dipped in the appropriate sauce then laid on the trencher for eating. A knife might also be employed by the guest to cut the meat off of a bone, or to cut it into more manageable pieces, then set aside while the food was brought to the mouth with the fingers. Diners were also expected not to gnaw on bones with their teeth, poke their fingers into eggs, spit across the table, wipe their mouths on their sleeves, put their elbows on the table, slurp their soup, belch, feed scraps to the dogs while eating, or butter bread with their thumbs.

Both knives and spoons, used for soups and puddings, were employed at a feast, but were considered personal possessions and were supplied for the most part by each individual diner. Only the most important of guests might have a spoon or knife provided for them. Forks did not come into general use until sometime in the seventeenth century, though variations of them were used to spear meat in the kitchen or sometimes to serve sweet or very sticky dishes.

Wine service depended on a guest's social status. It was the custom to mix water with wine before it was drunk and most guests were given their wine already watered from supplies not on the table, so the quality and quantity could be precisely controlled. More important guests would have a flask of wine left on the table for them, along with a bottle of water to mix their own. This was done both for health and moral concerns. Temperance and moderation were the mark of a sensible man. However, it was easier to disapprove of those in the lower classes than it was to judge themselves, or their peers.

Not only were guests and hosts sensitive to rank, but also servants, better than anyone, knew who was moving up the ladder of success and they paid little attention to someone they deemed unimportant. Not only did a lesser guest receive less attention, fewer choices, smaller servings as well as having to share with others, they were also seated the furthest from the fire. During a cold winter feast, it could become very uncomfortable and had to be endured with as much stoicism as everything else. Most guests though, however poorly treated, would never dream of refusing an important invitation when given.

Meat and fowl dishes were not carved by the lord of the manor, but by special carvers trained to handle any type of carcass with grace and ease. In this as in other important jobs, noblemen were usually served by noble youths sent to them for education and training in domestic and chivalric service. It was a good way for noble sons to advance, especially second and third sons who had no chance to inherit their father's estates. Carvers had specific techniques and tools for each type of service, from cutting a meat pie, to 'unlacing' a capon, to 'departing' a crayfish or 'displaying' a crane, and good ones paid lavish attention to every aspect of their job. Inept carvers were an embarrassment and not to be tolerated, as their chore was to make things as easy and as agreeable for the host as possible. After the lord and honored guests were served, carving knives were placed on the table so that other guests might carve their own portions.

The majority of banquets followed a three-course convention, but one totally unlike modern day three-course meals. Each course had anywhere from seven to fifteen different dishes, whether meat or poultry or fish, and all served with the appropriate sauce. Most courses lasted several hours and an entire banquet could last most of a day. Dishes within a course could be ordered any number of ways, depending on the cook's wishes or those of the host. Each item might be served by genre— different meats followed by different fish, followed by different fowl; by gastronomic concerns—cold versus hot dishes, or moist versus dry; or by some arbitrary zoological hierarchy—whole footed birds first, sorted by size for instance, in some kind of animal pecking order.

For instance, a typical banquet might include:

FIRST COURSE:	SECOND COURSE:	THIRD COURSE:
1. Meat in pepper sauce	1. Venison in frumenty	1. Blaundesorye
2. Seymé of Veal (a kind of veal stew)	2. Jelly	2. Quince in comfit
3. Boar's head and tusks	3. Stuffed pig	3. Egrets
4. Salmon Sounds (Salmon belly)	4. Peacocks	4. Curlews
5. Cygnets	5. Cranes	5. Partridge
6. Fat capon	6. Roast venison	6. Pigeons
7. Pheasant	7. Coney	7. Quails
8. Heron	8. Bittern	8. Snipes
9. Crustade Lumbarde (A marrow & fruit tart)	9. Pullets	9. Smal Byrdys
10. Sturgeon, great luces	10. Great tarts	10. Rabbits
11. A subtlety (Large, usually edible sculptures)	11. Fried meat	11. Glazed meat-apples
	12. Leche lumbarde (A wined date confection)	12. White meat leche
	13. A subtlety	13. Glazed eggs
		14. Fritters
		15. Doucettes (pastries)
		16. Pety perneux
		17. Eagle
		18. Pottys of lylye
		19. A subtlety

While the abundance of foods was important, not everyone was given the same choices. Those guests at the high table had the greatest choice, while the lower tables had very little if any. Of the perhaps ten or so dishes offered to the lord and his important guests, only three or four might be offered to lesser diners. On those few occasions when everyone was offered the same dishes, the size of the helping varied drastically according to the guest's importance.

It was a cook's job to make the food not only taste good, but to make it as decorative as possible, using any method he could devise. Good cooks had several methods and used them to good effect. Painting and coloring were one option. Foods could either be colored by the use of spices or herbs—for instance, saffron colored foods yellow, saunders red and parsley green—or they could be painted as if the food were a canvas and the cook an artist. Spices and herbs made good 'paints', as did various fruits, blood and of course, eggs. Sometimes meat and fish were served in their own jelly, fish especially, so they appeared to be 'swimming' in their own element. Often they were painted with spices to represent the heraldic crest of the host or an honored guest.

Another way that cooks made foods decorative was by creating fanciful 'monsters'. Calculated to delight the eye as well as the stomach, these were made by cutting in half both a capon and a pig, boning them, then sewing the forequarters of one to the hindquarters of the other. The bodies were then stuffed and roasted, then painted with spices and herbs before being served. Other foods, such as peacocks or boars, were roasted whole, then laboriously re-plumed or painted before being presented—with gilded tusks and beaks—for the delight of all the guests.

Pageantry was just as important at a feast as the food, and music played an essential part. Trumpet fanfares, drum roles and shrill pipe tunes signalled an important event, such as the hand-washing ceremony, and the beginning of each course. Softer, quieter music was played in the background as guests ate and talked, and between each course or at the end of the meal, music was used to entertain. For most of the feast, players were stationed in one location, but during the intervals, sometimes they would stroll through the hall, stopping here and there to play. Singing was popular and everyone enjoyed carols. They were easy, simple songs composed of multiple stanzas, usually sung by the musician, followed by the chorus (or burden) sung by the audience.

Medieval hosts loved to surprise their guests and they were great practical jokesters, often going to ridiculous lengths to achieve their goals. What modern day hosts would frown upon, they considered enchanting and fun and might be found to do anything from making a guest's wine turn unexpectedly red, to making a dead chicken jump off the table, to employing puzzle jugs, the medieval version of a dribble glass.

The dead time, after one course was cleared off and before the next one was brought, was the perfect time for entertainment, and medieval diners enjoyed many different kinds, such as jugglers, animal trainers, conjurers, comedians and storytellers. In later medieval periods, other forms of entertainment evolved: disguising, mumming and the interlude.

'Disguising' involved strangers or sometimes a few of the guests, dressing up in elaborate costumes and masks and making a grand entrance into the hall. Once there, they would usually perform a dance or sing a song before sweeping out as mysteriously as they entered, leaving guests to wonder who they were. Mumming was similar. Those who took part might play a game of dice with the host or offer presents or even dance, but always in complete silence, except for the accompanying music.

Over time, both of these entertainments grew more sophisticated and became more like plays or interludes, called that because they were played during the interludes between courses at a feast. The plays were short enough to fit between other festivities and could be played all in one sitting, or it could start at the beginning of a banquet and progress bit by bit as the meal went on. It was usually completed by the time the feast was over, but sometimes the ending was carried over to a later meal, like supper.

Stolties or Subtleties were another way that cooks could surprise the diners. These were large sculptures created to decorate the dining hall. Often they were edible, being made from spun sugar, or pastry or marzipan, but the bigger ones especially could be made of wax or papier-mache. They could depict anything from human and animal figures, to elaborate castles and fortresses and the more permanent ones were often kept after the feast or given to favored guests.

It was a combination of all these things that made a feast, but ceremony transformed the plain and simple into the extraordinary and made any feast a properly festive occasion.

FAST OR FEAST

THE ROLE OF FOOD IN RELIGION

Each week had three fast days sanctioned by the Church, Friday in memory of the crucifixion, Wednesday as the day that Judas accepted money to betray Jesus, and Saturday as the day consecrated to celebrate Mary's virginity. Of these, Friday was the most rigorously observed and only the very young, very old, or very sick were exempt. Four times a year these fast days took on a special seriousness and were called Ember Days: early in Lent, just after Pentecost, in September and in December during Advent. On these days, the items served might differ, but the usual amounts still had to be prepared, then given away to the needy.

Lent was the longest fasting period, six weeks in imitation of Jesus' forty-day fast in the wilderness. We still observe Lent to this day, but not with quite the same zeal or commitment. In the Middle Ages it was a penance time, a hardship to be endured and gotten through with as little inconvenience as possible while still following all the churches codes and rules. Unlike the other fast days during the year, where the only change was from meat to fish, Lent also meant eating less. Meals were reduced to only one a day, usually at noon.

No animal born or bred on land could be eaten during Lent as they signified man's failure and God's curse upon him. Other animal products such as butter, eggs, cheese and milk could not be eaten either, though the restrictions were not as great. Only fish had escaped the curse by living in water and could be eaten with impunity. Since the Church taught that all of God's creation was good, they had to walk a fine line between what was said and what was done, and emphasise that while meat was good, it must be given up during Lent as a penance and a daily reminder that man was flawed.

During this time, because everyone was eating fish, it became scarce and very expensive. In order to have enough to last during Lent, a household would have to stock up months in advance and store the fish during the winter. The same held true for the Easter feast. A haunch of beef had to be bought in November and hung in the chimney to smoke until Easter. Those who possessed the means travelled from one estate to another, supplementing herring and stockfish from the fresh water stews (ponds) on their property.

As the six long weeks progressed, the desire for forbidden food grew and it was up to enterprising cooks to find new and ingenious ways to provide what the diners wanted without breaking any rules. One way this was done was by taking a much-loved dish, and by substituting ingredients, make it as close to the original as possible. The Mock Egg is a good example. First an almond puree was made then sweetened and divided into two parts. One part was left white and the other was colored a golden yellow with a combination of spices. The content of a real egg was blown out, the shell washed, then filled with the yellow and white mixture. It was then roasted in the ashes of a fire and served as a hardboiled egg.

Monasteries were restricted to fish diets except for a few exceptions that were exploited whenever possible. For instance, they could only eat meat that was hunted, so a few monks got clever and let dogs onto the monastery grounds to chase the chickens and pigs, thus making them hunted prey.

The Medieval Church never missed a chance to make a profit and took advantage of any situation. While the rules for meat were never relaxed at Lent or Advent, it was possible to pay a bribe to the Church in order to gain permission to eat butter, eggs and other dairy foods. Enough money was collected to have certain Church towers and other structures paid for by these dispensations. Some Abbeys made money by imposing fines on boats and carts that transported fish across their borders, plumping their own profits in the process and driving up fish prices.

Many people believe that the Church had a stranglehold on the fish market and that they created a third fast day a week as a way to increase profits. While this may or may not be the case, it was certainly true that during Elizabeth I's reign, after the Reformation had loosened the Church's grip on its people, that most fast days ceased to be observed. While some were still honored, particularly Fridays and Lent, the use of fish was no longer as automatic as it had been. This led to a decline in the number of English ships at sea and so reduced the size of the navy, that in 1563 a document was drawn up establishing Wednesday as an official fish day.

Summary

Any author, or would-be author who intends to spend any amount of time in a medieval setting, either real or of his own design, would benefit greatly from seeing how medieval people in our own world lived. Most people who haven't done any research in this area would expect to find that those who lived in the Middle Ages were simple, uncomplicated people who didn't wash, didn't care about their health and ate nothing but stew. This is simply not true. Cooks took pride in the cleanliness of their kitchens and of themselves, and while it's true that people didn't bathe as often, they were just as repulsed by rotten food and foul odours as are we. They were also much more complicated than we give them credit for; the richness of their culture and the extensiveness of their laws attest to that. They took great care of their health, both spiritually and physically; at least as much as they understood diseases and their cures without our modern medical knowledge. And while their customs and manners seem crude and harsh to us, the fact that they had manners and followed them says much about how they lived.

In summary, it must be noted that while cooking and eating habits have changed greatly from medieval times until now, the richness of presentation and the pride of a cook in his creations, carries forward to this day and can be seen in all walks of life. If you choose to write fantasy set in the Middle Ages, you should strive to capture the heart and soul of what were once a complicated and culturally rich people.

Bibliography

Fabulous Feasts—Medieval Cookery and Ceremony, Madeleine Pelner Cosman (New York: George Braziller, 1976).

Fast and Feast—Food in Medieval Society, Bridget Ann Henisch (United States: Pennsylvania State University, 1976).

The Medieval Cookbook, Maggie Black (New York: Thames and Hudson, Inc., 1992).

The Medieval Kitchen—Recipes from France and Italy, Odile Redon, Francoise Sabban, & Silvano Seventi, trans. Edward Schneider (Chicago & London: University of Chicago Press, 1998).

Daily Life in Medieval Times, Frances & Joseph Gies (New York: Black Dog & Leventhal Publishers, Inc., 1990).

Everyday Life in the Middle Ages—The British Isles from 500 to 1500, Sherrilyn Kenyon (US: Writer's Digest Books, 2000).

Health and Medicine

MICHAEL McRAE

INTRODUCTION

Riding into town on the back of his pied gelding, saddlebags all but empty and his stomach much the same, the journeyman tried in vain to avert his eyes away from the leper sitting hunched in the mud by the gate. He pretended to not hear the croaky voice, a voice begging for alms, alms for the poor, alms for the sick, alms for the desperate and downtrodden. Drizzling rain had found its way through the traveller's worn riding cloak, daring to touch his flea-bitten skin with icy fingers, and chilling him to the bone. His left hand, scarred with burns from his years as an apprentice, clenched his second-last copper piece in anticipation of the warden at the gate. Even as he approached the guard, he could not help noticing the leper's hair lip, the smoky cataract dominating one eye, the white and crimson pustule bulging on his cheek. The journeyman thanked the gods for his own poor health—he was left to but imagine the foul stench of the beggar as he passed beneath the city's portcullis, his miserable nose clogged beyond use.

Whether it is on the steppes of southern Russia, the mires of western Africa, the icefields of northern Europe or the beaches of America's east coast, man has encountered famine, malnutrition, pestilence, or simple misfortune. Humans are made to break down—a simple, but important, fact of nature.

So, a simple question—are the inhabitants of your world any different?

Perhaps they are—maybe you have decided that your races are untouched by the gnarled hand of Nergal, the Babylonian fever-devil. Indeed, they could be untainted by ill fortune, free from harm, creatures of forever. In which case, feel free to ignore this section.

However, if you declare your fantastic subjects to be biologically fallible in any way, read on. You might be writing fantasy, but that is no excuse to altogether abandon reality.

The human body is a biological machine. As such, it is subject to the corruptive forces that living in a hostile world expose it to. To continue using this analogy; cogs can slip, levers can snap, it can run dry of oil or simple commands can be misinterpreted to cause problems. Knowing how this happens, why it happens and the consequences of such breakdowns is essential in the creation of a believable character.

- How long does it take for a certain wound to heal?
- What are the consequences of certain diseases?
- What medical problems can I give my character?

Such questions can do little but enhance a story.

To better understand this chapter, consider the term 'disease' as a malfunction of the human body. This could be caused by a 'pathogen' (any living agent that directly causes a disease), a toxin, a breakdown in the body's functioning or even an absence of nutrient from the diet. Much of this chapter looks at 'epidemiology'—the movement of a pathogen through a population. Therefore, a little bit of information about the history of society and the interactions between it and the cause of disease is provided.

Fantasy worlds are limited only by the writer's imagination. Yet it is rare that they fail to mirror our own history in some form. The writer decides where on the meandering road to scientific 'enlightenment' their created world is introduced—what sciences have been explored, what technology have they unleashed onto their world, what understanding have they of their universe, and so forth.

Keeping all of this in mind, I have broken this chapter down into the following sections in an attempt to address as simply as possible the variety of ailments that have plagued us, and the cures (both the effective and the not so effective) that we have surrendered ourselves to:

- The History: The Nomad, The Birth of Civilisation, The Age of Enlightenment;
- The Science: Pathogens, Example Diseases, Pregnancy, The Human Body;
- The Fantasy: Health and Medicine in a Make-believe World

This chapter's intention goes beyond the mere topic of health and medicine. While the content focuses mainly on the history of disease, I hope that these words inspire you, as a writer, to remain aware of the need for a sense of reality in your make-believe world. There is an incredible amount of information here, more than you will ever need to know. However, not everything you will need to know about health and medicine is provided here as a reference. Remember, just because you are writing fantasy, it does not mean that you can forget going to the library to do some good, old fashioned research.

THE HISTORY

THE NOMAD: PREHISTORY TO 5000 B.C.

Prehistoric Homo sapiens communities consisted mostly of family-based groups that moved periodically through a set territory. Studies done in anthropology on modern nomadic groups indicate populations ranged from small bands of ten to twenty members up to fifty or sixty related individuals.

In accordance with seasonal variations, a nomadic existence provided the members of the group with a variety of foods. Migrating between different environments meant throughout the year the members of a group could eat a variety of meats, grains, fruits, and vegetables. This is important considering malnutrition would not be seen as a problem for such societies, unless a staple food happened to be missing from the environment for an extended period.

Another advantage of nomadic existence would be the ability to avoid vectors of disease, such as decaying animal carcasses, contained herds of livestock and human waste. Not maintaining herds of animals for food decreased the chance of being infected with a disease. In other words, association with the breeding ground of a pathogen was often brief, limited to contact with an infected animal retrieved from a hunt or perhaps exchanges with a neighboring tribe, leaving little chance for the individual to become infected with a contagious disease.

This ties in with the fact that nomadic groups would have rarely associated on a day-to-day basis with many foreign groups. Pathogens had very little chance to move through the wider population—should one nomadic group become infected with a type of pathogen, there would be very little chance that this disease could be passed on to another community before all members of the infected group succumbed and died. The down side of this, of course, is that resistance to many different diseases would be difficult to attain. Simple diseases such as influenza could be deadly, given that it would be unlikely that the group would have had previous contact with the disease at all.

Pathogens responsible for low to non-existent mortality rates, such as most parasites and fungi, would be common within nomadic individuals. Worms, ticks, lice, and ringworm all would have been quite prevalent in the typical body of a nomadic human. Such infestations would have little to no effect on the wellbeing of an otherwise healthy individual. Grooming habits adopted from experience would be culturally entwined—removal of lice, for instance would be something bound within the hierarchical structure of the family, much as it is with many modern primate groups.

Medicine would be limited to what could be found in the environment. Based on the principle of association, certain plants would have been found to provide therapeutic relief from common maladies. However, this was mixed with a good deal of placebo in the form of ritual and pure psychology. Science, as a methodology for understanding the world, was basic at this stage; hence sickness was attributed to unseen factors. Disease and spirituality often went hand in hand. Foul water supplies would be called 'cursed', bad foods 'evil', and so forth. Likewise, cures would be associated with goodness and positive spirits. Hence why shamans and so-called 'witch-doctors' were healers and priests in one.

Surgery was rare, although present in the form of simple (although rather invasive) procedures. Some scholars argue that the suturing of wounds was regularly practiced, and evidence of 'trephination', where a section of skull is removed to relieve built-up pressure, has been found in some stone-age skeletal remains. The reasoning behind these practices was probably based on association rather than any form of induction, hence trephination was more than likely aimed at removing bad spirits than relieving the pressure of excess fluid on the brain.

Homo sapiens, as an animal, has adapted to a nomadic lifestyle over millions of years of various evolutionary stresses. His biology is suited to moving constantly and adapting to environments that change through a variety of conditions. In five thousand years the human species has created a new way of existence, one he has had little time to biologically adapt to, one where the environment is manipulated to suit the species, rather than the other way around. This has caused problems that no pre-historic individual could have possibly foreseen.

Welcome to the Age of Pestilence—The Age of Civilisation.

BIRTH OF CIVILISATION:
5000 B.C.—1600 A.D.

There is a general consensus that the first settlements of civilisation were erected between 10,000 B.C. and 8000 B.C., and occurred in what is today central Mesopotamia. Ultimately, this event was significant because it was mankind's first victory in his stand against nature. By manipulating the generation of crops and the production of animals for the first time in history, humans could remain in one place on a permanent basis, leading to the establishment of a rather sedentary lifestyle. They discovered that by annually tending wild grasses, spreading seed artificially, and maintaining small herds of grazing animal, they were able to create a stable community that did not need to be subjected to the rigours of constant travel.

There was, however, a cost.

Diseases caused by microbes can only succeed under strict conditions (see the section on pathology). These conditions were prevalent in early settlements. Permanent food storage and waste deposits, close association with various animal species, the ability to support extended population sizes in a contained, geographical area; all of this contributed to an increase in the frequency of major disease outbreaks. Changes such as these increased the chance a single individual would come across a dangerous pathogen.

The populated world had become an incubator for the worst kinds of diseases. Once, a plague would wipe out one or two small families of nomad before disappearing. With the help of a settled population, a single species of pathogen could circulate swiftly, breeding within congested pockets of population before moving on to another settlement, moving constantly for centuries. Plagues were able to spread like wildfire, and often did with devastating effectiveness.

As settlements increased in number, so too did populations. Larger population sizes, mixed with improved technology, meant geographical regions could specialise in agricultures that were well supported by their surrounding environment. A vicious circle was established where trade was boosted by regional specialisation, and regional specialisation was supported by an increase in trade. Throughout the ancient world, interlinking communities continued to spin mercantile webs, linking the Asian east with the European west. The most famous of these highways later became known as 'The Silk Road.' However oceanic highways hugging the coast enabled faster trade between countries otherwise separated by time, distance and water.

This was to have a massive impact on the movement of a disease through the world.

Following the downfall of the Roman Empire, trade routes remained strong out of a reliance on another region's agriculture. The value of exchange, however, fluctuated wildly. Knots of population formed where poverty was strife. Feudalism only exasperated this phenomenon by containing what little wealth existed in specific sections of the community. The western world became a cluttered network of communal 'nodes'. The progress of technology had crawled to a near stop because few could afford to risk change, and due to regional poverty, it remained this way for close to a millennium. All of this contributed to the conditions that allowed plagues, malnutrition and poor hygiene to become everyday phenomena.

An absence of progressive technology meant health and sanitation systems were rather basic, and often altogether non-existent, increasing the prevalence of common illnesses. At this stage, medicine was reliant on (often ineffective) age-old remedies and superstitions anchored in folklore.

Borrowed from old-world practices inherited from the experiences of past civilisations, a few measures were used to slow the movements of epidemics. Quarantine, for instance, was an early concept adopted to prevent a disease from entering a community. It was also known that infected corpses were sources of contamination and therefore needed to be destroyed or contained. It is likely that the practice of burning or burying the dead came from this. While various religious practices protested against the incineration of a corpse, it was frequently adopted in many towns that cremation be legally enforced, should it be suspected that the individual's death was the result of a contagious disease. Such understanding of the basic tenants of an epidemic could be seen in the practice of a form of 'germ warfare' during sieges. Infected human corpses and body-parts, as well as pestilential animal bodies, were catapulted over the walls of besieged cities in an effort to wipe out the contained population through sickness.

Herbal remedies, albeit mixed heavily with superstitious actions and colorful ceremony, remained the most common form of effective treatment for any type of malady. As a potion, a salve, a poultice or a vapour, almost anything in nature from mud to animal excrement to honey was made into a cure. Many of these had good reason to be effective. On the other hand, many did not.

The true nature of disease, however, continued to elude mankind. The alleged causes were as varied as the diseases themselves. One school of thought offered during the late Middle Ages saw contagion as airborne poisons, passed through the air in the form of bad smells. Perfume could combat this, as the foul air was purified by the pleasing fragrance (the large 'beaks' worn by doctors combating the plague during the Middle Ages were filled with perfumed rags for this reason).

In some parts of the western world, malevolent spirits and evil curses were blamed for non-contagious diseases such as neurological conditions, cancers, metabolic diseases and so forth, and could be banished only through ritual and prayer. Christian dogma saw disease as a repercussion of immorality, a sort of divine punishment—the physical ailment often a reflection of the damaged soul.

Spirituality and disease remained intrinsically bound throughout the dark ages. Contrition and penance, blessing, fasting and even financial 'indulgences' (payment to the Church for divine favor) were means of healing in the Christian world. Monarchs, often linked with divinity, possessed the ability to heal with a touch, especially with diseases such as scrofula.

With the passing of the centuries, the socio-economic status of both the eastern and western world became increasingly dependent on foreign trade. The science of finance had improved considerably, releasing wealth into the community as opposed to locking it up in an inheritance system. Such a shift in the balance of power from feudalism to a capitalistic climate opened the way for colonisation, the rise of universal education (as opposed to ecclesiastic education) and daring new entrepreneurial ventures instigated by an educated elite.

The world was waking into an Age of Enlightenment.

THE AGE OF ENLIGHTENMENT:
1600 A.D. TO THE FUTURE

With recovering economies giving many the chance to pursue non-ecclesiastic study in the west, there came a desire to return to a Golden Age like that which had existed in ancient times. Contrary to modern popular opinion, much of the knowledge created during the scientific Golden Age of Rome and Greece was being harboured by the Islamic Middle East, and not by the monastic centres of the western churches. Indeed, medicine was comparatively advanced in the Middle East as far as basic healing went. There are even tenth century scriptures detailing the use of a rabbit by a Muslim holy-man to detect a young girl's pregnancy. However, as with Christianity, Islamic doctrine provided a stumbling block for many forms of experimentation, such as human dissection, impeding any radical progress.

With the revival of researching ancient Roman texts as sources of inspiration, some old theories concerning the cause for human illness returned with vigour. Freedom from fundamentalism meant sinister causes for non-contagious disease were no longer acceptable. Although never completely absent, the ancient Greek notion of 'body humours' became highly fashionable again in the sixteenth century.

The concept of 'balancing humours' continued until well into the eighteenth century, with many physicians still referring to such outdated theories as late as the mid nineteenth century.

This theory maintained that an individual's health was kept in check by the balance of four essences present in the body's liquid 'humours'— melancholia (black bile), sanguine (blood), phlegma (phlegm) and choler (yellow bile). These essences also affected a person's state of being (or sense of 'humour'). Note that a person could be 'melancholy', or sad, if there was a surplus of black bile in relation to the other humours.

To remedy this, early physicians would attempt to artificially balance the humours. Blood letting, heat and cold therapy, steam baths and diets were all forms of accomplishing this, and were rarely successful. Indeed King George III, diagnosed as 'mad' as a result of what is now thought to have been a disease called porphyria, died as a direct result of the methods employed by his physicians to balance his humours. He was alternatively chilled, over-heated, had blisters put onto the soles of his feet and bled in ever increasing amounts until he finally died.

As late as the early 1700's, surgery was limited to the butchering practiced by 'barbers', who were little more than men trained in the use of a knife. Removal of rotten teeth, overgrown cancers and infected limbs were commonly done within this profession, as well as shaving beards and the like. The survival rate of their patients, needless to say, was rather low. For any other ailment, apothecary (druggists) or old-fashioned herbal remedies were used.

It is interesting to note that it was not until the 1850's that non-herbal based medicines became popular. Sulphur drugs, introduced in 1852, raised concerns amongst the English general public. The equivalent of modern 'New Agists' were uncomfortable with so-called 'unnatural' remedies. Until then, most drugs were made primarily from plant and animal extracts. Exceptions, such as the use of mercury for syphilis, existed, but were by far in the minority.

During the seventeenth and eighteenth centuries the gentry adopted various fashions to disguise what diseases they could not cure, thus allowing them to distinguish themselves even further from the commoners. White face make-up hid blemishes and pox scars and the effects of poor nutrition, while wigs allowed them to cut their hair short and still have long hair. Not to say this helped combat lice very well—wigs were all too often infested with all manner of parasite, including lice, mites and fleas. Yet powdering them was rumoured to have helped, to some degree.

Gout was also a condition prevalent in the gentry of the day. Caused by a build up of uric acid in the system, it affected those who ate too much meat by forming crystals in the fluid of joints. Other conditions caused by over consumption of certain foods, and malnutrition due to an absence of other foods, were common. Scurvy, caused by lack of vitamin C in the diet, was a huge problem in places where fresh fruit and vegetables were hard to come by.

As religion slowly released its oppressive hold on the pursuit of scientific endeavour in the west, the newly risen 'educated' elite took great delight in examining nature anew, inspired by the texts of ancient wisdom. Hippocrates was reborn as a scion of medical knowledge. Aristotle, Plato, and Thales were viewed as scientific saints. However, great care was taken to still comply with the Christian scriptures in regards to innovative discovery. While the Church tolerated the act of searching for universal truth, nothing was allowed to be published that could contradict basic doctrine. Hence pre-modern medicine became a bizarre hybrid of religious superstition, ancient science and modern experimentation.

This era witnessed the birth of a concept called 'the scientific method'. New-age philosophers such as Francis Bacon reinvented science in the mid-seventeenth century as a means of observing nature. As a methodology, it decreed that scholars should follow a set pattern that complied with a logical progression based on the process of 'induction' (making a single theory from many known facts). This 'scientific method' gave rise to a new school of thought where knowledge was born out of reason and not of pure speculation.

With this concept becoming popular, the tide had turned once and for all. Antony van Leeuwenhoek's perfection of the microscope in the middle of the seventeenth century instigated the era of the microcosm. Another world opened before mankind's eyes, where tiny animals moved through a minuscule environment. Sperm, plant cells, pollen...a completely new realm was available for research. Although it would take another century or two to change the accepted 'truths' behind the causes of various diseases, it was being observed that there was more to Mother Nature than devils and sorcery.

The nineteenth century saw the rise of such greats as Robert Koch, Joseph Lister and Ignaz Semmelweiss, who paved the way for control over bacterial disease and infection. Lady Mary Montagu has the dubious credit of being the messenger who brought the process of inoculation across from the Middle East to Britain, an art practiced by a few Muslim communities in order to vaccinate themselves against various diseases. However the first to truly inspire the medical world of the benefits of 'vaccination', and therefore control over viral contagion, was Edward Jenner.

Louis Pasteur, and his methods of controlling microbial growth, and Alexander Fleming's discovery of penicillin only further enhanced man's growing ability to cure disease, rather than just prevent it.

In short, mankind recovered from the ignorance of the Middle Ages by shrugging off the oppressive chains of 'infallible' religious dogma and looking objectively at nature by using a set method of inductive reasoning. New paradigms of thought, new ways of discovery, new methodology and a new hunger for objective evidence granted mankind with a revival of his Golden Age after all.

THE SCIENCE

PATHOGENS

Pathogen, as a term, comes from the Greek 'pathos' meaning 'suffering'. Today it refers to any disease-causing agent. It can be argued that this includes any single 'thing' that can cause biological breakdown—a chemical, a teratogen (mutagens that cause abnormalities in a developing foetus) and radiation—could technically be included. However when most people talk about pathogens, they are usually referring to living things.

There are essentially four types of organism responsible for most of the world's contagious diseases: viruses (debate ongoing on whether they are a living organism or not. For simplicity's sake, we will include them here), bacteria, protozoa and fungi. Each has its own method of infection, reproduction and transmission.

As noted earlier, pathogens need some essential conditions in order to spread. Most need something called a 'vector' (a place to breed in between hosts, or an agent of transmission between hosts—this could be an animal, water, food, water-particles, host-cells, clothing, objects and so on) and a community of hosts (a single host would offer a restricted environment in which to breed and evolve). Early civilisation provided both of these essentials in varying amounts, with few stresses controlling their growth.

An effective pathogen is one that:

- Breeds quickly
- Breeds large numbers of virile offspring (in other words, the offspring don't all die as soon as they are introduced into the environment)
- Possesses a life cycle that has a minimal impact on the health of the host

- Has an effective, yet simple, method of transmission that gives it access to a wide variety of hosts
- Employs a variety of methods to remain hidden from the host's defence system.

The 'aim' of a pathogen's existence is not to make somebody sick. Like any other living thing, its essential aim is to create a generation of offspring that is capable itself of making another generation of offspring, and so on. Only clumsy pathogens tend to kill their host. This is why most parasites tend to live in harmony with their environment—human parasites such as worms and fungi have minimal impact on their host due to millions of years of coexistence. Viruses and many bacteria, being relatively new entrants in terms of existing within mankind's social circles, are hence relatively ineffective.

Even though it is less than likely that you will describe the exact cause of an affliction in your story, knowing it yourself will be of benefit. Using the following information may be useful should you want to create a unique plague, such as one based on sorcery or divine punishment, for your world.

Note: When a parasite has little to no negative impact on its host, and its host has little to no negative impact on the parasite, and neither can survive without the benefits provided by the other, the collective of both host and parasite is known as a 'symbiotic organism'.

Ever thought of having a race of elves that need to grow a special fungus on its skin to survive?

VIRUSES

Viruses are little more than tiny packets of coding information contained within a protein shell. This information, similar to that use by all organisms, finds its way into a host cell and highjacks the cellular machinery in order to reproduce itself. As they contain no means to self-reproduce and have no real metabolism of their own, they are not usually considered 'alive'. However, they do express a sense of life through their host. Hence viruses have been an interesting pathogen for many fantasy and SF writers on which to base story concepts.

The average size of a single virus particle is so small that three billion of them could fit into this full stop. All living organisms on this planet are vulnerable to at least one type of virus. As such, they represent the most successful form of reproduction on this planet.

The host's response to the presence of the virus is essentially what elicits the symptoms of an infection, and gives rise to the disease. Fevers, blisters, rashes, swollen lymph glands and acute aches and pains are all part of the body's natural defence against a virus. Because many (although not all) viruses rupture cells in their effort to reproduce, the body reacts by segregating the infected site and filling it with chemicals (blisters), sending white blood cells to 'search and destroy' (pustules—battlefields of dead white blood cells), increasing the temperature to sabotage the operation of key proteins (fever) and re-directing the use of a body's energy to repairing damaged tissue (fatigue). They are all responses initiated by the host. Rarely is a symptom solely caused by anything a virus itself makes.

Because they lack a metabolism themselves, viruses are incredibly hard to 'kill'. Antibiotics are useless against them. Modern drugs focus on disrupting their reproductive process by knocking out any specialised tools they create within the host's cell, or by focussing the body's own defences on the intruder itself.

Viruses are transmissible through all manner of factors. Direct contact, airborne particles, contact with a contaminated object, food and water, contact with an infected animal—the list is endless. However, most viruses cannot last long outside of the body of a host. For instance, H.I.V., responsible for the disease A.I.D.S., can barely last fifteen minutes in the presence of a U.V. source (such as the sun). To compensate, many viruses can 'hide' by inserting their genetic material into their hosts' own, emerging when the host is stressed and unlikely to be able to launch an effective defensive.

BACTERIA

These organisms belong to a classification of living things called 'monera'. This group contains single-celled organisms that have a comparatively simple cell layout. Bacteria are the most diverse class of living thing on this planet—genetically speaking, the two most different organisms known to mankind are bacteria (i.e. in comparison, they have very few points of genetic similarity).

It is both the presence of a bacterial cell and the products of the bacteria's own metabolic processes that cause symptoms in an individual. Cholera, for instance, creates proteins that manipulate the cells in the lining of the intestine to leak fluid into the gastrointestinal tract (helps disseminate the bacteria into the environment through diarrhoea), while the very presence of the tuberculosis bacterium is enough to elicit an immune reaction responsible for the symptoms.

Bacteria have always been by far the easiest pathogen to control. This is because a) they possess a complex metabolism and b) that metabolism is unique to bacteria. Hence drugs that interrupt their metabolic processes will have little to no effect on the host. Many herbs and animal products possess antibacterial properties which mankind has taken advantage of. Honey, for instance, has been known since Egyptian times to have antibacterial and antifungal properties.

Transmission factors for bacteria are as diverse as those for viruses. The soil, bodies of water, animals, and plants all harbour a plethora of bacterial species pathogenic to humans. A few bacteria produce spores— small, robust capsules that contain the bacteria's genetic material and little to no water. Spores can last years, as they have no active metabolic processes that can be damaged. They can be frozen (no water means no damage due to ice crystals), heated (special 'heat shock proteins' help prevent damage), and even irradiated to a small degree without dire consequence. They are produced in times of stress, and can be 'revived' when conditions are once again favorable.

Pathogenic bacteria can also be found in individuals that otherwise express no symptoms. These 'carriers' can shed bacteria while they themselves remain unharmed. A perfect example of such a carrier was Irish cook Mary Mallon, who immigrated to New York in the late nineteenth century. A carrier of typhoid, 'Typhoid Mary', as she became known, unwittingly contaminated the food of the numerous families she worked for. In all she was responsible for three deaths and forty-seven cases of illness resulting from typhoid infection. Mary herself was unaffected.

FUNGI

As fungi are more closely related to humans than bacteria, diseases caused by them are somewhat more difficult to control. Their metabolism and cellular morphology are not all that dissimilar to those of their hosts, therefore there are few drugs available that can kill or stabilise a fungal infection. There are, luckily, very few types of fungi that are pathogenic to humans. Those that do establish themselves are usually commensal— they cause few or no problems as far as health goes. The most common cause of dandruff, for instance is a fungus—a case where the colonisation of a fungal organism has no effect on general health.

Those that do cause problems do so inadvertently through their metabolic bi-products (often changing the environment within the host enough to encourage a secondary infection such as a bacteria) or through the irritation they cause via their physical presence.

Most pathogenic fungi are 'opportunistic', in that they can exist in nature without infecting a host but often find an opportunity for nutrients in the presence of a host's body. Most of these feed on keratin (a substance present in hair, on fingernails, and on skin). Hence the sites where most pathogenic fungi tend to grow.

Fungi can transmit themselves through either spores or through pieces of fungal body. The most common sources of infection are other individuals or artefacts that have been in recent contact with an infected host (clothing, utensils etc.).

PROTOZOA

Protozoa literally means 'first animal'. They dominate most of the world's bodies of water in terms of number, however very few protozoans are pathogenic to humans. The ones that are include several species of filamentous worm, some amoeba and organisms such as plasmodium, the pathogen responsible for malaria.

To an even greater extent than with fungi, protozoa have very few metabolic quirks that can be attacked by drugs. Such is the reason why malaria remains one of the hardest diseases to control in the modern world.

In most cases, the symptoms arising from a protozoan infection is the direct, physical effect the organism has on the host. For instance, loa loa, a filarial worm that is transmitted through the bite of a small fly, can cause blindness as a result of its infestation of a host's eyeball. Malaria causes weakness through physically destroying the red blood cell it inhabits during early stages of development.

Transmission relies on either contact with a contaminated body of water, usually through ingestion, or through an infected intermediary vector such as a fly or mosquito. For these reasons, protozoan infections are often limited to tropical climates where temperature accommodates high rainfalls and larger numbers of animal vectors.

EXAMPLE DISEASES

The following are several examples of prominent historical diseases caused by pathogens. Take note of the symptoms if you wish to mention them in context within a story.

TYPHOID

Cause: Bacteria, *Salmonella typhi*
Transmission: Contaminated food and water.
Poor sanitation is often responsible for major outbreaks.
Symptoms: Prolonged bout of diarrhoea, fever over 40°C, head and joint pain, fatigue. The mortality rate in absence of any antibiotic therapy is 10—20%.
Significant Dates: Typhoid has been a menace since the early days of civilization due to poor management of human waste. It was finally recognized as a transmissible pathogen, as opposed to a

direct agent of poor water quality, in 1839 by William Budd.

Other: Often confused with 'typhus', the two have been interchangeable terms throughout much of history. The diseases themselves, however, are very different in cause, symptom and transmission. As strange as this is, such confusion has often been the case with a great many diseases through history, something that seriously complicates researching historical epidemics.

BLACK DEATH—BLACK PLAGUE, BUBONIC PLAGUE

Cause: The type of pathogen responsible is presently under debate. Formally accepted as the bacteria *Yersinia pestis*, new research suggests that this is a false assumption.

Transmission: Again, under review. Once understood to be causes by the transmission of *Yersinia pestis* through the bite of a flea carried by the black rat, *R.rattus*, recent research argues that historical epidemics of Black Death may have been caused instead by a filovirus, not unlike the disease 'Ebola'.

Symptoms: Varied depending on particular epidemic. However, common link of all Black Death plagues was the presence of dark colored, swollen 'buboes', or lymph glands, caused by the infection agent. Pustules, dark skin blemishes and fever also tend to be associated with historical epidemics.

Significant Dates: Multiple Black Death epidemics have raged through populations throughout history, although there are several eras of European pandemic that tend to stand out more than the others as being significant. Roman historian Livy recorded a number of epidemics in the Republic around the birth of Christ. There were multiple mentions of a disease resembling the Black Death throughout the west during the Dark Ages, the last being recorded in 767 A.D. Then, strangely, not a single plague of this nature was mentioned in any text for nearly 600 years. The next recorded epidemic came in the 1330's. From then on, there was a major bubonic plague roughly every ten years somewhere in Europe until 1720, with the last major outbreak in Marseille, France. Today, epidemics of Bubonic Plague refer only to *Yersinia pestis* outbreaks.

Other: Plague, from the Latin plaga meaning 'to strike and wound', is often synonymous with this disease. It is thought to have originated in the Chinese highlands sometime B.C., and to have been amongst the first epidemics known to mankind.

ST. ANTHONY'S FIRE—HIDDEN FIRE, DEVIL'S FIRE, HOLY FIRE, IGNIS SACER (SACRED FIRE), ERGOTISM (MODERN), ERYSIPELAS (MODERN)

Cause: fungus, *Claviceps purpurea*

Transmission: Consumption of the fungal body

Symptoms: Convulsive ergotism (affects the central nervous system)—anxiety, vertigo, hallucinatory sensations such as prickly skin, noises and stupor.

Gangrenous ergotism (caused by degeneration of blood vessels at the extremities)—described as sensation of ants running over extremities, followed by pain, blistering, redness, eventual blackening of flesh caused by the death of the limb.

Significant Dates: The 1692 Salem witch trials are one possible social manifestation of this disease. Caused by eating grain contaminated with the fungus, convulsive ergotism can give rise to symptoms like those exhibited by the accused. It is possible that ergot has been responsible for numerous cases of demonic 'possession' throughout history.

Other: As with many historical accounts of various diseases, there are several different conditions called St Anthony's Fire. This has made it difficult to pinpoint exactly what many of these conditions really were, leaving much open to speculation.

The fungus *Claviceps* contains a chemical that is similar to the drug LSD (lysergic acid diethylamide), or 'acid'. It causes hallucinations, and has been thought to be the basis for many legends such as the werewolf and other 'were' animals, where consumption of the contaminated grain gives the individual visual and sensory hallucinations.

SCROFULA—KING'S EVIL

Cause: bacteria, *Mycobacterium tuberculosis*

Transmission: consuming cow's milk that is contaminated with the bacteria is the most common method of infection. This same bacteria causes 'consumption' (tuberculosis of the lungs) when the bacterial particles are inhaled. Scrofula occurs when the bacteria infects a lymph gland, causing swelling to occur.

Symptoms: Scofula is essentially tuberculosis of the lymph gland that causes swelling. It is seldom fatal.

Other: It was believed in medieval times that scrofula could be cured by the touch of a member of the monarchy, most often the king. In a single year of his reign, England's King Edward I touched 1,736 individuals with the intention of curing them of this affliction, charging a penny per touch. Because symptoms rarely fail to resolve themselves over time, this act appeared to be truly miraculous.

LEPROSY—HANSON'S DISEASE

Cause: bacteria, *Mycobacterium leprae*

Transmission: Direct contact with an infected individual for prolonged periods, or direct contact with a transmission vector such as an article of clothing.

Symptoms: True leprosy (as opposed to other skin conditions called leprosy) gives rise to symptoms such as bad odour (from multiple secondary infections more than the leprosy itself), livid or black skin discolorations, lack of sensation at extremities, skin ulcers (again, secondary infections), and swollen mucosal tissue (eyelids, lips, tongue etc.).

Significant Dates: In 1179 the Third Lateran Council convened to make reforms to the religious bureaucracies of Christendom. It was declared that all lepers were to be identified and segregated from the rest of the community. The new laws ensured that individuals declared as 'lepers' were to alert others to their alleged condition by wearing identifying garments (a yellow cross and often a red sash), carry a noise-maker (a clapper), and bear a long stick for collecting alms (to avoid contaminating others).

Other: The word 'leprosy' historically refers to two things. One is what is mentioned above—Hanson's Disease. It is a difficult condition for a healthy person to contract. As an infection, it destroys nervous tissue at the extremities. The term 'leprosy' also refers to any one of a number of skin conditions, from acne to psoriasis to eczema. When first translating ancient Jewish texts such as Leviticus into Greek, early scholars adopted the word 'leper' from the Greek word 'lepra', referred to by Hippocrates as a 'white scaling of the skin'. This is the case, again, where the name of a disease is not necessarily a direct reference to a known pathogen. The use of the term 'leper' has more social connotations than medical ones. Keep that in mind.

SMALLPOX

Cause: virus, *Variola* (major and minor)

Transmission: Direct contact with an infected individual, inhalation of airborne particles (possible within several metres of infected host)

Symptoms: Massive numbers of small pustules, bouts of fever and severe muscle pain mark a smallpox infection. In the worst cases, haemorrhaging of major organs occurs. Smallpox pustules evolve through stages of development as they grow, die off and form scabs. New lesions are pink, middle-aged pustules are a darker color with white dots in the centre and dead pustules are covered with a dark-brown/black scab. Should the host survive, their skin is forever scarred with the pockmarks.

Significant Dates: During the late eighteenth century, physician Edward Jenner discovered something strange about certain individuals who underwent the process of variolation. This process involved artificially inoculating an individual with a disease through scratching pus from a smallpox blister into a person's skin, a practice brought to the western world by the wife of the British ambassador to Constantinople, Mary Wortley Montagu. The process actually gave the individual smallpox, yet the symptoms experienced that were not as severe (95%-98% of those who became infected with smallpox through variolation survived to have near miniscule chances of ever becoming infected again). Jenner, however, noticed that this method of variolation did not give rise to any smallpox symptoms at all in patients that had contracted cowpox at some point during their lives. He proposed that using pus from a victim of smallpox was not necessary to give an individual protection against the disease—rather, cowpox or a similar contagion could give the same response. This was the first step towards providing the public with a safe form of vaccination (word vaccination from vacca, meaning cow).

Other: Smallpox is so-called due to the nature of its pustules in comparison with 'great pox', or syphilis. Variola major had a death rate as high as 30% in the west, and much greater in susceptible populations such as the indigenous of America and Australia. Smallpox has a history that reaches back to the dawn of civilization. The mummified remains of Egyptian pharaohs have been found to bare the signature scars of smallpox infections.

Typhus—War Fever, Ship's Fever, Jail Fever, Camp Fever, Fleckfieber, Tabardillo

Cause: Bacteria, *Rickettsia prowazekii* (not to be confused with 'rickets', a disease caused by vitamin D deficiency in children).

Transmission: The bacteria are passed on through the human body louse, Pediculus corporis, and sometimes the head louse, Pediculus capitalis. Other forms of typhus are spread via the bites of fleas and mites.

Symptoms: A high fever coupled with a distinctive rash. The rash has earned typhus the names Fleckfieber (spotted fever) in German and Tabardillo (red cloak) in Spanish.

Significant Dates: It is generally accepted that circa 1490 is the time when typhus first arrived in Europe (although descriptions of a disease not unlike typhus appeared in Greece in 430 B.C., in an event called The Plague of Athens). Usually bound with war (hence the title War Fever), typhus raged in violent epidemics through the midst of camping armies. During one historical campaign where the Iberians attempted to remove the Moors from the Spanish peninsula, 17,000 Spaniard soldiers died of typhus while camped at Gianada. That was six times the number of casualties who died during the war. Such catastrophes have occurred numerous times throughout history, often deciding the outcome of the war itself.

Other: Typhus comes from the Greek, typhos, meaning 'stupor', or 'mad'. Typhoid, drawn from the same Greek word, was often confused with typhus, in spite of the many differences.

SYPHILIS—THE GREAT POX, MORBUS GALLICUS (FRENCH POX), DISEASE OF NAPLES

Cause: Bacteria, *Treponema pallidum*

Transmission: The first disease to be declared 'venereal' (from Venus, the goddess of love), syphilis is transferred primarily through bodily fluids.

Symptoms: The symptoms occur in three stages, with periods of 'latency' in between each stage.

Stage 1) The incubation period of roughly three weeks between infection and first symptoms. A painless chancre (small lesion) appears at the site of infection (almost always a mucous membrane). This remains for about a month before healing completely. Three weeks pass in a period of latency.

Stage 2) A rash of lesions appear over the body's surface (occasionally on internal organs as well), accompanied by fatigue, and perhaps a fever. These symptoms again disappear after a few weeks, sometimes returning briefly once or twice in subsequent months.

Stage 3) In populations with a historical exposure to syphilis, the third stage occurs in only 30% of sufferers. The symptoms marking this stage often don't appear until a few years have passed since stage 2. The rash of lesions experienced in stage 2 revisit the host in vast numbers, often striking vital internal organs, and even appearing on bone. Death occurs as a result of organ failure, or from lesions attacking the nervous system.

Significant Dates: In 1493 King Charles VIII launched an offensive against Spain to gain control of the kingdom of Naples (then under Spanish influence). His forces were so ravaged by syphilis that he was forced to withdraw and admit defeat. A large proportion of the soldiers, many of them mercenaries from all over Europe, returned to their homelands with the disease. The name 'Disease of Naples' and 'French Pox' came from this.

Other: Syphilis has always had connotations of being a whore's disease. Passed amongst the noble classes and the gentry, it was both viewed as a curse against the immoral and a physical manifestation of the sin of lust. Many hundreds of essays, papers and commentaries have been written about this disease over the centuries. Due to its sinful reputation and its outward appearance, syphilis has been the focus for the talents of medical quacks and charlatans through the centuries out after a quick buck. These pseudo-physicians touted Mercury salves and steam baths as the only cure, although vitriol and arsenic were also prescribed in large doses.

INFLUENZA—GRIPPE

Cause: Virus, *Influenza*

Transmission: Airborne particles and direct contact with body fluid from an infected host.

Symptoms: Sore throat, excess mucus production, fever, aching joints, chills, headache, fatigue.

Significant Dates: As influenza has a short incubation period of roughly two days, and a high transmission rate, this pathogen has been one of the few to achieve pandemic (wide range epidemic) status. Although the death rate is only about 1% (usually very young and very old, from complications such as inflammation of the brain or pneumonia), its high infection rate means millions of people can die during a single pandemic. Although ancient texts may indicate possible epidemics, the first written account was arguably 1512 in Europe. During the early twentieth century, more people died from the post Great War influenza pandemic than in the war itself.

Other: Influenza received its name during the eighteenth century, when scholars deduced that the symptoms were caused by the astrological 'influence' of the heavens. It has always been seen as a rather innocuous disease. However, due to an absence of historical exposure in their populations, it wiped out vast numbers of indigenous people in America, Australia and the Pacific islands.

For this reason, coupled with the observation that many animals such as ducks and pigs appear to be vectors of the disease, it is thought that influenza has been around ever since mankind first started farming many millennia ago.

PREGNANCY

Although it is not a disease (in spite of the presence of a rather powerful parasite called a 'foetus'), pregnancy and the issues surrounding it deserve to be mentioned here, if for no other reason than to alert you to its importance in the history of health and medicine.

Two things happened to *Homo sapiens* in its endeavour to becoming an intelligent, bipedal animal—it stood upright and its head grew in size to accommodate a larger brain. These two advantages, unfortunately, came at a cost.

To accommodate bipedal movement, early humans born with more robust pelvises and narrow hips had an advantage over their relatives. Narrow hips meant an ability to stand upright for longer periods and more control over a bipedal gait. At the same time, a change in environment meant there was a greater opportunity for intelligent individuals to be favored—hence those with 'bigger heads' became the breeders of next generation's children.

Such narrow hips on the mother and a big head on the offspring meant it was incredibly difficult for both of them when it came to the birthing process. Female humans have more problems of a more serious nature than any other animal when it comes to childbirth. Sadly, this is one realm where medicine has in the past done more harm than good.

Until the nineteenth century, it had been widely accepted across most of the world that the male was the one who bore the sole responsibility for passing on the genes. The sperm had always been the seed (sperm actually means just this) and the woman was simply the field (hence terms like 'barren' and 'fertile' were never used in conjunction with a man). The woman, as a field, could influence the growth of the child through what she ate and what she did, but the child was essentially the product of the father. This analogy has been around since biblical times, and remains ensconced in world culture in spite of new knowledge. This is important when noting familiarity in the features of a child—nobody in the Middle Ages would comment 'he has his mother's eyes'. This obviously just did not happen.

Interestingly, with the advent of the microscope it was exclaimed that a human 'homunculus' (a little man) could be seen inside the head of the sperm. Woodcuts from the seventeenth century show this in detail. It is a perfect example of subjectivity in science, where assumption dictated the interpretation of an observation.

Before this time it was unimaginable that a man who was capable of ejaculating could also be infertile. Women determined as barren who fell pregnant to other men were often executed as witches (not to mention as adulterers!).

I alluded to the fact earlier that the mother's actions had an indirect effect on the development of the child. It was believed for centuries, and still is in some folklore, that a child's appearance was a direct result of what the mother saw during gestation. It was improper, therefore, for a mother to go to a zoo when pregnant, in case her child took on the characteristics of a monkey, a giraffe, or worse still (as exclaimed by Joseph Merrick, the infamous Elephant Man, of the actions of his own mother) something a touch more disfiguring. Flowers and beautiful artwork was the order for mothers during the eighteenth century, while in ancient Greece they would gaze upon marble statues in an effort to give their unborn children god-like bodies.

I mentioned that childbirth is one field where medicine has done more harm than good. Once, only other women could be present during the birth. As physicians became more respected members of society (late eighteenth to early nineteenth century), they looked on the lucrative business of midwifery and ironically declared that it was not a realm for the uneducated. Obstetrics became a new field for physicians who had previously had little to do with the unique aspects of the female body. The invention of the forceps became the ultimate 'weapon' for these doctors in the early 1800's—difficult births could be remedied easily with this tool, something midwives had no access to. It slowly came to the point where mothers were discouraged from being in control of the procedure, allowing the doctor to deliver the child unaided, as such. Chloroform was used in the late nineteenth century (Queen Victoria herself used it during the birth of one of her children), further diminishing the role of the mother during the procedure. Reclining back on a bench to allow greater access to the womb (something called the 'lithotomy position', since it was the exact position used to remove kidney stones) enabled the doctor to 'remove' the infant more than enabling the mother to deliver the child naturally. Where once intervention was a worst-case procedure, by the twentieth century it had become an 'all-case' procedure, often for the worse.

Only now is the wider profession slowly recognising this.

However, not all is doom and gloom for modern medicine. Throughout ancient times, indeed up until Frenchman Jean-Jacque Rousseau's controversial publication 'Emile' in 1762, swaddling newborns was touted as being the only way to prevent spasticity in children. Swaddling was the process of binding babies tightly in bandages to prevent movement. It was thought the uncontrolled 'flailing' of infants needed to be discouraged early for proper motor-skill development. Rousseau proposed that children needed to get back to nature as early as possible and argued against this practice. Today it is an almost barbaric thought to subject a baby to such a condition.

Please make note of this fact—it is a myth that most people during the Middle Ages did not live past fifty. In fact, the majority of people, including the commoners, lived well into their sixties and seventies, with a large number making it into their eighties and older. The misunderstanding arises when you fail to take into account the inflated infant mortality rate. If there are twenty people born in any one year, and ten of them die at childbirth, while the other ten live until they are one-hundred years old, the average life-span of this small population is fifty years old (average age of ten one hundred-year-olds and ten zero-year-olds). Hence it does not mean that few lived past fifty.

All of this information might play a role in the design of your various races, or of certain communities, within your fantasy world. Pay heed to this when you read the chapter on race creation. Maybe your elf has a small head, and childbirth is an uncomplicated matter. Or your halfling birth is regarded with fear for the mother, who rarely survives such an ordeal. Perhaps the development of the baby is influenced by the presence of a chosen 'soul-mate', who is selected to remain with the child until puberty. Regardless, paying attention to details such as these can turn a simple, boring creature into an amazing character that readers will want to know more about.

THE HUMAN BODY

It seems like a strange irony that in this modern era of safety and technology, injury is proportionately responsible for more deaths this century than in any other time in history (including during those unsafe times in the great Industrial Revolution). But then again, if you consider that today the motor vehicle claims countless lives worldwide, and medicine is decreasing the number of disease-related deaths every year, it is maybe not such an amazing fact.

This is not to say humans were any stronger, or resilient, in the past. The nature of the injuries, and the types of mishap, however, would have usually related directly to what the individuals had exposed themselves to in their line of profession. Those in the industry of agriculture would risk injury from their tools (axes, adzes, hoes), herders from their livestock, tanners from the chemicals in their workshop...and so on. Aside from the impact of war (which still had little effect on the statistics when it came to injury related death), it was not until the industrial revolution that injury started to rate a mention in a population's mortality rate.

Most injury, when suffered, was rarely fatal. Wounds tended to heal well enough on their own, if kept relatively clean. Numerous bodies excavated from the past show fractured bones that have healed, while ancient mummified remains from as far back as early Egypt show healed scars of hideous wounds, many with signs of suturing. What often killed the unfortunate soul was therefore not the wound itself but the infection caused by an opening in the skin. During times of war, very few soldiers died as a result of a blow to their bodies. Indeed, weapons were not designed to kill outright (see chapter on combat and weapons). It was the infection that followed that often leads to an early grave. The next most common cause of death due to an injury was internal injury. This led to haemorrhaging that, if undetected, would allow the patient to bleed to death from the inside.

When injury was suffered, it was in the hands of the surgeon to set things right. Although I mentioned earlier that it was essentially the barber who handled all matters surgical, at least until the sixteenth century, this was not always the case. While it is indeed true that barbers represented the majority of surgical practitioners, there were devoted surgeons throughout the Middle Ages who studied the mechanics of the human body, men who kept alive the Greco-Roman medical practices in spite of the religious condemnation of their day.

The medieval medical school of Salerno held out against ecclesiastic influence in spite of the presence of a monastery at nearby Monte Cassino. Gaining prominence late in the tenth century, this school was open to both male and female scholars and based its teachings on the surviving anatomical writings of ancient Greece and Rome. It was the reason why Hippocrates continued to be such an influence on medicine at the time.

Other centres of learning, such as Verona, Bologna, Naples and Montpellier, further increased the field of learning in human anatomy and surgery. Note most of these are Mediterranean cities—the world respected the learning that came from this area. Surgeon Guglielmo Salicetti wrote perhaps the most magnificent text of the entire period of medieval surgery in 1296. Titled Cyrurgia Magna, it detailed everything from setting bones, to care of hair and face, to blood letting, amputation, cauterisation and even, believe it or not, cosmetic surgery on breasts and face.

While such surgery was crude, it worked often enough to be continued through the centuries. Quite a few basic beliefs of the time, while incorrect, survived well into the nineteenth century. It was believed that a wound without pus was one that would not heal. Pus was seen as necessary— hence a wound could smell wrong if it was not infected. Not until Joseph Lister came along was this view challenged, and even then had difficulty changing centuries of belief.

It comes as little surprise to us today that aspects of anatomy and the role organs play in the health and functioning of an individual was so misunderstood. With the ban on dissecting cadavers, and with the risk inherited in operating on a living person, there was no room for anatomical exploration. Those operating during the Middle Ages had to rely on roughly drawn manuscripts which had simple explanations, basic sketches and a great deal of myth surrounding them.

English physician William Harvey, for instance, did not discover the role the heart played in the circulation of blood, until the seventeenth century. Before this point, most scholars accepted the fact that blood circulated either as a result of the effect various spirits had on it (animal spirits given in the heart, and vital spirits in the brain, as per the Greek physician Galen), or via the heating of blood by the heart (which accordingly acted as a furnace). This is not to say that Harvey was the first to propose a model for the cardio-pulmonary system—as early as the twelfth century Muslim Ibn-an-Nafis proposed that the blood moved through the heart and lungs as part of its journey. Harvey, however, first published the mechanics.

Other organs were given strange roles at various times in history. The liver made the blood, according to Galen in the second century A.D.. Alcmaeon, in ancient Greece, proposed that the brain inspired sleep when filled with blood, and awake when blood was removed. Strange as that may seem, it was closer to the truth than the other purpose of the brain held by scholars of his day—to produce semen! (For what purpose women then had a brain, one can only imagine.)

During the Middle Ages, many thought the brain was a radiator for the blood, intended to cool it during its journey, while other organs moderated the balance of humours.

An unusual concept that also dated from ancient Greece (and is still, believe it or not, believed by a select few in this day and age) regarded the functioning of sight. It was thought that a sort of 'fire', originating in the eye, radiated out towards an object in focus to result in vision. This 'reverse seeing', where sight is caused by something that comes out of the viewer, was cited often through history, and was not dispelled until the first principles of 'optics' were proposed in the early seventeenth century.

As you see, what we take for granted as basic biology in this modern age has not always been the case. Ethics surrounding experimentation on human life have, for better or for worse, had an impact on history's understanding of the body's functions. This is important when referring to what knowledge a person may have in a society where understanding is basic, due to a reliance on ethics. Likewise, a society with little regard for the value of a human life, or the ethics surrounding it, may have greater knowledge of how a body functions. Keep this in mind when creating a background for your fabricated community.

Health & Medicine in A Make-Believe World

This chapter has offered little more than a cursory glance at the nature of disease and its place in history. I have left out a great deal, either intentionally or accidentally, from the areas covered. The advent of anaesthesia, forms of alternative medicine, ancient Chinese medicine, female sanitation (and the fabulous 'floating uterus')—as I said at the beginning, I could go on forever. Yet providing you with boundless numbers of facts and figures has not been the aim behind the chapter.

The intent has been less to inform and more to inspire you, as a writer, to consider your fantasy world as a warped reflection of the real world. I hope the information here has been enough to give you a starting point to base some research on.

I'm sure the following question has played on your mind at least once so far—'Why should this matter in my fantasy world?'

This is a valid question. 'Why?' indeed. Who cares if you are writing about a hamlet situated in a pseudo-English, medieval, high-fantasy setting and you say, 'everybody in the village noticed that the child had his mother's eyes', or, 'Arnulf tapped his finger against his temple and said, 'I think real good with my brain'? In your fantasy world, this might actually be the case, right? Fair enough.

However, let me answer you in this way—a little bit of knowledge about such a thing as disease or the concepts surrounding basic biological functions in history can a) enhance the sense of reality surrounding your story and b) prevent the reader from being turned off through an anachronism. You might be writing fantasy, but you still want the reader to feel a connection with your world in order for them to be able to 'escape' into it. Good fantasy is like a pair of worn slippers that are not their usual color—comfortable to slip into, but a little different to what you are used to. Showing ignorance is a fast way to disconnect the reader from your fabricated realm, no matter how well written it is.

So how far do you go? There is no strict answer to this, unfortunately. It is up to you. After all, if you slip up and say, 'Arnulf's skin still bore the scars from his bout of typhoid', how many readers will truly care (or even know) that typhoid does not give any visible scars? 5%? Less?

The next question is, 'Are you comfortable with that number?'

You do not have to remain completely faithful to historical accuracy if you do not want to. After all, unless you are doing alternative history or basing your story in a factual setting, they might have actually employed modern-type obstetrics in your twelfth century medieval setting. To go further with this example, it is not important for you, as a writer, to necessarily address your anachronism by saying 'Arnulf's orcish wife was lying flat on the bed, patiently awaiting the doctor's arrival, as had been detailed by the late master physician, Doctor Hasan, in his doctrine 'Orcs and Giving Birth—The New Obstetrics.' Yet just by being aware of the difference between your world and the real world will influence the design of your creation to make it more of a tangible realm of possibility than a simple, make-believe story.

SUMMARY

Fantasy is about making stuff up. Let's not get too technical here— writing in a genre such as this is about creating new things in order to have a reader experience something different to their everyday lives. Maybe it is for pure escapism, perhaps you are making a social comment. But it cannot be forgotten that no matter the reason behind why you are writing it, fantasy fiction is about something that is essentially not real.

That said, readers must still be able to associate with the picture you are painting. Even if your entire world is completely fabricated, there has to remain a sense of reality to act as a bridge between your world and the reader's. If that bridge is shoddy, people will not feel comfortable crossing it. Everybody makes assumptions when they read script in a given context. It is up to you, the writer, to anticipate to the best of your ability the assumptions that will be made by the reader about your work.

The issue of health and medicine has been a constant pressure on the evolution of human society since our ancestors loped across the African plains on all fours. It forms a strong part of our cultural psyche and has influenced everything across the globe from our cuisine to our poisons, our science to our art, our communal wishes to our collective fears. Knowing a little bit about it can make all the difference between a tale that is merely interesting and an epic that is absolutely fascinating.

BIBLIOGRAPHY

I highly recommend the following texts:

Blainey, G., (2000), *A Short History of the World*, Viking Press, Victoria, Australia

Kiple, K.F. (Ed), (1997), *Plague, Pox and Pestilence: Disease in History*, Phoenix Illustrated, London

Lyons, A.S., Petrucelli, R.J., (1987) *Medicine: An Illustrated History*, Abradale Press, New York

Root-Bernstein, R., Root-Bernstein, M., (1997), *Honey Mud Maggots and Other Medical Marvels*, Macmillan, New York

Magic

Tom Dullemond

*"Any sufficiently advanced technology is
indistinguishable from magic."*
—Arthur C. Clarke

Introduction

Magic is an inextricable part of fantasy—be it a heroic romp through the
woods to defeat an ancient wizard with your mystical blade, a simple downtown
suburb where the neighbors lurk in strange shadows, or a highly advanced
technological society whose citizens teleport with hardly a thought.

Magic is arguably the common theme that binds all of fantasy literature
together—if not literal magic, then a sense of wonder and immersion in
a fantasy environment. For practical purposes, however, this chapter
will focus on literal magic. Although other chapters in this book will
invariably deal with magic in their own way—magic being as integral to
fantasy writing as it is—this chapter will analyse magic and the impact of

magic on your fantasy world, denizens, wars, and societies.

You'll see how fundamental factors of magic in your society—scarcity, difficulty, and price—affect the kind of 'workable' or 'believable' societies that can exist in your world. If everyone has access to cheap, easy magic, why would anyone need a wagon, or ride a horse?

This chapter is divided into two parts—the first will introduce a tool to help define the magical properties of a fantasy society, and the second will discuss both the impacts of magic on society and some basic 'types' of magic.

By the end of the chapter you should feel confident enough to step into your fantasy world without fear of being overwhelmed by technical questions such as, 'Why are your evil wizards still using swords when the Skull of Garghul gives them all the offensive power they could possibly need?'

This chapter is not intended to define magic, but rather to refine your understanding of its almost limitless power in fantasy literature—and to give you an understanding of how to write about your realistic magical worlds or societies.

SECTION ONE—SO DAMN POWERFUL!

The presence of Magic has a greater impact on society than we can possibly imagine, living in our mundane little world. We have no direct experience of true 'magical' effects, and so when we wish to write about a magical society we need to examine several important factors to help define our framework—completely separate from whether a wizard needs to wave a wand and mumble his grandmother's secret name. Without at least a basic framework, the power of magic may unbalance our world and make it far more difficult to create the kind of conflict from which great stories are made.

This is a little system I devised for my own writing, and one I will share with you now. It's a quick and simple little tool that looks at three factors of magic: scarcity, difficulty, and price. Any magic system can be said to fall on a point somewhere in a big three-dimensional space, with 'Scarcity 0, Difficulty 0, Price 0' in one corner and 'Scarcity 10, Difficulty 10, Price 10' in the opposite corner. The bigger the rating, the more powerful, rare, wonderful (and perhaps terrifying) that magic is perceived to be in your society.

So what does all this mean, and is this some crazy *Dungeons & Dragons*™ derivative? I'm a writer, not a role-player!

The SDP method is a tool that can be used to analyse the magical 'rules' (or lack thereof) that you've created, and help you consider the impact of magic on your society. 'So Damn Powerful' is merely a little mnemonic to help me memorise the three factors, since the higher the rating, the more impressive a magical feat appears to be in your society. With that information you can adjust your magical system to fit your desired society better, or your society to fit your desired magical system. Here is a brief explanation followed by some examples.

S IS FOR SCARCITY

The scarcity of magic in your society is an indication of the number of people who have access to magic, and whether or not they have the materials or skills to use it once they have access to it. If a dictator has confiscated all the Holy Statues of Aliria the Love Goddess, for example, and these were the only way to use magic, then the scarcity of magic in your society would increase significantly, irrespective of the ease of using the statues to access the magic.

A society where magic is plentiful (Scarcity 0) will be a society where every single facet of life can potentially be tinged by magic. Regardless of the Difficulty or Price attached to using or activating this magic, this level of scarcity indicates a society completely composed of and infiltrated with magic. It is not, however, an indication of those who know about magic or those who practice magic. A society with a magic scarcity of 0 is a place where every single person has access to magic, but they may not know it exists, or be able to use it. The key factor is the population's access—Scarcity indicates the potential of every person to 'do' magic. A society where every person has a magical talisman to remain linked to 'the source of all magic' would be a good example.

Conversely, a society with a Scarcity of 10 is a place where magic can only be found in the rarest of places, times, or people. The perfect example is a common ploy in fantasy—the Chosen One, a unique individual who has magical powers. Another example would be a single well of magical energy, found only in the deepest, darkest belly of ancient underground ruins. Or perhaps a magical power that only manifests when the three moons align above the left tower of the Castle of Doom, which only appears in our world once every thousand years.

Scarcity is an indication of the difficulty of accessing a source of magic, be it internally or through some external device, of a random individual in the population.

D IS FOR DIFFICULTY

This determines how difficult it is for an individual, once he or she has gained access to a source of magic, to learn how to use that magic. Difficulty is simply an indication of how hard it is to use or control the magic to produce a specific effect once all required components (times, sacrifices, songs, etc) are in place.

A Difficulty of 0 is a society where, once an individual has access to magic (dependant on Scarcity) and has acquired the necessary ingredients or made the sacrifices (dependant on Price), a mere thought is sufficient to manifest the magical effect. There is absolutely no training required—any ignorant peasant or child can perform magic. Clearly, a society where Scarcity and Difficulty are 0 is one where anyone has the ability to access magic, and the capacity to use it at will. Whether they do so or not is entirely dependent on the third factor, Price.

A Difficulty of 10 is a society where, once an individual has access to magic, the chance of successfully using this magic for the purpose they intend is almost nil. Decades of training, inhuman precision, or absolute gruelling luck are required for the magician's desire to be made manifest. This may involve the etching of perfect patterns, singing of beautiful songs, expert timing, or perfect concentration on the desired result—who knows? For whatever reason, it's just exceedingly difficult to use magic, regardless of the Scarcity or Price.

Of course, this may not necessarily mean that nothing happens when a caster attempts to use magic. Magic might still be easy to use—just impossible to control.

P IS FOR PRICE

Ah, yes—the price of magic. It might be easy to access magic and it might be easy to use it. But what is the price of using it? Do you go mad? Must you sacrifice your youth? Is it wealth or rare ingredients, or something more sinister? Is using magic punishable by death? Or will the commoners merely come to your house to burn it to the ground? The cost of accessing and using magic is indicated by the value of the Price factor.

A Price of 0 means that, once an individual has gained access to a source of magic, and has learnt how to use it, they can do so with no ill effect whatsoever—no social, mental, or physical repercussions will follow from their displays of magic. In a society where the Price of magic is not an issue, those individuals who have access to it and the skill to use it have no reason not to use it. Once they have mastered their art (regardless of the Scarcity of magic or the Difficulty of using it), they will not need to think twice about wanting to use their powers.

A Price of 10 is extreme—the ultimate cost. Using magic in this society would generally cost you your life. A caster might be condemned to death for using magic in public, or the magical energies released might cast the soul from his body or burn him to a crisp. When the Price of magic is this great, magic, no matter how low the Scarcity or Difficulty, is a rare occurrence indeed.

Bear in mind that all this is relative—if your society is in the grip of a religion that does not value personal life, then magic that consumes the body is not such a great price. A greater price might be the defilement of your religion's holy symbols. Essentially, a Price of 10 is a cost that few in your society would be willing to pay.

WHAT DOES ALL THIS MEAN?

What this means is that you can use the SDP method to outline a magical society instantly, almost at random. It's a tool for creativity that lets you make some assumptions about how magic might be viewed in a particular society. When it comes down to it, Scarcity, Difficulty and Price are all factors relative to the average person in your society. Therefore, whenever a magical event happens in your society, you can use these factors to work out roughly what that average person would think, or how they would react.

OK, that's great, but now that I know what this tool is, how do I use it?

Here's where we get to the meat and bones. You can use SDP as a starting point to your magical universe.

Let's try some ratings and see what kinds of fantasy universes they inspire.

SDP OF 5, 5, 5

This is a good middle range, so what might it mean? Well, a Scarcity of 5 would suggest that a significant portion of the people in this society (let's say half for argument's sake) have access to magic, or an affinity to magic that allows them to use it. This could mean that there are two races in your society, and that one is innately magical. Because the difficulty is also 5, we can also say that at the most, half of the magical race is trained in the use of magic. A price of 5 indicates that those who are wizards must pay a formidable price for the use of their powers. Let's say their senses are overloaded and useless for a period of time after they use their magic and that this period of sensory deprivation has driven some wizards to madness.

Now this is only one possible configuration for this SDP rating, but one that allows us to establish a magical civilisation quickly. How do people of the magical race react to wizards in their midst—those highly trained individuals who must sacrifice so much and risk insanity when they use their power? And worse, how do those of the unmagical race react? If someone uses magic, one thing is certain—the onlookers will be impressed and most likely fearful of this power, but aware that the practitioner is likely to be weak and helpless after their exertion. And what if someone in the unmagical race was to use a wizard's power?

SDP OF 10, 10, 10

This is very extreme. In one possible interpretation of these numbers, no one but perhaps a single individual in this society has magic. The individual may never gain the skills or knowledge required to use her innate power, and when she does, she will most likely destroy herself and all she holds dear. Hooray.

An alternate interpretation is a society where magic is plentiful and accessible through magical amulets, but highly unpredictable. A single benevolent king has confiscated all magical conduits, because mastering the magic is near impossible—experimentation by those not skilled enough has resulted in terrible accidents that have taken the lives of hundreds of innocent citizens. Even those very few who have mastered the magic do so at the cost of their fragile bodies. The true masters discard their bodies when they cast their spells, and let their souls inhabit new bodies. Anyone found using magic is trapped in special soul-cages and killed on sight.

Now let's examine this for a moment.

Until the king confiscated everyone's amulets, maybe half the population had access to these amulets that granted magical power. The scarcity might have been 5, then. The gathering of the amulets under one king, however, explains the current scarcity of 10. Similarly, before magic was outlawed, the self-destructive nature of using magic might have meant a price of 7—remembering that the soul is not destroyed, so the caster does not pay the ultimate price. With the outlawing of magic, however, magic is now penalised by death of the soul, not just the body. This explains the adjustment to a price of 10.

You can see how without much planning at all, we've been able to conjure up a society, a basic system of magic and legal repercussions for any characters living in this world.

Remember that the higher your society's SDP rating, the more impressed or afraid a casual bystander would be when an individual creates a magical effect, independent of the actual power of the spell. A candle flame appearing on the end of someone's fingers in a society where magic is very Scarce would result in loud laughter and disbelief, or terrible fear and a desire to retreat, since the watchers wouldn't know about magic. If magic were also very difficult, then even those who did know about it would be impressed. And of course, if the Price of magic were great enough, even those unimpressed by the difficulty of a magical feat would be astounded at its mere appearance. That is, if they didn't disintegrate you on sight with the King's Witchfinder Wand of Death in order to collect the bounty on your head.

SDP OF 0, 0, 0

A magical world where everyone can access magic, anyone can use magic, and magic costs nothing.

This is a bizarre, free-for-all universe limited only by the power of the magical effects you allow. If magic in your society is merely the ability to create fire at varying strengths, then with this SDP rating every member in that society, from the youngest baby to the most withered Old One, will be able to do so, and will do so, as there are no social, mental, or physical repercussions. A society like this would quite possibly have advanced metallurgy or manufacturing (or cooking) skills, since the acquisition of heat sources is instant and limitless.

Also note that the Price rating of 0 indicates that not even a fuel source is required for this fire (else 'wood' or 'coal' might be a needed component and the price would go to 1 or more, depending on the rarity of this material).

SDP OF 0, 0, 7

This might be the above society, but with the added requirement of an extremely rare fuel source. Perhaps this race of wizards is stone-bound, living only in chthonian caverns, and there is no wood to burn—perhaps the magical skill is fading with the generations, ever since they were vanquished to the caves by their archenemies, the water-weirds, who live in swampy woodlands. And your heroes have to free their people before the magic is entirely lost.

SUMMARY—YOUR MAGICAL SOCIETY

A magical society's structure is highly dependent on several important factors, some of which relate to how magic is accessed, used, and paid for. I've refined this into the SDP ratings scheme used above, but its sole purpose is to help you flesh out your magical society. Pick three ratings values at random and try to build a society to match it—the options are limitless.

In the next section we will have a look at some examples of magical systems and the corresponding impacts on the world in which they exist.

SECTION TWO: WHAT MAGIC CAN DO FOR YOU

Contrary to the heading, this section is not about making your life easier by magicking that winning lottery ticket into your pocket. If I could do that, I wouldn't be writing this chapter.

What we need to examine in this section is how your magical world affects the logic of your world. If magic is fairly accessible, to the extent that many larger villages might have a 'wise man' with magical powers, you really need to extend the influence of those powers logically into the past.

For example, let's argue that your fantasy world is based culturally on late medieval England except that wizards exist and sell their not-inconsiderable skills to the highest bidder. In a world where magic is moderately powerful and available, it is a replacement for—or, at worst, a supplement to—technology and skilled human labour.

Who needs a translator if a wizard can weave a translation spell or hand you a magical amulet that will translate every word you hear?

Not only does this world make the job of translator obsolete, it might not even know what a translator is, not ever having had a need for one. Perhaps only the poor use human labour for this kind of menial task, since the rich all have mystical artefacts to provide the same service.

Who needs a wagon if a wizard can magically transport your goods into your warehouse?

Indeed—and who needs oxen or horses as beasts of ongoing financial burden if magic can provide this service? I guess we'll just eat the horses then. Hors d'oeuvres, anyone?

Who needs a castle if a wizard can turn the stones to mud beneath your feet?

TYPES OF MAGIC

Magic needs a means of being accessed. You need to know how a wizard casts their spells. Do they merely have to think about something to make it happen? Do they ask their god to do the magic for them? I've identified five basic types of 'methods' used in modern fantasy literature to create magic. Although the boundaries between these methods are sometimes wafer thin, they help to classify magic use somewhat.

'HOLY JOE' WIZARDS

This kind of magic is the domain of priests and religious types. The magical effect is provided for a nominal charge (several candles lit at a certain time of day; a rosary of prayers; the burning, still-beating hearts of unbelievers, etc) and the magician is a conduit for this divine (or unholy) power. The type of spells and effects this kind of wizard produces is dependent on the nature of the god, gods or spirits providing the magical effect. The success of these spells, however, is entirely up to the deity involved.

The defining characteristic for this kind of magic is that an external supernatural being is wholly responsible for producing the magic.

'GREEN THUMB' WIZARDS

Magic from the ground and plants. It can be considered a sub-type of the 'Holy Joe' wizard if the source is an 'earth-mother' or similarly distributed deity.

Mary Gentle has an excellent non-traditional example of this kind of magic in her novel *Rats & Gargoyles*, where the generally despised Tree-priests can heal with a touch, channel life-energy and become surrounded by the scents and sounds of nature as they do so—a stark contrast to her world's otherwise urban miasma.

'Green Thumb' magic relies on the presence of living plants and animals, or a 'living' earth, to provide a magical life energy to perform magical effects. *Star Wars'* 'The Force' is a good example, though it borders onto the next category of 'One Power' wizards (below).

'Green Thumb' Wizards of this kind can often be found congregating in forests, and spend lots of time communing with nature and smoking pipe-weed. Sometimes backwards they must speak.

'I Wanna' or 'One Power' wizards

These wizards simply 'will' something into being, and it happens (depending on their skill and willpower, of course). David Eddings has his magical heroes use the Will and the Way—a glorified version of really, really, really wanting something to happen. Robert Jordan's *The Wheel of Time* series has his magicians tap into a pool of magical energy to weave their spells—girls get the clean pool in which to stamp their feet and tug their braids, while boys get the dirty pool and generally go insane. Countless other writers use variations on this One Power method of magic, and it is a tried and true trope of Fantasy writing.

Generally, the prestige and power of this kind of magic is determined by scarcity—only chosen people or specially bred individuals have access to these limitless sources of energy, and their training allows them to bend this energy directly to their will.

'One Power' wizards are usually limited by several factors: their strength of will, the price of using magic (as in Robert Jordan's world, where male wizards go insane), or the difficulty of their craft. However, once these factors have been conquered, they merely need to think in order to 'do' magic.

'Pattern' wizards

A very general definition of those wizards, whose magical effects are generated through specific rituals, patterns, songs, or runes. Regardless of where the magical energy comes from, these magicians can't simply wish for a spell to be cast, or pick from a list of alternate futures (see Kewpie wizards below). They have to spend a lot of time picking the right herbs, mixing them up, and drinking potions. Alternatively, they might spend a lot of time singing, dancing, or waving their hands—the distinction between a drunk and a pattern wizard is that the drunk has to try an awful lot harder to bring the house down.

It is clear there is some overlap here, especially with the 'Holy Joe' wizards. If you really need to know exactly into which category a wizard falls, simply find out what is more important to the success of the magic: whether the rituals are executed correctly (Pattern), or whether the god is watching (Holy Joe).

'QUANTUM PHYSICS' OR 'KEWPIE' (QP) WIZARDS

This breed of magicians is a more recent phenomenon, extending the science of quantum uncertainty up from the world of photons and electrons to our macroscopic world. This magic relies on the conceit that large objects (eg. cats) are capable of existing in many states at once, much like quantum particles. Since we only see one of these states at any time, the author postulates that there is a constant splitting of reality into parallel universes, one for every possible state/event that could happen. The wizard's ability to influence which alternate branch he/she will follow is what creates seemingly magical effects. Need the roof to collapse to make your escape? Simply flick through your Rolodex of possible futures to find one where the roof did collapse, then make sure that your consciousness continues in that world.

Quantum Physics wizards are often used to inject a bit of science into a novel or story dealing with magic. A prominent use of this kind of magic was in Margaret Weis and Tracy Hickman's series, *The Death Gate Cycle*. Initially the wizards in this world seemed to be Pattern wizards, but the authors finally decided on rules for their magic system by the sixth novel in the seven novel series. From that point on, their heroes stopped simply 'doing' magic. Rather, they started 'grasping the possibilities' and picking their own futures, bringing down roofs and the like.

Generally, Kewpie wizards exist in borderline SF novels, fantasy novels whose authors demand a plausibly scientific basis for their magic, or hard-SF novels, where this ability is not even classed as magic. An excellent example of this kind of 'magic' is Greg Egan's hard-SF novel *Quarantine* where the logical extension of this method is explored. Your hero might choose a particular possibility out of the alternate universes to experience, but that doesn't mean those alternate universes didn't happen, and there were plenty of universes where the bad guy's bullet did hit the hero. We just never get to read about them.

IMPACTS OF MAGIC

MAGIC AND WAR

Traditionally in human history, anything that could be used to hurt or kill someone was used. Will your readers really believe that your society of peace-loving neo-Celtic druids exist happily alongside any other sort of human society, without those societies being even the slightest bit interested in the military applications of those friendly tree huggers' magic?

I think not. Let's pretend for a minute we've decided to create a world like this:

> The happy and peace-loving Glowen Druids spend their lives congregating in great Glowen forest and smoking pipe-weed. They use their gifts peacefully; mending broken branches, helping lost coneys and communing with the trees. Violence is unknown to them, and they reject the vile meat-eating warriors of neighboring Princely, who spend their days doing what humans do. The druids are the only known people to practise magic. They take in like-minded individuals and train them in the use of magic, because all people have the gift—they just haven't opened their eyes to love and peace.

Doesn't this sound simply lovely? What an exciting place that forest must be! Well, let's take this magical society and bring it to life to see how the world unfolds.

> Princely's ruling king has an adviser called Pete, who hears of the magical powers of these druids. 'Aha,' thinks Pete, 'perhaps these magical powers might come in handy for my lord, who has been in an unending arms race with his enemy, the King of Doldrom.' One evening, Pete creeps into the druids' forest with a solid wooden club, and brings his lord a little memento—one gift-wrapped druid with magical powers. The druid's fellows try to rescue their friend but cannot do so. Their oaths of peace are little use against King Princely's heavily armed soldiers.

> Within a year, King Princely's R&D department has managed to isolate how the druids 'do' their magic. By the end of the decade, King Princely has access to a wealth of unique combat spells and magical weapons. Their peaceful origin is no guarantee of peaceful intent, however—King Princely's spells tear down walls with powerful oak roots which magically spring from the ground; they cripple horses and other four-legged animals in his enemy's army; they wither limbs and rot food. Princely's arrows sprout poisonous thorns on impact that tear and infect a soldier's flesh; his mangonels loose balls of foetid spores that choke a man's lungs.

Hey, what's happening to our happy little fantasy world?

> The King of Doldrom goes into a panic as magically grown trees and violent woodland beasts slaughter his men. He

calls in several of his best assassins, and they sneak into Princely and steal one of the King's advisers' unpublished research papers. The King of Doldrom withdraws his troops strategically, long enough for his men to learn some of Princely's magical techniques. He then releases all his soldiers from his service, sells his castles, and trains only wizards for his army. 'What use are horses,' he thinks, 'when magic cripples them instantly? And what use is my castle when its walls can't offer protection?' The war drags on—land is destroyed, people are killed, yadda yadda yadda.

What went wrong? War is a constant race of weapon versus armor—offence versus defence. Solid castles kept people out, until offensive technology rendered them useless—the cannon's destructive power ensured that new castles were more decorative than defensive. After all, why have solid walls if several cannon can reduce them to rubble in a day? Having a world where everyone can learn magic relatively easily means that the offensive power magic provides will drastically change the world on all levels—especially when it is introduced rapidly as in the above example.

The impact on weapons technology is also significant. Why encumber your troops in heavy protective armor when the enemy is armed with vorpal blades that slice through steel like butter? Why develop explosives and firearms if your magical troops cast exploding balls of fire to disrupt the enemy? How do you supply troops when the enemy poisons your food from afar, or calls down a storm to turn the battlefield into an unmanageable morass? How do the medieval battle tactics you've so painstakingly researched hold up against an airborne attack from flying wizards or magical mounts?

If magic exists in your world, it is highly likely that is has always been a part of that world. That means that whatever technological development exists, it will have been shaped by the presence of magic. And what it means is that it is not realistic to create a medieval fantasy world based on a historical culture, and then throw plentiful magical items and people into it. The likelihood that a medieval European culture could have developed in your world if magic had always been present and accessible is low. Why? We've looked at the potential impact on the military, so read on.

MAGIC AND POLITICS

Right. This king has an adviser, right? And this adviser is also a magician. What? Oh, yeah, every king has a magician as an adviser.

Sound good so far? Of course. What magical world doesn't have kings with magicians as advisers, right? Read on.

The King of Krishna has recently hired a magician to be an

adviser. His impoverished kingdom has lagged behind the rest of the world for some time now, and he needs to increase his prestige a little.

In the first week his magician adviser tells him that his three most trusted advisers are really agents for the King of Princely (who is currently destroying the world with his army of magically augmented soldiers) who have been magically disguised to look like his old advisers. The magician promises to cast a spell to detect lies, so that the king will be able to interrogate his court in the morning.

The next day the King of Krishna asks each member of his court several pointed questions. He's horrified to learn that all of them are liars, the King of Doldrum has bribed five of them, three of them are illusions, and one of them is a zombie! He turns to ask his adviser what to do, only to discover a knife in the man's back. As the adviser collapses, bleeding, to the ground, he points an unsteady finger and mumbles, 'in...invisible ass...assassin...'

The King of Doldrum, watching all this many hundreds of miles away through his scrying mirror, laughs at the King of Krishna's terrified face.

The King of Princely, watching the King of Doldrum watching the King of Krishna, suffers a sudden, fatal, and completely understandable aneurism as he tries to keep track of what's going on.

Okay, so what went wrong there? Nothing, really, except that several basic magical means were employed to infiltrate the King of Krishna's court to assassinate his adviser. Treaties, truces, declarations of war and pledges of peace—all these things are affected by the use of magic. Is the king really the king, or merely a magically disguised intruder or some magical construct? Espionage becomes simple indeed with scrying magic. But for every magical effect there is an equal and opposite magical effect—there has to be a war of escalating power as counter-scrying spells are invoked to cloak the king's private chambers in an impenetrable magical shield.

Will this happen in your world? No, probably not, unless you want it to. But what I'm trying to show is that unless you devise your society's magical rules with these factors in mind, there may be no reason for your world not to be this out of control. If your reader comes to understand the role of magic in your world and asks, 'Well, why doesn't King x just use power y to find out about the plot against him? What kind of idiot king is this, anyway?' then you're in trouble. You need to be aware of the implications of your magical system, and if you don't want the kind of political situation in the example above to arise, you'll need to make sure your magical system can't be used to do those things. Perhaps magic is too risky to use for frivolous activities like scrying? Perhaps wizards are haughty beings who will not stoop to mundane and dishonorable tasks like spying. Perhaps it's not possible to create illusions?

MAGIC AND RELIGION

This is a dangerous field—firstly, you need to decide what kind of religions your society worships (see the chapter on Religion Building). Then you need to decide whether these religions are real or simply political constructs. That is—do their gods really exist?

You need to ask this question because magic makes it very easy to fake religion. Do you want to give your flock an epiphany? Or do you want to let them witness a miracle? If the gods regularly perform miracles like this, then a magician doing the same may go undetected by the public (though the gods, when they find out, might be a little upset). Conversely, if the gods don't exist, then the magician will be able to convince a good many commoners that his/her tricks are divine favors. Or a priest might augment his old god's powers by performing the healing miracle himself, or by spicing up his sermons with some flashy effects. Then again, the magical powers themselves may be a divine gift (see 'Holy Joe' wizards above).

Magic, however, can be a threat to established religion—even to the gods themselves! Why pray to the rain-god for rain if the local magician will make rain for you for a couple of shekels?

Now—if the gods' powers depend on how many worshippers they have, then magicians whose powers emulate those of the gods—especially for common tasks like healing the sick or helping to ensure a good crop—are a direct threat to them. By providing the same services as the gods, wizards are forcing the gods either to undercut the magicians (by providing their gifts for free and on demand) or to destroy the magicians directly (or at least threaten them). This threat of destruction may mean that magicians are reluctant to provide their gifts to the general public. However, it may also mean that the gods are pathetic, comical creatures, competing for their very lives against mortals in a harsh economic climate. Imagine the severely reduced god of thunder knocking on doors with a special offer— three lightning bolts at your greatest enemies for fifteen ducats, and if you buy now you get a free lightning rod to protect your family.

MAGIC AND MERCHANTS

You may already have read about the various means of ripping off customers that bakers developed in medieval London (see the chapter on Medieval Food). How much worse would the corruption and fraud be if magic were added to the recipe for bread? Illusionary weight, false gold, fragrance spells to hide rotten ingredients, mental tricks to confuse customers or convince them they're buying something they're not. The list goes on.

Generally, magic is very beneficial to merchants who want to rip off their customers. Magic makes it easy to disguise the true nature of poorer-quality objects, or to create fakes easily. However, the prevalence of magic can also influence the value of objects. Spices, generally worth a fortune due to the incredible cost and risk of transporting them half-way across the planet, might not be so expensive if magicians can transport them easily. Would wizards compete directly with merchants? Or would the wizards vie for the merchants' attentions, devising more effective spells to transport or protect their goods?

In a world where magic is prevalent, the risk of transporting goods across the country might also be greatly reduced. Perishables could be kept fresh for longer and caravans could be magically warded from raiders.

Magic might even reduce the importance of crafts. If it is possible for a wizard to carve a wooden bowl magically, then the craftsman who takes several hours to produce the same wooden bowl might be out of a job. Or magic could have the status of mass-produced products in our society—people might want to spend the extra few florins on the handcrafted wooden bowl, much as contemporary people often appreciate handmade objects over those constructed in a factory.

Is magic a commodity? Are there magic shops that sell potent magical items to commoners? Beware a nation where every citizen with money has access to violently accurate crossbows or hideously keen blades, especially if that access is enshrined in law.

Again the question is, are you sure the magical system you have created will not result in an economic meltdown in a real society? And more importantly: does the mundane society you have created mesh with the magical society you have created? They are both intrinsic parts of the same system—you can't have one without the other.

MAGIC AND FOOD

With magic, suddenly the greatest risk of food spoilage is potentially a thing of the past. We can either magically suspend food, leaving it as fresh as when it was picked, cooked, or harvested, or we can create magical cold rooms. Magic might allow perishables to be imported that could never have survived the journey before. Special ice-fruits could be kept at freezing temperature during their trek down from the great mountains, to be served fresh at the King's banquet a thousand miles away. Magic is also a much simpler way to keep drinks and refreshments cool than chopping blocks of ice off a mountain slope, as the Persians did over a millennium ago. These factors have the potential of reducing the rarity of certain perishables, by making it easier to maintain or transport them.

Magic can also add a great deal of entertainment to a banquet. Who needs carvers when the king's personal magician can manipulate the carving knives from a distance? Meals can be decorated magically, or hidden in illusions. Baked fish can be made to swim, poultry might flap around the banquet hall and boar heads sing. In between meals, the magician might even provide fireworks (as Gandalf does in the movie version of *The Lord of the Rings*).

Or the magician could create a magical poison and kill every single guest without leaving a trace. Hey, you can't spend fifty years studying your art then end up entertaining peasants in a hall with fireworks all the time.

MAGIC AND THE LAW

When magic falls in the hands of criminals, look out. Invisibility to break into houses, destructive spells to thwart the law—potentially, there is no limit. Whose gold is safe if a thief can use mundane skills to break in, and then use magic to leave an almost exact copy? And what lock could stop a magician?

On the other side of the law, guards and officers may have a whole swathe of magical effects available to them. No ordinary thief could avoid a magical alarm, or survive a magical firetrap. Or a spell could be used to recreate a crime scene, as happens in Raymond Feist's and Janny Wurtz's *Daughter of the Empire*. How do criminals avoid this? Here's another situation where you might expect criminals and lawmen to try to stay ahead of one another in a magical arms race.

Oh man—so what do I do now? I've already got a European medieval world with magic in it. Can I fix it?

That depends on what you're willing to do. You don't really need to change anything if you don't want to, as long as you are confident that your readers will accept your world the way you have portrayed it. Hopefully, reading this chapter will have made you aware of the potential danger to society of allowing magic to run rife—things we take for granted, such as the value of gold, become meaningless if magicians can create them almost at will.

In general, to ensure that your chosen society does not collapse due to the impact of magic, you need to know your boundaries. Magic needs boundaries—scarcity, difficulty and price—to ensure that it doesn't take over your story against your wishes. You need to make sure that the challenges facing your heroes cannot be overcome too easily by using the magic system you've created. This is not because solving them too easily with magic would upset your reader (which it would), but because not solving them with magic would upset your reader even more! If your wizards can select from the myriad possible futures, then what excuse can you as the writer offer your readers when the hero is shot? 'Surely,' the reader would ask, 'there is a possible future where the bad guy missed?'

If you create paths to solutions in your world, and your characters deliberately ignore them because otherwise the 'story wouldn't work', then you know you have a problem. No reader believes a non-magical story where heroes need to cross a river but ignore the bridge ahead of them in favor of the narrow and dangerous path along some cliff, just so you can add tension to the scene. Similarly, if you've made it clear that there is a simple spell to determine whether an individual is speaking the truth or not, then you cannot have a tense scene where the heroes and their wizard friends struggle to believe someone's tale about a conspiracy to kill them. If you played the scene properly, and along the rules you defined earlier, then there would be no struggle—the wizards would simply cast the lie-detection spell, and the problem would be solved. You need to make sure you don't spring this kind of plot-hole trap on yourself.

So think carefully about your magic system before you implement it. You can't simply say, 'My world is similar to England in the year 1500. There are wizards around, too, by the way.' You need to think of the repercussions of magic in your world, and you also need to ask yourself—if magic has been around since my people lived in caves, then why does my society still have x, where x is something that can commonly be done using magic.

The easiest way around this dilemma, of course, is to limit magical ability to a few specific individuals—that way the impact on society is restricted severely. However, if you want to add magic to your world more directly, you will need to exercise careful consideration. If you don't, I guess I'll just have to pick a future where you did.

Mythology

THE STORIES WITHIN YOUR WORLD

VALERIE GRISWOLD-FORD

INTRODUCTION

Marissa held her breath as her grandmother lifted the ancient yew bow gently from its hiding place beneath the floor. Still in the niche lay a quiver with twelve shining silver arrows.

"Our family has carried Diana's bow for generations," her grandmother said, handing the artifact to her. "Now it is your turn, Marissa. Use it well."

The Merriam-Webster Online Dictionary defines the word "myth" as "*a usually traditional story of ostensibly historical events that serves to unfold part of the world view of a people or to explain a practice, belief, or natural phenomenon.*" When you as a writer create your world, the mythology you choose to weave through your story adds yet another level of depth and believability that draws the reader in. Whether used as a major plot point or simply as part of the background, mythology grounds a story, giving readers and characters alike something concrete to base their perceptions upon.

It doesn't matter whether you create your own mythology or use a historical mythology, as long as it meshes cleanly with the world you have created for your story. Used properly, mythology can add deeper dimensions of color to your world, and give your characters a natural direction for their actions, words and feelings. However, a mythos that is incomplete or inconsistent with the setting, such as Vikings that believe the world was created by Ra, the Egyptian god of the Sun, can jar a reader out of the web of belief you have created and cause him or her, at worst, to abandon your story in disgust.

There are many excellent sources for those who wish to use an existing mythology. There is a suggested book and website listing at the end of this chapter for anyone wishing to delve deeper into the world of mythology. But what about those who wish to create their own mythology?

Writing your own mythology has the added bonus of allowing you to explore your world, its religions and cultures that you have created in deeper ways. The myths of your cultures will be a direct extension, not only of their religion, but of the way they live, breathe, love and interact with one another. Why do your warriors wear leopard tails on their helms? Why do maidens sacrifice yellow-feathered birds on the first full moon of the spring? These answers can be found in the myths your people tell.

Furthermore, mythology is not simply found in low-technology cultures. Even today, mythology can be found woven through our highly technological society. The stories found in the *Bible* are myths used by some to explain our presence on this planet, and new myths are still being created to explain things we do not understand, including phenomena like UFOs. Legends of Bigfoot, the Yeti and the Loch Ness Monster still circulate. Mythology is alive and well.

One of the interesting characteristics of myths is that because they are oral in nature, they change as they are passed from region to region and generation to generation. Thus it is possible to have many versions of the same general story in circulation, each version with its own special characteristics that illustrate the region, culture and time period it is found in.

There are several general kinds of myths that are common to all cultures: creation myths, which explain the history of a city, nation or people; myths that explain natural phenomena; heroic myths; and apocalyptic myths. All are fodder for a creative author to flesh out their world with.

CREATION MYTHS

Only the ocean existed at first. Then Ra (the sun) came out of an egg that appeared on the surface of the water. Ra brought forth four children, the gods Shu and Geb and the goddesses Tefnut and Nut. Shu and Tefnut became the atmosphere. They stood on Geb, who became the earth, and raised up Nut, who became the sky. Ra ruled over all. Geb and Nut later had two sons, Set and Osiris, and two daughters, Isis and Nephthys. Osiris succeeded Ra as king of the earth, helped by Isis, his sister-queen. Set, however, hated his brother and killed him. Isis then embalmed her husband's body with help of the god Anubis, who thus became the god of embalming. The powerful charms of Isis resurrected Osiris, who became the king of the underworld, the land of the dead. Horus, who was the son of Osiris and Isis, later defeated Set in a great battle and became king of the earth. (Egyptian creation myth, *The Book of Gods, Goddesses, Heroes and Other Characters of Mythology*)

Creation myths appear in every single culture on Earth. Man appears to have a primal need to identify how and where his world and people came from, and the stories like the one above illustrate early peoples' attempts to explain their origins. World creation myths follow a certain formula: first there is either a void, or a great ocean, which in turn gives birth to one or more gods. These gods then create land and then people. In some of these myths, there is a war between the gods and monsters, with the gods winning and taking control of the land and peoples (as in the Greco-Roman and Norse myths). In others, the mortals cause themselves to lose favor with their gods, which results in either the gods withdrawing to another plane or the mortals being thrust out of the paradise they were created in (as in the Garden of Eden story of the *Bible*).

When writing a world creation myth, look at how and where your people live. Are they in a mountain valley with a river running through? Beside an ocean? In a tropical or arctic environment? Do they share their home with other sentient races? Are they a nomadic people or do they have a permanent settlement? Their gods and, by extension, their religion and creation myths will reflect the area they call home.

On a narrower scale, many ancient cities had their own creation myths to explain the founding of the city. For example, two brothers, Romulus and Remus, who were suckled by a wolf, supposedly built the city of Rome. However, they argued over what to call the city, and Romulus killed Remus in a fight. Romulus then built his city, and called it Rome. Gods or their partially mortal children may have started your cities. Perhaps the city's founders were refugees from another city, or even another world. This kind of story, while it may have very little bearing on your plot, adds a deeper flavour to your city, making it come alive in ways that you may not have expected.

The questions that need to be answered when writing a city creation myth are similar to those that are asked in world creation myths. What is the area like? What drew the city's creators to the area? Where did they originally come from? Were there other sentient races in the area first? How did they deal with them? The answers to these questions will help you to shape the culture you are dealing with.

Myths Explaining natural Phenomena

Fire. Weather. The turning of the seasons. Man came up with myths to explain the presence of these phenomena in his world. Myths in this class are much narrower in scope than creation myths, and are far more individualised by region. These myths are especially helpful in characterising the gods and beliefs of the region you are working in. This class of myths, along with heroic myths, is often the fodder of ballads and tales, and is useful in helping along the plot of a story. Of all the types of myths, these are the ones that will give a great deal of color to your world.

These myths usually arise side by side with the religious practices of your culture, as they can be used to provide the explanations for the rituals performed by the people. Again, these myths are going to be heavily influenced by how and where your people live.

A good example of this kind of myth is the story of Persephone, the daughter of Demeter, goddess of agriculture in Greek mythology. Hades, god of the underworld, stole Persephone away and made her his queen. Demeter, distraught over her daughter's disappearance, swore she would allow nothing to grow until Persephone was returned to her. She wandered the world, neglecting everything, and the world grew cold and dead. Finally, Zeus ordered Hades to returned Persephone. However, before he did, Hades tricked her into eating six seeds of a pomegranate, ensuring that she would return to him for six months of the year. Thus, say the Greeks, we have six months of winter, when Demeter mourns for her daughter, trapped in the underworld. In spring, when Persephone returns to the upper world, everything blooms again.

Heroic Myths

A bow-shot from her bower-eaves,
He rode between the barley-sheaves,
The sun came dazzling thro' the leaves,
And flam'd upon the brazen greaves
    Of bold Sir Lancelot.

A red-cross knight for ever kneel'd
To a lady in his shield,
That sparkled on the yellow field,
    Beside remote Shalott.
—Alfred, Lord Tennyson, *The Lady of Shalott*

Along with the myths discussed in the preceding section, heroic myths are the most commonly used by bards, poets and musicians to entertain people. These myths show up in songs, poetry, tales and plays of all ages. It is these myths that embody what their culture holds dear, be it strength, goodness, godliness or intelligence. Heroic myths do not necessarily pit man against the gods, although this is a common theme in earlier myths: the example above is part of the story of Sir Lancelot, one of the knights of Camelot. The enduring quality of heroic myth is well illustrated by this story: Camelot and its many heroes are still being used in fantasy stories today and will most likely continue to be popular.

Many fantasy novels themselves are heroic myths, and creating these myths can often suggest to an author what may eventually become a prequel to the current story. However, authors can get too caught up in creating the myth, and neglect the actual story they should be telling. Just remember that the myth is background for the story. It is not the story itself.

Heroic myths have most, if not all, of the following qualities: it follows the life of a hero, usually from birth; the hero faces many challenges, not the least of which is the enmity of at least one god; and he or she has a long, perilous journey to complete, which takes most of their life. Good examples of these myths are the *Odyssey*, which chronicles the ten year journey of Odysseus home from the Trojan War, and the Aenead, which chronicles the ten year journey of Aeneas after the Trojan War to eventually found the Roman Empire. Another good example of the heroic myth is the story of Camelot, as mentioned above: good King Arthur and his Knights of the Round Table, who embody the ideals of knighthood: chivalry, honor and courage.

When writing a heroic myth, the following questions need to be answered. What are the qualities your people hold the dearest? How did your hero come to be born? Of who? Which god or gods dislike him or her, and why? What obstacles do they need to overcome, and what is the outcome? Not all heroic myths end happily: the myth of Hercules ends with him being poisoned, albeit accidentally, by his own wife and dying. In fact, the more tragic the ending, the more heroic the hero seems to be. Sir Lancelot and King Arthur are two more good examples of this.

APOCALYPTIC MYTHS

Some say the world will end in fire,
Some say in ice.
From what I've tasted of desire
I hold with those who favor fire.
But if it had to perish twice,
I think I know enough of hate
To know that for destruction ice
Is also great
And would suffice.
— Robert Frost, *Fire and Ice*

The last main type of myth that has been encountered is the apocalyptic myth, that which foretells the end of the world as we know it. These myths, too, have survived to the present day: even now, there are stories of a giant asteroid that will destroy life on this world one day. The ancient stories of the Twilight of the Gods, in Norse mythology, and the Apocalypse, in the *Bible*, mirror the notion that man holds: that everything must end. Flood myths, which appear to be fairly universal, are also part of this category.

If you decide to include an apocalyptic myth in your culture's repertoire, the following questions need to be answered. How will the world end? Will it be a war between gods? If so, what will be the catalyst? Will the final end be a great battle, or a flood, or a firestorm or other natural disaster? Will anyone survive? This question is in regards especially to flood myths, where one family or city is usually saved because of their piety. These types of myths usually have the gods becoming disgusted with the lifestyles of the mortals below, and deciding to destroy them and start over.

Apocalyptic myths often reflect the theme of destruction and renewal in many cultures: the idea of a "great wheel" turning and turning on itself. It is important to remember that these myths tell of the destruction of the world, as it is currently known. There is usually a rebirth at the end of the story. The dove returns to the Ark with an olive branch at the end of the Noah story, and he proceeds to repopulate the Earth. The battle of the gods ends and the world is rebuilt at the end of Ragnarock in Norse mythology. It is the end of one era and the beginning of another.

SUMMARY

Mythology is a powerful piece of background information for any writer. It adds color and depth to a world, and allows the writer to explore the cultures he's created. However, it should be used sparingly, or it can become a tedious information dump that will turn off the reader.

Likewise, mythological stories can take over and overwhelm the plot line if not watched carefully. Using mythology in a story is like cooking with a pungent spice: too little, and your food is too bland. Too much and you lose the flavour of the original food. Don't let your mythology drown out the story you're trying to tell.

BIBLIOGRAPHY

Several books and websites for you to consider, if you are interested in learning more about mythology:

Great Irish Tales of Fantasy and Myth, edited by Peter Haining. This book has some wonderful tales from Ireland.

The Golden Bough, by Sir James Frazer. This is a very dense book, but if you are looking for information on mythology, this is pretty much the definitive book.

www.bulfinch.org: *Bulfinch's Mythology*, put online. This is a wonderful resource for anyone interested in mythology.

www.pantheon.org/mythica.html: *Encyclopedia Mythica*. You can search for specific gods, heroes, and myths on this site.

www.cybercomm.net/~grandpa/gdsindex.html: *The Book of Gods, Goddesses, Heroes and Other Characters of Mythology*. This is a good beginning resource for those interested in mythology.

Religion

JULIE PEAVLER-McCORD

INTRODUCTION: WHY INCLUDE RELIGION?

The simple answer is that religion is an easy source of tension and plots. If you're stuck for a motive for war or personal conflict, religious difference works fabulously. Need to explain why your villain, or your hero for that matter, is doing something dreadful or illogical? Religious beliefs will explain it. Want to lay down some hints of what's going to happen and then play against them later? Prophecy, usually passed down through religious writings, makes a marvellous tool.

In addition, fleshing out a culture's religion, even partially, will be a great help in making the culture come alive and making it distinct from its neighbors. Strange local festivals left over from "the old ways" make for great color, and you can even plumb your culture's god-names and symbols for new ways to let your characters cuss. After physical differences, alien belief structures are one of the easiest and most effective ways to set apart a created race from "humanity."

HOW TO INCLUDE RELIGION

If you're writing in a real-world setting, the job is relatively easy. You need to research the existing beliefs of the people in question. There are many decent encyclopedias on world religions now in existence; or a search on Beliefnet (www.beliefnet.com) might be another place to start. These general resources should be able to point you toward more specific references on your chosen religion.

If you're working with a created world, however, the job becomes more complicated. For some, that's the fun part, actually, but it can be daunting if you're not experienced in the field. Just remember as a foundation that as with everything else, it's your world, your rules. All you have to do is make it internally consistent. Don't make your main character a dope-smoking thief who adores the Lawkeeper God unless that juxtaposition is going to be part of the story. You could build an amusing or dramatic explanation around this kind of contrast, but if you conjure such an inconsistent image and then never explain it, it will hang over the reader's head like an unanswered question.

This chapter will take you through a basic step-by-step thought process for creating a religion. Along the way, it will introduce and explain a number of religious and philosophical terms that are useful in defining religions and religious sects. Then it will give some thoughts as to how religion affects the individual character.

RELIGION'S ROLE IN SOCIETY

First and foremost, religion serves as an answer to life's big questions: "Where did all this come from?" "Why are we here?" "What should I be doing?" "What will happen after I die?" In pre-scientific cultures, religion is the only available answer to such questions; and even in high-tech cultures, it often remains the most emotionally satisfying answer.

Culturally speaking, religion also creates a pattern for sharing experience, providing rituals for meaningful life passages like birth, coming of age, marriage, and death. In the process, it binds the people closer together. Religion is instrumental in deciding what virtues a culture strives to attain and what sins it seeks to avoid. Religious thought is also a frequent source of secular law and power processes.

Philosophy of the World

This is a natural place to start building a religion. In fact, in creative terms, it is easier to start here and then create gods who fit the philosophy than to do the reverse. This step involves deciding your religion's attitudes about where the world came from, and the basic relationship between spirit and matter.

This first step, and most of those that follow, require that you either know something about your created culture (see the Race Creation chapter), or are willing to create the culture to be consistent with what you do with the religion. Although it is not that unusual for aspects of culture not to match aspects of religion (just look at Christianity's role in modern American culture for an example) if they do not mesh in the key elements, you will eventually need to explain why not. In most cases where a culture has religion at all, culture and religion are deeply linked together. Apply anything you already know about one to your development of the other.

Animism

Animism is a belief that all things that exist have souls. This belief is quite common in "primitive" cultures in close touch with the natural world. An animist religion is probably well populated with souls of many types, including the souls of the dead, spirits of place, and animal souls, perhaps even plant, mineral, and created object souls. There is likely to be some system set in place for communication with all these souls. Each type will have gifts it can offer the sensitive human; on the other hand, each is also likely to place certain demands on people. For example, in cultures that believe that the dead still contact the living, they often either need or demand some kind of offerings from their descendants. If these are not received, then the souls of the dead are made unhappy or uncomfortable, and they may retaliate by bringing bad luck or sickness to their families. If the offerings are prompt and generous enough, the spirits reward their families with protection and insights.

Animism creates a special problem for the writer, in that you must know at least something about the flora and fauna local to the created culture. Special characters or powers are often attributed to various animals and plants in an animistic system, and to write convincing animism you must construct a logical system. For example, in many places, the strongest predatory animal takes a Hero role and is considered brave and powerful, unless it is inimical to man (e.g. Lion, Eagle, Wolf). A smaller predator or scavenger often takes the role of Trickster, a character with less strength but more cunning (e.g. Jackal, Raven, Coyote).

POLYTHEISM VS. MONOTHEISM

Put simply, a polytheist has many gods and a monotheist has one. These two states actually represent different views on what a "god" is. Quite often in polytheistic religions, there is no single Creator; the universe simply comes to be, or is a child or by-product of several different primal forces acting on one another. The "gods" do not appear until several generations into the process, and in a sense they represent its completion. The "gods" then take control of what already exists, imposing an order on it. None of them is all-powerful or all-knowing, although some will be very powerful and know a great deal. Each is charged with ordering one or a few particulars of existence, and in cases where several jurisdictions overlap confusion will often result.

Monotheism, on the other hand, assumes a single Being, which is all-knowing and/or all-powerful, and this Being is normally credited with all of Creation. This Being may well have a number of attendants who are semi-divine (e.g. angels) and who fulfil some or even many of the functions of a polytheistic god, but these are not given the status that polytheistic gods enjoy; they are seen as strictly secondary.

IMMANENCE VS. TRANSCENDENCE

Immanence means that God or the gods are present in the physical world; it goes nicely with animism. Transcendence means that God or the gods reside outside the physical world and are not directly linked to it, but instead interact with it from beyond.

The Christian God is usually thought of as a transcendent god: He is a Creator outside of the Creation, watching it from elsewhere. By contrast, a deity like the Greek Earth goddess Gaea is immanent, because she is actually expressed in the physical world. The physical world is Gaea; it is not something she built, but something she is.

Some mystics have always been able to combine these two ideas, because mystical experience does not have to confine itself to logic or linear thought. However, unless you are a mystic yourself, this is probably more complicated than you will want to get in a novel.

CULTURE & PLACE IN RELIGIOUS DEVELOPMENT

Philosophers like to debate whether men create gods or the other way around: as a fantasy author, you can have it either way, but you should try to match the gods to the people who worship them.

For example, people in a harsh climate tend to have a harsher view of the gods and of the afterlife. Other factors influence this: for example, in ancient Egypt, where it was possible to build monuments that lasted forever, it was also possible to imagine that the soul might live forever surrounded by pretty things. In Mesopotamia, where everything tended to rot, the afterlife was full of darkness and decay.

A culture that has grown up around agriculture is more likely to have a mythos in which seasonal change is important. Commonly in this world, this has been expressed in terms of an immortal Goddess who seasonally loses and regains either a lover or a child. Sometimes the seasonal cycle is seen as applying to humanity as well, and a belief in reincarnation develops. The mythos of a herding culture will not share the same features. The mythos of a culture built on a series of wanderings and conquests is likely to show similar behaviour by the gods.

Gods influencing nature will be seen through the lens of how nature treats your people and location. For example, on Earth, there is a tendency for the Sun to be described in gentle, benign terms in moderate or cool climates, but to take on a wrathful or destructive aspect in very hot places. A calm sea might be seen as a generous mother, while a wrathful sea is a short-tempered man. A clear river full of fish might be a kindly old fellow, while the lake people keep drowning in is the home of a beautiful but hateful lady.

This kind of cultural influence will even affect myths and deities that are shared by more than one culture. A study of Greek versus Roman mythology is helpful for understanding this, as so much of Roman myth is actually borrowed from the Greeks. To the intellectuals of Athens, the god of war, Ares, was an uncultured brute; the same figure in conquest-loving Rome became Mars, a great hero and founder of Rome itself.

WHO ARE THE GODS?

Now that you have developed a sense of your culture's general mindset toward the world and its gods, it's time to actually start developing the gods themselves. How many are there? Did they create the world? If not, how did it come into being, and how did the gods gain control of it? What does each of the gods do? How do they relate to each other? Do they get along, or are they in conflict?

Try to resist the temptation to simply borrow the stereotypes we all learn from reading Greek mythology and game books. It's easy to fall into the trap of thinking that the Sun is naturally represented by a god who favors writing and music, the Earth is a stern but loving mother, and so on, because that is familiar. A wider reading of world mythology will cure this; a few experiences of bloodthirsty Sun goddesses and male Earth figures should be enough to start opening up new possibilities.

Part of the fun of god-creation is choosing what powers the god is best known for having, and then deciding how they hang together. You can start to imagine the process by looking at the symbols of a god you know about and working backwards. Athene, normally a Greek goddess of culture and civilisation, has a horrible-looking Gorgon's head on her shield, showing her powers of protection and, according to some, rulership over women's mysteries. How did the head get there? Well, there used to be this terrible monster named Medusa—and so on.

Actually, it is more fun and better writing to experiment with fresh combinations, and it helps with developing other parts of your world. It's cheap and easy to make a simpering blonde Love Goddess, but it will really teach you something about your world and your culture to figure out how somebody ended up as the God of War, Music, and Rivers.

Remember not to fall back onto stereotypes, and remember to keep the gods at least somewhat consistent with the culture. For example, we remember the Greek goddess Aphrodite mostly as a goddess of love, beauty, and pleasure. However, in Sparta, she had a warrior aspect. This is because Sparta was a very warlike culture, so just about every deity ended up with some warrior aspects. The *Star Trek* universe does this one better: the first Klingons are said to have killed their gods.

Also decide at this point how involved the gods are in worldly affairs. There is more room to play with this in fantasy than in other genres, even if you are working with a "real world" setting. In Tolkien's Lord of the Rings, several deities are mentioned, especially Elbereth, the Star Goddess. Although she does not take any direct action, her influence is felt through the elves, and invocations of her are effective weapons against dark forces. In Homer's *Iliad* and *Odyssey*, the gods take a more direct approach, often appearing with advice or even acting directly for their favorites or against their enemies.

THE MYTHOS

When you have gods, you need something for them to do. The stories of the history and teachings of the gods will color the symbology used by the church and the virtues extolled by the culture.

The important thing in writing mythology is to free-associate imagery. It's like writing a dream sequence in a way. If you are creating the mythology first, then you can go wild with the myths and figure out what they mean later, as if analysing a dream, applying what you've learned to how the culture develops. If you've already created the culture, then you'll want to choose your symbols more deliberately, with what you already know in mind.

Here are two examples from old writings of mine. In the first, I created the myth with only a vague notion of how the culture behaved. It ran like this: Erslo, the Creator, made the world, and formed the first man and woman out of clay. He left them to their own devices for a while. When he came back and asked them how they were doing, they complained that it was dark and scary, and they heard sounds, and there was nothing to do. Erslo, angry at their ingratitude, tore out his own heart and threw it into the sky, where it blazed and became the sun. "There," he said, "you have light. And you will toil in the heat to gain your way in the world." He left them to their own devices again. Later, regretting his temper, he returned and asked again how they were doing. Again they complained, saying that there was always either too much light or none at all, and that in the night strange things still came to them and frightened them. This time, Erslo did not have the heart to be angry; so he plucked out his left eye and threw it into the air, where it became the moon, slowly opening and closing. "Now," he said, "I will always be able to watch over you."

In the second, I knew that I wanted the myth to support a neopagan-like idea of a paired goddess and god of the wild, calling those who had forgotten them back to worship. So I got this: Bordering the kingdom in question was a vast and dangerous forest; many men had been lost within it and never returned. Lord Tyril and his companions were riding in the wood on a hunt, but could find no game. They became lost, and could not even find a creature to eat. Deep in the wood, they found an old woman that promised them that, with her blessing, they would find a meal; but they must thank her immediately after the kill, and save her all the bones. Later, a great white hart bounded across their path. They shot it, and Lord Tyril dropped to the ground and gave thanks to the old woman, even though his companions scoffed. He also made sure to gather the bones after they had eaten. Late at night, while Tyril's companions slept, he saw the woman come to the camp and chant over the bones, which transformed into the shape of a great, bearded man with antlers on his head. They told Tyril that they were the Lord and Lady of the wood, and that he must tell of them to the neighboring townsfolk, so that they would know how to honor them in return for safety in the forest.

PRAYER, AND WHAT GODS PROVIDE

Outside of special initiatory cults, polytheistic gods tend to offer basic, prosaic items: money, health, cows, wives, good crops, and so on. They might go so far as to improve one's skills in their chosen field, offer protection from rival tribes, or deliver an occasional glimpse of the future. Truth be told, many of the common folk will feel the same way about monotheism as well: God's importance is primarily that He (or She, or It) can give or withhold the rain this season.

To people on the bottom of Maszlo's Hierarchy of Needs (those concerned mostly with day-to-day survival), prayer and religious worship therefore are primarily a matter of making sure that no one important is angry with you. So you do whatever is the minimum: you go to church every Sunday, or you sacrifice one goat every year, or you make sure to pour beer on the hearth stone before you drink any and say "Hail Bubba." In the case of polytheism, there are usually rites to be done at home over the course of daily life, to ensure the goodwill of whatever deities affect what you're doing at the time. You say a quick hello to the Kitchen God as you make dinner, or to the Goddess of Weaving as you prepare your loom, in whatever way your culture has deemed fit. These little rites may be done with full awareness by a religious-minded person, or barrelled through half-heartedly.

A little higher up on the hierarchy, people might start worrying about trying to be a virtuous person by their religion's definition, and their place in the afterlife. Remember, again, that what is considered "virtuous" and what a positive or negative Eternity looks like will depend on the values you've chosen for that culture. For example, a people who value strength and valour in battle above all else probably don't have a Heaven full of peaceful harp players, nor will they probably see meekness as something to which they should aspire. They are more likely to have something like Valhalla, where dead Viking heroes could spend every day in practice combat and every night drinking mead with their friends and pretty Valkyries.

Above these are the mystics, people who are so enthused about God or the gods that they wish to attain a state of constant awareness of them. Depending on how the rest of the religion plays out, the mystic might want to bask in the infinite majesty of Deity as an eternal servant, or to be reabsorbed into Deity completely, or to become self-identified with Deity so that he or she actually wields similar power and wisdom. People at this level will probably have special processes that they must undergo: extended or frequent periods of prayer and meditation, vision quests, initiations.

THE NATURE OF THE CHURCH
PHYSICAL STRUCTURE

Even this aspect of your people's church or temple will probably reveal something about their beliefs. In cultures where God or gods are believed to live in or beyond the sky, one has to build upward to attract their attention. From this principle we get pyramids laid out in the form of constellations; huge chalk drawings designed to be seen from the air; and churches built with high, vaulted ceilings. People whose gods are more accessible to the surface-dwellers will probably build out rather than up, resulting in large Greek-style temple complexes. Gods and spirits who reside beneath the surface will more likely be honored from within underground catacombs, or simple enclosures built into the earth. Very nomadic or very naturalistic cultures will not have temples at all; instead they will select or create certain kinds of outdoor setting, or enclosures that can be erected and taken back down quickly.

What belongs in the church or temple will depend on what your culture considers sacred. Gold, silver, and gems are always popular, because they're shiny and pretty. A culture that sees a particular animal as sacred may either have creatures wandering the temple grounds, or offer the animal in periodic sacrifices, depending on other factors (like whether cats are considered tasty and whether anyone wants to clean cow dung out of the rectory). Artistic interpretations of gods and myths, according to what your culture finds attractive, are likely—although you may want to think about whether your culture considers it sacrilegious to depict their gods this way. If it is acceptable, there may be specific stylised ways of showing them; perhaps a particular deity is always shown holding a certain item, or in the company of a certain animal, or performing a certain gesture.

What is considered a sacred item is largely a matter of common sense. If your priests sacrifice animals in the temple, there are probably special ritual knives for the purpose. If there is a ritual sharing of drink, there are special cups. If, in developing your myths, a deity has built a special connection with a particular symbol—a solar wheel, or a cross, or a fish—then that symbol probably appears in some form, either as a sacred object or as a decorating motif.

POLITICAL VS. ECUMENICAL INFLUENCE

There are two ways in which a particular branch of a religion—which for simplicity we will call a sect—can vie for power. A sect can try to gain ecumenical influence, which means that it attempts to change (or maintain) the orthodox views and practices of the religion as a whole. Or it can focus on gaining political power, influence over how the culture is governed on a secular level.

Naturally, a really ambitious sect will try for both.

CONSERVATIVE VS. LIBERAL

A conservative sect is heavily invested in preserving the status quo of the culture. It stands for "traditional values"; it expects followers to keep to these, and depending on its political clout, exerts pressure on the culture itself to maintain these values. A conservative sect often plays a reactive role against perceived cultural changes, or external forces.

Conservatives might become more powerful during a war against a culture with a different religion, or during an influx of immigrants with different cultural values, for example. Pat Robertson (political) and Billy Graham (ecumenical) are examples of a conservative religious figure.

A liberal sect, on the other hand, is usually looking for a better way of doing things, by whatever its definition might be of "better." Compared to a conservative sect's version of the same religion, the liberal sect will be more tolerant of ideas from outside of tradition, and may even adopt some of them. If it has enough political power or ambition, a liberal sect will attempt to make changes in the status quo to reflect values it feels are lacking. Martin Luther King (political) and Matthew Fox (ecumenical) are examples of a liberal religious figure.

EVANGELISM VS. PLURALISM

An evangelistic sect actively recruits new members. Historically, in our world, evangelistic sects and religions are a minority, unless you include cults. Current evangelistic sects include branches of Christianity, Islam, and Hinduism (the Hare Krishnas).

Since evangelism is not the normal state of affairs, it must be accounted for somewhere in the creation of your culture. In the case of Christianity, for example, factors that lead to evangelism include Christ's teaching of caring for others, including those outside one's ethnicity or caste; belief in eternal punishment for non-believers; and the adoption of Rome's love of physical conquest applied to a spiritual level. Belief that one's own religion is the only correct one is often, but not always, among the factors. Among our modern world examples, this belief applies to Christianity and Islam but not to the Hare Krishnas.

Pluralism holds that there is no one absolute truth, but several. This mindset allowed the majority of polytheistic religions in history to get along with one another with comparatively few conflicts, at least on a religious level. Christian missionaries throughout history have often complained of their frustration with pluralists, who will happily place Christ among the half-dozen other figures on their altars and go on with their lives without really absorbing the idea that he is supposed to replace the others, not join them. Likewise, the pagan Romans who conquered Gaul were content to worship local deities, under Romanised names, along with their own while they were stationed in that territory. Back in Rome, they also borrowed favorite deities from elsewhere; for example, Isis, an Egyptian goddess, was a particularly popular import.

It should be noted that pluralists can believe that their path is the best option, just not that it is the only correct option. Therefore, pluralist groups tend not to evangelise. Instead, they gain membership either through the children of previous followers or through people who actively seek them.

ASCETIC VS. ECSTATIC

Ascetics believe in self-denial. Usually, but not always, this stems from a fundamental belief that spirit and matter are separate—they believe in transcendence rather than immanence. The belief arises that in order to strengthen the spirit, one must deny the body; so to belong to an ascetic-oriented sect, one must undergo whatever self-denials are favored by that sect. Examples include dietary restrictions (vegetarianism, for example), fasting, vows of chastity or poverty, and in extreme cases, limited forms of self-torture, such as flagellation. Typically, an ascetic sect will demand more of this kind of behaviour from its clergy, monks and nuns than from its laity.

Ecstatics, in contrast, feel that one of the surest paths to spiritual growth is intoxication of the senses. Their rites might include orgies, bouts of heavy intake of alcohol, other drug use, eating of raw flesh, and other practices that would be unthinkable to the "mainstream" of the culture. Interestingly, flagellation can also appear at this extreme.

It is quite possible to combine these two. An ecstatic might undergo a period of ascetic behaviour, leading up to a major festival of ritualised excess. On the other hand, an ascetic period inflicted on the masses might find itself preceded by a "last chance at sin" festival, as Lent is preceded by Mardi Gras and Carnival.

ORTHOPRAXY VS. ORTHODOXY

Orthopraxy is "right action." It is an emphasis on pious behaviour—whether one attends the right festivals, says the right prayers, and behaves correctly according to the virtues favored by the religion and culture. The majority of old "pagan" religions focused on orthopraxy.

An important point of orthopraxy is that it does not require any particular belief. In theory, it would be quite permissible to disbelieve in the gods, or dislike them, or have any number of peculiar ideas in contrast to the teaching of the religion—as long as one's behavior was still correct.

Orthodoxy is "right belief." Here, what one thinks does become important. Orthodoxy came into its own with Christianity, where Christ taught that thinking of committing a sin was as bad as committing it in fact. In a religion that cares about orthodoxy, there is likely to be more tension between different branches of the faith (because they have differing beliefs), and more concern about things like hypocrisy (words or deeds not matching beliefs).

SECTS WITHIN A RELIGION

If a religion harbours multiple sects, you will need to decide how they relate to each other. There are two common responses. In peaceful places and times, different sects will usually tolerate each other, perhaps with a slightly patronizing tone of "not quite as good as us, but close enough." However, in times of stress, sects can turn on each other, especially if there is not an external enemy to unite against. Conservative and liberal sects are particularly likely to turn against each other; and a conservative sect that is orthodoxy-oriented is very likely to start "cracking down" on rival sects if it has enough political authority to do so.

SPECIAL CONSIDERATIONS OF FANTASY

The sect-building level is a good place to start looking at special considerations unique to your world. Are there psychics? Wizards? Non-human races? If so, each sect or religion is likely to have a set stance on them, either welcoming, neutral, or hostile. One sect might see psychic or magical power as a special gift from the gods, and actively recruit practitioners into special positions within the church; another might call such powers an abomination and seek the destruction of anyone who wields them. The different sects of a single religion may all share the same views on this subject, or they may not.

WHAT IS EXPECTED OF THE FOLLOWERS?

CLERGY

Clergy normally keep up the temples, perform whatever rituals are appropriate for holy days and life-altering events, and advise followers on correct behaviour (orthopraxy) and beliefs (orthodoxy) as dictated by the religion. In some cultures, each of these functions goes to a different group; in others they are combined. Being clergy might be a full-time job paid by the government or donations from the masses, or for a minority faith, it might be part-time volunteer work.

Other codes of conduct will depend on the religion. Certainly clergy will be expected to keep to the orthodoxy and/or orthopraxy of the religion. In a faith with ascetic leanings, clergy may be asked to restrict their diets, or take a vow of chastity. There may be limits placed on who can become clergy, according to the prejudices of the culture. A patriarchal culture is likely to accept only male clergy, while a culture whose other powers are decided by blood lineage will probably apply a similar rule to clergy, keeping it within certain families.

LAITY

What is expected of the masses depends to an extent on whether the religion leans on orthodoxy or orthopraxy. However, since it's always harder to monitor what people think than what they do—unless psychics form a major part of your world construction—the basics will tend to be correct behaviour. Followers should attend whatever major festivals are appropriate, show deference to the clergy of their religion, perform whatever prayers or sacrifices are called for, and generally try to be seen as upholding the correct values—hospitality, say, or honesty.

In the case of orthodoxy, followers will also be expected to at least pay adequate lip service to whatever specific ideas about God or gods, virtue, the afterlife, and so on, have been put forward by their church.

Religion and the Character

By now you should have a fairly good idea of what religious life will mean to a character that comes from your culture. There are a few broad types of individual to be aware of in this regard.

The Simple Folk: this character believes in his or her religion in a very basic, rudimentary way. If a Christian, for example, the Simple Folk goes to church at least on major holidays, has a vague understanding and belief in the major tenets, and feels warmly toward Jesus. This may or may not have any further impact on how the Simple Folk lead their daily lives. The Simple Folk sort of believe because it seems like the thing to do, and perform just enough of the required religious functions and rules to feel like a believer. It's safe to assume that the majority of people in your world are Simple Folk unless your plot requires otherwise.

The Believer: this character is more deeply involved in his or her religion. He or she goes to church (or temple, or whatever) on a very regular basis, studies whatever texts or practices are intended to augment the faith, and makes an honest effort to bring his or her life into closer accordance with the "virtues."

The Zealot: this character believes so intensely in the letter of his or her religion that the spirit is lost. There is no tolerance for different views, and quite often the zealot is able to rationalise heinous acts in service to the faith. A bishop during the Spanish Inquisition who honestly felt that he was saving souls and protecting Christendom from the Devil would be an example.

The Manipulator: this character may or may not believe in his or her religion. He or she might fall into any of the other categories, including Skeptic, where personal belief is concerned. The important thing is the way that the Manipulator deliberately uses other people's beliefs to control their behaviour. In contrast to the Zealot, a Manipulator would be, for example, an Inquisition bishop who was well aware that most "witches" and "heretics" were innocent, but thought that the hunt for them benefited the church and his own personal ambitions.

The Zealot and the Manipulator are easy plot devices in period and fantasy fiction, because they are highly motivated to create conflicts and intrigues in pursuit of their ends. They can even be played against each other, as in the Zealot or Believer who devotedly follows a Manipulator and then learns the truth. This conflict can lead nicely to another personality type.

The Skeptic: this character has lost faith. He or she may once have been a Believer or even a Zealot, but something has happened to shatter his or her belief in religion, and perhaps even in basic decency. Stephen Donaldson likes to write Skeptics; Thomas Covenant the Unbeliever is a good example. In this case, Thomas loses faith because of his leprosy and his failed marriage. Even confronted time and again by deific beings, other worlds, and the reality of his own powers, Thomas drags his feet, because whatever the cost of not believing, the risks inherent in opening himself again seem even worse.

SUMMARY

In this chapter we went through one basic method for constructing a religion and thinking about how it would affect plot and character. We have seen that religion is closely bound up with other subjects like culture and local environment, so that whatever you create for one will affect the others.

In basic terms, the key to creating a detailed religion is to work in stages. In the above process, we started from the most general or universal, and moved in toward specifics. If you had created a culture first, it would be possible to use the same process backwards, looking at specific customs and working out what they meant about sect, then religion, and then view of the world. By careful attention to each step, moving in either direction, one could create a fairly detailed and complex system.

However, it is not actually necessary to have the religions of your world fully fleshed out in order to use them for tension. For example, in C. J. Cherryh's *Fortress* series, some aspects of the plot are driven or exacerbated by conflict between three different religious orders. The differences between these are never fully explored in religious terms, except for their comparative tolerance for magic; but we understand their comparative powers and ambitions in political terms.

In other words, it would be possible to focus on just one or two aspects of the above list, creating just enough information to satisfy the needs of your story or novel, without having to delve too far into aspects that are less interesting to you.

Arms and Armor:

LIVE FAST, DIE YOUNG, LEAVE A BEAUTIFUL CORPSE...MAYBE TWO

TOM DULLEMOND, MICHAEL McRAE AND TEE MORRIS

INTRODUCTION

This chapter will focus on armor, several specific weapons and how to employ them effectively, as well as things to bear in mind when creating your own Fantasy arms and armor.

Due to the enormous scope of this topic, discussions must remain brief—however, each section of this chapter provides an excellent starting point to expand your knowledge of arms and armor and make you appreciate the importance of their use in a fantasy setting.

OVERVIEW OF ARMOR (TOM DULLEMOND)

All pieces of armor need to come with the following warning, to discourage foolish warriors from charging blindly into battle:

By wearing this armor, I, _____of _____ Generic Warrior, acknowledge that I will still be killed by any effective blow. However, the maker of this armor warrants that wearing this armor will reduce the 'kill-zone' surrounding me by an unspecified amount, and that a certain (unspecified) number of 'border-line' blows that would have only just killed me previously, might now merely maim or cripple me. I indemnify the maker of this armor for any injury or death I might experience in the course of wearing this armor.

What is important here is the definition of 'border-line' blows. If a powerful sword-blow cuts you in half, you will die. If a weak sword-thrust penetrates your inside thigh, you will most likely bleed to death in thirty seconds. The end results are the same, but the types of blows are wildly different. Armor exists to help sort the weak killing blows from the powerful killing blows.

Where the first death cannot be prevented by wearing armor, the second can. Both deaths are just as dead (depending on your religion—see the Religion chapter!), but by wearing a piece of armor that requires a certain amount of force to penetrate, it is possible to 'edge-out' certain blows that would have killed you had you not worn that armor. It's a minor but relatively important distinction.

Armor is not going to save your life every time. It's basically there to maximise your chance of living by either deflecting a weapon or minimising the damage when a successful blow doesn't hit just the right spot. But when it does hit the right spot, you could be wearing a suit of plate worth a small kingdom, and the sword that hit you is most likely going to cut you open. So the goal of combat remains: do not get hit. Even in your most powerful suit of armor you don't want to take a chance.

There are three rules of wearing armor. I've made them up myself, but they are valid rules nonetheless. All warriors wearing armor need to remember these; else they will certainly be killed in battle.

The first rule of wearing armor:
If someone hits me hard enough, I will still be dead.

Weapons are not toys. They are designed to kill, and not even a half-inch metal plate is going to stop them if they come at you hard enough.

The second rule of wearing armor:

If someone hits me in the right spot, I will still be dead.

Armor is not a seamless suit of metal. It needs to be flexible enough to allow the wearer to move. What this means is that somewhere there is a gap or a join that offers less-than-optimal protection. Suits of chain may not have such gaps and joins, but they are essentially suits with lots of holes in them. Anything pointy with a diameter smaller than those holes will go straight through.

If someone finds the weak point in your armor, they won't need to worry about rule one to kill you.

The third rule of wearing armor:

If I'm not paying attention, someone will teach me the importance of either rule one or rule two, but probably both.

Essentially, if you're standing still, admiring the clouds, anyone can come up to you to practise rules rules one and two. They will have ample time to aim, find a gap, or swing their weapon with maximum force. If your hero is not paying attention on the battlefield (either because he is busy fighting someone else or simply an idiot), anyone can come up to him and kill him with relatively little effort, even if he is wearing a suit of plate. So having your hero stand imperviously contemplating a flower, while barbarians are pelting spears at him (which bounce off his armor), is an unrealistic scenario. Unless you want to raise your reader's interest in the scene by deliberately making it unrealistic, this scene belongs in the 'bad idea' bin.

Finding the 'right' suit of armor is a balance between the need for agility and protection. Since there are two ways to avoid injury on the battlefield—by dodging or deflecting an attack or by wearing thick armor—you need to organise your priorities. In a one-on-one situation, where you pit your skills against another, you want to rely more on your own talent to avoid being hit than on your opponent's lack of talent to hit your armor in the right spots. In this case, minimal constriction for maximum flexibility is important. However, if you are in a war or other chaotic battle where at any time an arrow, rock, broken blade or other weapon could strike you and there's nothing you can do about it, you have to stop caring about avoiding the unavoidable—you just want to make sure that when you're hit, you're not going to be injured.

BASIC ARMORS

Armor falls into three basic categories:
- Armor made of leather, fabric, or a combination of both.

- Mail—sheets of armor made by linking small metal rings together in a specific pattern to create a fully flexible metal 'cloth'.
- Rigid armor made of metal, wood, plastic, or some other solid material.

PADDING

Padding is needed to absorb the impact of blows that do not penetrate the armor. Once the armor has been penetrated, of course, the force of the impact (which will kill you in several days from internal bleeding) is not as important as the result of the impact (which might kill you a lot quicker than that). Padding is a crucial 'backup' to traditional armor, especially considering that a very large proportion of deaths in combat are due to massive bruising and internal bleeding. Remember, although your armor might have turned the cutting damage of the sword-blow, the impact of that force still needs to be reduced. The breastplate took care of your opponent's sword edge and some of the force. The rest of the force is going to crack your ribs unless you do something about it, which is where padding comes in. This is generally constructed of felt, thick linen, or some other tough fabric.

Padding also helps 'fit' armor better. A breastplate can sit snugly around a padded jacket, instead of rattling on your bony frame. Did I say bony? I meant well muscled.

ARMING CAP

A small padded cap worn between the head and helm, to ensure that blows to the helm aren't transferred directly to that most important of body parts, the head.

Practical example: hold a metal saucepan upside down on your naked head. Tap it lightly with your fingertips. Now tap a little harder. Repeat until you find your limit (for reference purposes, your limit is just before it starts to hurt). Now place a folded-up handtowel between the pan and your head. Repeat the previous exercise, and stand amazed at your increased impact-resisting ability. Then try not to think too much about why you are standing in your kitchen with a saucepan and handtowel on your head.

GAMBESON

A padded suit worn beneath armor, particularly chain.

LEATHER

Leather armor ranges from your basic hyena-hides (rancid strips of spotty fur) to advanced cuir-bouilli (leather panels made by soaking thick leather in a mixture of boiling paraffin and beeswax, then bending them into shape).

Mail

Often redundantly termed 'Chain mail' by role players around the world, 'mail' or 'chain' refers to sheets of armor made by linking small metal rings together in a specific pattern to create a fully flexible metal 'cloth'. Various methods of linking the rings, all based on the same basic pattern, produce variable thicknesses of mail—a knight might want the extra thickness on his shoulder, chest or gloves, where padding is more important than flexibility. Mail is best at protecting against slashing blows, but because of its flexibility it is comparatively lousy at absorbing impact. Similarly, because it is essentially full of holes, it doesn't provide the best protection against piercing blows such as arrows, either. Mail works best with secondary padding beneath it. There are stories of Crusader knights walking around looking like pincushions—although their hauberks (see below) could not stop the Saracen arrows, their thick felt gambesons were sufficient to protect them. Of course, 'normal' bows, not designed for speed and for use from horseback as the Saracens' were, could penetrate more easily, so don't use this example from history to have your knights become impervious to one of the most dangerous weapons on the medieval battlefield!

Coif

Worn over a padded cap (Arming Cap) and usually under the helm, the coif is essentially a mail sock with a big hole in it for the face and possibly a small flap to tie over the chin. It is excellent for providing additional safety from slashing attacks to the neck and throat.

Hauberk or Byrnie

A hauberk is a full suit of chain, generally long-sleeved, with or without integral gloves (mitts) or an integral coif. A byrnie is essentially the precursor to the hauberk, much shorter in length and with shorter sleeves and no integral coif or mitts. If you were writing in early medieval periods, sometimes inappropriately referred to as the 'Dark Ages', your heroes would be wearing byrnies.

A full hauberk is very heavy and clumsy (and unusable) without an arming belt to help distribute the weight. The belt is cinched tightly around the waist so that the weight of the bottom half of the armor hangs from the waist, not off the shoulders. It effectively separates the total weight into two more easily worn parts.

CHAUSSES

These are essentially mail stockings. Full chausses are complete pants legs that are tied to a belt, much like mail versions of hose (see 'Medieval Clothing'). They are often tied just above the knee to help distribute their weight (just as an arming belt helps distribute the weight of a hauberk). Half chausses are chausses that are open at the back and laced shut.

LAMELLAR

Lamellar armor consists of hundreds of small plates or 'lames' sewn onto cloth. The lames could be metal, wood, horn or leather. This armor has been in use throughout history in one form or the other from the early ninth century B.C. until as late as the sixteenth century A.D.

PLATE

This generally refers to rigid metal armors, either full body harnesses such as were being developed in the fifteenth century A.D, or smaller pieces of plate armor, such as greaves for the lower legs and bracers for the forearms.

CUIRASS

A single piece of armor, which covers the torso. It can be fashioned of leather, iron, or bronze. The ancient Greeks wore cuirasses made of bronze and fashioned to follow the body's musculature. A cuirass is generally open at the front, back, or both, and fastened with straps or laces (as the Roman cuirasses were).

GORGET

A solid collar to protect the throat.

GREAVES

Armor to cover the shins and calves.

BRACERS

Armor to cover the forearms.

KNIVES (MICHAEL MCRAE)

What is a knife? More to the point, what is the difference between a knife and sword?

If you answered 'size', you would be only 90% correct. Think about this: The Roman gladius, typically described as a sword, had an average blade length of approximately two feet. The Anglo-Saxon 'scramasax' also had a blade length of two feet, yet was by most definitions a knife.

So what is the difference?

Strictly speaking, very little. It could be argued that the Japanese katana is in fact a rather long knife. The Norse 'langseax', in spite of its classification, could be more akin to a sword. However, there are some subtle differences in the way knives and swords are used, differences which are reflected in their design throughout the ages.

Typically, knives are offensive weapons of precision. They are rarely used for defensive strategies, as opposed to most swords, which the combatant can use to parry their opponent's weapon. Rather, knives rely on speed and agility to wound an opponent. Hence most knives, such as daggers, dirks and stilettos, are small in size. Where swords are weighted towards the guard for optimal control, knives are usually weighted considerably towards the blade tip or towards the handle, depending on the design's intention. The scramasax, for instance, is blade heavy to achieve maximum power for its size. Most stilettos, on the other hand, have a weighted handle to give the opponent maximum control over the 'business end'.

For simplicity, this section will describe a knife as being any pointed blade under one foot in length that has either one or both sides sharpened.

The 'seax', a type of knife commonly used for combat in the Norse regions, spread through the western world during the dark ages. A single edge of the blade was sharpened, this side being longer than the unsharpened end. They often had a small guard, or no guard at all, and lacked a pommel. The seax, in all its forms, was primarily a 'hacking' weapon used in close-distance combat against opponents who were often armored in thick hide or chain. It had the advantage of being powerful, able to break bones through any pliable armor, yet was somewhat unwieldy and not as agile as most other knives.

Up until the thirteenth century, the knife as a melee weapon seems to have played a minor role in battle throughout the world. Few cultures held the knife in esteem as a practical military weapon. Seen more as a tool, knives rarely occupied a high place in the armory of any soldier. They were usually carried by their owners for utilitarian reasons, to be used as weapons only if pressed.

Within the course of the crusades, however, prestige made way for practicality—'peasants' weapons,' formerly little more than axes, adzes and fruit-picking bills, took new roles as weapons of war. Infantry soldiers were equipped with daggers, or 'cultellus' (where the word 'cutlass' later came from, as well as 'cuttlefish' and 'cutlery') as part of their standard kit. They were used blade-down as stabbing weapons, often to further wound or kill fallen soldiers in progressive stages of a battle.

Knives steadily became the choice for a secondary weapon—small and light, they were easily carried on the hip opposite to that which carried the sword. Most forms of knife were versatile enough to complement the sword as a back-up weapon. In other words, where the sword failed, often a knife could succeed.

As the Middle Ages progressed, the humble knife succumbed to technological advances and diversified into an array of small weapons. *The Maciejowski Bible*, created in the thirteenth century, displays a large number of combatants using various knives as primary weapons.

Changes in armor further diversified knives. Faced with increasing amounts of metal plate to get through, combatants used a style of weapon with a narrow blade called a 'stiletto'. These weapons were used offensively through gaps in the armor where the blade could be inserted. In later eras, as rifles were adopted as the soldier's weapon of choice, knives were adapted to fit the end of the rifle's barrel as a 'bayonet', to be used where the gun was an inappropriate choice of weapon. Again the knife is used as a secondary weapon.

Hence the knife's design relies primarily on its intended use. Throwing knives, for instance, are balanced towards the tip, focussing the force behind the blade. If the blade happens to strike a target, the blade has a better chance of being driven forward rather than have the handle carry forward on its own inertia. To use such a weapon, the knife can be held by the handle or the blade (depending on the thrower's preference). What matters is the number of complete turns the knife completes before it strikes the target. If the blade points towards the target on release, each revolution of the blade in flight must be complete. If thrown handle first, an additional half-turn is needed. To judge the number of turns needed (and therefore, the exact distance the thrower needs to be from the target) takes practice and experience. The smallest error in distance can make all the difference.

The one thing most knives have in common is that they are primarily offensive weapons. By this it is meant they have little capacity for defence. While this is not a hard and fast rule (the Japanese 'si' could be classified as a knife by some definitions, and yet it is primarily defensive in use), it covers most knives, or knife-like weapons.

Therefore knives in combat must be used in a style that enables the combatant to defend themselves by some means. This often means using the free hand as a defensive weapon. Parrying through redirecting the opponent's strikes with a quick swipe of the free hand is often effective. However, in a one-on-one knife fight the knife itself can be used 'offensively' in a 'defensive' manner. Confused? Think of it this way—a strike made by your opponent opens them to attack, hence immediate retaliation against any exposed regions (for example, the offensive forearm) while manoeuvring your body away from the strike will defend you against the attack while attacking them at the same time.

Whether it is a tiny dagger, a massive langseax, or a needle-thin stiletto, the humble knife is hardly a weapon to be trifled with. When asked, 'Does size matter in a weapon?' nine out of ten knights surveyed will say, 'Of course.'

Just don't turn your back on that one that smiles and says, 'No.'

THE EPEE BLADE (TEE MORRIS)

I was asked by Tom to give him a hand with this chapter as his speciality was rooted in twelfth century Century weapons and he knew I had some hands-on experience with "less manly" weapons.

Well, I prefer to describe the epee blade the way Obi-Wan Kenobi describes a light sabre to Luke Skywalker in George Lucas' *Star Wars*: *"An elegant weapon for a more civilised time."* The epee blade is a signature weapon for swashbucklers, highwaymen, and swords-for-hire. Zorro used one to leave behind his moniker. Errol Flynn's Captain Thorpe lived up to his name of *The Sea Hawk* in sacking the enemy ships of the British Empire. And can we deny the skill of *The Princess Bride*'s Inigo Montoya who had dedicated his life to fencing?

Go ahead, Tom, you tell *these guys* they aren't manly!

Writing for an epee blade is a little different from writing for the broadsword. The epee blade would be considered a "light weapon" in that it is easily wielded with one hand. That is the biggest difference between your general broadsword and an epee blade. From here, it is a domino effect in the gaps between the two weapons. They are both swords, and they are both blades. Beyond that, they are two very different weapons.

The general attack for a broadsword is similar to the attack for a battle-axe. You come to your opponent in arcs, cutting either on the diagonal or across the target. The epee, however, is a quick weapon. Its main intent is to work underneath an opponent's blade and stab or cut, not hack. Depending on how you look at it, the wound from an epee can prove to be far worse than a broadsword's or two-handed sword's blade as the epee inflicts more internal bleeding wounds.

There are some things to know in writing for the epee blade. There are certain factors and settings where epee blades work and where a better weapon would be utilised.

THE WIELDER'S ARMAMENT

Alright, picture the battlefields of the far-off Realms of Hyriana. High above the summit of Death Mountain, dark clouds surround the hold of the Evil Lord Ressnik. The various races have answered the challenge of Lord Ressnik and meet his forces at the base of his stronghold. Filling the air is the sound of metal clashing against metal as the Evil Lord and his forces lumber to the battlefield. They begin to pound against their metal breastplates as they draw their elegant, thin epee blades.

The united races of Hyriana look at one another a little exasperated. It is clear the Evil Lord Ressnik is a moron.

Yes, while Ressnik may be able to call upon the Forces of Darkness, he made a horrible judgement call in arming his armies. When you're fighting with an epee blade, movement is essential. The combatant needs to move and has to move fluently. Dressed head to toe in metal armor, movement will be hindered. To effectively fight with an epee, your hero or heroine should not be dressed in anything bulkier than leather armor. Most of the time, epee-wielding heroes are dressed in simple clothes and cloaks. The cloaks these combatants wear can also be used as a weapon (see the later section on epee fighting styles), but in all cases the clothes never hinder movement, as heavy armor tends to do.

So if your hero or heroine is working with epees, have them dress for success. Keep the clothes light and liberating. If you are worried about vulnerability, have them dress in layers or light armor such as leather or chain mail (in moderation). Remember that armor not only limits certain movement, but also slows your attacks.

THE KILLING BLOW

Even if your hero is wielding a full *Schlager* blade (see later section "Evolution of the Epee") and completely lost in the heat of battle, *you cannot behead anyone with an epee blade!* The neck is a thick collection of muscle and sinew and to cut off an opponent's head requires a lot of force as well as a lot of blade, and the epee blade just doesn't have that ability.

So why use an epee? How can you kill your opponent with this weapon?

As mentioned earlier, the lethal strikes are quicker and not so much as *hacking* at your opponent as it is *cutting* or *stabbing* your opponent. When people died from the wounds of an epee blade, it was not from blood loss. Death from epee (and bullet) wounds usually came from internal bleeding, especially if the wound was dealt in the stomach. Thrusts are the more lethal attacks dealt from an epee blade and far easier to make with a light epee versus a heavy broadsword. It would not be unheard of for a broadsword to face off with an epee as both weapons have advantages. True, a broadsword could easily break an epee in two. However, the epee can easily sneak in underneath the more massive broadsword attacks. Depending on the weight of the sword and the momentum of the attack, a broadsword could make its wielder open for attack from a smaller, lighter weapon, such as an epee. The risk for the epee wielder is that they must get in underneath the blade, attack, then retreat fast enough so that the broadsword does not come back on them and take off an essential body part, such as a head!

Another option for epee blade fighters is to cut the skin. While rapier cuts are rarely lethal (unless the epee's tips or edges are anointed with a poison as Laertes' blade in Shakespeare's *Hamlet*), they can take an opponent down from blood loss. Targets are key when trying to cut your opponents. The best target for rapier cuts are usually the neck (if you can get close enough) or wrists, inner wrists being the preferred targets as they can not only promote maximum blood loss but can also disarm your opponent.

If you intend to write for the epee, make sure your attacks are kept quick and either a thrust to the belly or a cut across the neck or wrists. Remember that you cannot take off an opponent's head or a limb with a rapier. The blade isn't heavy enough. With your targets clear and your movements swift, your epee fights will sing in your Fantasy novel.

THE EVOLUTION OF THE EPEE

Before there were broadswords, Egyptians and Romans were winning wars with long bows, spears, and *short swords*. Short swords were no longer and usually as wide as a man's forearm. As the art of war evolved, so did weapons. Bigger usually meant better, and in the European region the broadsword was given form, beginning with executioner's swords that were the earliest known two-handed broadswords. However, in the Middle East and Asian regions, two-handed swords were not so much "broad" as they were sleek. "Bigger" did not necessarily mean "better", and from the tactics and disciplines developed to these unique blades come the foundations for combat with the rapier.

The first rapier was called a *Schlager* blade, named after its creator. It was a heavy blade, not as heavy as a full broadsword but designed to be used only with one hand, work underneath the tactics of a heavier two-handed sword, and give the option for the combatant to use a second weapon such as a second sword or dagger. (See later section on variations of fighting with a rapier.) Schlager blades were subtle over time, the shape of the *forte* (the area of the rapier blade closest to the hilt) changing in shape and thickness. What was developed more than the blade itself was the guard. In the original version of the Schlager blade, the hilt was a simple, curved design with several *quillions* (extended flourishes of metal from the hilt). Then came the *swept, cage,* and eventually the *cup* hilt, each design making the hand a harder target for the opponent's blade. From the development of the rapier came several variations of a *short sword* (the duelling weapon of the seventeenth century) as well as the epee blade.

In comparison, the epee blade is half the width of the original Schlager blade, but easier and faster in its attack. It can also be used with second weapons, making it a versatile weapon in one-on-one combat.

VARIATIONS ON A THEME:
RAPIERS AND SECOND WEAPONS

A clear advantage over the two-handed broadsword with rapier combat is the incorporation of a second weapon. Due to their weight and the fighting tactics, the heavier two-handed broadsword rarely lends itself to use of another weapon. With the rapier, you have several options that can be used against either other combatants armed with rapiers or even heavier broadswords.

RAPIER AND DAGGER

The Rapier and Dagger combination is the most widely used in film, television, and stage. In this variation, the dagger is used as the "killer blow" weapon while the rapier can block or deflect the incoming blade. If the incoming blade is a heavier broadsword, a good, solid dagger can deflect it if there is enough power behind the dagger defence. Otherwise, the dagger can easily slip in underneath a rapier parry. It can be either a cut or a thrust to the earlier mentioned preferred targets of the stomach or wrists.

RAPIER AND BUCKLER

A *buckler* is a tiny shield, either made of thick wood or all metal and covers half of a forearm. It is not as heavy or as practical as a full shield, but the intent of the buckler is to deflect an incoming blade. Against a broadsword, bucklers can be easily destroyed (especially if the buckler is wooden) but many times the buckler is used as a striking tool against the fighters themselves. A common rapier and buckler strategy is to deflect the incoming blade with the rapier and then striking the opponent in the face with a buckler.

CASE OF RAPIERS

If your hero is not ambidextrous, I would not recommend this rapier variation. If your fighters are skilled with both left *and* right handed combat, give them this fight. A *case of rapiers* is two rapiers wielded by one fighter. In these fights, unless the opponent can parry both blades to one side, the attacks do not relinquish. As one blade is deflected, another blade is already coming in for a second attack. Combat with a case of rapiers is fast-paced, quick, and dangerous if the opponent is armed only with one. It is a challenge for combatants and to write effectively. If you want your hero to use two rapiers at the same time, do some research. Fighting with two weapons simultaneously, a case of rapiers especially, is very different. You take a chance of sounding extremely foolish if you don't understand the balance and co-ordination demanded.

Rapier and Cloak

This is my favorite on many levels. The rapier and cloak fight is for the swashbuckler hero and the hardest to defend against, depending on the hero's taste in fashion. The second weapon in this variation is exactly what it sounds like—a cloak or a cape. The combatant wields the cloak almost like a bullfighter, aiming either for the head or face in an attempt to distract the opponent. An additional option for the cloak is to weight it down by sewing into the hem of the cape lead pellets or weights. Then the cloak, instead of being used as a distraction becomes a weapon itself in striking the opponent's face or trapping the opponent's arm. The cloak can also wrap around and entrap the attacking weapon and disarm the opponent. It doesn't get more swashbuckling than the rapier and cloak fight, and it can be a lot of fun for the writer to create for the reader.

So while Tom may think the rapier is a "less manly" weapon than a broadsword, the rapier is a versatile weapon that can add a lot of depth and excitement to your novel's level of combat. Again, keep the pace of the fight quick, your blows either cuts or stabs, and know your weapon. Know the anatomy of your rapier, be it a full Schlager blade or a slim, sleek epee blade. While the epee is not as powerful or as sturdy as a two-handed broadsword, the rapier is designed for swift attacks and agility. Above all, have a great time with it. Rent a few of the classic swashbuckler movies and watch the fighter's techniques, or rent Danny Kaye's *The Court Jester* to watch "comedy combat" at its finest. Enjoy the fluidity and grace of the rapier fights and let it happen in your writing as well.

Mr. Kiss Kiss, Bang Bang—Firearms (Tee Morris)

As you have seen in the previous chapters I've penned, you will notice that I have a soft spot in my heart for the nostalgic swashbuckling antics of Errol Flynn. The man wrote the book on how to make chicks swoon, villains tremble, and kings and queens praise his name on high! Single-handedly, Errol Flynn raised the bar for adventurers to follow. Hollywood knew this and wanted to make sure that Errol looked as good as possible.

This meant that "historical logic" was thrown out of the window.

When it comes to firearms and fantasy, research is a necessity. (See my chapter on "Research in Fantasy.") If you are setting your Fantasy in a world that is post-fourteenth century, then you have the potential to introduce firearms to your characters and your story. While cannons have been documented to exist in China in the thirteenth century, firearms were not introduced to society until the fifteenth century, according to some Firearm History timelines offered up in print or on the Internet. Even with the introduction of the first firearm (less of a gun and more of a "portable cannon"), the firearm did not reach Europe (not *England*, but *Europe*) until nearly a century later.

So before you arm your pirates, highwaymen, and cavaliers with firearms, take a look at the history behind the hand-held pistol.

FROM BLACK POWDER TO BULLETS:
A BRIEF HISTORY OF FIREARMS

While this section of *The Complete Guide*™ *to Writing Fantasy* is one that brings a smile to Charlton Heston's face, you do not have to be a card-carrying member of the National Rifle Association to be well versed in firearms. Print and electronic resources can either give you an overall history of gunpowder and firearms, or you can research a specific firearm such as the Colt Winchester or the Sharpe rifle. (A rifle is a rifle? Hardly.)

So we begin our understanding of firearms with the invention of gunpowder or *black powder* as it was called in its early day. While we do not know which came first—the chicken or the egg—we do know that the gun would not have come to pass without the invention of gunpowder. While it is still uncertain exactly who invented gunpowder (from here out, referred to as black powder) it is documented that the Chinese Sung Dynasty in the tenth century were using black powder primarily for fireworks displays. It was in the mid-thirteenth century that the Chinese invented the first firearm that was a bamboo tube loaded with stone projectiles. However, according to Sportshooter.com and their history of Black Powder, Arabs in 1304 were using bamboo shoots reinforced with iron to shoot arrows. It would not be until the mid-fifteenth century (1429-1430) when the *culverin*, a portable cannon supported either on stands or wielded by two people, was introduced in the Battle of Orleans.

See (http://www.sportshooter.com/reloading/historygunpowder.htm).

THE MATCH LOCK

In the late fifteenth and early sixteenth century, a new weapon far more portable than the two-man culverins and the small cannons of China was introduced. The *matchlock pistol* is the first firearm that resembles the weapon modern society would recognise as a "gun." These firearms were originally developed by the Germans between 1460-1480. The key element of matchlocks was a large fuse that remained lit at both ends at *all times*. This was known as a *slow fuse* and would be attached to a component similar to a hammer. On pulling the trigger, the lit end would fall into a small chamber of black powder known as a *flashpan*. The black powder would ignite through a small hole in the barrel (called a *touchhole*) that would ignite the powder in the barrel and fire the bullet. If for some reason the slow fuse attached to the pistol's hammer was extinguished, the shooter would quickly lift the other lit end hanging by the gun's side, touch its lit tip to the touchhole, and ignite the powder that way.

Sounds like a Wile E. Coyote chain reaction Road Runner Trap from ACME, doesn't it? Well, in a sense, early pistols were about as reliable as those wacky inventions Wile E. would invest his hard earned money into. Matchlocks were reliant on many factors. Weather. The fuse. The heat of the fuse's tip. Wind conditions. If any of these factors were off in the slightest, matchlocks ran a fifty-fifty chance (closer to seventy-thirty, depending on the historical re-enactor you talk to) in firing.

THE WHEELLOCK PISTOL

The Germans continued development of the pistol with the advancements of the wheellock pistol, a weapon popular with the Landsknecht mercenaries of the fifteenth century Holy Roman Empire. The principles of the wheellock are the same as a matchlock, but the slow fuse is replaced by a metal serrated wheel located near the flashpan. The hammer-like mechanism pulls back the wheel and is held in place by a spring-loaded lock. Once the trigger is pulled, the wheel rotates against a set of iron jaws that creates sparks. These sparks ignite the powder in the flashpan and the pistol fires.

Again, weather and wind conditions factor into the chances of a wheellock pistol firing. While the matchlock fuse remaining lit is no longer a factor, the wheellock parts wearing out and not creating enough sparks to ignite the powder is. The extra moving parts also become problematic. If the spring-lock jams or if the wheel does not lock into place, you have a weapon in your hand with a lot of potential but little stopping power.

THE FLINTLOCK

The wheellock was a definite step forward and were state-of-the-art in weaponry for nearly an entire century. Then in the late sixteenth century (roughly around the 1580's and Queen Elizabeth I's reign), the flintlock pistol was developed. It promised a happy medium between the matchlock and wheellock pistols. Attached to the hammer of the pistol was a hard stone or metal block, known as the *flint*. Also attached to the barrel was a small piece of steel that either pivoted up for the flint to strike, or down and out of the hammer's reach. The flintlocks could be considered the earliest firearm to offer a *safety*. The pistol could remain loaded and ready to fire, but unless this second steel attachment (called the *frizzen*) was in the "up" position the bullet would not fire. When the frizzen is locked in the up position, the hammer back, and the trigger pulled, the flint strikes the frizzen causing sparks to be directed into the flashpan, which fires the pistol.

Flintlocks were more widely used and less expensive to produce as there were fewer moving parts than the wheel lock. They were, however, not as reliable as wheellocks or matchlocks as flints and frizzens tended to wear out after frequent use. Their popularity came from their ease to repair if something were to go wrong and their increased loading speed.

For centuries, the flintlock remained a popular firearm and gave birth to many variations. One popular off-shoot was the *musket*, a rifle version of the flintlock pistol. Still, the environment soldiers would be fighting in could easily affect the reliability of these early firearms. This uncertainty made pistols and rifles a *secondary* weapon to the rapier, sword, or battle-axe.

THE WAY OF THE GUN

When I was co-writing with Miss Lisa Lee, our world of *MOREVI* also extended into Tudor England under the rule of King Henry the VIII. At this time, wheellocks were in use so the Pirate Captain Rafe Rafton was quite skilled with a pistol. Our editor and publisher noted in her first critiques that Rafe would use his "advanced weapon" only as a "last resort," a reason that did not make a lot of sense with her. If opponents are armed with swords and our swashbuckler hero has a pistol with hammer pulled back, does he not have an advantage over them?

In stopping power, yes. In reliability, absolutely not!

In my chapter on research, I mention exactly how reliable early pistols were, particularly in situations of war and combat. (I also mention how important it is to research.)

First there is loading or priming the pistol, be it a matchlock, wheellock, or flintlock pistol. A portion of black powder is poured down the barrel, then the bullet is (literally) shoved down the barrel. *Wadding* (a piece of cloth or some palpable substance) is stuffed down the barrel in order to keep the powder and bullet in place. Another small amount of gunpowder is placed in the flashpan. Your pistol is now primed and ready.

After all, you are allowed one shot. Only one shot. Once that shot is done, you repeat this process once more.

Think about that for just a moment. How fast do you think you can do all this while the enemy is charging at your hero? Going back to my love for Errol Flynn movies, I still wince when I see his Captain Thorpe in *The Sea Hawk* fire his pistol three times in a two minute period while moving quickly through a South American swamp. Granted, it is Hollywood. You just have to "go with it." Still annoying when you not only know how long it takes to reload a pistol (while moving), but you also take a closer look at his surroundings. Captain Thorpe is moving through a humid swamp; he and his men kicking up water everywhere. If that powder became even slightly wet, provided it even remained in the flashpan as he ran, he would be lucky if the pistol fired once.

The fact still remains a pistol can travel farther and faster than a blade. Pistols are far more powerful than swords, right? Yes, but power is not the issue here. Keep in mind these are pistols of 1540, not 2002. Compare a wheellock pistol (the more reliable of the three pistols covered here) to a modern AK-47. An AK-47 in full automatic combat mode fires over one hundred rounds per minute. Its average reload time is ten seconds depending on an individual's training and agility. Its reliability (reliability defined here that if you pull trigger, the weapon will fire) would be rated somewhere between 80%-100%, leaning more to the 100% level. Now the wheellock pistol of the sixteenth century fires *one* round per minute and has an average reload time of *five to fifteen minutes* depending on the individual's training and agility. Its reliability could be anywhere between 25%-50%, regardless if you loaded it properly. If it did fire, the bullet's path would be far from straight due to the shape of the bullet (as bullets were made by hand) and the weather conditions.

So why did people use pistols? Because they were new, not efficient. Pistols were used as a first wave for an army. If you have a long line of riflemen, your chances of doing widespread damage with bullets greatly increases. As for individuals, they are a final option in combat situations or daring weapons to use in duels.

MODERN FIREARMS

For those of you working with urban fantasy, alternative history, or science fiction, you may want to work with more modern weapons, familiar weapons to all of us from movies and television. The more modern pistols and rifles are regarded as "signature weapons" just as rapiers and broadswords were in The Renaissance. James Bond, and his fellow Secret Service agents carried the Walther PPK's. Mickey Spillane's Mike Hammer named his Colt Automatic "Betsy." And when facing beings from the Eighth Dimension, no one handles firearms better than Buckaroo Banzai. (I still dig the way Peter Weller shoots one being, spins his six shooter *behind his back*, and takes out another coming from the other direction. Now that's style!).

It would be great to be as well versed in weapons as *The Terminator* or even *Team of Darkness* author Tony Ruggiero who worked closely with the United States Navy SEALS. (He would tell me what he did with them, but then he'd have to kill me. You know how that goes.) Sadly though, unless you are the serious hardcore sportsman, a survivalist, or ex-military, you know as much about guns as what you see in TV and film. We could easily dedicate a chapter on modern firearms, but instead let's take a look at the highlights of the more modern firearms of the late nineteenth century and today.

THE PISTOL

The Six Shooter. The Peacemaker. Saturday Night Specials. Heat. There are as many words and slang phrases to describe a pistol as there are calibres. The *calibre* of a gun— .22's, .38's, and .45's—all refer to the diameter of the gun's barrel and consequently determined the type of ammunition used in them. With ammunition, you can use *blanks* (bullets that only make a loud noise and show, but have no projectile in the bullet's casing), *semi-magnums* (bullets that are used mainly for target practice that do not come to a point and are not fully packed with metal), and *full magnum bullets* (bullets that come to a tip and are usually heavier than semi-magnums, causing the most damage to a target). Bullets also come in various makes ranging from hollow-point (*dum-dum* or *talon*) bullets where the bullet tip collapses inside its cavity creating sharp lead shreds that tear muscles and organs (causing internal bleeding) to the modern-day *glaser* bullets that explode on impact into tiny teflon balls. The glaser bullets' velocity cannot penetrate thick material, approved for used by Sky Marshalls and they will not breach the cabin or fuselage.

There are a wide score of pistols in the world. Different makes and models, automatic and semi-automatic. What is essential in your research and application of working with firearms is knowing what weapon your hero is using and how it reacts under fire. Know and understand the differences between a six-shooter and a semi-automatic. How is loading a Smith & Wesson Magnum different from loading a Smith & Wesson Auto Mag? Which one has better stopping power? If you want to find out more about working with firearms, loading times, and efficiency, go surfing on the web under "Gun Manufacturers" or take a look at the related links page of the National Rifle Association (http://www.nra.org) who will also provide many other web sites beyond gun manufacturers.

THE RIFLE

Rifles are the two-handed swords of firearms. They tend to have more range and can either be built for accuracy or widespread damage. Matchlocks, wheellocks, and flintlocks came in rifle sizes as well as pistol sizes, and muskets proved to be very reliable (relatively) on the battlefields of the seventeenth and eighteenth centuries. In the nineteenth century, *lever-action rifles* like the *Winchester .45 Long Colt* were developed by Colt, and mainly used by infantry and frontiersmen as they made their way west across America. By this time in history (post-American Civil War), flintlocks were weapons of the past. Winchesters and other lever-action rifles now had a different way of firing bullets. Instead of a flashpan, the powder was cased in the bullet itself. The hammer would have a sharp spike tip and strike the back-end of the bullet, propelling it out of the barrel and to its target. To this day, both rifles and pistols work this way.

Today, rifles tend to be used for one of two things—accuracy or maximum damage to a single target. Films like *The Negotiator* or *Leon: The Professional* (not Fantasy or science fiction films, but still VERY good movies) showcase how accurate high-powered rifles can be as well as how accurate they are in the hands of a skilled marksman. With laser sightings, a simple dot against a target can guarantee where the bullet's path will end once the trigger is pulled. If rifles are not used for accuracy, they can deal a large amount of damage to one single target. In *Terminator 2: Judgement Day*, both the Terminator and Sarah Connor use rifles (Schwarzenegger's rifle was a Winchester while Linda Hamilton's was a pump-action shotgun.) to slow down the more advanced T-1000. You can easily see the amount of damage dealt to the "Liquid Metal Assassin" when they open fire with their weapons at such close range.

However, don't be fooled by the "Hollywood Factor." Yes, it was cool watching Schwarzenegger cock his Winchester by swinging it around in an arch, letting the momentum do the work. Yes, it was cool (and something extremely sexy) watching Linda Hamilton pump the shotgun with one hand. But know this—rifles are still considered "heavy" weapons. The amount of force needed to do what they did in *Terminator 2* (particularly Hamilton's one-handed pump action, a move often duplicated now) would be nothing less than superhuman. The firearms used there were rigged to do that so that they would look cool. Keep that in mind.

THE MACHINE GUN

It was in the American Civil War that rifles took a far more lethal turn with the invention of the *Gatling Gun*. This was the cross between a cannon and a rifle, a stationery weapon able to fire through rotating barrels a total of six hundred rounds per minute. The Gatling Gun was the most lethal of firearms right up through World War I. A "portable" version of the Gatling Gun, the *Thompson Machine Gun*—better known as the *Tommy Gun*—became the choice weapon of New York, Chicago, and Kansas City mobsters. By today's standards, the Tommy Gun is a quaint antique in comparison to the Uzi, Mach 10, and other semi-automatic and automatic weapons seen in television and film. These smaller, lightweight firearms are not built for accuracy but more for widespread damage. "Sweep-and-spray" is the technique used in firing such weapons. You see a terrific display of the "sweep-and-spray" destruction technique (as well as an extensive variety of modern machine guns) in the Agency's Lobby sequence in *The Matrix*.

WEAPONS OF THE FUTURE

At present, lasers are used merely for targeting purposes. While science fiction tends to promise the wide-use of laser pistols, we are currently in the infancy of the twenty-first century and we are still nowhere near the invention of a blaster, light sabre, or even a simple Type 1 Phaser.

In the IBM commercials of 2001, Avery Brooks was asking, "Where are the flying cars?" No doubt today there are those gun enthusiasts asking, "Where are the phasers?"

So when you create your worlds of Tomorrow, how advanced is your arsenal going to be? Look at the *Aliens* series. Man has begun colonising outer space and has mastered the science of suspended animation and space travel. However, firearms are still nothing more than automatic pistols and glorified AK-47's with grenade launchers. The future is looking a lot like its past, is it not?

But is that lazy writing? Take a look at the development of the firearm in our own world. For centuries, the flintlock was the basis of both the pistol and the rifle, upgraded from age to age but still nothing more than a basic flintlock. It would be nearly three centuries and a score of wars and revolutions before the Gatling Gun and the Colt .45 would be introduced. The evolution of the firearm in your writing is strictly up to you though. While we don't have the "flying cars" of 2001, we do have two-way video communications (video conferencing), communicators (cellular phones), electronic libraries (the Internet), and even Tricorders (the Palm Pilot, a stretch, but still, think about it). We have these advancements as our society is inspired and driven by a need for education and communication. What if we were more aggressive as a race? Oh sure, we have aggressive factions of the human race, but as a whole humans are a benevolent bunch. What if, as it is in Roddenberry's *Star Trek* Universe, we were something more akin to Klingons? Then perhaps we would have more advanced weaponry (as seen in the latest *Star Trek* franchise, *Enterprise*, where the Klingons have a new weapon unknown to the Humans called *photon torpedoes*) instead of communication and data-exchange devices. The development of your world's arsenal is strictly up to you, but before arming everyone with laser pistols and video wrist watches, think about where your society is headed and where they are at now. This will surely guide you in what advancements, if any, the world's arsenal technology.

KNOW YOUR WEAPONS, BUT KNOW THEY ARE WEAPONS

In closing I would like to pass along some sound advice. Perhaps you are like me and you want to write from first-hand experience. Say then you have a friend who is heavy into historical re-enacting (like some of my friends are) and say they offer to you, "Come on out to my place and we can do some target shooting."

Two words: remain aware.

In 1984, Actor Jon-Erik Hexum, an actor who showed a lot of potential in the somewhat innocently-fun and short-lived SF television show *Voyagers!* was quickly establishing himself as an action hero in his new television show, *Cover Up.* His frustration over a filming delay drove him to goof around with one of the show's .44 Magnum prop guns. He put the gun to his head and pulled the trigger. Even though the gun was loaded with blanks, the explosive charge inside the blank discharged at point-blank range. It cost him his life, less than a month shy of his twenty-seventh birthday.

In 1993, after numerous low-budget martial arts movies, Brandon Lee—the son of the Dragon himself, Bruce Lee—was about to break out with his own *Enter the Dragon*. It was a gothic, paranormal epic called *The Crow.* The word in Hollywood was that this film would not only lift Brandon to the status his father obtained with *Enter the Dragon,* it would bring him into his own status as an action film hero and as an actor. In between scenes, a crewmember was testing one of the guns for a future scene. The gun was "dry fired" (meaning the crew member simply pulled the trigger, thinking there was nothing in the barrel) to uncock the hammer. This dry fire inadvertently knocked the tip of another blank into the chamber. Instead of a cleaning and final check to confirm the guns were empty, the crew reloaded the "props" with blanks. This uncleaned gun with the blank in its chamber was fired directly at Brandon Lee. The second blank turned the first blank lodged in its chamber into a projectile or a "live" round. It was not until the shooting of the scene was finished when it was noticed that Lee had been actually shot. He died at twenty-eight.

In 1999, I was performing with murder mystery troop in Washington, DC. I was goofing around with the realistic looking prop guns. Taking "cop show" poses and things of that nature. I had seen others in the company do this and assumed these prop guns were merely that. Prop guns. I had worked on shows before where primed weapons were part of a show but these weapons were also closely supervised by a "weapons master." I had pulled the hammer back on this one pistol and could not ease it back into the safety position, so I simply pulled the trigger, expecting a dry fire.

The gun went off in my hand.

Unbeknownst to me, the prop pistol was loaded with a blank. I saw the charge's flame shoot from the gun. Fortunately, my other hand was clear of the gun's barrel. The pistol itself was pointing down and away from others. Still, I was caught completely off guard. After receiving a lecture from the director, I asked why in the month and a half I had been with the company I remained uninformed that the guns were "hot."

The director replied, "Tee, *everyone* knows I keep a live round in these guns. In case I want to have an effect."

I quit the company that night.

It does not matter if the guns are loaded with or without blanks. It does not matter if the firearm you are studying up close and personal is an antique or in use. It does not matter if the weapon in question is a firearm, a sword, or even yourself in the case of martial arts. A weapon is a weapon, not a toy. If you do wish to study firearms weapons, or combat of any kind, safety is key. Be certain to work closely with someone well versed in whatever weapon you are researching, and make certain they are also competent in their craft. Make sure your expert is careful with his or her weapon as well. And when you are researching, remain aware. Of your environment. Of your behaviour. And of the behaviour of others. You have a responsibility to yourself and others in working with weapons. When this responsibility is waived, injuries, deaths, or having your wits completely frazzled is bound to occur. Accidents will happen, but the more prevention you can take will assure you, your trainer, and anyone close by. You will find that a hands-on study of weaponry, firearms, and even martial arts will benefit your writing. This approach, however, should *never* be done without proper supervision. When working with weaponry of any kind, there is no room for carelessness.

Remain aware.

WEAPON CREATION (MICHAEL McRAE)

So, you want Daid'denan the Elflord to have a cool crossbow, eh? Or maybe you want that fancy warrior race of Bod-gani to be wielding giant axes? Perhaps you imagine that annoying thief, Snoop Pussy-puss, carrying a pair of wickedly sharp claws in case of a run-in with the law.

In any case, weapons can be the perfect supplement to that new race, that divine hero or that most insidious villain. The right kind of weapon can make a character look strong, weak, clumsy, lawless or humorous. Of course, the wrong type of weapon can do the same thing, albeit when you least want it to.

So how do you go about matching a weapon to a character or a race? Or more importantly, how do you go about devising a unique weapon that suits the style of character it is intended for?

The following is a suggested method that can be used to either create a unique weapon or assign a historical weapon to a unique race or character. Simplicity is the key here. Unfortunately, magical weapons are not addressed here. The influence of magic on weapons is a whole different ball game.

STEP 1: PICK A STYLE

A IS FOR AIM,

B IS FOR BLUDGEON,

C IS FOR CLEAVE

Before you make this first step, ask yourself this question: Why do I want to invent a unique weapon?

If it is honestly because you think it would look rather cool, then please reconsider. Barf the Barbarian might at first come across as rather intimidating carrying around a 'Lumbar 2000' Spring-axe, but it may be creating more questions than you are interested in answering. Why does he have this weapon? Is it a one-off creation? What is the significance? Why isn't he using a two-handed axe like the other barbarians?

Weapons reflect the culture of the character hence reflect the race. And vice versa—the race can affect the weapon (see Race Creation). Use this fact wisely. The weapon your character uses in the story might seem insignificant at first; however, it says quite a bit about them. Is the culture of the character technologically advanced in nature? Refined? Industrious? Sporting? Clandestine?

So, the first step in tailoring a weapon to fit is: 'Pick a weapon style descriptor'. In other words, how does the weapon 'work'? In effect, the style of your weapon should reflect the nature of your character's culture, or your race's culture. Some examples of 'style' are:

·	Bludgeon	Hack	Pierce	Poison
·	Ballista	Slice	Garrotte	

Assigning a style descriptor to your intended weapon at this point will help maintain a bond between weapon and character throughout the process. Bludgeon might give connotations of brutish, oversized creatures, while slice might insinuate a lithe, agile character. Would a small thief use a bludgeoning weapon? Or a monstrous ogre use a small blowpipe? Perhaps, but this step forces you to acknowledge that a weapon helps to define the character.

While there are no hard and fast rules on what sort of descriptor suits what sort of culture, use a little discretion and historical research. And don't forget, you are not assigning a weapon yet, just a style of weapon.

STEP 2: EYE FOR AN EYE

CHANGE BEGETS CHANGE

The family tree of weapon technology is as knotted and twisted as any ancient oak. At its lumpy base lay the humble stick and the innocuous rock. Its heavy limbs are carved with the words 'sword', 'club', 'axe' and 'knife'. Climb out into its canopy and there sprout the leaves of modern warfare—Panzer, Glock, ICBM.

Tracing this genealogy through the ages, as complex as it often is, relies on a simple concept. Change begets change.

Casting a stone at another's skull with a well-aimed throw is the most basic form of ballistic combat. In anticipation of this, the victim of the attack might well devise a form of protection that would absorb some of the impact of his enemy's weapon, such as a hyena skin. In response to this advance in his enemy's technology, the initial attacker would need to do something different in order to be successful in any subsequent assaults. He might need a stone that would go faster, in order to be able to make the 'ballistic-absorption-device', or 'hyena skin', ineffective. Or he might need to aim better, in order to strike an area that the hyena skin does not cover.

In any case, the attacker would need to take advantage of a weakness in the enemy's technology to get the better of them. Change begets change— the motto of progress. Nowhere is this more apparent than in the global history of war.

The first forms of armor would have been little more than sun-dried animal skin. Made to protect against the blows of stone, bone and wooden weapons, they would have been crudely effective. With the advent of using metals such as bronze, and later, iron, better weapons would have been created in order to get past such simple armor.

The technology for constructing armor could only go so far, however. Tanning, for instance, might have made for sturdier leather; however, when faced with weapons that could be sharpened into blades and points, even the hardest leather armor could only do so much. The answer to this predicament was to invent a covering that was flexible, like leather, yet could prevent the cutting of a honed edge or the piercing of a sharp point. Loops of interlinking metal, called 'mail' or 'chain' (chain-mail, in spite of its common use in the vernacular of many role playing games, is like saying 'chain-chain', and 'plate-mail' makes no sense at all), was an effective form of armor that remained in common use for nearly two millennia after it was first devised. In response to chain, heavier weapons that could crush bones through chain—such as mauls and two-handed axes—were developed. Plate armor developed to get past this hiccough, stilettos to get past the plate. And so on.

Without going into details for every advance in weapon technology through the ages, it is easy to see that the creation of a weapon is never in a vacuum. Creating a unique weapon relies on several factors. However, none is as important as the reason it is created in the first place. The old adage 'If it ain't broke, don't fix it' works well here. Why was the weapon initially made?

Hence, Step 2: 'Eye for an Eye'. Your weapon style must now be given a precedent—a reason for its creation. Was it designed in retaliation against the sudden were-bear attacks in the summer of '49? Or did the Al'khira redesign their armor in a way that prevented normal darts from pushing through? Is the cleaving weapon a one-off, made by a weapon smith for your father to defeat Biju the Peg-leg master swordsman? Once you have an incident in mind, you can create a weakness that can be taken advantage of. Biju's Peg-leg for example, or the flammable nature of the Al'khira's new armor, or the fact that were-bears happen to lower their heads just before they attack could all be inspiration for a new weapon.

Doing this will give you a sense of appreciation of 'why' you have a unique weapon. At no point in your story's plot does it have to be explained. The important thing is that you can justify the weapon's existence.

Step 3: That sword is so...yesterday!
Why, that's not a paperclip!

By now you should have a good idea of a) what style of weapon your character would use and b) what the weapon was made in response to.

Again you are reminded—simplicity is the key! Bigger is not always better, smaller not always more discreet, and more pointy-bits are not always more evil. Keeping in mind the reason behind your weapon's creation, ask yourself: What sort of implement was this weapon based on. A small sword? An axe? A spear? A potato peeler?

Seriously, many weapons began as simple tools. The glaive, a weapon that formed the foundations for countless billed weapons, was once a humble fruit picker. Hence you are not limited to existing weapons. Many farm tools such as axes and pitchforks were used in times of war as weapons, don't forget, and were potentially quite effective.

Be aware that the 'foundation implement' on which you are basing your weapon, does not necessarily have to reflect the style descriptor (although it does help). Sure, it might be a bit hard to modify a frying pan to 'slice', or a rapier to 'bludgeon', but with some trial and error it might be possible to create something not only unique, but also rather believable.

STEP 4: STOKE THAT FORGE, BOY!

WHAT DOES THIS BUTTON DO?

The final step. To the drawing board! Time for the physics.

Do not be afraid of some trial and error here. Jumping between Step 3 and 4 is not only allowable, but also encouraged. Play with different foundations—maybe a hammer doesn't work, or perhaps using a spear is not quite right. Be creative.

When you are happy with all of the above steps, modify the foundation item to suit the weakness in the incident that led to the weapon's creation. Look at historical weapons for inspiration—hooks and barbs to catch flesh and cloth, rings to snare hooks, the balance of a weapon to give power to the swing or control over the blade...and so on.

The physics are the most demanding. As this is fantasy, the weapon does not necessarily have to work in practice, but it does have to be believable. This is a case where 'it works in theory' is good enough. Making the actual weapon and testing it is not required (not to mention, not advised!). However it should still work in the confines of your story.

All weapons have weaknesses. If it is blade-heavy, it is hardly very agile. If it is long and thin, it will be rather inefficient in parrying a heavy broadsword. If it has lots of small spikes, a lot of training might be required to avoid injuring yourself while using it. Being aware of the parameters of your weapon will help retain an element of reality. A great big, dual-bladed axe with a spiked ball on its end could look rather menacing, and hurt lots when it strikes. But how effective would it be in combat, considering it would be nearly impossible to use to parry incoming blows?

Again, all relies on the style of your story. If it is to be written in the style of an ancient legend, then a dwarf carrying a six-foot long maul might be appropriate. However, if it is more akin to typical High Fantasy, then it does not matter how strong Biju the Peg-leg sword master is, he will not be able to use his massive two-handed sword as a fencing foil.

The way a weapon is designed will always influence the way it is used beyond the physical attributes of its wielder.

You call it a 'Peacemaker', I call it 'Justice'

The name says it all. Well, maybe not all, but it does say quite a lot. The name of a weapon should again reflect the culture of its origin. The word used will always convey connotations of existing cultures, present and past.

Descriptive words are rather technological and hence reflect a rather western ideal. Animal names, or words that are 'nature oriented', echo indigenous cultures such as the American and Australian natives. For example, 'Stinging Bee' is not very European medieval. Likewise, 'Barbed Maul' is a little bland for a pseudo-African native's weapon.

Refer again to the chapter on Race Creation—creating names. The rules there apply equally to the making of weapons.

My uncle has one just like it!

Creating a special weapon can be the spit needed to polish off that race of elves, or to spruce up that daring hero. They can speak volumes about the alien nature of a character, the advanced technology of a species or the dark forces employed by an antagonist. However, discretion must be used.

History has already seen the rise and fall of unique technologies. Indian swordsmen, Japanese ninjas, Spanish conquistadors, Moorish raiders and even Pacific Islanders all used weapons that were unique to them. Why not borrow from their experience? If you want a small spiky thing to throw in front of a running horse to make it throw its rider, why not use caltrops instead of making up your own device? At least most people recognize the term 'caltrops', and you don't have to spend half a page explaining your own unique version of them.

Weapon construction should be the spice in the soup, not the meat and vegetables. Use it sparingly, and even then, only if you really think your story needs it. Then again, Snoop Pussy-puss would just not be the same without those Simbalese Climbing Claws of Death.

Combat (Tom Dullemond)

What is more exciting and nerve wracking than a good battle between your heroes and their nemesis' henchmen? A minor skirmish can weaken your heroes just enough to make their final showdown a little more dangerous. But what if you get it wrong? How does the reader come away from your tale if you screw up your battles? Last impressions are lasting impressions.

The effectiveness and realism or believability of your combat scenes relies on the same thorough understanding and research as the realism of your clothing, religions and food. However, in our modern society we do not generally experience the mind-numbing fear of certain, unavoidable death facing an oncoming horde of screaming soldiers, or the cold certainty that you will survive that grips your guts when you face a more evenly matched or even outnumbered foe.

The problem is that, unless you have actually been in those sorts of combat situations, it is difficult to convey that experience to the readers-tripping over bodies as you and your fellow knights retreat slowly, praying that one of the enemy flanks will fold beneath your commander's last rally so you can overrun them before you stumble in a rabbit hole and sprain your ankle; watching your sword rust before your eyes in the thin drizzle that makes the grass treacherously slippery underfoot; watching your champion challenge the enemy before the amassed shield walls, then seeing him cut down moments later.

This chapter will follow our hero Berk on his misadventures as he tries to kill goblins in the most interesting way possible. It will conclude with a full example from start to finish of how to stage a battle and describe it effectively.

TIME KEEPS ON SLIPPING

TIMING

Combat scenes need to flow. Think of them as you would an action scene in a movie. Unless you slow the action down by means of some literary device, your characters do not have the time to analyse or debate:

- their foes' religion, fashion sense or sexual preferences;
- the intricacies of the heroes' interpersonal relationships;
- the weather; or
- the execution of their combat skills.

Why? Because—unless the writer specifically indicates otherwise—an action scene happens in real time. Why? Because it's action. Action happens in the real world, not in some metaphysical thought scape. To get the reader to work themselves into a lathered frenzy, gripping your book tightly as they curse their reading ability, you need to control the flow of your tale minutely, speeding up and slowing down appropriately as the pace of the battle changes.

> Berk chopped down at the goblin with his small hatchet, tracing a silvery arc towards the brute's ugly, misshapen head, trying to control his stomach at the thought of goblin brains staining the cool, crisp morning air.
>
> The blade connected with a sickening crunch, much like the sound Me'Evil had made in the final minutes of his life,

when he had fallen to his doom from the heights of lost Trenn. Berk wondered how the goblin thought of him-his careless murderer. But it was either the goblin or Berk. He pulled the hatchet free and the goblin's twitching body collapsed to the ground.

All right! Now a blow that would have taken a second at the most to execute took far longer than a second to read. But as of yet, the actual combat involves only Berk and his hapless victim, and so you could just get away with this kind of extended scene—it's almost in deliberate slow-motion. However, if several other combatants were around, the reader could be excused for hurling your book across the room. Why? If a single blow requires two long paragraphs of exposition, an entire battle may take the rest of the day to read.

A good guide to writing effective action scenes is to group events into sentences depending on their proximity in time. By that I mean: if two events happen closely together, your action will flow better if those two events happen in the same sentence.

Compare:

Berk chopped down at the goblin and watched his hatchet cleave into its head.

Berk chopped down at the goblin. He watched his hatchet cleave into its head.

The second sentence adds a significant break between the act of swinging the hatchet and the act of head-cleaving, although there is no break in real time. Generally this gap needs to be eliminated or glossed over. In our first—overly long—example, this gap was filled with inner contemplation and reminiscences-a trick whose effectiveness is short-lived, as it can become both obvious and tedious.

AVOID LISTING

The easiest way to avoid listing actions is to use the word 'then' sparingly.

Berk chopped down with his axe, then watched the goblin collapse. Then the imperator's elite guard broke down the door, and then the old guard...

In the above example only the first 'then' really fits. Generally, starting your sentence with 'then' should be avoided completely.

Berk chopped down with his axe, then watched the goblin

collapse. Suddenly, the imperator's elite guard broke down the door. The old guard...

What you are trying to do is avoid simply listing the actions in your combat scene. Although listing actions does work sometimes, and may even be unavoidable in shorter sections of combat, it can quickly becomes tedious if your battle lasts for more than a few paragraphs. I find it helps to think of your action in terms of a movie scene—the camera angle changes as the action scene unfolds. Merely listing your actions is a lifeless way to portray combat.

VARIETY IS THE SPICE OF LIFE

There are only so many ways of describing a sword blow or a sword, and unfortunately you have to use them all—over and over and over again.

So what can you do?

> Berk swung down at the goblin, burying the blade of his axe in its forehead. The second goblin leapt towards him, and Berk swung his axe in a wide arc, parrying its powerful swing. It sneered and swung its rusty sword at his neck. Berk dodged the swing and kicked the goblin in the knee, bringing it snarling to the ground.

Okay-clearly there's way too much 'swinging' happening here and too many 'axes'. The prose may not actually be repetitive, but it sure feels that way. Berk needs to be swinging, chopping, hacking, cleaving, attacking and lunging. To add variety to his 'axe' you might like to name the weapon—certainly a common historical practice. The alternative is saying, 'Berk swung his weapon' which sounds odd, seeing as it's not just a weapon, it's an axe—see Milena's comments regarding 'Charlie the fair-haired warrior' in 'Fantasy Without Clichés'. A weapon could be anything from his fist to a two-handed magical sword. A weapon's given name would obviously have to be established earlier in the writing, but it's hardly difficult to do that. We'll name Berk's axe 'Nailfang'.

On a side note, the same rule applies for enemies. If somehow, through an overheard conversation or some other literary device, Berk (and by proxy the readers) finds out what the goblins are called, it gives you more flexibility and precision when describing the action. Instead of three goblins that need to be kept apart through vague descriptions such as 'the bigger goblin' or 'the smellier goblin', you can actually refer to them by name—Gib Og and Krag Tob, for example.

> Berk chopped down at Gib Og, burying Nailfang's blade in its forehead. He braced his foot on the goblin's neck in order to pull the axe free. He turned just in time to see the

second goblin, Krag, leaping towards him. Berk swung his axe in a wide arc, parrying a powerful blow. Krag sneered and hacked with its rusty sword at Berk's neck. Dodging barely in time, Berk kicked the goblin in the knee, bringing it snarling to the ground.

Notice that each of the actions happens in its own little sentence, grouped together by timing: chopping and striking; leaping and parrying the leap; sneering and attacking; dodging and kicking and collapsing.

Planning

Planning is the key to a successful action scene. It is vitally important that bad guy A, who's on his knees in corner B, doesn't hit hero C, who's fighting in corner D on the other side of the room. Because writing is a fairly slow process and reading is much faster, the readers will catch this kind of error where you might not since they have a fresher three-dimensional image of who is where in the room.

Another reason to plan your fights is to remove the random factor from combat. This may sound strange, since as a writer you are ultimately in control, but what it comes down to is that in the heat of writing, you may add something minor into the combat that will drastically affect story elements later on. It's a lesser example of a more common plot flaw where something your heroes might have done as a logical response to current events ultimately spells their doom (if uncorrected by some heavy-handed rewriting). In a combat situation this kind of slip-up is deadly. I recall being stuck for two weeks because all but one of my heroes was unconscious and the bad guy could have defeated them all with ease. Recovering gracefully from this kind of situation without the reader feeling that the scene is manipulated requires some careful editing and potentially a lot of rewriting.

Marco! Polo!

No amount of planning, however, can help you if you are unable to communicate your careful plan to the reader. A combat scene on paper is like playing a game of Marco Polo, where the person who is 'it' is blindfolded and calls out 'Marco!' and is answered by the others. The readers are 'it'—they don't know where all the players are in this game, and you aren't allowed to tell them outright, because doing so would mean having to list their actions and positions, making for a dull and lifeless scene.

So how do you get around this? The more characters in the scene, the harder it becomes to keep tabs on them, but it is very important that you do so and that you allow the reader to do so. The reader knows what is happening only from the few pieces of information you are releasing. If anything you describe is misinterpreted or vague, then the reader might imagine that hero A jumped to the right and is now near evil overlord B, whereas you might have intended (and are therefore assuming) that hero A jumped to the left and is now near evil henchman C. This is a fundamental screw-up, and when your reality becomes sufficiently different from the reader's reality, they are instantly lost because what they're reading suddenly makes no sense, as the hero beats up the henchman and sneaks up behind the evil overlord. 'Wait a minute,' says the reader. 'How can he sneak up on the overlord? The overlord would have seen him when he leapt towards him before. Oh, I am so confused.'

REALISM

The best and most exciting way to get a feel for combat—and without the stink of blood and guts it's still not even completely realistic—is to become involved in a metal weapons re-enactment group. The second best way—and the easiest and cheapest—is to go to a medieval or Renaissance fair. One thing to remember about Renaissance fairs is that they are fundamentally the hunting grounds of weirdos and madmen. Having been involved in the movement for six years, and even having served a stint on the managing board of one, I feel qualified to make that sweeping statement.

Regardless of archetypes, the fairs are dominated by Egos. Therefore, venturing to a fair to do some research requires a combination of luck and skill to pick the right person to whom you should direct your questions. If a medieval group you approach does not use metal (replica) weapons or allow vertical attacks to the head (headshots), don't waste your time unless you have enough time to waste. The ubiquitous SCA generally falls into this category—although the SCA members are fonts of knowledge, and you are assured of finding someone in their group who can help you, you would be better off asking a group that actively performs a more accurate combat re-enactment (for those in the dark, the SCA uses rattan swords wrapped in copious quantities of electrical tape for safety reasons. This allows a wholly inaccurate style of fighting which is fun to watch but not much use for your fantasy story—you're there for research, remember!).

Re-enactors are, on the whole, eager to show off their knowledge and share their experiences. Although the following section will save you some time by giving you answers to a few frequently asked questions on the subject, there's nothing like going out to a fair and hefting a sword.

Here's a list of things to try to do at a medieval or Renaissance fair (remember to be polite and always to respect another's property—these people are under no obligation to let you touch or try anything on this list):

Tell the person in charge of arms & armor that you are a writer looking to do some research into the particular period of their group for a new project you are considering. Make sure the group you are talking with is one in a period you are interested in—learning about Renaissance politics and weapons technology is probably of little use to your medieval English war scene). Re-enactors are often rabid fantasy readers so be prepared for an enthusiastic response.

Ask about holding some or all of the weapons. You'll need to try a range of weapons—for a perfect medieval sword experience I would suggest (in this order): dagger, short sword, long sword, hand-and-a-half/bastard sword; zweihänder/two-handed sword. After swords, ask about polearms (glaives, guisarmes, spears, etc), maces and mauls, axes and finally try out bows and crossbows—if you're lucky. Safety standards are often very high and strict rules may preclude you from touching, let alone swinging, these weapons. Never swing a sword after you've been allowed to hold it (see step 4). You've been allowed to hold it, not brandish it with all the skills of a grade-schooler on Prozac. Remember your role is 'writer', not 'embarrassment to combatants'. Also, in order to convince them to let you swing it you must first show them that you can be trusted to obey simple instructions.

As you progress through the different weapons, ask about fighting stances and grips—actually having this demonstrated to you so you can try it is a lot easier than explaining it to you in this chapter. At this point you want to start getting to an understanding of the capabilities of these weapons with respect to defence and attack, weight and speed. If there is a willing and agreeable complement of re-enactors, ask for a slow-motion demonstration on how to fight with different weapons—sword and shield vs spear; sword vs sword; sword and shield vs sword; sword vs axe; spear vs dagger (I've seen it done, and the guy with the dagger won!); and so forth.

Examine footwork, stance, balance, and the kinds of swings, thrusts and parries the combatants use. As this is hopefully a personal demonstration, you will get a better look at the methods than during the field battles the group might perform during the day for the general public.

Ask about being allowed to make some basic attacks.

Depending on the group's safety standards you may not be allowed to do this at all, but your chances are increased if there is a clear space easily demarcated for battle (to avoid bystanders getting an axe blade in their skull, for example). Alternatively, you might be invited (or invite yourself) to a training night/day for the group, where you can do some training for yourself. The group I was with required at least six months of regular training before members were allowed to fight free form at a public event. For metal weapons and head blow combat groups, safety is very important, and injuries ranging from stitches to broken fingers or ribs are not unheard of, though uncommon.

Ask about armor, specifically the types of armor used, the 'comfort' level of each, and the amount of trouble and time it takes to put on. Also find out how many people are required to don the armor—a full suit of chain, for example, is difficult to put on by yourself—the sleeves of your padded gambeson ride up and you're hard pressed to pull them back out by yourself. At least one person needs to help you. To speed things up you need two, though more than that starts becoming a little ridiculous.

Ask about being put in a suit of armor—at our shows, we regularly dressed members of the crowd and interested children in full gear (watching a small child trying to balance in a suit of chain is worth the effort). To fully appreciate the reality of being encased in armor you should try walking around with twenty kilograms (around forty pounds) of metal on your upper body. You become surprisingly top-heavy and will be off-balance and uncomfortable until you acclimatise. Ask one of the re-enactors to give you a push, and then try to correct your balance without falling on your arse to everyone's amusement. It's best to wear some comfortable clothes over which a suit of armor can easily be fitted. Now strap on a shield and wield a sword, and— depending on your earlier experience with basic sword training (step 4)—go back to the safe zone and swing the sword around for a bit. Without taking your training further and actually becoming involved in combat on the field, this will be the memory you should most try to recall and bear in mind when you write about a battle. You are uncomfortable in your grandfather's inherited armor; you smell; if it's summer, you're hot; you're tired, and swinging a sword is the last thing you want to do, because you're as likely to fall over as hit anything. And when I say swing the sword around, I mean four or five times! Obviously a long-term combatant will be much better trained than you are, and will have developed muscles suited to the occasion, but imagine that same long-term combatant after two days of war and hours of fighting. That's probably more like how you feel after your four or five good swings.

When writing combat scenes, such hands-on experience swinging weapons can be incredibly useful. But even if you've never hefted a sword or mace, you intuitively know certain things about weapons and people. Heavy things are slow, and light things are fast. This is really all you need to know to get to the first step of realism in combat—getting the timing right. Compare the following two sentences:

> Berk lunged at the goblin, swinging his sword to and fro to force it back.

> Berk lunged at the goblin and swung his sword to force it back.

In the second example, Berk simply swung his sword. Both sentences occur in the same timeframe, but the second sentence only has a single action, not a flurry of swings—and since a long sword simply can't be moved back-and-forth as rapidly as the first sentence suggests in a short timeframe, the first sentence is difficult to visualise without imagining Berk's sword as an aluminium toy.

Bear in mind that a long sword is not slow—far from it. But you are swinging three kilograms (six pounds) from the end of your arm. You can move that weight rapidly in arcs, over your head and diagonally all you want, but you're not going to be moving it very rapidly 'to-and-fro'.

If Berk really is swinging his sword backwards and forwards, then we need to bear in mind our earlier section on timing. Swinging the heavy sword to and fro might take several seconds to do, yet the sentence that told us about it took less than a second to read. Since this is an action scene that we are following in real time, we can't compress and uncompress the flow of time at will—if a sentence takes more or less time than simply reading it, we need to indicate this. During a battle, the action needs to flow consistently —the sentence with Berk to-ing and fro-ing attempts to make the reader imagine that action happening in a much shorter timeframe than that in which it really occurred. Better to quantify the time required by saying something like:

> Berk lunged at the goblin, swinging his sword to and fro to force it back as he advanced slowly down the hallway.

With a small addition the sentence has been 'locked' into the rest of the scene—instead of an action that is happening within the timeframe of reading the sentence, we've indicated that this is happening within the timeframe of 'slowly advancing down the hallway', which could be long seconds indeed, and gives Berk plenty of time to swing his sword.

Similarly, the time required to reload a pistol (see 'Arms & Armor') or load a crossbow bolt is important to know when trying to write realistically.

RESEARCH

Tee Morris discussed 'knowing' your weapons in his chapter on Research. You need to know that the pommel on a sword is a counterweight. You need to know what a crossguard is, and what it is for. You need to know how rapidly an arrow can be loosed. You need to know that blocking an attack with your own weapon is practically impossible—you are not physically going to stop a sword coming down at your head—and that deflecting the blow or avoiding it altogether are your only options unless you have a shield, and even then your options are limited.

The chapter on Arms & Armor goes into more detail about the nature of weapons and armor, but here are two simple tips:

TIP 1: ACHRONISMS

This is a simple rule. Learn it well and repeat it daily. Let it be your mantra towards accurate Fantasy combat. I have seen professional writers ignore this rule in the field's best magazines, and I cringe. Repeat after me:

'I do not fire arrows or crossbow bolts. I loose them.'

Why not? Ask yourself this: what does 'firing an arrow' mean? Is there any fire involved? No. And flaming arrows don't count. The term 'Fire!' refers to 'firing' the blackpowder in pistols or cannon, not mechanically projected missiles. Arrows were loosed in combat centuries before cannon were fired.

This warning was prompted by having recently read the following line coming out of the mouth of a medieval-type heroine in a fantasy novella in a respected Fantasy & Science Fiction magazine: 'Tell the archers to hold their fire.' Unless you use firearms or cannon, excise the imperative 'Fire!' out of your vocabulary, please.

The previous quote is an example of the easiest way to tell your readers that you have no idea what you are writing about and that you are a lazy researcher. Incidentally, in a different novella by the same author, the hero shrugs his chain vest on over his undershirt without padding (see the chapter on 'Arms & Armor' about why this is stupid). Anyway, I rest my case.

Just remember: you can't ever get away with telling people to 'fire' their arrows. Telling a medieval person to 'fire' their arrows is like telling them to make their horse go faster by 'stepping on the gas'. It's simply the wrong word for the action you are describing.

TIP 2: BE CAREFUL ABOUT THIS

Be careful when you use the word 'slice'. Slicing is a verb that connotes precision and control, two things that are not reminiscent of your traditional medieval sword. A Japanese katana or a razor-sharp dagger might slice, but a broadsword certainly won't: it'll slash or hack. If your hero's sword 'slices' an opponent, your reader may feel a momentary disorientation as he or she tries to imagine how a heavy sword hacking into an opponent could leave a nice slice.

CHEATING

The easiest way to write a combat scene is not to write it, but to gloss over it using a technique I have dubbed 'Cheating'. A prominent fantasy writer who shall remain nameless has used this method on occasion in his writing. Essentially, cheating is a way to try to hide that you don't want to write the combat scene at all. However, it is fairly blatant and therefore it rarely works unless there is a specific reason for including it, and in those cases the reader will usually forgive the author.

Yes, there is a place for cheating! It is possible to write every combat scene by cheating—as long as you are aware that somewhere during the narrative your readers will catch on that you don't actually know anything about whatever you are trying to hide.

If used sparingly, cheating conveys a sense of blazing power and skill—the battle is over before the reader (or anyone else except for the character that is cheating) has had time to register what is actually happening. The technique works when you need to display character skill, but like other techniques mentioned in this chapter, overuse can become tedious and even ludicrous. Also, you run the risk of looking like you don't know anything about combat and are trying to hide that fact from the reader.

Cheating unfortunately has the side effect of making the reader feel cheated. Fantasy readers want in on the action—they want to see their heroes performing great feats. Being told about the battle rather than getting to see it 'live' is often disappointing.

In practise, you can cheat by describing the action in 'code' or 'jargon'. The Martial Arts often have forms to describe certain attacks—'Leaping Tiger' or 'Washerwoman with Two Pails' for example. These names usually share a passing resemblance to the physical actions required to perform them. By not telling the reader what the codes are, you can throw out some general descriptive terms and pretend that a battle happened.

> Berk flinched and moved into Washerwoman with Two Pails. The lead goblin charged but Berk dispatched him with Flying Swallow. As the other two goblins charged, the Star

Rose over the Hills and they collapsed to the ground with their chests slashed open.

Phew, that was close! Remember that even when you are cheating, timing is important. The above paragraph forces the reader to make three assumptions: Washerwoman with Two Pails, Flying Swallow and Star Rises over the Hills are all fast attacks—the goblins charge, the Star Rises, the goblins are dead.

You see, the same rules apply to cheating as to normal combat description—weapons can still only travel at a certain speed. You are cheating with respect to the actual description of the combat, not the timing.

The main thing to bear in mind when you are cheating is that the combat is invisible to the reader during the 'jargon' bits, and that the result of the 'jargon' bits needs to be explained, else your reader will be unsure of where the characters end up positioned relative to one another (see the previous section 'Marco! Polo!').

MAGIC IN COMBAT

The same rules for magic as listed in the Magic Chapter count for combat—traditional forms of combat may be completely changed by basic applications of magic. Your wizards might have a spell that turns metal to stone, or worse, heats metal magically. If these kinds of spells are generally available to war-wizards, then soldiers will be turning to materials other than metal to produce weapons and armor, for who wants to run the risk of being trapped in a stone shell or cooking inside their own personal oven? This constant arms race between magical and mundane weapons of war needs to be considered when introducing offensive and defensive magic to your battles.

Apart from that, just like any other weapon, the magical spell exists in its own timeframe. If you write:

Berk snapped the goblin mage's staff in half with a wild swing, knocking the horrid creature back, then felt a fierce ball of heat slam into his gut. He collapsed to the ground, rolling twice and feeling Nailfang slip from his grip. Looking up, he stared helplessly as the mage approached, and watched as another ball of fire grew in its gnarled hands.

Right—the first ball of fire seemed to grow instantly, but the second took several seconds. Magic needs to work consistently, or its inconsistency needs to be part of the magic (in which case it is consistent!). Your advantage as a writer is that there is no 'maximum' speed for magic other than that which you define yourself. However if spells take ten seconds of chanting to cast, then the first ball of fire to hit Berk in the example simply came out of nowhere—certainly there was no time to cast the spell between being knocked back by Berk and hitting him with the fireball.

Another trap of using magic is that spell effects are things that your reader would not generally be able to visualise as easily as regular weapons, most of which tend to be variations on the 'swing a stick around' theme, something which can be vaguely analogised to swinging a baseball or cricket bat. This increases the burden on you to ensure that the combat elements are still in the right place after a magical effect. If someone is thrown into a tactically beneficial position by a magical explosion and is going to sneak up on evil overlord B, then you'd better tell your readers that—without telling them, of course. Hey, no one ever said this was easy.

EXAMPLE

We're going to run through an example of combat—from deciding who and what is involved, through to planning the fight, through to writing it. We'll be exploring Berk's schlocky High Fantasy battle in full.

THE CAST:

Berk and his trusty hatchet Nailfang. Berk is our hero, and it is his mission to kill everyone in the room. Berk is wearing a fashionable byrnie inherited from his grandfather, which is a little tight across the shoulders. His left boot sole is worn shiny and sometimes slips on wet surfaces. An old wooden shield is strapped to his forearm.

Gib Og, leader of a small Goblin Warband. Gib sports a trendy wooden club sprouting several rusty nails and wears an ill-fitting collection of abandoned metal plates.

Krag Tob, second in command of the Goblin Warband. Krag carries a rusty short sword and wears what looks like poorly tanned hides.

Gobbading Gub, third and final member of the Warband. Gobbading is a little runty for a goblin, but wields a two-handed axe with a certain finesse belying his stature or unfortunate smell.

Ghastard Grobo, an independently wealthy goblin wizard. He has hired Gib Og's warband to retrieve the lost Skull of Sasha, a powerful magical artefact hidden in a fearsome puzzlebox. It takes him several seconds to create his magical spells.

THE SCENE:

Berk has tracked Gib Og's band to this small cave, the antechamber to the larger Cave of Sasha where Ghastard Grobo is trying to unlock the secrets of the puzzlebox, which holds the Skull of Sasha.

Gib, Krag and Gobbading are arranged through the room for maximum effectiveness. Gobbading stands beside the entrance with his axe, so that he can hack Berk to pieces before he even gets in the room. Gib and Krag are further in the room (out of immediate range in case Gobbading screws up) on opposite walls. Gib is closer to the entrance than Krag. Ghastard is in the main room cursing and spluttering over the puzzlebox. Occasional puffs of smoke drift into the smaller cave.

THE ACTION:

Berk walks into the room and rolls out of the way as Gobbading tries to hit him and misses. Gib and Krag run forward, but Gib is closer to Berk. Berk attacks Gib with an overhand shot. Gib parries it but Berk whacks him in the head with his shield. Gib falls back just as Krag runs at Berk. Berk sidesteps Krag's thrust and chops him in the back of the head, killing him instantly.

Gobbading has recovered and makes an overhand attack at Berk. Berk twists and the heavy axe just misses him, catching one of the shield straps and cutting it free. Berk throws the now-useless shield at Gib, collecting him in the head and knocking him back to the ground. Berk turns to face Gobbading. Gobbading snarls at him and Berk throws Nailfang in response, collecting him between the eyes.

Berk grabs the heavy axe as Gobbading's lifeless corpse collapses to the ground, then turns to face Gib.

Gib has regained his footing and is shouting for help from Ghastard as Berk moves towards him, giving his new toy a bit of a practise swing. Gib steps forwards, makes a feint with his club, and then ducks to the side as Berk overcompensates with the heavy axe. He swings at Berk and hits him in the chest, knocking him back. But the blow is a glancing one. Berk recovers from the impact and spins around, collecting Gib in the side of the head with the flat of the axe blade and sending him staggering. He steps in towards Gib and as the goblin turns around he chops him in half.

Berk hears evil laughter and turns just in time to be obliterated by evil goblin mage fire.

THE EXECUTION:

We're going to convert the above plan into prose now. The section of the plan that we are converting is listed in the first column, followed by the actual prose, then a description of all the characters at the end of the converted section (see if the prose is clear enough that you agree with this positioning) and finally a space for some notes on techniques used or decisions made.

Plan	Prose	At end of Section	Notes
Berk walks into the room and rolls out of the way as Gobbading tries to hit him and misses.	*Berk walked carefully into the room, alert to any sound. He smelled Gobbading an instant before he spotted the glint of torchlight on its huge double-headed axe. Without a thought he hurled himself to the ground, rolling clumsily forward on one shoulder as Gobbading's axe thudded into the dirt behind him.*	Berk is on his knees. Gobbading is recovering from its swing. Gib and Krag are waiting in the shadows.	The axe is slow, which is why we get the chance to do some description. Berk's forward roll is fairly slow as well.
Gib and Krag run forward, but Gib is closer to Berk.	*Gib and Krag had been cowering in the shadows, but now that their underling had failed they charged him, although Krag was easily twice as far away as Gib. Berk smiled—that would be their undoing.* *He hefted Nailfang and faced Gib as it closed on him.*	Berk is standing facing Gib. Gib is almost on him, with Krag trailing behind. Gobbading is presumably either still recovering from his attack or lumbering towards Berk's unprotected back.	A bit of chatter and exposition here to fill in the gap between Gib and Krag charging and reaching Berk.
Berk attacks Gib with an overhand shot. Gib parries it but Berk whacks him in the head with his shield. Gib falls back just as Krag runs at Berk. Berk sidesteps Krag's thrust and chops him in the back of the head, killing him instantly.	*The instant the goblin-leader came into reach, Berk stepped aside and hacked down at its head, bracing himself with his shield in case it tried to ram him.* *Gib clumsily parried Nailfang aside, then spun around Berk and stepped in with a powerful swing of its crude, nail-studded club. Berk deflected the blow and smashed his shield solidly into its misshapen head, smashing it backwards.*	Berk hasn't moved much. Gib is on the ground, trying to recover his footing. Krag is dead. Gobbading must be pretty close by now...	Lots of examples of an entire action being put into one sentence. Long sentences here string together all the related events, so there are no time-gaps between striking, hitting, and killing.

Plan	Prose	At end of Section	Notes
	Gib collapsed, cursing and spitting blood, just as Krag charged into the fray. *Berk sidestepped and Krag thrust his rusty sword into thin air, losing his footing. Without a thought Berk spun and attacked, and Nailfang sank deeply into the back of Krag's head, pulling free in a thin spray of foul black blood. The goblin collapsed to the ground, thrashing out his life. Berk took a deep breath and frowned at the sudden smell.*		Notice also how the combat actions provide gaps for several players to perform their actions in sequence— almost exactly like a choreographed fight— reducing the need to describe multiple simultaneous actions and confuse the hell out of everybody.
Gobbading has recovered and makes an overhand attack at Berk. Berk twists and the heavy axe just misses him, catching one of the shield straps and cutting it free. Berk throws the now-useless shield at Gib, collecting him in the head and knocking him back to the ground.	*Gobbading's familiar stink alerted him an instant too late. He started to turn around but the heavy axe swung down and skimmed a fraction of an inch past his left forearm, glancing off his mail sleeve but slashing through half the straps holding his shield in place.* *Breathing heavily, with the shield dangling uselessly from his tight left fist, Berk stepped out of Gobbading's reach, twisting his head to find Gib. The goblin leader was climbing back to its feet, and Berk hurled the now useless shield with all his might at the cursing figure, smashing its head a second time and knocking it back over.* *It gave him time to deal with the real threat of Gobbading and its vicious axe.*	Berk is now without a shield, facing Gib but preparing to deal with Gobbading. Gib is on its back again. Krag is still dead. Gobbading is behind Berk, raising its axe.	The last sentence is a filler that allows the reader enough time to imagine Gobbading pulling its heavy blade back up for another attack and Berk turning away from Gib to finish Gobbading off.

Plan	Prose	At end of Section	Notes
Berk turns to face Gobbading. Gobbading snarls at him and Berk throws Nailfang in response, collecting him between the eyes. Berk grabs the heavy axe as Gobbading's lifeless corpse collapses to the ground, then turns to face Gib.	*He turned lithely, now unencumbered by his shield, and watched Gobbading close in with the axe raised high for a vicious diagonal slash.* *There was no time for fancy axe-play anymore—Ghastard could have the puzzlebox solved at any time. Berk lifted Nailfang and hurled it at Gobbading's head just as the battleaxe began its downward swing.* *Nailfang sank into Gobbading's forehead with a terrible crack, and Berk stepped in as the huge axe began to fall, twisting the solid wooden handle out of Gobbading's suddenly lifeless grip.* *He kicked Gobbading's crumpling body aside and turned to deal with Gib.*	Berk has a big axe. Gib is presumably getting back to his feet the second time. Krag is still dead. Gobbading is now also dead. Nailfang is in Gobbading's forehead.	See how the act of throwing Nailfang and hitting Gobbading has been separated into two sentences? The tiny delay between throwing and connecting can be represented by splitting the two actions into two sentences—something you might not want to do if Berk was using Nailfang in hand-to-hand (and therefore very fast) combat.
Gib has regained his footing and is shouting for help from Ghastard as Berk moves towards him, giving his new toy a bit of a practise swing. Gib steps forwards, makes a feint with his club, and then ducks to the side as Berk overcompensates with the heavy axe. He swings at Berk and hits him in the chest, knocking him back.	*"Mashter!" Gib stammered through broken teeth and streamers of bloody snot. It had finally regained its footing and faced Berk across five yards, separated by Krag's lifeless corpse and Gobbading's still twitching body. It trembled as Berk took a single step forward, experimentally swinging his new axe in a slow arc above his head, loosening his shoulders.* *"Mashter!" Gib cried again. "He ish here!"*	Krag and Gobbading's dead status hasn't changed. Gib is in hand-to-hand combat with Berk. Berk is off-balance. Ghastard may or may not have heard Gib.	Had to use different words to describe Gib's attack, blow or swing. Had to sit down and visualise Gib's feint and subsequent attack, and had some difficulty trying to describe it concisely while still giving enough information to the reader.

Plan	Prose	At end of Section	Notes
	Before Berk could approach any closer, Gib lunged forwards, his club held high. Berk lifted the axe quickly in an attempt to parry, but Gib ducked aside at the last moment, bringing the club down and around for a sideways blow. Cursing at the feint, Berk tried to swing the axe down to deflect the attack, but its momentum was too great.		
	Gib's nail-studded club smashed into Berk's chest, knocking the breath out of him and forcing him a step back.		
But the blow is a glancing one. Berk recovers from the impact and spins around, collecting Gib in the side of the head with the flat of the axe blade and sending him staggering. He steps in towards Gib and as the goblin turns around he chops him in half.	*Berk spun with the force of the blow, extending the battleaxe and smashing the flat of the blade into Gib's head as he stepped past. Gib staggered forward, his arms thrown wide for balance.*	Everyone except Berk and Ghastard are dead.	There are more 'filler' phrases as we slow down the action now that Berk is armed with a slow double-headed axe.
	Berk regained his balance, wincing at the pain in his chest, and waited until the goblin had fully recovered before swinging his huge axe back and around. Gib had time to turn and see a flash of reflected light before the razor edge cut him in two.		
	Its upper and lower half sagged together, guts and blood and unidentifiable goblin innards slopping around its twitching legs. Berk kicked the steaming pile contemptuously.		

Plan	Prose	At end of Section	Notes
Berk hears evil laughter and turns just in time to be obliterated by evil goblin mage fire.	*"Very impressive!" a dark voice cackled from the small corridor leading to the Cave of Sasha* *Berk swallowed dryly, whirling with the battleaxe. Gib's blood trailed vilely from its edge as he faced the twisted shape of Ghastard Grobo, goblin mage, and the flickering fire in its gnarled hands.* *"Curse me for a fool!" Berk cried—his lust for battle had clouded his judgement; Grobo was by far the greater foe, yet he'd wasted his time fighting Gib's band.* *Luckily his shame was short-lived, for the flames flared in Ghastard's hands and leapt across the intervening space, engulfing Berk in foul goblin magic and burning the flesh from his bones.*	Everyone except Ghastard is dead.	We're giving Ghastard time to cast its spells. Although it could have been watching from the moment Gib shouted its name in the previous section, to avoid confusion we are giving it time to blast Berk. In any case, Berk could never have run fast enough.

Farewell, Berk. It was fun having you around. I guess the heroes will come by your bones later in the story.

The above section was not written in one attempt by any means, despite planning and preparation, after you finish your battle scene you need to revisit it as a reader. Only at reading speed does the flow of combat become visible; only when you reread the action can you tell that the axe chopped too quickly, or that sword swings took too much time.

Repeat that a couple of times (like I did) and you will see the action come together. Given practise, the timing of swinging and chopping and hacking will become second nature to you.

SUMMARY

Combat and action scenes succeed on the strength of your description—actions need to occur in a continuum where the reader is able to visualise that action without having to speed up or slow down time themselves. It's your job to ensure that the reader can easily translate your description into the actual event inside their heads. Unlike more static descriptions of flowers and hairstyles and castle walls, you can't afford to give your reader time to work it out. This is nail-biting stuff, and if the reader misinterprets your hero's sword swing, spear thrust or acrobatic tumble, suddenly their image of who is where in the battle will differ from yours. When that happens, the next time a critical piece of good luck, timing and skill comes together to defeat the enemy, your reader will cry, 'Oi! Berk was over there, you hack! How did he throw his axe in time to knock the evil wizard's staff out of his hands?'

Writing your combat scene is a complex juggling act of avoiding lists, repetition, the word 'then', time dilation and anachronisms, while ensuring you know what's going on and making doubly sure that the reader is 'seeing' exactly what you are seeing, lest you confuse their little world.

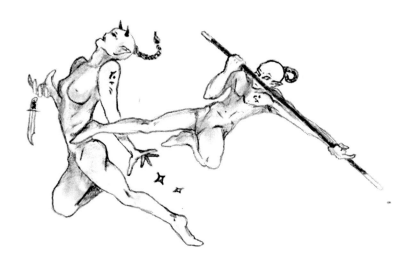

Martial Arts and Fantasy

TWO GREAT TASTES

THAT TASTE GREAT TOGETHER

TEE MORRIS

Chances are, before 1999, if you were to go to a movie that featured martial arts (and I do mean prominently featured martial arts) you would find yourself sharing a theatre with maybe ten other people spread out across with the couple or two playing "Find the Junior Mints" in the back row. It would be a movie badly dubbed into English, a non-existent plot, and plenty of impressive martial arts sequences. For many years, it was Jackie Chan who dominated the martial art movie circuit before

1999. So why is all this before 1999? In that year, a movie came along that not only redefined the genre of the martial arts film but also raised the bar for *all* films, especially when it came to visual effects. This movie was the second film from these two directors. A science fiction-martial arts adventure that took reality and bent it like a spoon in a strong grip, only to reveal the true reality that "there was no spoon."

This movie was *The Matrix*.

For the first time two very distinct film genres met and played well with each other. While you may think, "*The Matrix* is a SF film, not a martial arts movie," take a closer look at the airtight writing from the Warchowsky brothers. Sure, it's SF on the surface, but you have many impressive fight sequences that incorporate many martial art techniques. Then you have Neo's visit to the Oracle as well as the character of Morpheus. Wise teachers. Lessons passed to those seeking guidance. Mind over matter. And you even have an Eastern mystical element in *The Matrix* where Neo simply "takes control" of the environment and stops bullets in mid-flight.

All of these aspects can be found in the early works of Jackie Chan and Jet Li, but are even more dominant in the restored opening of Bruce Lee's classic film *Enter the Dragon*. This works well for science fiction, but is there really a place for martial arts in fantasy? In 2000, director Ang Lee took the martial arts movie to an even higher plane by giving us the "artistic epic" of *Crouching Tiger, Hidden Dragon*.

The answer is "Yes."

Now for those of you out there who are conjuring up martial arts in fantasy as the wire work action and cartoon-slapstick sequences from Hercules and *Xena*, take a look at *Crouching Tiger, Hidden Dragon*, Ang Lee himself describes it as "Sense and Sensibility (another film of his) with martial arts", but with the superhuman feats of the heroes and heroines. This along with a haunting, mystical ending, easily classifies it as an epic fantasy. While this section deals with "Eastern Martial Arts" know that "martial arts" includes hand-to-hand (or "fist-a-cuffs" as it is referred to by stage combatants) combat. A drunken pub brawl may not look pretty, but it is "martial arts", the word "art" being defined here however you wish. From this point on, understand that the term "martial arts" refers to the ways of hand-to-hand combat originating in the Pacific-Asian regions. Key to incorporating martial arts or creating a martial art unique for your world (and it will be these little details that truly make your world unique and memorable as Tina Morgan talks about in her Worldbuilding chapter) is understanding what the martial arts are, what their history is, and the philosophies surrounding each martial arts style.

The Rules of Engagement

The Canadian comedy troupe "The Frantics" have a sketch famous among the martial arts community called "Boot to the Head". It tells the unfortunate story of an overenthusiastic student who "...has the pyjamas, paid his fifty bucks, and now he wants to learn how to kick a little butt." He is then taught the lesson of "Boot to the Head" by his wise sensai. (This is the Japanese word for "teacher" or "master.") The opening dialogue from the instructor does sound extremely trite and annoyingly stereotypical, as if plucked from those earlier mentioned bad *Karate* movies or perhaps from an episode of Kung Fu, but for those of you who have ever studied or are currently studying a martial art, you know we live by a strict code of ethics. These are ethics that date back thousands of years, even before there was a code of chivalry established by knights of Europe and England.

Perhaps one reason why there is so much philosophy intertwined with martial arts is because the people who first created the martial arts were priests, passive men and women who lived a life of isolation and chose to meditate on the mysteries of life, always searching for the higher planes of enlightenment. It was not uncommon in Ancient China for seasoned warriors to "burn out" after serving under numerous generals in countless civil wars. These skilled swordsmen and tacticians would retire to a life of solitude, study, and placidity, free from the burden of taking life at the command of a lord. As most of these monks swore off using weapons, raiders and highwaymen targeted these men of peace as "easy scores" for themselves. There were also the never-ending supply of warlords and their occasional uprisings against the ruling dynasty. After a few decades of being prey to these outside threats, these monks began to devise ways of defending themselves without the use of weapons. This self-defence became what modern society now knows as the martial arts.

Can you imagine the first gang of Western raiders who stumbled on a "defenceless" monastery and thought these priests were "easy pickings"?

Eventually, these self-defence techniques were incorporated into the fighting styles of the military. One martial art in particular was created and developed specifically for the warrior in mind (*Kendo* which means "The Way of the Sword"), but even with this style comes an understanding of learning the martial arts strictly as a means of defence. You do not pick up a martial art so you can "get all Chuck Norris" on someone. You learn a martial art to open your mind to possibilities once thought impossible, to discover a strength you did not know you possessed, and to defend yourself if attacked. That is the way of all martial arts and that is the discipline all true martial arts follow. I'm starting to sound like a Jedi Knight, am I? Before Lucas even placed a lightsabre into

Alec Guiness' hand, the martial arts have followed these ethics. In their lessons with a master, students discover a hidden power. And it was not uncommon for one or two students to be lured by a "darker side", abandoning disciplines and edicts for the quick fix of power and strength. A true martial artist abides by ancient disciplines, and these disciplines keep him or her honest.

This is one reason why it is not at all odd that Lucas incorporated *Kendo*-style fighting tactics into the fighting tactics of his Jedi Knights. If anyone in Lucas' *Star Wars* universe, which as we all know is in "a galaxy far, far away," would know martial arts, it would be the Jedi.

While the martial arts believe in a life of peace and tranquillity, it does not mean you cannot inflict damage on an opponent. The discipline is merely the reaction to another's action. Or, to put it more bluntly, someone has forced your hand to open up a can of "Whoop-Ass" on them. True martial artists never attack out of malice or without provocation. They will fight to defend themselves, resorting to their martial art as a last resort. Martial artists prefer a "peaceful out" to an argument, but once unleashed, the martial artist will not stop until the opponent is down and remains down.

This is the way of the martial artist.

How Do You Like Your Martial Arts? Hard or Soft?

When I was first looking into the martial arts, the first thing I learned is that there are two styles—hard and soft. Perhaps another way of describing the two styles is aggressive and passive. When writing martial arts into your Fantasy, you will want to know the difference between a hard or soft martial art.

A "hard" martial art is a martial art that follows a simple rule: if someone pushes you, push back. Hard. A lot harder than they pushed you. These are the more aggressive martial arts that are made popular in film and television. Punches and kicks are distinctive in hard styles, and here the martial artist's body truly is a weapon. *Tae Kwon Do* is an excellent example of a "hard" martial art. Translated, "*Tae Kwon Do*" means the Way of the Hand and Foot. Its roots are in Korea and it is the most popular of all the martial arts styles in the world. Students of *Tae Kwon Do* study in a do jang (a studio) and classes are led by either a *Sa Boo Nim* (teacher) or a *Ta Soo Nim* (master). To learn the ways of *Tae Kwon Do*, a student will learn a series of attacks and defences called forms, or *poom se*.

Another "hard" martial art is *Aikido*. Its origins are in Japan and concentrates on power generated from punches and kicks, much like *Tae Kwon Do*. Does this mean that *Aikido* and *Tae Kwon Do* are interchangeable? Hardly. While *Tae Kwon Do* attacks involved thrusts and on-line attacks,

Aikido punches and kicks are less thrusting and more circular in execution, the techniques similar to *Kendo* but involving the whole body in the attacks. Unlike *Kendo*, *Aikido* concentrates on the body, the sword merely an extension and the body itself working through it. *Aikido*'s punches and kicks also go by different names. The forms vary greatly between the two arts, and the traditions and levels of achievement vary.

"Soft" martial arts are the antithesis of the hard martial arts. Instead of the martial artist's body becoming the weapon, it is the attacker's energy and aggression that the martial artist utilizes. Instead of "pushing back when pushed" a soft martial art will let the attacker push until they are off-balance, then that lack of balance is used against them. Soft martial arts also tend to be less aggressive and more for personal health and betterment. One of the most popular soft martial arts is *Tai Chi*, a slow, detailed series of movements that work to relieve tension and promote relaxation. While it looks easy, it's not. The hands must end at a certain point. The feet must be placed precisely. Otherwise the student's centre of energy or "chi" is off-balance. And while these movements are executed, movements must be slow, even, and controlled. The exercises are, in reality, a variety of "take-down" tactics, designed to use your opponent's own weight and momentum against themselves. This use of the opponent's size and strength against themselves is applied in sparring for *Tai Chi*. Unlike sparring in *Tae Kwon Do* or some other hard martial art, *Tai Chi* spars in bouts of "push-hands" where the object is to use the opponent's centre of balance (energy, in a philosophical sense) to "push" them off-balance. Again, in this sparring, the movement is slow, controlled, and fluid.

While I can't really go into every style of martial art in existence for there are many, I can introduce you to a few of them. Do know these two modern traits of the martial arts, however:

- 1. *Karate* is, in modern times, a catchall word used for many styles of martial arts. (There is a style called *Karate* but just because the studio you happen to come across says "*Karate*" on the door, that may not be the style that is practised there).

- 2. The 'belt' is another trait of modern martial arts. When the martial arts migrated to the West, eventually hitting the East Coast of America and continuing back to where they originated from, the colour belt levels (i.e. at the writing of this chapter, I am currently a Brown Belt in *Tae Kwon Do*.) were used as a way to measure progress, the goal to reach the Black Belt level. If you are writing a Fantasy novel and incorporating historical martial arts, there are only two levels: the student and the master.

Now that you have a good idea of the difference between a hard and a soft martial art, you can decide exactly which martial art you want to write about, or what kind of martial art you wish to create for your world. For example, in *MOREVI: The Chronicles of Rafe & Askana*, Lisa Lee and I created two forms of martial arts native to Askana Moldarin's fictitious realm. One martial art that we called Tan Te Kassa took its foundations from *Tae Kwon Do* as we are both students of it. Another called Yelan-Chi possesses the fluidity of *Tai Chi*, the kicks of *Tae Kwon Do* and the agility of gymnastics.

Creating your own martial art is not as easy as it may sound. You need to create not only the attacks and defences, but also the philosophy or purpose behind the art. What are the advantages of Yelan-Chi over Tan Te Kassa? What is the philosophy behind the art? The more details you can create for your martial art, the stronger and more believable you make it.

COMMON KICKS AND PROBABLE PUNCHES

While there are many styles of martial arts, there are common threads between each of them. There are basic kicks and punches in each martial art universal in their application, advantages, and description. The names may vary as well the techniques in executing them, but here are just a few common kicks and punches easily recognised both visually as well as literally in narration.

FRONT KICK

With front kicks, the attacker is coming from the front. This is a direct attack, either to the head or chest. It is a *driving* kick, meaning to execute it the defender drives forward, through his target, dealing more power to the target.

SIDEKICKS

The sidekick is perhaps the most easily recognisable of martial arts. It, too, is a driving kick, but the sidekick is executed by the defender pivoting in place and sending the foot forward in a sideways fashion. The target areas can be either in the knee area (low), the chest (mid-level), or the head (high-level). Unlike the forward assault of a front kick, the sidekick has a variety of attack-and-defend angles. A "reverse sidekick", for example, allows for the defender to evade first by turning in place, then continuing the momentum into a sidekick, stopping one step forward from the starting position. The "spin sidekick" also allows the same evade tactic as the "reverse sidekick", but the momentum of the sidekick brings the defender back to the starting point as the body follows a full 360-degree motion.

ROUND KICK

The round kick (also called a "roundhouse kick") is a glancing kick, not as powerful as the driving kick of a sidekick or a front kick but still effective if executed properly.

The attacker is usually to one side of the defender, and the kick follows an arch-like path (while the afore mentioned sidekick is more of a thrust) to either a mid-level or high-level target. Round kicks can be thought of as a "jab" with the foot.

CRESCENT KICKS

If a sidekick is looked at as a "punch" and the round kick is a "jab", then a crescent kick could be the "slap" with a foot. Now before you think "How much power can there be in a slap?", think about what you're slapping with. Perhaps the most powerful muscles of the human body are the legs and feet as they provide support and momentum. A crescent kick follows a larger arch pattern, the travel of the kick following a half-circle or tall, crescent shape from which the kick gets its name. The crescent kick can also be executed as a "reverse crescent kick" and a "spin crescent kick." To complicate things even more, the crescent kick can also be executed as a "butterfly kick." This kick begins as a reverse crescent kick, but in mid-turn the kick switches to the opposite leg. What makes crescent kick so popular and useful to master in the martial arts is that crescent kicks can work as an attack or as a block.

PUNCHES AND HAND STRIKES

Now we get into the common hand techniques shared between the martial arts. The punch is the most common of attacks, found in all martial arts and hand-to-hand combat styles. The punch is a strike executed with the fist. A strike dealt at full force. Much like a sidekick, the punch is meant to drive into the opponent. You can probably guess you do not have to be a martial artist to punch someone. All the great action stars who don't know a lick of martial arts are masters (in their own way) of the punch. Being such a common form of an attack, the punch tends to lend itself in all genres to humour. Can your character make a proper fist (because if you tuck your thumb inside your fingers, it is guaranteed you will dislocate your thumb)? How does your character take a punch? Or are your heroes suffering just a hint of vanity like these animated superheroes:

>Tick: "We need battle cries! You know, those things we shout just before going into battle?"
>Arthur: "What? You mean like 'Not the face! Not the face!'?"
>Tick: "Hmm...lacks force, chum."
>—from *The Tick*

Or maybe you've got your hero facing a hulking henchman, and the first punch he or she throws does nothing to phase him! The punch allows for power and ferocity, as well as a hint of levity when needed.

A jab is the glancing blow of a punch. Instead of punching to drive into your opponent, the jab works like the tip of a whip. The defender throws a punch only to pull it back quickly. A jab may not deal as much damage as a full-blown punch, but the advantage is swiftness and speed. The jab can be dealt repeatedly, dealing damage gradually. When jabbing an opponent, you are not trying to take them out with one punch, but merely wear them down.

A backfist is a variation of the jab theme only instead of leading the jab with knuckles, your striking tool is the back of your hand. If your hand is open, it has some damage capability but very limited. However, a hand in a taut fist will easily send an opponent's head swimming. The most common target for a backfist is the temple. Once a backfist is dealt, it is quickly pulled back to be dealt again.

Knifehand and Palm Heel Strikes are dealt with other parts of your hand. The knifehand sounds exactly like what it is. The hand is formed into a "blade", fingers kept closely together and fingertips even with one another. The striking tool of the hand is the outside edge of the hand and dealt like a punch; a driving strike that can easily break boards—and bones—if necessary. Palm heel strikes use the hard bottom portion of your open hand as a striking tool. The thumb and fingers are pulled back, the strike dealt like a punch.

All of these kicks and punches have variations in their attacks. You can create combinations of punches and kicks, and depending on the skill of your heroes and villains, they can be either simple and basic or far more complex. The more complex the kicks and combinations, the more formidable an opponent.

But remember the world you're creating and the realism you need to create a truly wonderful fantasy.

East Meets West: The Plausibility of Martial Arts in Fantasy

So what kind of world have you created for your Fantasy novel? Is it a Celtic-based society? If you have modelled your world from a European influence there is a possibility you have no place for the martial arts in your world. Such was the case in 2001 with the swashbuckling film The Musketeer, its heroes a little hard to believe as Europeans that moved with all the grace of black belt masters. Then there are the Fantasy offerings like The Beastmaster and Sheena where you meet characters who, in no way, would have contact with an Asian-based or—inspired society. But what about the fantasy classic, *Conan the Barbarian?* How did writer Robert E. Howard and screenwriters John Milus and Oliver Stone pull it off so well? The world Howard built was a blend of Norse myth along with cultures of the Far East where the great swordmasters accepted students and trained them in the disciplines of combat. As far as Conan's screenwriters, they effectively made the Chinese Connection with one line: "He was sent far to the East, a great honour." So as far as Conan's world was concerned (which, in the film, was apparently our Earth, before Atlantis sank into the Atlantic, as stated in the Prologue), it was made clear that he was sent to the "Far East" where he learned sword fighting from the "great masters." No. Conan was not jump sidekicking or vanquishing his foes with a graceful spin-crescent kick, but he was learning a variant of *Kendo* in his time east.

But what if your fantasy is set not in a different world but in the history of our own? Then you have some research to do. Trade routes between China and Europe were actually dated back to the 1200's, but explorers could have sailed the oceans and circled the world earlier than that. From these trade routes came exotic imports such as silk and tea, but it was also documented that some sword masters trained in Italy and even the Germany provinces at fighting schools starting in the 1400's. Knowing this, it becomes more and more plausible that a combatant of the early Renaissance would learn a martial art. Why couldn't a sword master from the Orient take under their wing a particular student, a gifted fencer who shows exceptional skills with a rapier, and teach them a different discipline that would make those skills even sharper, more precise? And in this great age of learning and enlightenment, wouldn't such skills be embraced by one willing to learn? It always pays off, doing your homework.

True, I'm kicking around a lot of hypothetical ideas and concepts here, but here is where the details come in to crafting a fantasy that is "believable." So the concept of a "believable fantasy" sounds like an oxymoron, but there is a fine line in the sand of writing fantasy that writers continuously strive not to cross. As I said in my chapter for characters, there needs to be just enough reality in your cast to give the readers a sense of connection. Take Peter Parker of *Spider-Man.* Can we as an audience relate with someone that holds the power of a spider? Probably not. But what about Peter Parker? He's got the crush on his high school's hottie, tends to be a bit on the shy side, and has a tough time talking to girls. That little trait makes him as a person a bit more familiar.

This same familiarity holds true with the combat you incorporate in your book. If you have a character that is an explorer and is exposed to various cultures and philosophies, then it would be highly likely that he or she would know the martial arts. But let us say your character has lived all their lives in a community that prefers solitude from the outside world. How believable would it be to see Frodo Baggins suddenly launch into a flying sidekick? Albeit, if he could, he would do a lot of damage with those monster feet of his, but it's unrealistic. Or what if you have a seasoned soldier, fresh from overseas campaigns, as your principal hero? Would he posses the skill of a master, or would he know just enough to benefit him in battle? Again, it depends on the world, the characters, and the martial arts you create.

The R&D invested in your character and your character's world will depend on how plausible martial arts are in your story. Never use something in a story simply because "it's cool" and never take a leap into the hypothetical ("Well, my character knows Jujitsu because…") unless you can back up your arguments with sensible facts ("He dated a chick who took a couple of lessons from a travelling priest," is not a good argument). You have heard me say this before: sweat the details. The better you can justify aspects of your work with facts, not opinions, the stronger the final story will be.

YOU HAVE FAR TO TRAVEL, GRASSHOPPER…

Now just because I have thrown at you a good amount of background on martial arts does not mean you can call yourself "knowledgeable" in the martial arts. I speak from a decade of stage combat experience and four years of martial arts training, and I consider myself only "well-educated". Hardly an expert. Hardly a master. There are times I have questions, and when I do I turn to resources that will hopefully point me in the right direction. Here are some exercises and ideas designed to help you in developing a "Chinese Connection" with your Fantasy realm:

If possible, find a school where you can observe and take notes on the style taught there. Try and schedule an interview or several interviews with the school's master. There is a reason why they are called "masters" and what they reveal may surprise you. If you cannot pay them for their consulting, give them a mention in the book's acknowledgements. It is a gesture they will appreciate.

Take a look in your local bookstore for resources on the martial arts. Some, like *The Complete Idiot's Guide to the Martial Arts*, take a beginner's approach to the martial arts, providing a dictionary of terms and techniques for various styles. These books do not teach the martial arts, but do educate you as to exactly what they are. Other books will focus on only one style of martial arts, giving detailed descriptions of various attacks and what damage they can inflict. It would also benefit your martial art if you read on the philosophy of various styles. One resource I highly recommend (which was recommended to me by my first *Tae Kwon Do* instructor) is *Zen and the Martial Arts*, written by Joe Hyams. A quick read, this book goes into the spirituality and influence the martial arts can have on life. Then there is the book *Striking Thoughts*, a collection of writings and words of wisdom from The Dragon himself, Bruce Lee. Both books will help you in your development of a philosophy and "way of life" for your Fantasy martial art.

SUMMARY

The incorporation of martial arts and Eastern philosophy can bring a new aspect to the world you are creating in your Fantasy novel. Contact with an Eastern-based realm can enrich your world in its spirituality and philosophy, and this contact can bring a new form of combat to your heroes.

Before writing about or creating an original martial art, writers should observe instructional videotapes or (even better) classes of nearby schools. Watching martial arts movies is not the same as observing a class as many "Hollywood" martial arts tend to be a mish-mesh of all martial art styles. Also, the more modern martial arts movies are filled with wire work. While it worked great for *The Matrix* and *Crouching Tiger, Hidden Dragon*, it is quickly becoming a crutch for many television and film martial artists. Watch a *Judo* class or an *Aikido* class. Observe carefully how their punches are dealt and kicks are executed, take notes on how the students' bodies move, and then adapt these ancient techniques to the fighting styles in your work. If the master of the school you're visiting has time, ask for an interview concerning the philosophies and histories of his or her martial art and the different kicks, both simple and advanced.

Martial arts also possess a philosophy of spiritual growth. Make sure that if you incorporate a martial art, whether it is an existing art or one of your own creation, adopt a philosophy for it. Research Eastern mythologies and religions to give your martial art a depth and texture that will add a dimension to your characters and to the cultures you create. Between the style of combat and the spiritual aspect of the fighting style, you now have avenues to explore of an individual's growth, the decisions and morals of combat, and ascending to higher, spiritual planes.

Humour in Fantasy

DARIN PARK & ROB DURNEY

BUT THE FUNNY THING IS:

Webster's Dictionary defines "comedy" as:

A light amusing play with a happy ending; A literary work treating a comic theme or written in a comic style; and Humorous entertainment.

A politician travelling through Scotland looked out of the train window and saw a number of black sheep.

"That's interesting," he said. "All Scottish sheep are black."

"No, no," warned his agent. "Don't make positive statements like that. Best just say, 'Some Scottish sheep are black.' Isn't that right, Jim?"

Jim, a statistician, replied, "Well, on the evidence so far, the only thing you can say is, 'Some Scottish sheep are black on one side.'"

WHAT DO YOU FIND FUNNY?

Addicted to both comedy and fantasy as I was a growing lad, and even when I stopped growing vertically and just continued growing horizontally, it came as no surprise that I would eventually start writing in the fantasy-comedy genre. Little did I know (and even though I know better now, it is far too late) that I had chosen perhaps the most difficult literature to write.

For comparison value, let's imagine an ordinary type of story, with little or no humour and say that it's like riding an elephant in the jungle while ducking low-lying branches. Now, the humorous story is like riding that same elephant...hanging on to its belly...upside down...with no straps... screaming all the way.

If the previous image gave you a little grin, then you're well on your way to understanding how humour works

WHAT MAKES US LAUGH?

Comedy. That's the easy answer. Almost too easy.

Actually, it's not easy at all. Comparatively, trying to find the right sequence of words or word patterns to evoke humour is much like trying to defuse a bomb in a parking garage, blind-folded, with a miniature poodle wrapped around your leg humping it like a maniac.

There are only two wires. Cut this one and the bomb goes off. End of story. In other words, the joke has bombed. Cut the other one and the timer stops. No boom. A brisk shake of your leg sends the poodle sliding across the car park into an open drain, where you hear the dog's high-pitched yapping fade rapidly away, which causes you great pleasure. You feel a smile spread across your face and there is peace inside for a job well done.

You begin to walk away. Ominous click. You stop and turn only to be stunned by a light so bright you see the face of God through your closed eyelids. All hell breaks loose. Through shielded eyes you see debris showering around you in huge chunks, although it is noiseless because the blast of the bomb has deafened you. The cement floor beneath your feet buckles and gives way and pitches you downward where you land on your back far below with a lung shattering, "Whomp!"

Miraculously, you survive. You realise this because of the throbbing in your head. You raise your head slowly, painfully, looking around from your prone position. You don't care that you are in the middle of a pile of debris, unscathed by the explosion or the fall. You don't care that a building has collapsed around you and has littered a one-block radius with pieces of concrete and throat-clogging plaster dust. All you are intensely concerned with is the rhythmic jerking of your leg where that damned poodle has re-attached itself.

If you found the previous passage funny, then you understand the joke. That's your number one priority: making sure the reader gets the joke.

That was an example of the "serious" story with cause and effect to create an absurdity, which serves as the punch line.

APPROACHING HUMOUR INDIRECTLY

There is more than one way to approach humour in writing. The first and foremost thing to remember is not to try and be funny. Trying to be funny is like attempting to be the life of the party by trying to "one up" the person who just told a joke that left the audience speechless with laughter. Or even worse, telling the same joke because you remember the punch line better. It will be anti-climactic and it just won't work. What you have to do is pretend that everything is perfectly normal. Walk your reader down the proverbial garden path. Sneak up on him if you have to. But instead of the cliché monster that emerges from the shadows and bites off his head, you surprise the reader from a totally unexpected direction. That is the crux of all humour writing.

USING "NOT"

If you're really serious about writing comedy, try looking at the works of two masters of the genre. Douglas Adams and Terry Pratchett have a similar device for creating a funny scene. It's called the "not" descriptor. Here's an example of how it works using negative comparison:

"He has the same stealth and agility with magic that fish have with mountain climbing."

And here is the not statement:

"It floated in the air without means of visible support in much the same way that a brick does not."

Once again, comparison is on the negative side. If it's slightly ludicrous, immensely ridiculous, then it's always humorous. Well, maybe not always-on a scale of one to ten, possibly a five. But, if you get fifty percent of your audience laughing that means you've sold half your novels. Now you can put your money in the bank and not worry about the other fifty percent, as you've already been reimbursed for the immense amount of time and energy you've put into making a cohesive novel that is a fairly enjoyable read for anyone with a functioning funny bone. The other fifty percent have probably already flung your book against the wall, gleefully watching it slide down with a broken spine.

Everyone knows the speed of light. That's not very funny. But to quote Steven Wright, "What's the speed of dark?"

Using long drawn out sentences (set aside with commas throughout) creates a long-winded passage that can, if handled properly, create a bit of humour in the minds of those whose brain cells still communicate, and cause those who read by merely moving their lips to eventually pass out from lack of oxygen (see physical humour). Never write your material with invisible ink—for some reason the reader never gets the joke.

To reiterate, use the not statement, ludicrous imagery, long sentences with practically no logic (just to confuse the reader as to what you are actually doing, which is exceptionally useful in those instances when perhaps you don't know yourself). And while doing all of these things, make your characters behave as if everything that is happening is perfectly normal. The reader gets the joke while the characters do not.

Absurdity

Absurdity plays a key role in humour. Let's use another example from Steven Wright.

> "My roommate has a pet elephant. He lost him. He's in the apartment somewhere."

And speaking of elephants, if you have two inch elephants in your story, make your characters act as if there have always been two inch elephants in the world. You can call them "personal pack-a-derms" or some such.

Rules—Break Them

Have everyone run full tilt to wherever they're going because it's against the law to walk. Now, create collisions, preferably with people carrying armloads of something or other that can crash splendidly and make a mess of everything.

Have an invisible sun hanging in the sky and make everyone wear sunglasses because the light is too bright.

If you do have ridiculous schemes and plots, make sure it all hangs together. Even insanity has rules, and that is: it's against the rules to be sane. If someone floats six inches above the ground when holding his or her breath, then everyone has to be able to do the same thing. The rules apply to everyone.

If trees talk, they're not allowed to have dumb conversations. They'd have to be great intellectuals because they are such slow and deep thinkers and spend many waking hours just pondering life, the universe—everything. Use common sense when choosing your comedy motif.

Be aware of things that have come before. Be original. For instance, you are not allowed to have a world supported by four elephants being carried on the back of a gigantic turtle swimming through space. Someone is already doing that one.

There are certain other rules that must be remembered (or copied just inside your sleeve where the observant reader or editor will never see it) or else your attempt at humour will, at best, have no effect and, at worst, find you caught in a Chinese thumb trap by a coin-hungry toddler in the middle of a four year-old's birthday party at Chucky Cheeses with two hundred of her closest friends.

Rule number forty-two (who numbers these rules anyway?): let your reader in on the joke. This is the humour writer's version of the "common background" theory. You must give the reader enough information to actually get the joke. Let me explain—no, that would take too long, let me sum up, instead. Suppose you have whisked your readers away to the farthest reaches of our galaxy, or to a small deli in Hobokan (there is no appreciable difference). You sit them in a restaurant where they overhear the following conversation:

> First alien: Why won't you introduce me to your sister, Phlemarelda?
>
> Second alien: Because the thought of a Gilignian whorebeast having to suckle an illegitimate Spasnovian Iglicker is too much even for me to bear.

Now, while the writer has fallen out of his chair, laughing so hard he is in danger of relieving himself into his lucky boxers, the reader is left to wonder if perhaps he didn't get off the wrong exit on the Jersey Turnpike. Had the author explained beforehand, in any of the acceptable methods which include flashback and exposition (but specifically excludes tattooing), that Gilignian whorebeasts have only one teat the size of, oh, a #2 pencil eraser and Spasnovian Iglickers, the most oversexed race in the known cosmos, at birth have heads the size of blue ribbon watermelons with lips like Mick Jagger, the reader at least has a sporting chance of "seeing" the absurdity of the remark and getting the joke. Never assume the reader has the same background as you. Some things can be assumed as common knowledge but in a unique, just developed fantasy/science fiction world, it is necessary that you provide as much information as needed.

AVOID CLICHÉS LIKE THE PLAGUE

Comedy, like writing, can suffer from the plague of clichés. Advisers whose breeches tear in the crotch when they bow to the king, or the king who utters, "Take my jester—please!" are not going to endear you to your readers. In fact, if you listen ever so quietly you will be able to hear their collective moans over these tired old favorites. An excellent way to introduce a humorous element to your story is to use the technique of "writing the absurd."

While the idea of a fish that flies might not be funny, a knight who is afraid of horses would be an absurd comedic device. Suppose the aforementioned royal adviser has an underarm hair fetish and spends all his time trying to come up with new and inconspicuous ways of getting people to raise their arms.

Perhaps a report is found circulating the outer galaxies that a recent study of life forms on planet Earth has determined that armadillos are the most intelligent life form despite their propensity for developing a vehicular suicide fetish soon after reaching full maturity.

What if that pack of Juicy Fruit in your purse or on your dashboard is actually a sentient life form? Absurd? You bet! Hit the reader from an unexpected direction!

It bears repeating that you should not try to be funny. Likewise, do not try to "set up" those funny situations. Just as in real life, if you tell your story true, and your characters are living a real existence, the opportunities for them to end up with egg on their face will occur naturally. The trick is for you, the writer, to recognise these situations and slip in the unexpected. When a horror story has shown you every place in the bedroom but the inside of the closet, it is easy to tell where the monster is. The comedy that works best is the comedy the reader doesn't see coming. The more serious the circumstances, the more ripe the situation is for something funny to happen.

Comedic Methods

High Comedy (or Comedy of Manners)

A type of comedy depicting and satirising the manners and customs of fashionable society, the life and problems of the upper class.

Low Comedy

Comedy that gets its effect mainly from action and situation such as slapstick, horseplay, etc. instead of through the use of witty dialogue. This also encompasses the farce, which is based on broadly humorous and highly unlikely situations.

Within the two "classes" of comedy there are predominantly two comedic methods: verbal comedy and physical comedy. There used to be a third, but psychokinetic comedy was determined to be unconstitutional and discriminatory by the United States Supreme Court in the landmark case of Bubba Leroy Johnson vs. the 1-800 Psychic Hotline Union.

VERBAL COMEDY

Verbal comedy utilises tried and true methods like the "one-liners."

"Is that a serrated two-handed broadsword in your pocket or are you happy to see me?"

The Call: "Why is it always the same thing every time I come home?"

The Windup: I've been a good son, Mom, but this time you have gone too far.

The Pitch: "I will not go as Jimmy Olsen's date to the Alternative Senior Prom. I look horrible in chiffon."

If you are going to use verbal comedy, most likely you are going to have a particular character that has this bizarre, "I'm the class-clown-who-never-grew-up" personality trait. Their comedic style will develop as you get to know them better. You will know what things they find funny and what things they are likely to poke fun at.

Physical comedy is the variety popularised by men such as Jerry Lewis, the Three Stooges and by comedians today like Jim Carey. Since your reader cannot actually "see" what is going on, it is up to you, the undaunted writer, to narrate the comedy of the scene. Make use of mental imagery as much as humanly possible. This will be easier at times than at others.

For instance, if I say that a young girl curtsies with all the grace of falling out of a wagon, you can mentally picture someone falling out of something and, instantly (or much more slowly if you are from the south like me) your brain makes the connection that perhaps everything isn't bending exactly the right way.

An excellent example of physical comedy is the character made famous in the Pink Panther movies by actor Peter Sellers; Inspector Clouseau. He was a bumbling, incompetent idiot with a servant who was ordered to attack him when he least suspected it, resulting in hilarious violence. Or he might catch the crook by falling out of a window and landing on him. Not much different than the knight who is thrown from his horse while charging a dragon and, while flying through the air screaming like a maiden, soon finds himself hanging off his lance which has perchance impaled and killed said dragon. So what does the knight do? Confess his great fortune? Expound on his cowardice? Certainly not! He struts back into town, dragonhead in tow, lying through his teeth! And your readers are the ones in on the joke! Unexpected circumstances with the result of your character holding the winning hand at the end of the scene is a great laugh motivator.

However, if you are dealing in unfamiliar terrain, you will have to give the reader enough mental clues to make the connection. For example, you might be back at that restaurant in the third quadrant of the Lollipop Cluster. You have every type of alien imaginable flying, morphing, oozing and tentacling around the place.

Funny? Not yet. You are there to meet a specific ambassador in hopes of signing a peace treaty with his war-like race since your peace-loving race failed to develop anything in three million years to defend yourselves except an odd variety of flower that sings, "Do You Really Want To Hurt Me" repeatedly when plucked. You believe yourself a dignified race, which have grown beyond the barbaric need to flex your painted-on muscles.

Funny? Nope. Needs a little bit more. The ambassador arrives. He smells. He's hairy and his third eye keeps telescoping out from his forehead to stare up the waitress' leather mini.

Funny? Almost. Well, ok, a little, but that's not your mark. Your dignified representative cajoles, argues, and pleads his cause. After much diplomatic mumbo-jumbo, and three gallons of Validian Goolie Juice, the barbarian agrees not to wipe out your entire race. All that remains is to seal the bargain. Grunk, your aromatic comrade, suggests (actually insists) on the traditional method of sealing the deal. He strolls over to the massive Zili Death Beast noisily slurping his special of the day, six-eye soup, and proceeds to urinate into his large bowl, insisting while he does so, that you have the honor of dispatching it in single combat.

You have arrived!

PARENTHESES—INSIDE JOKE

More than anything else, readers love to be in on the joke. When explaining something to the reader put it inside parentheses (like this) and they feel as if they're being let in on the secret. This also creates a rapport with the reader. (Don't you just love rapports?) (**publisher's note: use this sparingly, and very carefully, as it can pull the reader out of the story.)

UNDERSTATEMENT

A simple, effective way of breaking the ice with your readers, understatement is another comedic device that your readers will recognise without any necessary background information.

Say you learn before meeting Princess Julip that she is very protective of, and is never seen without, her pet "Pookie." Instantly your reader might picture a Persian cat or some other cute cuddly creature. Naturally upon seeing the princess strolling the grounds with her gigantic sabretooth megator cat the reader is taken aback. THAT'S Pookie? It's not any different than the largest guy at the local tavern being known as "Tiny" or "Mom" of Mom's Diner fame being the nasty, overweight, cigar smoking, stubble-bearded grease slinger whose head is, as we speak, poking through the kitchen window.

How about the guy who has to drive ten miles to pick up his date for a special evening? Tux, bouquet of flowers, car waxed—he's ready. He sets out, directions in hand. Along the way you throw a few obstacles in his path: a washed out bridge, a tornado, a car-jacking and subsequent mugging. You get the idea. He arrives, on time and undaunted, to her uptown residence. Opening the door, she is met by the dishevelled, muddy and beaten young man holding a slightly wilting bouquet of stems. The socialite, apparently a total ditz, merely inquires: "Did you have any trouble finding the house?" To which your young hero would naturally respond, "Uh, no problem at all." Understatement.

SARCASM

Perhaps your hero has been carrying his wounded comrade for six days since having to eat their horse to keep from starving. He staggers into town, bent, exhausted, and obviously struggling under the heavy load (your reader might also wonder why he didn't remove his friend's armor first). A passerby asks if he is in need of assistance. "Nope, could go on like this for days," replies your irritated character. This, dear comedy writer, is sarcasm.

All of us, well most of us anyway, know someone who uses sarcasm. Sarcasm is comedy with an edge. Sarcasm can be funny when it is not being rude. You run the risk of turning your character into a smart-ass if it is used all the time. Perhaps you have a character that is grumpy or crotchety all the time. Sarcasm is an excellent way to elicit a laugh or two from the reader. Just remember, if the character is a grump, a curmudgeon, etc., then the character is NOT a comedian so every other thing out of his mouth shouldn't be an attempt at humour. The humour should be in the way it relates to the story or how other characters react to him.

Wife (whose husband has just fallen out their second story bedroom window): Honey, are you ok?

Husband (lying sprawled in a horribly contorted position on the front lawn): Fine, dear. Just send Timmy down with a couple of band-aids and some gauze.

Another good example of sarcasm is comedian Bill Engvall who uses sarcasm to alert us to stupid people who should be required to wear a sign.

Man drives into a gas station with a flat tire.

Attendant: Got a flat? (He is obviously the stupid one)

Motorist: Nope. Was drivin' around and the other three just swelled right up on me! Sarcasm.

Remember, sarcasm can be funny when it is not mean-spirited.

EBB, FLOW & HIGH TIDE

Comedy writing is no different than that of plotting an ordinary novel. However, the author must have a working knowledge of what is funny and what isn't. Spend some time watching comedy shows or reading humorous books to gain some insight. Pay careful attention to how the joke develops, note when expectation is highest, and the final line or situation that causes the audience to erupt in laughter. Then use what you have learned and incorporate the techniques into your own work. Be original. There is no humour in using old material. Readers enjoy looking at the world through a comedian's eyes, so try to be as fresh and innovative as you can.

Within the full scope of your novel will be chapters, of course, but inside those chapters will be the little stories that will dictate the overall tone of the completed work. There will be the quiet lead-in, the pace that quickens as you get closer to the punch line, then the coup de grace or actual punch line. The story will then resume along its normal course until another situation arises. To create tension, have the character encounter one situation after another that grow progressively more difficult to hurdle.

For example, let's send your character on a quest. It could be a quest for a magical device or something as simple as milk. But it has to be something that is really needed and the character will go to the ends of the earth to get it. As he leaves the front door, there is a major earthquake. Does our hero falter? Of course not. He absolutely needs to get that milk. He travels up Johnston Street, which is the normal route he always takes for his milk. Unfortunately, there is a gap in the street due to the earthquake and it's impassable. Now he must take a different route.

Already, the tension is rising because the character is in unfamiliar terrain. He decides to try Timmons Street and discovers that there are looters and gangs taking advantage of the earthquake, and raiding shops along that street. He thinks he can slip through without being seen but he's spotted. The looters pull out weapons and begin shooting at him. He dives behind a vehicle for protection. There is a looter already crouched there with his own gun drawn. Our hero kicks the looter in the head, who immediately falls unconscious. Now our hero is armed.

He rolls across the hood of the car, taking a couple of shots as he does. The other looters duck as bullets hail around them. Weaving erratically, our hero reaches the end of the street. He is now across from the store where his favorite milk resides, the only store that sells that particular brand. He must get it from there. Just as he makes it across the street, several police cars screech onto the scene, called out by the looting. They see our hero with a gun and naturally assume he's one of the thieves.

Car doors fly open, policemen squatting behind each, guns drawn and levelled. As the bullets begin to fly, our hero dives the remaining few feet to the store, crashing through the door in a shower of glass. The police remain outside, guns at the ready. There is the amplified sound of a voice demanding that he turn himself in.

But, there in the back, in the store's only cooler, is the milk that our hero must have. Shoving shoppers and store salesman aside, he runs to the back. The storeowner knows our hero and can't understand why he's being so aggressive. The police by now have decided to raid the store to see if they can't apprehend our hero. As he reaches the back, there are gunshots and the cooler explodes in a colorful spray of two-day old deli sandwich shrapnel and punctured milk containers. The fluid flies everywhere and our hero slips and falls at the base of the cooler. He can feel the crunch of glass along his leg and arm where he's fallen and knows that he's cut. He turns, and in a sitting position with his back to the cooler, starts shooting towards the front of the store. Some customers scream and duck out of the way as the cops fall back.

Our hero spies one container of milk that hasn't been hit by bullets. He reaches for it and moves it just in time. Where the container was, a bullet ricochets. With his prize underneath his arm like a football being held by an unstoppable running back, he throws himself through the rear door that the police haven't covered because they don't realise it's there. Running hard, he spins around the corner of the store, along the back of the police cars where the police aren't looking, and back up the street where he previously encountered the looters. He is tired and dripping blood but he grits his teeth, preparing once again to do battle. The arrival of the police, however, has scattered the criminal element, and it's now clear sailing for him.

He makes it home, and drops panting into a chair in the kitchen, the milk grasped firmly in one hand. He is shaken with emotion, his fingers quivering. The phone rings, and despite great difficulty holding it in his hand, he finally gets it to his ear.

"Hello?" he says, wheezing horribly.

"Mr. Johnson, I believe you forgot to pay for that item when you left the store," comes the storeowner's familiar voice.

By following the sequence of events above, you can see how you can take an ordinary every day event and turn it into an exciting adventure with a humorous ending. By using the ebb and flow of an action story, we've created climax, anti-climax, and finally the punch line.

The trick is climaxing the funny section at just the right point. Knowing when this is most effective can only come from experience. The more you write, the more experienced you will become at knowing just when the "tide" is right for the line that will cause your reader to "gut" laugh. You know you are doing it correctly when your fan mail can be easily distinguished from your bill collectors by the conspicuous absence of death threats.

Parody

And what discussion of humour could be complete without at least a brief glimpse at that most irreverent and satirical of forms, the parody, This type of humour is found in many guises, from short stories and editorials to political cartoons and skits. The art of imitation has long been used as a means of poking fun at the silly or larger than life events and personages of history.

The only thing that varies with parody is the scale. If the parody is of an individual, there must be sufficient clues that the reader will recognise the figure being parodied. For example:

Your hero, the gladiator Rockus Balboacus, has just defeated yet another colossus in the colosseum when amidst the throng of Romans seeking to touch his blood-spattered biceps we are made to hear our hero bellowing "ADRIATICA!"

Obviously anyone who has seen any of the "Rocky" movies will recognise the only Spartan in Rome who says "Yo." And in the recognition, rests the humour.

Parody can also be used on a larger scale to poke fun at things that society at large finds silly or humorous. I wrote a story once, in which the main character, a gumshoe-style detective, takes a case that takes him into the seedy, unseen world of professional wrestling. Taking cart blanche with the almost obscenely silly story lines currently being used in the name of sports entertainment, I created my own "pay-per-view" style wrestling event with matches such as the "Weapon of Opportunity Match," an "Electrocution Match" in which the ring ropes are electrified, etc. As you can see, by taking the things we find silly and pushing them "over the top," you can poke fun at just about anything. It really depends on the type of story you are writing as to how much or how little parody you use. The entire story, a part, or even just a character can all be parodied. It is simply another tool in your Humour Writer's Utility Belt.

Summary

The best way to write comedy is with full knowledge of what makes people laugh. Laughter is created when a situation that has become tense, critically so, is suddenly released from tension and instantly into relief.

Actually, a joke is like a story in itself, involving all aspects of writing, including the climax and anti-climax.

There is no "one" way to write comedy, just as there is no "one" way to write fantasy, or mystery, or science fiction or, indeed, any genre of writing. It's a safe bet that what makes you laugh out loud is a prime candidate to be placed into a story situation to share with your readers. Look at everything around you and the every day situations that you see. Carry a notebook with you. When you see something that makes you smile or laugh, write it down. Then try to use that situation to its best effect in the story you write. Life is the best teacher for those funny moments. He who laughs last truly laughs best.

Research

The More You Know, The Safer You Are

Tee Morris

Perhaps this chapter's presence perplexes you to no end. Research? For a fantasy novel? Aren't we just making this stuff up as we go? This is the misconception of many, in particular literary snobs who believe that the Fantasy genre is merely the "flying by the seat of your pants" approach to writing, making up the Laws of Nature as we go. At one time, Science Fiction was regarded in the same fashion, but this was before the advances in technology that we have seen in the past century. Now, even SF authors turn up their nose at the Fantasy genre! I will never forget the time I was sitting on an authors' panel—four authors, three Fantasy and one Science Fiction—and the Science Fiction author turns to us and ask

"I've a question for the panelists. What are your opinions of the use of magic in your work? I've always found the use of magic as a crutch."

The silence was absolute.

Perhaps some of this animosity comes from an opinion that Fantasy is a relatively "new" genre. This is not an opinion, but a misconception. Take a look at William Shakespeare's work, *The Tempest*. It doesn't get more Fantasy than that. Perhaps having Fantasy blindly lumped in with Science Fiction has upset a few, and there are some authors who take a lot of pride voicing their distaste with that grouping. These SF snobs love to voice how writing that is "a cakewalk" because Science Fiction, to be quality Science Fiction, possesses a basis in scientific credibility. Even with soft science fiction, some sort of theory, be it cooked up by Einstein or Hawking, gives credence to the events of the book. With Fantasy, according to this argument, there is no need or real urgency for this. Fantasy novels are set in realms of magic, and an author can make up the rules and build worlds without a care to the consequence. We rewrite history on a whim. We leap into a story with no regard to the past, present, or future. It's not "real" work. Right?

Wrong! This is simply not true.

Depending on the world you build and the era of your adventure, research is not only important but also essential. Research extends deep into your writing, down to the choice of words you choose for your characters to speak. While you as a writer are looked upon to create worlds of fantastic creatures, characters, and high adventures, you also need to know what you are writing about and how to write it in order to make your writing real. Without a dose of Reality, the Fantasy becomes too far-fetched and loses the reader's trust in the world you create. This is the challenge in creating your Fantasy novel. Finding the right time and place in our history to make it your own. You may be reading this thinking, "This is starting to sound a lot like a homework assignment for a History paper!" Well, rest assured, it is nothing like that...

A History essay or term paper is merely a one-page book report compared to the amount of research that goes into one Fantasy novel.

So let's take a closer look at some of the things you will need to research for your Fantasy novel. We will be looking at areas you may need to do some reading on, or even get some formal training (if applicable) before you begin writing. Another option is to check your research at the end of your rough draft, but this could mean serious re-writing in your second draft that can lead to a domino effect of changes throughout your novel. This effect can leave to even more research for you to carry out. The aim of this chapter is to give you an honest and realistic perspective on how to look at your novel before you begin and after the rough draft is complete.

THE ERA OF YOUR NOVEL

When you begin your novel, whether in outline format or at Page One, ask yourself a simple and poignant question: What era is your world set in? It would astound you how many people respond with 'the Middle Ages'. Okay—when in the Middle Ages? Are we talking the 1100's? The 1200's? Who is sitting on the throne? Have cannons or firearms been introduced yet? Fundamental questions such as these are going to set the rest of the tone of your book, and your research. Now while this may sound like a review of the worldbuilding chapter, this chapter could actually be considered its addendum. Once you have built your world, you must fill in the details through research of other worlds and cultures of the age you have set it in.

You might be thinking, "I don't understand, Tee. This is Fantasy. I can do what I want. Right?" Well, to an extent. Let's take a look at this passage, set in an Ancient Egyptian setting. See if you can pick out the glaring inconsistency of this little paragraph.

Queen Sebi sank to her knees before the giant statue of Sebt-Nim, the God of Death. She implored Him to take her life in place of her child, Ramashan. She closed her eyes, concentrating on the prayer. But when her eyes shut tightly, the shadows she saw before her eyes merely took form. She could see the young heir to the throne, his head sinking deep into the pillows of his bed as he fought to take in the sweet air of his kingdom, granting him another moment of life. The soft mattress gave him some semblance of comfort, as if he were floating on a cloud to the blessed arms of Ara, the Goddess of Light; but Sebi—even in this conjured image before her—could see in his eyes the fear of passing so soon into the Afterworld.

Now where is the inconsistency? Well, provided I built this fantasy world in an Ancient Egyptian setting, the "bed" young Ramashan slept in would not have a soft mattress or pillows. Beds of that era hardly resembled the kinds of bed we are accustomed to. This is a simple example of an inconsistency or what is more commonly referred to as an anachronism. With anachronisms, history is juxtaposed or rearranged with little or no consequences to known history. *Xena* and Hercules would pull off glaring anachronisms with tongue firmly place in their cheeks, giving the audience an obvious wink and a knowing grin.

It is details like this, however, that you as a writer must stay true to in order to give your work a hint of realism. Otherwise, you undermine your writing. So when setting your Fantasy, try not to be too vague in what time it is set. The Middle Ages. The Dark Ages. The Fourth Age of Man. Yeah, that's great, but how about a year? Months and dates are even better because you can fill in even more details. Does it snow in your realm? If your realm is set in a deep desert, probably not. If your kingdom is set in a mountainous region, is there a difference between summer and winter? Here, your research would lead you to books on the regions of our own world like Switzerland and Austria. What is the climate like there? What do they import? What do they export? The more details your research answers, the easier it is to build your world and write your novel.

When writing your novel, knowing how steeped into history your story goes will determine how much research is involved. A growing sub-genre in Science Fiction and Fantasy is the Alternative History genre. This is the ultimate "What If..." kind of novel for those curious about the outcome if a single event in history were changed. It could be something as major as a battle in the American Revolutionary War that turns out differently. It could be something as traumatic as the assassination of Winston Churchill. It could also be something innocent, such as Albert Einstein meeting Charlie Chaplain. Whatever the significant event, history as we know it is altered and rewritten. In this genre, the research is essential and demanding. You, the author, must not only know inside and out the historical time period in which you have set your novel, but you must also consider the changes, both dramatic and subtle, to the known timeline of the world. It will be your research that dictates how much known history is altered, but this Alternative History must happen within reason. I say "within reason" because Alternative History cannot be anything overtly wacky such as, "If Albert Einstein ever met Charlie Chaplain, space travel is developed twenty years earlier and by the year 2000 we not only have bases on the Moon but we are now experimenting with time travel." It would be something more along the lines of, "What would England have been if under Spanish rule?" This is Harry Turtledove's Ruled Britannia where up-and-coming playwright William Shakespeare is asked to write a play that will rally the English nation to rise up against the occupying forces of Spain. Alternative History does require a lot of extra research, but the end result can be quite rewarding.

Combining history with your Fantasy can also be tricky. In this instance, you are not writing Alternative History so much as creating a "familiar" background for your reader. In the case of *MOREVI: The Chronicles of Rafe and Askana*, written by myself and Miss Lisa Lee, the historical backdrop was Tudor England under the reign of King Henry the VIII. Here, it was our responsibility to know our Tudor history in detail. Some authors would find this meddling with history inhibiting, but our challenge was legitimising the combination of historical figures with characters of Fantasy. In our work, Queen Askana Moldarin was in search of allies and crossed a gateway between her realm and Rafe's in order to meet with King Henry, a completely neutral superpower that could—if she gained His interest—supply allies. The interaction was a lot of fun for both Miss Lee and myself, and in the end the story allowed for us as writers to explore one of the greatest monarchs of the millennium as a human being rather than an untouchable king.

History and Fantasy can work together, provided the events are believable, credible, and free of anachronisms (as mentioned earlier). For example, in an *early* draft of *MOREVI*, Lisa and I took our characters to meet William Shakespeare. (This guy makes the rounds in this genre!) While the scene itself was a lot of fun and provided some levity, the "Temporal Anomaly Police" were also busting down our creative hideout, as this was a blatant anachronism that could not be overlooked. William Shakespeare would not be known in London for another fifty or so years, so that scene was one of the first to be cut. Now that is a more dramatic example, but here is one we discovered in the rewrites.

To remain true to the story's timeline, we needed a different English Queen on the throne. In the first draft, the wife was Anne Boleyn. In our rewrite, it changed to Kathryn Howard. In a pure Fantasy with history providing only a basis, not a backdrop, this would not have mattered much. With the change in Queens for *MOREVI*, a domino effect occurred. (A domino effect Gene Roddenberry, Ray Bradbury, and any other author who wrote about the dangers of meddling with history would have relished!) Our researched revealed a definite "changing of the guard" in the Royal Court. There was a different Chancellor in power, meaning that Thomas Cromwell would not have been our principal adversary rooted within the Palace. Changing court villains also meant changing character motivations, both for the villain and the English Queen in her animosity for Askana Moldarin. This is the pitfall writers face when incorporating history with Fantasy. One change and the fallout can easily run throughout the entire book.

Am I saying, "Do not incorporate history with Fantasy"? Absolutely not. What I am saying is be ready to do some serious research in writing that rough draft, and if there is a slight change in anything historical, then make certain you are ready to research your facts (from multiple resources, not just one—more on that later) and that your resources support, not contradict, your story. When incorporating history, make sure the history itself compliments the plot, not overpowers it. I tell people, when asked about the historical accuracy of *MOREVI*, that the book is as historically accurate as the story allows me to be. If Lisa and I were completely accurate in our Tudor history, the privateer captain would flash his daring smile with far fewer teeth in his mouth, would be covered in sores from some kind of sexually transmitted disease, and would have shot Askana and her cohorts on sight as being in league with the Devil. That is *if* Askana didn't kill him first in his intrusion into her Palace and for crimes against her crown.

Another obstacle to avoid is throwing in so much history that your story becomes a "Who's Who" in history. If historical figures appear, make sure their presence is essential and realistic to the story. Otherwise, you take the risk of your Fantasy work resembling an episode of Irwin Allen's *Time Tunnel*. (In this short-lived television show, the heroes stumbled through major event after major event of history. I still believe the writing sessions for their scripts were a couple of guys with a fifth Grade history book and a six-pack of Budweiser. But that's just me...)

The rule of thumb in history for your Fantasy novel: let the history help, not hinder your story.

TALKING THE TALK: APPROPRIATE WORDS FOR YOUR AGE

You have your age selected; now you begin your adventure. Now let's imagine we are working on a novel set in a circa 1300's society. Our two heroes have their weapons drawn and backs against the wall, knowing full well there are a roomful of enemy soldiers on the other side of the door.

> Gareth tightened the grip of his broadsword, taking in a full, deep breath of the stale catacomb air.
>
> "I know the adrenaline is going," Samuel said, "but you have to keep it under control."
>
> "Easy for you to say, knight." He raised the blade in his grasp a little higher, "but I intend to enjoy this rush to the fullest. Forgive my warrior's faux pas!"
>
> "Bloody buccaneer!" Samuel spat before kicking open the door.

Can you find the words these thirteenth century characters shouldn't be using in casual conversation? While "faux pas" is French for "false step," the word itself was not first documented to be in use until 1676. The word "buccaneer" was not documented until circa 1690.

The real offender, however, is the word "adrenaline." While heroes have felt the rush of adrenaline in the heat of battle and just before the kill, the actual word "adrenaline" was not documented until scientists actually extracted it from a test subject in 1901. These characters should not know any of these terms, adrenaline in particular. By knowing the origins of words and their first documented uses, you will be able to develop your characters and their speech patterns much easier. I'm not saying you need to make all of your language "historically accurate." If that were the case, all dialogue featured in Fantasy novels would resemble Shakespeare or even Chaucer's *Canterbury Tales*. Just be careful, though, in the words you choose. Instead of adrenaline, describing the effect of adrenaline as "a rush of blood" or "quickened pace." There are always alternatives. The best way to check the origins of a word is to refer to a collegiate dictionary. *The Merriam-Webster Collegiate Dictionary* and its companion CD-ROM give a detailed explanation on the "date stamp" given to a word looked up.

Keep in mind, the date is not its first use but the first documented use. Some words you look up could have been in use before its documented year but the year itself gives the word a basis in history. I tend to give my own words (not ones I create, but words I choose for dialogue) a "grace century", refusing to go one hundred years past the century I'm using for the basis of my society. If, however, you are working with Urban Fantasy (a sub-genre that sets Fantasy elements in modern, everyday settings) you will want to stay closer to the documented years.

While some words carry dates that fit your story's century, it is a good idea to dig deeper and find out how the word is used in context of the era. Many times, words can "evolve" and become something different with time. I encountered this when writing with Miss Lisa Lee. She dropped into a dialogue between one of our lead characters and another character the word "turncoat." It was being used and understood in this instance as another word for "traitor." While we know this as being a synonym for "traitor", the character of Rafe—a privateer from King Henry the VIII's realm—would have understood it as something very different. "Turncoats" in the fifteenth and sixteenth centuries were considered "cheapskates," as they would turn the cuffs of their coats to give it a "new" appearance. Finding out the history of words is actually easy, especially if you take this search online. This study of the origins of words and phrases is known as etymology and there are numerous websites, both personal and professional, that follow this study of linguistics with a passion. Here are a few examples of online resources dedicated to the art of etymology:

- http://phrases.shu.ac.uk/meanings/index.html
- http://www.word-detective.com
- http://www.uselessknowledge.com/word/origins.html

Take advantage of these resources, and if they do not have your answers, follow their links to other online resources that can trace your vocabulary back to its original applications and origins.

But what about narration? Are you limited to only the words and sayings of the time period in which you have set your adventure? This is a choice for you, the writer, to make. In most cases, keeping your narrative more modern than your character's speech is acceptable, but how modern is up to you. There is definitely more leeway and freedom, depending on your story's point-of-view. If your story's point-of-view is in first person or a limited third person, then you are confined to age-appropriate words. When your story's narrative is told from a grander scale, then you have the luxury to use words that perhaps the characters would not know. Your end decision needs to be final and must be adhered to with discipline. If your characters are speaking at one moment like twentieth century intellects, then sound like Othello or Hamlet a few chapters later, the reader will notice. Find the happy medium and take advantage of resources both written and online to make sure the words you choose are appropriate.

THE ART OF WAR: WEAPONS AND COMBAT FOR YOUR ERA

You may notice this chapter ties in with *Arms, Armor, and Combat*, elsewhere in this book but again it all comes back to research and the era that you have set it in. If you have set your Fantasy novel in a time where black powder is still a relatively new substance, can you expect to have your hero wield a pistol? What kind of pistol is it? A flintlock? A wheel lock? Is it a pistol or is it a rifle? If the society you have created does know and utilise pistols, they will no doubt know about and use cannons in combat. If they know cannons, are they used only on land campaigns or has your society expanded their capabilities with black powder to use it on the open waters? Here, your research goes into the history of war, strategy, and combat. You will need to establish with your society exactly how advanced the sciences and technologies are. If black powder has not advanced beyond fireworks, then how skilled are the blacksmiths and forges of your society? Do the craftsmen of your realm create steel that is sturdy or lighter than other realms' weaponry, or have they a technique in smelting that achieves a balance between both?

To truly understand the evolution of combat and warfare, do a search online for historical re-enactor groups and start up a dialogue. Top-notch historical re-enactors can tell you everything you wanted to know about the specific time period that is their speciality. The most common historical re-enactor groups in the United States are set in the Revolutionary War and American Civil War (or "War of Northern Aggression", depending on which side of the Mason-Dixon Line you were raised on) eras. If you direct your web browser to http://www.landsknechts.org, you will find yourself in the domain of "Das TeufelsAlpdruken Fahnlein Landsknecht" or "The Devil's Nightmare Regiment." This group based in Crownsville, Maryland is dedicated to the German mercenaries of the fifteenth and sixteenth centuries. Your search for historical re-enactors will show you web pages and web sites for eras dating as far back as Ancient Romans and as modern as the 1980 Soviet Union soldier fighting in Afghanistan. Many of these re-enacting groups are history buffs that enjoy stepping back in time and love talking about their time period. Whether professional or amateur, these re-enactors can either answer your questions or guide you to a variety of a resources that will aid you in understanding what weapons came first, which ones were reliable, and what kind of tactics were used in that time period.

The importance of knowing what tactics were used and what weapons were relied upon also plays an important role in polishing and sharpening your work. Returning to the pistol, I had someone ask me, "If your hero has a pistol and knows how to use it, why does he refer to it as a 'last resort'? Wouldn't a pistol be better than a sword?" Unfortunately, this is a misconception perpetuated by Hollywood that guns are better than swords. Swashbuckler movies from Errol Flynn's days right up to *The Mask of Zorro* with Antonio Banderas and Catherine Zeta-Jones depict heroes and heroines firing pistols with full confidence that they would fire and they would be accurate. However, if you dig into the history of the gun, you soon discover why swords were still used alongside firearms right up to the days of the Revolutionary War. Guns were far from reliable. There was a fifty-fifty chance, provided you loaded it properly, that it would fire. If it did fire, due to the shape of the bullet and the weather conditions, you might hit your target. Now, let's say your target is a soldier wielding a long two-handed sword and is fifty yards away from you. You fire your pistol. You miss. You now have to reload. This is a process that, if you are skilled at doing under the strain of battle, will take anywhere from five to ten minutes. This same process can take ten to fifteen minutes if you are a beginner. So you dump in some powder down the barrel, drop the bullet into the barrel next, stuff wadding down the barrel, then pull the hammer back, place another small amount of powder in the chamber, and then aim.

Your pistol is primed and ready for firing.

Unless you called a "Time Out!" to the charging soldier, his blade is probably buried into your belly and you can't fire your pistol as a last act of defiance because your hand jerked back and the powder in the chamber has fallen out. So much for the reliability of the pistol.

Once you have the weaponry decided for your characters, it is a good idea to research the capabilities and limitations of the weapons in questions. One example that springs to mind is the rapier, which I discuss in detail in the weapons chapter. No matter how hard you swing or how heavy your rapier blade is, you cannot behead anyone or hack off an opponent's limb with a rapier. Rapiers, much like pistols of early make, did not deal blows that killed right away. Most victims of rapiers and early pistols would die hours or days later from the internal bleeding these weapons would cause. Being familiar with the weapons used by your characters will also help you in creating the general appearance and build of your character. If your fighter is skilled in two-handed sword, broadsword, or axe combat, he or she will be of a stockier build, perhaps wide shoulders and developed upper body strength. Archers tend to sport upper arm and chest definition, along with specific calluses on their fingertips (unless they are using a specially tailored glove, then the calluses would not be so prominent). Fencers and fighters skilled in rapier combat will not only have developed and defined muscles in their upper body but their legs will also be developed from the different lunges and intricate footwork absent in fighting with a broadsword.

Two excellent resources for understanding and researching the evolution of the sword are Richard F. Burton's *The Book of the Sword* and *Renaissance Swordsmanship* by John Clements. These books not only trace back and document different tactics in fighting, but also give you the anatomy of a sword. This type of detail proves helpful, especially when writing combat sequences.

For example, what if our adrenaline-junkie swashbuckler Gareth runs into the roomful of soldiers, his broadsword held high, and he does the following:

> The unsuspecting guard turned, his frothy mug of ale in his hand held outward as the broadsword began what appeared to be a slow plunge deep into his belly. Gareth felt the weapon stop at the pommel and could see the weapon clearly protruding from the Uldorian's back. He took a quick sip of the soldier's ale before pushing the corpse free of his blade.

If you take a good look at this attack of Gareth's and you know how a sword is built, you would know this attack is impossible. Why? Because the pommel is the bottom tip of a sword's handle. If Gareth were to in fact, "bury his sword up to the pommel", he would have struck the soldier with a force equal to that of *The Terminator*. His blade, hilt, and hand would be wrist-deep in guts. To fix this passage, the writer must have a basic understanding of a sword. You must know sword not only in its use but also its basic construction. Know that your hero's sword is run up to the hilt. Running a sword up to the pommel would be overkill.

Pardon the pun.

Two Heads Are Better Than One: Confirming Your Resources

When you do your research—whether it is online, print, or otherwise—it is always a good idea to have two independent sources for your information. Writers tend to have one reliable resource for the bulk of their work, that one authoritative voice that they will rely on. For myself, if I want to refer to the be-all and end-all expert concerning piracy and privateering, it is David Cordingly, the author of Under the Black Flag. While I rely heavily on his works for solid, historical background, I tend to consult other online resources for confirmation on a key fact that is essential for my work. By having the research confirmed by two independent resources, you remain assured that your facts are straight.

Now what if your resources contradict one another? Here, your research becomes complicated. For example, when I was working on research of Tudor England under the rule of King Henry the VIII, I would find both online and in print several different interpretations of exactly what kind of individual Henry was in his lifetime. One resource paints King Henry Tudor as being a great leader, tower of strength, and the symbol of the Renaissance arriving to England. Another resource depicts the King as a tyrant, ruthless on the brink of wild paranoia, and heartless in his treatment of wives and daughters. Even in the research of *getting published*, one "reliable resource" will tell you one way of approaching publishers and agents while another will completely contradict what you have just read. So who wins out?

Both do. Your cross-referencing is not to match resources word for word, but to find the common thread between the two. It would be terrific to think that all historical research is objective, but that is simply not the case. Returning to the earlier example of King Henry, his second wife, Anne Boleyn, also comes under the subjective fire of historians everywhere. The descendants of Boleyn are usually writers of historical works that depict her as a victim while other resources written by distant relatives of Jane Seymour (the woman King Henry married after Anne Boleyn) make her out as being a defiant, headstrong, and somewhat irritating nag. So the research calls for you, the writer, to find a commonality in the different opinions and biases in your subject matter. An extra challenge, but not an impossible one to meet.

The most stimulating and perhaps most fun research a writer can be fortunate enough to document for their work are hands-on research and real-life interviews. Universities, museums, and historical re-enactments can introduce you to a wide variety of historical authorities, both professional and amateur. If you are lucky enough, you might even establish a relationship with an expert in a specific trade or practice, such as sword fighting, herbology, or nautical skills. Close contact with these skills will only add detail and enhancement to your worlds and your writing that readers will appreciate. If your "living resources" and your writing schedules do not allow for that sort of "close contact", then take detailed notes of the interviews. When interviewing subjects, get their names, spell them right, and give a "shout out" to them in your book's "Forward" or "Acknowledgements" page. "Please" and "Thank You" are great words to use when asking for interviews, following-up your interviews, and being gracious for the time given to your project.

This may strike you as common sense, but sometimes writers tend to suffer "tunnel vision" and forgot those people who help them along the journey to creating an airtight story with a definitive edge. The bottom line: be polite! One reason why many do not grant interviews so readily to writers is due to the fact that writers will suck them dry for knowledge, trivia, and detail only to take them for granted, stooping so low as to ask, "And you are?" at the book signing where they are buying a copy of your work. This is a sure-fire way to guarantee that this resource will not return for help on your second book. Thank your living resources for their time and knowledge, acknowledge them somewhere in the opening of your book, and (at the very least) compensate them with an autographed copy of your work. Regardless if they ever read your work or not, it is the gesture that matters in the end.

So there you are. Your roadmap for research. You may think this is a lot of work in creating a Fantasy novel, but this is the reality of your imagination. Yes, the magic, the mystery, and the wonder can still be there, but it is the research you carry out and the depth of this research that will add detail to your world, your characters, and your writing. From here, the novel you envision will become far more than just prose on a page but a living world with real heroes, real villains, and real places that your readers will want to visit in future works that follow your first.

SUMMARY

In writing Fantasy, research is essential in making your work well-rounded, polished, and sharp. As the title of this chapter says—the more you know, the safer you are. Research provides validity to your work and also adds dimension and depth to characters, cultures, and realms of your creation. In the genre of Alternative History, facts must be double-checked and then double-checked again when your story begins to follow your new timeline. While research in your Fantasy is important, keep your research under control. Avoid losing yourself into the details of facts and history. Your research should assist and validate your story, not bog it down with trivia that clouds the world you create. Finally, remember that one resource should be a cornerstone, but not the only resource that you use. Cross-check various resources to find common threads and reinforcement in the development of your major and minor cast members.

Market Resources

Tina Morgan

Submitting Your Work

Whether you are querying an agent, magazine, or novel publisher, you should take the same careful steps:

1) Make certain your work is the best you can make it.

- a) Run spelling and grammar checks.
- b) View a print copy of your work—even when submitting electronically. Punctuation and misspellings are easier to see in print.
- c) Find someone to read over your work for mistakes and inconsistencies.

2) Research your market.

- a) Make sure the publisher you are querying accepts stories like the one you are submitting. Double check length, genre, style etc.
- b) Know the name of the editor/agent. Make certain you have gender and name spelling correct.
- c) Study the submissions guidelines and then FOLLOW THEM TO THE LETTER. Each publisher is likely to have slightly different guidelines, so you need to customize your submission for each.

3) Prepare your work in a professional manner.

- a) Do NOT send dirty or crumpled copies.
- b) Do NOT submit unedited work.
- c) DO remember that publishing is a business. Conduct yourself in a professional manner.

No matter how well you prepare your work, odds are you will be rejected at some point. You may receive rejections that show a serious lack of respect and professionalism: strips of paper, poorly worded sentences, spelling errors, sales pitches for the agent/publishers' books on how to write, dirty, crumpled and/or faint copies. Do not allow this to change the way you conduct yourself. Publishing is still a business and you will not succeed by sending out anything less than your best work.

Maintain a professional attitude can be difficult. Rejection hurts. Especially when it's single word scribbled across the top of your query letter, "NO." No one expects you to be unfazed when your hard work is turned down, but try to keep it in perspective. Just as your tastes in reading may differ from your best friend's or significant others, so will the editor/agents' taste vary from one magazine to the other. Reading books/stories published by the publisher you are querying will give you a better idea if they will accept your work.

GETTING STARTED

After months of pouring your heart and soul into your novel it's finally finished and the hard part is over right? I wish I could say it was. Unfortunately, today's publishing industry demands that we learn how to sell our own novels, first to an agent, or publisher, then to the public.

There are several publishing options open to the new writer: self-publishing, subsidy press, independent and traditional publishing. All three can be e-press or print. Each one requires the new writer to help market their book. Even if you are published with a large NY publisher, they are not going to spend the money advertising your book the way they would Stephen King, Nora Roberts, Daniel Steel or John Grisham. A first time or even mid-list author is not going to see their book cover being advertised on Wal-Mart TV as they're shopping. Without advertising, your novel will sit quietly on the bookstore shelves waiting for someone to notice the cover and pick it up.

Publishing is not for the timid. Unless you are very lucky and become one of the rare "Cinderella" stories, you are going to have to work for the dream of seeing your work in print.

FINDING AN AGENT

As self-publishing does not require an agent or an editor's approval, I'm not going to go into a lot of detail about the option. Suffice it to say, if you self-publish, no one is responsible for editing your work but you. Take steps to be sure your work is as clean as it can be. Hire an editor to look over your final copy. Make certain your manuscript shines. Self-publishing is one of the hardest things a writer can do. You are responsible for all facets of editing and marketing.

Self-publishing and subsidy press do not require an agent. Very few independent press ask for agented submissions, so don't let a disreputable agent try to convince you that you need to pay for their services if you choose to explore any of these publishing options.

Finding a reputable agent can be just as difficult as being accepted by a large publishing house. The publishing industry is full of sharks and con artists ready to separate the uneducated writer from their money. Don't let this discourage you. Study the industry and know what an agent is supposed to do and you'll be able to spot the scams without losing any money to them.

The first rule is money flows to the author, not the other way around. If an agent is asking for up-front fees, reading, editing, anything, then you're not dealing with a legitimate agent. Do not pay monthly fees for office expenses. One questionable agent asks for fees of $200 a month or more. This agency has charged hopeful writers thousands of dollars but never sold their work.

If an agent tries to refer you to an editing company, don't go. A few years ago, several agents were referring their clients to Edit Ink. They received kickbacks for every writer that signed an editing contract with Edit Ink. Lawsuits were filed and after a lot of delays and appeals, sentences were finally handed down. The owners of Edit Ink were ordered to pay large fines. The agents associated with them are either out of business or are still up to their questionable—though not strictly illegal—practices.

Agents make their money by selling your work. If they don't sell it, they don't get paid. Consider this, your work is yours, you own the copyright, you don't sell that when you sell the novel to a publisher. What you sell is the right to publish the work for a set amount of time. It's rather like a real estate agent that is managing rental property. Your agent is "renting" your novel to the publisher for a time specified in the contract. The agent receives a commission just like the real estate agent. If the rental property isn't rented, then no one makes money—same thing with your novel.

Just like the real estate agent, your literary agent is your middleman. He/she is there to help sell your work to an editor. A good agent will have a working relationship with editors in the genre in which you're writing as well as experience negotiating contracts. A good agent should be familiar with all the legal issues concerning your contract. They should know the ins and outs of the business and how best to sell the rights to your story. They know which rights should remain with the author and which ones they can bargain for at a later date.

After receiving numerous rejections, some authors may think that a bad agent is better than no agent, but this isn't true. Most fee-charging agents do not have contacts in the publishing houses. They are known for their dishonest practices and reputable editors/publishers won't talk to them. Do not sign with an agent if you are unsure about them. Signing a contract can lock you into a business arrangement you'll regret. Horror stories have been told about unsuspecting authors signing contracts and being forced to give a percentage of their profits to an agent who did nothing to sell their book.

Besides fees, there are other red flags: disputes with former clients, no verifiable track record of sales, and poor quality correspondence. One questionable agent I contacted sent what looked like standard form letters with my name typed in the blanks. These letters contained numerous spelling and typographical errors. If an agent cannot take the time to run a spell-check on their e-mails to their clients are they going to bother to do so when they're contacting editors? Unprofessional letters, e-mails, or web sites are a warning sign not to get involved.

Some unethical agents have highly polished web sites and correspondence. They might not even ask for a reading fee. They wait until you've sent them the sample chapters they've asked for, and then they hit you up for an editing fee. One of these agents has a very slick site. On it, she asks if you're tired of rejections and promises to get you published when no one else can. You should always keep this old adage in mind: if it sounds too good to be true, it probably is.

If an agent has a web site, check it out. Look for typos and misspellings. Look under the list of clients. If they tell you that their client list is confidential, they're lying. Legitimate agents are proud of their sales records. After all, if you see a title on their site that looks interesting, you might buy the book and that's more commission for them. If the list of clients is open but the publishing houses listed aren't names you recognise, do a search on them. The agent I referenced in the previous paragraph has hundreds of clients on her site. Unfortunately, the only sales that have been made are either to a self-publishing house or to a publisher she started herself. This is a conflict of interest. Also, remember that you don't need an agent to self-publish.

There are several books on the market that lists agents. These can be helpful but they should not be taken as a blanket endorsement. Always double-check an agent before signing a contract. There are several sites out there to help you in this search.

WRITER ALERTS & AGENT LISTINGS

This author's site includes a listing of reputable literary agents. Ms.

Collins will not include an agent she has not checked out personally. Nor will she include agents that don't return Self Addressed Stamped Envelopes (SASE).

- Preditors and Editors ™ is an excellent site for information. However, they do not endorse self-publishing so some companies that are legitimate self-publishers will show up as not recommended on their site. http://www.anotherealm. com/prededitors/

- Writer Beware—Writer Victoria Strauss runs this site on a strictly volunteer basis. She is very helpful and will respond to questions from writers she does not know. http://www. sfwa.org/beware/

Market Listings

One of the best things a writer can do to improve their odds of getting their novel published is to build a writing portfolio. By selling short stories and articles to magazines, newspapers and newsletters, a writer proves that they are not only marketable but also professional and determined. A new writer without any publishing credits to his/her name may have to start small with local newspaper and semi-pro magazines, but these credits are important. Each one adds to your credibility and shows an editor that you are serious about your writing career.

The e-publishing industry is in its infancy. E-zines come and go very quickly. I have listed a few of the longest running e-zines but instead of listing all the short-story sf/fantasy markets I'm going to give you some links to follow. These will take you to some very informative sites. Ralan's is one of the most extensive collections of paying and non-paying markets I've seen and he does an excellent job of keeping it updated. Fiction Factor and Writing World have market listings as well as articles over how to improve your writing, finding an agent, and building a writing portfolio.

Market Listings (alphabetical order)

- http://www.anotherealm.com/prededitors/peba.htm
- http://www.fictionfactor.com
- http://www.ralan.com/
- http://www.spicygreeniguana.com/index2.html
- http://www.writing-world.com

E-ZINES
ANOTHERREALM
287 Gano Avenue
Orange Park, FL, 32073 U.S.A.
Fiction Submissions: editor@anotherealm.com
Flash Submission: flashfiction@anotherealm.com
URL: anotherealm.com
Fantasy, science fiction, horror. Max 4000-word limit

ROGUE WORLDS
E-mail (subs & info): specficworld@hotmail.com
URL: http://www.specficworld.com/rgworlds.html
Science fiction, fantasy, does accept sword and sorcery

STRANGE HORIZONS
E-mail (subs): (See various departments)
E-mail (general info): editor@strangehorizons.com
URL: http://www.strangehorizons.com
Prefers urban fantasy, magic realism, "slipstream", dark fantasy okay, but no outright gore-horror, occasional surreal so long as it's readable. Science Fiction okay but must involve three-dimensional characters and interesting stories, focus can not be on science puzzles. No submissions where half or more of the story explains scientific or technological phenomenon

SCIFI.COM FICTION
SCIFI.COM
PMB 391
511 Avenue of the Americas
New York, NY 10011-8436 U.S.A.
E-mail (No subs, info only): sfeditor@www.scifi.com
URL: http://www.scifi.com/scifiction
No reprints, wants science fiction and fantasy stories with strong characterization. No sword & sorcery or space opera.

SPECULATION
E-mail (general): editor@speculon.com
E-mail (fiction subs): submissions@speculon.com
E-mail (poetry subs): poetry@speculon.com
URL: http://www.speculon.com
Science fiction, fantasy and cross-genre. No horror or exceptionally dark fantasy.

TWILIGHT TIMES
E-mail (general): publisher@twilighttimes.com
E-mail (fiction subs): fiction@twilighttimes.com
E-mail (poetry subs): poetry@twilighttimes.com
URL: http://www.twilighttimes.com
Fiction from 1000 to 6000 words. Essays to 3000 words. Poetry to 30 lines. Prefer a balance of dark/light SF, fantasy, cross-genre and literary works, but recent submissions have been largely dark fantasy, wants some 'up-beat' stories.

WILD CLOWN CHRONICLE
Email: webmaster@wildclown.com
Subs: http://wildclown.com/chronicle/submissions.html
URL: http://wildclown.com/chronicle/ezine.html
Short Stories preferably 2,500 to 7,500 words. Sciencefiction, fantasy, speculative fiction, horror, erotic adventure and open adenture.

PRINT MAGAZINES

ASIMOV'S SCIENCE FICTION
475 Park Ave. South
11th Floor
New York, NY 10016   U.S.A.
E-info (no subs): asimovs@dellmagazines.com
URL: http://www.asimovs.com
Does accept fantasy but no S&S

BLACK GATE
New Epoch Press
Attn: Submissions Dept
815 Oak Street
St. Charles, IL 60174   U.S.A.
E-subs & info: submissions@blackgate.com
URL: http://www.blackgate.com
When they say they want action oriented, they mean just that. The story must have action in it.

DNA PUBLICATION INC.
PO Box 2988
Radford VA 24143-2988   USA
E-mail (Queries only, No Subs): dnapublications@dnapublications.com
URL:http://www.dnapublications.com

DNA publications is the home of several major magazines in the horror/fantasy/SF genres: Fantastic Stories, Weird Tales, Dreams of Decadence, Absolute Magnitude, Mythic Delirium and Science Fiction Chronicles. Make certain you visit the site and read a few issues of the magazine you're querying. You don't want to waste your time submitting to a magazine that does not print your type of story.

The Magazine of FANTASY & SCIENCE FICTION
P.O. Box 3447
Hoboken, NJ 07030   U.S.A.
E-mail (no subs, info only): fsfmag@fsfmag.com
or GordonFSF@aol.com
URL: http://www.sfsite.com/fsf

PLAYBOY
Fiction Editor
680 North Lake Shore Drive
Chicago IL 60611   USA
URL: http://www.playboy.com
Monthly print; MYS, SUS, SF, HUMOR. Pays $5000 ($2000 if very short) for FNASR, 1-6k words, POA. "Serious contemporary stories, mystery, suspense, humour, science fiction and sports stories. Magazine's appeal is chiefly to a well-informed, young male audience. Avoid fairy tales, experimental fiction, pornography." No e-mail, sim-, or multi- subs. No reprints. Include cover with short bio. RT: 2 months. Various editors will handle fiction.

ZOETROPE: ALL STORY
The Sentinel Building
916 Kearny Street
San Francisco, CA 94133
E-mail (No subs, info/queries only): abrodeur@compuserve.com
URL: http://www.zoetrope-stories.com
Simsubs & multisubs OK. RT: 5 months.

E-PUBLISHING LISTINGS FOR NOVEL LENGTH FICTION
Short listing of e-publishers but some of the better ones
http://www.itl.nist.gov/div895/ebook2001/links/publishers.html

Atlantic Bridge Publishing
http://www.atlanticbridge.net/publishing/contracts/guidelines.htm

Awe-Struck Books
http://www.awe-struck.net/asubmit/authsub.html

CYBERMANBOOKS
A New World of Words
P.O. Box 1252
Yuma AZ 85366 U.S.A.
E-subs & info: info@cybermanbooks.com
URL: www.cyberManbooks.com
URL: www.desertlightjournal.homestead.com

Double Dragon Publishing
Email: info@double-dragon-ebooks.com
URL: http:// double-dragon-ebooks.com/index/html

Writers-Exchange E-Publishing
http://www.writers-exchange.com/epublishing/

Novel Length Print Publishers

ACE BOOKS
(Penguin Putnam)
375 Hudson Street
New York, NY 10014 U.S.A.
URL: www.penguinputnam.com

BAEN BOOKS
P.O. Box 1403
Riverdale, NY 10471
URL: http://www.baen.com/

BANTAM SPECTRA BOOKS
(Random House)
1540 Broadway
New York, NY10036 U.S.A.
Contact Info: www.randomhouse.com/backyard/contact.html
URL: http://www.randomhouse.com/bantamdell/spectra.html

DAW BOOKS
(Penguin Putnam)
375 Hudson Street
New York, NY 10014 U.S.A.
E-mail (No subs, info only): daw@penguinputnam.com
URL: http://www.penguinputnam.com/static/packages/us/about/dawsub.htm

DEL REY BOOKS
201 East 50th Street
New York, New York 10022 USA
URL: http://www.randomhouse.com/delrey/main.cgi
Information only, no queries: delrey@randomhouse.com

TOR BOOKS
175 Fifth Avenue
New York NY 10010.
URL: http://www.tor.com/

SMALL PRESS PUBLISHERS

101 Independent publishers
http://www.bookmarket.com/101pub.html

Big Engine
PO Box 185
Abingdon, Oxon
OX141GR
Information only, no subs: info@bigengine.co.uk

Dragon Moon Press
URL: http://www.dragonmoonpress.com

Edge Science Fiction and Fantasy Publishing
P.O. Box 1714
Calgary, AB T2P 2L7   Canada
E-mail (No subs, info only): editor@edgewebsite.com
URL: www.edgewebsite.com

Four Walls Eight Windows
http://www.fourwallseightwindows.com/

Morpheus International
http://www.morpheusint.com/

SUMMARY

If you remember these ten simple rules, there is no need to fear venturing into the publishing world.

· 1. Money flows to the author not the other way. Agents/

publishers do not charge editing fees nor do they recommend book doctors or editing services.

- 2. Editors are people too. They like to see their names spelled right, and they like to be treated with respect.

- 3. Rejection happens to the best authors. Stephen King was rejected more times than he could count before his first sale.

- 4. Perseverance pays off.

- 5. Find a good critique partner or qualified editor to go over your work before you submit.

- 6. Study your craft: how to write, proper grammar and sentence structure, plotting, characterisation, pacing, setting, world building.

- 7. Conduct yourself as a professional. Publishers/agents are in business to make money, without it, they can't pay their bills, they can't continue to print books.

- 8. RESEARCH. Do not sign a contract with anyone, agent/ publisher/editor/book doctor, without researching the contract, your rights and how the industry works. This is the best way to protect yourself.

- 9. Remember to have fun. That's why you started writing to begin with, isn't it?

- 10. This one bears repeating. PERSEVERANCE PAYS OFF.

Author Biographies

FOREWORD, HUMOUR IN FANTASY—DARIN PARK

Darin Park majored in English, culminating his education at Dalhousie University in Nova Scotia, Canada. He has published eight short stories, and his humorous short, "The Devil, You Say?" won the Publisher's Choice Award in *Futures Magazine* in 2001. Currently he is working on a novel *Once Upon A Time: Twice If You Screw Up* and expects to complete it by December of 2002. He originated the book concept for "*The Complete Guide™ to Writing Fantasy*" and it is his first major achievement in the fantasy realm.

ROOTS OF FANTASY—JOHN TEEHAN

John Teehan attended Rhode Island College where he majored in English Literature and Medieval/Renaissance Studies. Through a grant provided by the National Endowment of the Humanities, he spent time at the University of Exeter where he studied Old English poetry and composed his thesis on the religious poetry of *The Exeter Book*.

He has sold fiction, poetry, book reviews and non-fiction articles to a variety of professional science fiction/fantasy markets. "A Small Goddess" appears in a DAW anthology edited by Martin Greenberg and Mike Resnick. "Digger Don't Take No Requests" appears in Steve Miller and Sharon Lee's *Low Port* (Meisha Merlin).

John lives to write, but he's also been known to dabble in art, game design, and music. He is a freelance typesetter, active in fanzine fandom, and a member of the Science Fiction and Fantasy Writers of America. Since fall 2002, John has been the Production Manager and Art Director for the SFWA Bulletin.

CHARACTERISATION—LEA DOCKEN

Lea Docken lives in a large old haunted house near the Missouri River in the Midwestern United States with her husband and children.

She is an internationally published poet. Her articles and short stories have appeared in national and international publications.

Currently she is working on a Women's Spirituality book and a fantasy novel.

Lea is responsible for the Internet Fantasy Writers Association an online writers group devoted to fantasy.

Fantasy without Clichés—Milena Benini

Milena Benini holds a degree in comparative literature (well, actually, she keeps it in a tallboy). She started writing when she was twelve, and got her first professional publication when she was fourteen. She has written numerous short stories and some novels; her novel *Children of Chaos and Eternity* won the 1998 Sfera award for best Croatian SFF novel. She has also taught for many years, including classes in English literature and creative writing classes. She is a member of the organising committee of Pontes literary festival, gathering young authors from the whole of Europe. She was born in Zagreb, and still lives there, with her daughter, Leona, and her dog, Edmund. You can find out more about her at www.sff.net/people/Milena.

Plot Construction—Marko Fancovic

Marko Fancovic was born before the Beatles had a recording contract, in the small Croatian coastal town of Zadar. Most of his adult life he lived in Belgrade, but relocated to Zagreb after the war in ex-Yugoslavia. He neglected formal education in lieu of reading and writing, publishing his first SF story when he was seventeen but later abandoning fiction writing for comics writing, working with top Yugoslav artists and taking up comics reporting, journalism and criticism.

He taught at several courses in creative writing and comics writing, and was a jury member of every major SF/F competition. He works full-time as a journalist and part-time as a SF/F translator, having translated works by almost everyone from Lovecraft and Heinlein to Anthony Burgess, Philip K. Dick, Tim Powers and Ian McDonald.

Marko's had some pulp novels published under assumed names, recently started publishing stories again, has a large space opera planned which he is writing on-and-off, and is currently working out the concept for a sword and sorcery novel.

Medieval Food—Michele Acker

Michele Acker says of herself, "I started writing a little over two years ago and find that it has become a vital part of my life. I eat, sleep and dream fantasy and science fiction. My characters live for me in a way that non-writers don't understand, and when I try to explain, they laugh or give me strange looks. But that's okay, they don't have to understand, as long as they enjoy the final product. The collaboration that went into writing *The Complete Guide™ to Writing Fantasy* taught me a lot and gave me great respect for my fellow list members and writers. Though it is my first non-fiction project, I've had two short, science fiction stories published; 'Daddy, Why?' cowritten with Tom Dullemond in *AlienQ*, and 'How to Tell if Someone's an Alien' in *AntipodeanSF*."

MEDIEVAL CLOTHING—LAUREN CLEELAND

Lauren Cleeland says of herself, "I am a thirty-seven year old mother of four and wife of one. My interest in writing began at age thirteen and continues to this day. I am especially fond of fantasyand it was my first genre. I have since branched out into contemporary and historical romance, horror and psychological thrillers. I also write non-fiction pieces related to an assortment of topics, including human sexuality and morality, medieval history, especially Celtic and Catholic Catechetical and Apologetic works. I am currently pursuing a BA in Anthropology."

RACE CREATION, HEALTH & MEDICINE—MICHAEL MCRAE

Michael is currently teaching science and maths at a Queensland secondary school. When he is not battling teenagers over the merits of quadratics or the theory of evolution, he is working on his historical fiction novel. Michael has recently moved over into the speculative fiction genre afterpast studies in the semiotics of science. He lives in Brisbane with his co-writer and pet (who really does all the work, and who happens to be a rat) Cloacina.

RELIGION BUILDING—JULIE PEAVLER-MCCORD

Julie Peavler-McCord is a priestess and religious writer making the transition into fantasy writing. For three years, she was the main writer and editrix for *Guardian's Grimoires*, an ezine on magic and paganism. Previous publications include "On Faith and Skepticism" (PagaNet News, Beltane 1998) and "The Charge as Ethical Precept" (abridged, in PanGaia Magazine #35, Spring 2003).

MYTHOLOGY—VALERIE GRISWOLD-FORD

Valerie says, "This is my first publishing credit. I've been writing for almost twenty-two years and am working on my second novel. (The first will never see the light of day until after I die—GRIN) I am married and live in Central Massachusetts with my husband and the most spoiled Siamese cat that has ever been known to live. My other interests include the SCA (Society for Creative Anachronism) and beadwork.

Living World, Arms & Armour, The Martial Arts, Research—Tee Morris

Tee Morris has always been a writer at heart. He gained accolades for his writing witticisms in high school with an original satirical piece, *Forensics: Why Bother?*, winning him the championship title at the 1987 Mid-Atlantic Forensic and Debate Invitational. His works would appear on stage and in print at James Madison University where he received his degree in Mass Communications and Theatre, and at The Maryland Renaissance Festival, one of the largest festivals of its kind on the East Coast. It was here portraying the character of Rafe Rafton his historical-fantasy epic, *MOREVI: The Chronicles of Rafe & Askana*, would take shape.

In 2002, Tee Morris arrived in the writing world with several premieres all within months of one another. Along with his contribution to *The Complete Guide™ to Writing Fantasy*, he appears in the 2002 CrossTIME Anthology, available at Crossquarter Publishing with the science-fiction short story, "Asleep at the Wheel." Following this was the premiere of *MOREVI: The Chronicles of Rafe & Askana*, the debut work of Tee and Miss Lisa Lee, his writing partner and dear friend across the globe. This historical-fantasy epic is also available through Dragon Moon Press.

Currently, Tee hard at work on my first solo novel, *Billibub Baddings and the Case of the Singing Sword*. Also in the works, a collaborative work with EPPIE-nominated author Tony Ruggiero, a *Farscape* tie-in novel, and picking up the pen with Lisa again for a sequel to *MOREVI*.

Magic, Arms & Armour, Combat—Tom Dullemond

Tom Dullemond was born in Holland but has lived in Australia since 1988. He is a great fan of speculative fiction of all sorts, and has appeared in several small print anthologies, most recently Speculation Press' *'Heaven and Hell'* and Agog's *'AustrAlien Absurdities'*. His unpublished dark fantasy manuscript *'The Final Arcanum'* was short-listed for the 1998 George Turner prize.

Armed with degrees in IT and Medieval/Renaissance Studies, Tom is a programmer by day, and both a random assortment of projects and a father by night. He spent the last two years developing a submission management program named 'Write Again' which was released to the public in March of 2002, receiving excellent feedback from fellow writers.

Tom can be found roaming the Internet at www.asmoday.com. He lives in Brisbane, Australia, with his lovely wife Clare and beautiful little baby daughter Page.

WORLD BUILDING, MARKET RESOURCES—TINA MORGAN

Tina Morgan is the Assistant Editor for *Fiction Factor e-zine*, where she contributes non-fiction articles as well as preforming editorial duties. She has placed articles with several online magazines and newsletters, her latest with Scriptorium. She also writes fantasy short stories and novels, both alone and with her co-author, Ciara Grey. Her story, "What's in a Name" is due out with Dragonlaugh ezine this summer. www.fictionfactor.com

HUMOUR IN FANTASY—ROBERT DURNEY

Robert Durney was born in Miami, Florida in November 1963. He graduated from St. Thomas Aquinas High School in 1981 and from the University of West Florida with a Bachelor's in Creative Writing in 1998. He spent sixteen years in the Navy from 1982 to 1986 traveling the world from beneath the ocean as a submarine sailor. His writing credits include song lyrics, poetry, and various journalistic and creative pieces.

Rob has won numerous writing awards including recognition from the National Library of Congress, the Mary Meisel Award Foundation and the Florida Outdoor Writers Association and has published in the U.S., Canada, and England. A father of five and retired Navy Chief Petty Officer, Rob currently teaches Writing and English in his home state of Florida. Look for his first fantasy epic, *Drakkul's Maze*, set for completion and, hopefully publication, sometime in early 2003.

Index

Dragon Moon Press and Hades Publications, Inc. acknowledges the ongoing support of the Canada Council for the Arts and the Alberta Foundation for the Arts for our publishing programme.

The Alberta Foundation for the Arts
COMMITTED TO THE DEVELOPMENT OF CULTURE AND THE ARTS

Alberta
COMMUNITY DEVELOPMENT

Canada Council for the Arts   Conseil des Arts du Canada